Russian Teachers and Peasant Revolution

INDIANA-MICHIGAN SERIES IN RUSSIAN AND EAST EUROPEAN STUDIES

Alexander Rabinowitch and William G. Rosenberg, *general editors*

Russian Teachers and Peasant Revolution

The Politics of Education in 1905

SCOTT J. SEREGNY

INDIANA UNIVERSITY PRESS
Bloomington and Indianapolis

This book was brought to publication with the assistance of a grant from the Andrew W. Mellon Foundation to the Russian and East European Institute, Indiana University, and the Center for Russian and East European Studies, University of Michigan.

Manufactured in the United States of America

Library of Congress Cataloging-in-Publication Data

Seregny, Scott Joseph.
Russian teachers and peasant revolution.

(Indiana-Michigan series in Russian and East European studies)
Bibliography: p.
Includes index.
1. Education and state—Soviet Union—History. 2. Education, Rural—Soviet Union—History. 3. Teachers—Soviet Union—History. 4. Soviet Union—History—Revolution of 1905. I. Title. II. Series.
LC93.S65S47 1989 370.19'0947 88-45386
ISBN 0-253-35031-X
1 2 3 4 5 93 92 91 90 89

To the memory of my father, Joseph J. Seregny

Contents

Acknowledgments

As with most first books, this one marks the end of a long scholarly odyssey, sometimes confused, but often exhilirating. At times when I have lost my bearings or nerve, teachers, colleagues, and friends have helped me find my way. I owe a large intellectual debt to teachers at the University of Michigan. Horace W. Dewey, John V. A. Fine, Jr., William K. Medlin, Arthur P. Mendel, and Roman Szporluk all provided invaluable training in Russian and East European history, and some read this work at the dissertation stage. Among these I owe a special debt to William G. Rosenberg, in whose seminar my interest in the rural intelligentsia and the 1905 revolution had its genesis. Bill has been a relentless critic and supporter through all of the transmutations this study has undergone, and, as important, he has been a sympathetic friend. One could hardly ask for more in a mentor.

I have profited immensely from conversations about Russian education with Ben Eklof, who also provided incisive comments on portions of the manuscript. We disagree on some points of interpretation, but our work has always been complementary in the best sense of that word, and this study has been enriched by his work. Muriel Joffe read earlier drafts and has always provided encouragement, sometimes at critical junctures. Timothy Mixter was always eager to share his expertise on rural Russia. Terence Emmons, Gregory Freeze, Nancy Frieden, and Roberta Manning all provided sound advice in the conceptualization and early stages of this research. John Bushnell read the entire manuscript and offered many useful suggestions. My former colleague Allan K. Wildman read portions of this work, as did Hans Rogger. Jonathan Sanders generously shared his work on the Union of Unions. Nicholas Thorner provided valuable assistance and Rex Wade helped me keep my sanity in juggling this with another project. Will O'Daix provided critical technical assistance in the preparation of the manuscript.

I have received generous support from the School of Liberal Arts and Department of History at Indiana University, Indianapolis. I would like to thank in particular John Barlow, Bernard Friedman, and William Plater. Research and writing were facilitated by grants from the Fulbright-Hays Fund and IREX for research in the Soviet Union, a National Endowment for the Humanities Summer Stipend, as well as the Eggertsen Dissertation Prize from the University of Michigan. Joseph Placek and the Slavic staff at the University of Michigan Library acquired indispensable sources on microfilm, and the Russian Research Center at Harvard University helped make two years in Boston both productive and pleasurable. The Russian and East European Center at the University of Illinois provided an ideal research environment through its justly renowned Summer Research Laboratory. Valuable assistance was provided by the staffs of the Central State Historical Archives in Leningrad, the Central State Archive of the October Revolution in Moscow, the Saltykov-Shchedrin Library in Leningrad, the Lenin Library in Moscow, and by those "guys in the black coats" in the Newspaper Room at the Library of the Academy of Sciences in Leningrad who carted in those huge folios of provincial newspapers.

I would like to thank Janet Rabinowitch of the Indiana University Press for her assistance. Part of chapter 5 appeared previously as "Revolutionary Strategies in the Russian Countryside: Rural Teachers and the Socialist Revolutionary Party on the Eve of 1905," *Russian Review,* 44 (July 1985). My mother and late father provided an environment that fostered intellectual curiosity. Indeed, a handful of books on Russian history from my father's college days initially sparked my interest in this subject.

Russian Teachers and Peasant Revolution

The Provinces of European Russia

1. Introduction

During the half century between the Great Reforms of the 1860s and the Revolutions of 1917 Russia experienced momentous changes. A significant feature was the transition, halting and hotly contested, from a society where power and privilege were determined largely by rank and birth to one in which social mobility, education, and expertise demanded recognition. The end of serfdom ushered in sweeping economic and institutional changes and gave impulse to new social imperatives, while stimulating the appearance of new occupational categories to perform the tasks required by a modernizing society and conferring a certain legitimacy to the professional claims of these new practitioners. An important aspect of social change in late Imperial Russia was the rise of modern professions, virtually new groups which collectively constituted a "third force" or "democratic intelligentsia," standing between traditional elites of landowning gentry and bureaucracy and masses of workers and peasants.[1]

In broad terms the significance of the professional intelligentsia in Russian development is clear. Engineers, doctors, educators, and the like had to play a major role in the country's social, cultural, and economic transformation. Rural backwardness, in particular, enhanced the importance of professionals, who, through provision of vital services in the countryside and strong commitment to popular welfare (commonly equated with Western-style modernization), sought to dispel rural ignorance and stagnation and help integrate the peasantry into the wider society and nation. Prior to 1917 much of this burden was shouldered by professionals employed by new institutions of local government, the zemstvos (established in 1864). Agronomists, medical personnel, and other members of this so-called third element played a key role in whatever strides rural Russia made in the decades following Emancipation, and recently their activities have been the subject of historical study.[2] Properly so, since their recorded experiences provide a valuable perspective on the transformation of the Russian countryside during this era and, in addition, tell much about the institutional and cultural forces impeding or fostering Russia's advance along Western rails of development.

The zemstvo third element and other professional groups have also attracted the attention of historians concerned with the political conflicts raging in Tsarist Russia. Vocal elements of such groups were a strong source of criticism of the Tsarist order, contributing to the widespread disaffection of educated society *(obshchestvo)* with the Old Regime and, as conservatives alleged, to popular discontent as well. In general terms the roots of this opposition are clear. The very principles the professions espoused—service to society, merit, and expertise—challenged the dominant political culture, and sustained work in the rural milieu brought them face to face with social inequities. Attempts at professional mobilization and acquisition of autonomy and social space within the cramped interstices of traditional power and privilege swept many zemstvo professionals into open political opposition, particularly in the provinces where they provided cadres for the revolutionary parties, both Socialist Revolutionaries and Social Democrats, and for a nascent liberal constitutionalist movement based in the zemstvos. The political mobilization of Russian professions culminated, as is well known, at the national level during the Revolution of 1905 in the Union of Unions. Indeed, in the provinces the famous Liberation Movement of the early 1900s was grounded upon a liberal-radical alliance between progressive zemstvo gentry and radical professionals who shared to some degree a vision of Russia's constitutional and social transformation.[3] We have a fairly clear picture of the national movement, but much less is known about such mobilization at the local level, though it is obviously central to understanding how national politics were transmitted from the capitals to provincial society, how the periphery influenced the center, and how urban-based political movements and ideologies penetrated the village before and during 1905–6. At the same time study of professional movements can provide a much-needed picture of secondary and tertiary leadership during this period.

In order to examine these questions of professional and political mobilization we have selected for study one of the most humble, but arguably the most important, third element group, rural schoolteachers. By virtue of their numbers, their direct proximity to the village, and the centrality of primary schooling to the zemstvo's and society's entire mission, teachers occupied a prominent place in efforts at rural modernization, in the rise of Russia's professions, and, at least potentially, in attempts to bring the Liberation Movement to the peasantry. At the same time, Russian teachers were among the most improbable of activists. Memoirs, literary accounts, and zemstvo statistical studies reveal Russia's lowly teachers prior to the revolution as an inert, torpid lot, divorced by education, living conditions, and administrative constraints from the lofty concerns of progressive society; living in isolation within the village community, the objects of scarcely concealed peasant contempt and suspicion. Devoid of power or influence within rural society or the school administration, frightened of their own shadows, and oblivious to the burning questions of the day, rural teachers had earned the nickname "zemstvo rabbits." Shunned by local elites, including their better educated third element colleagues, they were objects of pity.

Historical treatments of Russian education and teachers have revised and reinforced this picture of isolation and torpor. Ben Eklof has recently demonstrated that Russia's infant rural schools accomplished more than previously thought in rearing a generation of peasant literates. Indeed, in his excellent study Eklof has produced hard evidence that teachers, despite their low educational credentials and abysmal status, were well suited, in a cost-effective sense, to teach the basics. At the same time, he has helped reinforce old stereotypes. In fleshing out a collective profile of rural teachers, based on a wide array of statistical and other data (on feminization, social status, qualifications), Eklof finds remarkable stability and continuity in the profession between 1890 and 1914, a period of rapid educational growth. But in this writer's opinion he presents an excessively static picture, failing to take into account the remarkable emergence of a professional movement among teachers and what this development tells us about Russian politics and society and likewise failing to examine teacher-peasant relations during critical periods of change in concrete detail at the local level.[4]

For, as we will chronicle, during the tumultuous year of 1905 Russia's "zemstvo rabbits" emerged in the forefront of the movement to mobilize the professions, catching many contemporaries, both opposition and government supporters, by surprise. Teachers, particularly those in primary schools, organized an All-Russian Teachers' Union with overt political aims which ranked among the most militant of professions in the Union of Unions. Though relative latecomers to professionalization, teachers emerged with a reasonably effective organizational base, program, and identity, all forged during the previous decade. Most surprising, rural teachers formed the backbone of this movement and immersed themselves in peasant politics through the peasant unions, political parties, and election campaigns to the State Duma.[5]

This experience forces us to revise the relatively static picture we have of rural teachers as perennial "outsiders," incapable of exerting much if any impact on peasant society outside the narrow confines of the classroom. Close scrutiny of teachers' activities during 1905 reveals their dynamic, changing relationship with local communities and does not support generalizations to the effect that "the third element intelligentsia, despite their idealism, real service to the people, and non-involvement in land relations, were in the peasants' view just as much outsiders—representatives of the establishment—as was the gentry 'second element.' "[6] By the same token teachers' activities during 1905–6 call into question time-honored assumptions about peasant isolation from Russian society and national politics. They should further help inform our understanding of peasant political mobilization during this period, a topic only now receiving serious attention from historians.[7]

What does this turn of events mean? As we will show, the political mobilization of rural teachers during 1905, which caught so many observers off guard, was conditioned by the dynamic of the revolutionary situation.

The disarray of official administration at all levels, pressure from educated society for teachers to take an activist stance in the village, and, not least, pressure "from below," from peasant communities, combined to thrust teachers into unaccustomed roles. These developments will be treated in the second part of this study, which demonstrates that teachers' low status and isolation within peasant society were not immutable conditions. Indeed, as studies of modern professions suggest, teachers' professional status depended on the changing perceptions of the key actors involved in the effort to build a school system in Russia—government, educated society (most notably the zemstvos), and peasantry. The politics of this effort were central to the rise of a teachers' movement in Russia and teachers' involvement in the 1905 revolution. Studies which take the longer view, as recent critiques of social history inform us, commonly err in muting the sharp political conflicts which served as lightning rods for broader social movements, especially in sparking self-definition, and which were in turn profoundly shaped by social forces. To approach it another way, the teachers' movement that emerged so dramatically in 1905 was more than the product of a unique political conjuncture, more than a blip on a wide, rather depressing screen stretching from the Great Reforms to 1914. The Russian teachers' movement emerged and ultimately failed for specific reasons, some generic to teaching as a profession, others embedded in Russian political culture. With regard to the latter, study of teachers' professional formation and political activism can inform our understanding of late Imperial Russia, its polity and society, as well as limits to reform.

The roots of teacher radicalism ran deeper than the events of 1905 and must be sought in the preceding decade, when teachers began to define their place within the larger context of Russia's educational and social development. In approaching this task they faced fundamental and formidable contradictions in their status within society. Ultimately, it was in attempts to resolve these contradictions that increasing numbers of rural teachers arrived at a remarkable degree of programmatic consensus and professional consciousness and were transformed into vocal opponents of the Old Regime. Consciousness, as we will see, was the byproduct not only of teachers' work and life experience, but also of the often conflicting priorities set by the key actors in popular education.

Observers of modern professions have often noted the low, "semiprofessional" status of teachers in primary schools. Teachers, as opposed to "pure" or established groups such as doctors, tend to exhibit a low degree of professionalization, largely as a result of low pay, feminization, modest social origins, high rates of turnover owing to lesser commitment, and subordinate status within a bureaucratic hierarchy that restricts autonomy. These conditions reinforce teachers' low prestige within society at large.[8] These generic traits to one degree or another are characteristic of rural teachers in late Imperial Russia. In Russia, in fact, certain features appeared hypertrophied. Subordination was extreme, not only to local school boards, state inspectors, and zemstvo employers but to a host of rural officials as well. Teachers lacked even the right of self-defense in disciplinary matters. Restrictions on professional association were, even by Russian standards, draconian. The disability of meager formal qualifications was severely aggravated by rural isolation and cultural deprivation upon arrival at the school. These problems were among the most corrosive of teachers' status in Russia, and, as we will demonstrate, issues of association and legal and cultural status lay at the heart of the teachers' movement.

Conditions aside, public recognition of the indispensability or urgency of services rendered strongly influences an occupation's progress toward professional status, as well as its bargaining power in demands for autonomy. Lacking both an esoteric knowledge base and services deemed by society to be urgent or important (as in the case of medicine or the military), teachers historically have not enjoyed high status. A British sociologist writes: "Teaching is the most profoundly contaminated (secularized) profession because with the rise of mass education its mystique is compromised by the fact that in general the tasks it performs are within the competency of all who have been taught themselves and since those upon whom it practices are children, many of these functions are substitutes for parental roles in any case."[9]

Russia, obviously, was not a country that had experienced mass education, but a largely peasant and unschooled society, quite different from one where low status inevitably accrues to "teachers in primary schools to which *everyone goes* to learn what *everyone knows*."[10] Indeed, during the last decades of the Old Regime one of the most pressing and constant concerns of educated society and many policymakers was the yawning chasm dividing educated, overwhelmingly urban society from the "dark masses," especially the peasantry. While sometimes exaggerated, the gulf between these two societies nevertheless has to be reckoned as one of the major weaknesses in the country's social structure, since it was ultimately the failure of privileged, cultured obshchestvo to make its vision of Russia's social and political development comprehensible and acceptable to the broad masses which derailed Russia's advance along the rails of Western-style constitutional and capitalist development. Jeffrey Brooks's provocative study of popular reading suggests that some progress was registered here, but the advance was clearly tentative and uneven.[11] In any case, the progressive intelligentsia perceived overcoming this gulf as a national imperative of the first magnitude, and this perception held crucial importance for Russia's teachers.

By the turn of the century key elements in society, including the zemstvos, came to attach urgent significance to popular schooling and in so doing embraced and fostered an image of the teacher's role that went well beyond the confines of the classroom and the task of imparting the "three R's" to peasant children. Progressive society projected an image of the rural teacher as a "cultural pioneer" and "public activist" fulfilling a mission of crucial importance in the country's social, economic, and even political development. Consciousness was not "delivered" to teachers, in any simplified Leninist sense, since the roots of professional identity went deeper and were more complex. But society's perception of teachers as the advance guard in a multifaceted "enlightenment" campaign among the masses enhanced the potential (and actual) status of teachers while exerting a powerful influence on the growth of a professional movement and the rise, in fact leap, in corporate consciousness among Russian teachers during the decade before 1905.

Teachers' internalization of this ideal was central to the movement, providing both the basis for claims to legitimacy as a profession with certain rights and prestige and for teachers' opposition to the Tsarist regime. To the extent that they accepted and aspired to the ideal of "cultural pioneer," which was laden with a strong ethic of service and sacrifice, teachers would struggle for radical improvements in status, which, they argued, were essential to their role as cultural agents among the "dark masses," as well as for public recognition as "experts" enjoying some measure of autonomy. That rural teachers did occupy a strategic position on the frontier dividing educated, Europeanized Russian society from the peasantry helped foster a unique professional ethos (compared to either generic models of the profession or contemporaneous European contexts) and placed them at the vital switches linking state and society with the masses. That they came to define themselves as a vital link between obshchestvo and *narod* brought many teachers into conflict with the government.

Any generalizations about state policy during this period should be qualified. Much evidence in recent years has suggested that the traditional view of the Russian bureaucracy as irredeemably obscurantist owes more to contemporary liberal critiques than fact. Indeed, the Ministry of Education (MNP) did not wholly deserve the name "Ministry of Popular Ignorance" and contained enlightened officials as well as routine-driven *chinovniki*. Allen Sinel, Eklof, and Brooks have shown that the government and Orthodox Church did more to foster education than previously conceded.[12] By the same token, society's commitment to popular education was not unqualified; nor was the zemstvos' record in this area, as we will see, unassailable. Nevertheless, one suspects that this revisionist adjustment unnecessarily obscures very real political dynamics. Education quite clearly was a battleground in turn-of-the-century Russia. As with most struggles the parameters were often fuzzy but the conflicts real—between zemstvos and bureaucracy, teachers and school officials, church and zemstvos, clerics and teacher—and they were perceived as being important, indeed mortal conflicts by the combatants, teachers included. Teachers' perception of the state as foe is more important to our study of the teacher's movement than any estimate, impossible to reckon, whether there were more obscurantist or enlightened school inspectors (though I strongly suspect the former).

More important is the fact that official policy toward mass education and toward teachers was highly ambivalent. Attempting to achieve two essentially irreconcilable aims—spreading basic literacy among peasants while seeking to cordon the village off from outside influences—state policy toward teachers alternated between concessions and repression. Official policy, we will argue, insured that the fundamental contradiction between the ideal of the rural teacher working against formidable odds to bridge the gulf between educated society and peasantry and the harsh realities of isolation and cultural deprivation became a source of increasingly militant professional activism. The perception that the government was responsible for perpetuating this contradiction insured that the nascent teachers' movement would embrace other visions of the future, whether liberal or revolutionary, and would advance a program in which professional and political demands were inextricably linked. As teachers, like other Russian professions, groped toward self-definition, they became increasingly aware that their interests could not be accommodated within the existing social and political order, either autocracy and unrestrained bureaucratic rule or the gentry-dominated and undemocratic zemstvos.

What follows, then, is a case study of the rise of a key profession in a traditional political culture and society undergoing rapid transformation. As often as possible, we will let teachers speak for themselves, since their perceptions were central to the emergence of a professional movement; we will, however, attempt to balance their perspective with other sources, an effort dictated not only by the historian's craft, but in order to place the rise of this movement within the broader context of political and social conflicts.

We should also point out that the teachers who spoke, who joined professional organizations, who entered politics remained a minority. It can be argued, however, that when compared with Russian political movements and labor organizations, let alone other professions in this period, teachers hardly appear more inert. What is significant is the dramatic emergence of a teachers' movement, a turn of events that stands as testimony to its compelling power, the force of national imperatives in popular education, and the sharpness of political conflict in Russia. By 1905, Russia's "dress rehearsal" or "moment of truth," activist teachers were a significant minority.

The question of the impact of the teachers' movement can be posed another way: how many teachers enlisted as active supporters of the Old Regime? It is often said that during the nineteenth century Prussian teachers helped instill loyalty to the state and inculcated national values and that French teachers, in the process of helping "make peasants into Frenchmen," fostered acceptance of the secular Third Republic and its institutions in the countryside. This might have been the end result of the Russian state's tentative commitment to popular schooling in the years preceding World War I, but we will never know. In the midst of the crisis of 1905, however, a significant minority of schoolteachers, and many of the most committed among them, were opponents of the regime. This fact, indeed the whole history of teachers' professional struggle in Russia, suggests that there were serious limits to reform under the Tsarist regime and highlights some of the broader reasons for its collapse.

2. Teachers and the Politics of Education in Russia

The dramatic emergence of a teachers' movement in Russia, as we have suggested, was closely related to wider conflicts involving state and society. The rhythms of the Russian teachers' movement followed the ebb and flow of public and official commitment to popular schools during the decades after the Great Reforms. The expectations of society and state both circumscribed and enlarged the boundaries of teachers' professional status, organization, and consciousness. While the beginnings of teachers' association were evident in the first decades of the zemstvo school, a compelling professional identity and ethos that would inform a professional movement, as well as the means to organize, took shape only in the wake of national crisis, the famine and cholera of the early 1890s. Therefore it is proper that we first sketch out the new imperatives involved in Russia's education campaign, ask to what degree new expectations about the teacher's role in Russian development were consistent with the human resources available, and place these issues within the context of the political dynamics of education. In doing so we will introduce the main actors involved in Russia's education drive and the teachers' movement: state, society, zemstvos, peasantry, and teachers.

The foundations of an elementary school system were laid in the years after Emancipation, and a modest "army" of teachers was recruited. In 1880 a government census counted 22,770 rural schools in sixty provinces of European Russia (including Poland and the Baltic regions). Twenty-four thousand, three hundred eighty-nine teachers labored in these schools (19,511 men and 4,878 women).[1] Much of the early development was achieved under the auspices of the zemstvos—within the thirty-four zemstvo provinces at this time there were between 9,000 and 10,000 zemstvo schools—but not necessarily through the efforts of local self-government.[2] As B. B. Veselovskii pointed out in his classic study of the zemstvos, an inordinate share of the burden for public education was borne directly by local peasant communities rather than defrayed through general zemstvo revenues. And Ben Eklof has suggested that much of the growth of the zemstvo school network before the 1890s stemmed from formal incorporation of *volnye* schools and "literacy schools" organized on peasant initiative. Both he and Jeffrey Brooks have shown that it was the peasantry's thirst for schooling, above all else, that spurred the growth of schools in this period.[3] During the immediate postreform era much of the activity and funding of the zemstvos was concentrated on teacher training, an important concern to be sure. As for the government, it provided very little aid for the establishment and upkeep of secular-run schools before the Revolution of 1905.[4]

An apparent lack of urgency characterized efforts of the elite to enlighten the rural masses, and as the era of Great Reforms receded, public interest in education waned perceptibly. By the 1880s there was much talk in zemstvo circles of "cheaper" schools for the peasantry, and many zemstvo men openly considered turning their schools over to the Holy Synod. Others spoke of "professionalizing" the primary school—shifting its emphasis from "general education" to the more narrow task of imparting trades and applied skills. These developments, of course, marked a shift from, if not a betrayal of, the earlier enlightenment ideals of educators like Baron N. A. Korf and K. D. Ushinskii and indicated a depressing complacency on the part of educated society toward the realities of rural Russia's ignorance, poverty, and illiteracy.

The period of the 1880s, the "quiet," is variously described as one of "reaction" or "small deeds." Both interpretations have merit. Reaction, particularly in the gentry-dominated zemstvos, was unmistakable, most evident in sharp cutbacks in zemstvo services benefiting the masses. At the same time grass-roots, nearly invisible, cultural work in the countryside proceeded, slowly and painfully, conducted by isolated but committed zemstvo activists and increasing cadres of third element specialists. Small deeds were accomplished against great odds, but these cultural activities went on in splendid isolation. Thus, not only were the modest gains that had been registered in danger of slipping away, but it also augured ill for substantial progress in the future.

As for rural teachers, they appeared isolated and all but forgotten by the 1880s. The prospect of teachers playing a vital role as "cultural pioneers" in the countryside, or for a professional movement to support this activity, looked dismal. Mobilization of teachers around a potent professional ethos, as the literature on professions suggests, was predicated upon a resurgence of public commitment to peasant schooling, especially on the part of the zemstvos, and this was not forthcoming until the mid-1890s.

The great famine and cholera that swept across large areas of Russia in 1891–92 had a devastating effect on educated public opinion. At one level, faith in Russia's position as a national power and in the autocracy as a system was severely shaken. For the intelligentsia, the experience of 1891–92 seemed to highlight prerevolutionary Russia's fundamental, potentially fatal, flaw: the cultural gulf between Europeanized, educated society and the "dark" masses, the narod. It was apparent that two "societies" coexisted within Russia—educated, privileged, mostly urban elites and the largely illiterate, disenfranchised, rural masses—and that the links between the "two Russians" were still basically characterized by coercion, suspicion, and hostility. Incidents of peasant hostility and suspicion toward the ministrations of relief workers, such as the "cholera riots" in small towns along the Volga, provided ample evidence of popular *temnota,* a term conveying peasant illiteracy, suspicion of outsiders, and their apparent fatalism in the face of natural calamity.[5] The famine and cholera exposed the myriad weaknesses of rural Russia: peasant poverty, agricultural stagnation, rural overpopulation, the inequities of the taxation system. Of all lessons imparted by the famine, none seemed as urgent as the crying need to spread public education, or "enlightenment," among the rural masses: to improve peasant agriculture, break down popular superstition, and somehow narrow the cultural divide separating urban, privileged Russia from the peasantry.

The "hungry year" galvanized educated society. The "quiet" *(zatish'e)* of the preceding decade gave way to a renewed commitment to the narod and a flurry of "public activity." Education figured prominently here, as many people who had participated in famine relief entered the adult education movement and the campaign for universal elementary schooling. Much of this activity centered on the zemstvos, which, by statute, bore direct responsibility in primary education, as well as various "enlightenment societies," particularly the Moscow and Petersburg Literacy Committees *(komitety gramotnosti),* which were revitalized during the early 1890s by a new generation of activists.

Until their disbandment by the government in 1896 the literacy committees engaged in feverish activity: they organized free libraries, published popular literature, and sponsored a debate on the prospects of universal education in Russia. When Vasili P. Vakhterov demonstrated in the Moscow committee in 1894 that by accepting a three-year course as the norm (the European standard was seven years), universal and compulsory schooling in Russia was not an unrealizable dream but, in fact, was possible within the present generation, the effect was dramatic. A participant later recalled: "We, youth, were electrified—it seemed to us that now we would begin to work, that the end of this disgraceful illiteracy was at hand."[6] Faith in the power of "enlightenment" to solve the many problems plaguing backward Russia swept up broad sections of educated society during the following decade, a commitment only reinforced by Russia's industrial transformation. Already by the mid-1890s, a series of authoritative studies of Russian industry demonstrated a positive correlation between literacy and workers' productivity.

Amid all the debate and prognoses public attention focused on the all-but-forgotten teachers in the Russian countryside. Educated Russians echoed Bismarck's remark about the Prussian teacher's contribution to the victory at Sedan, while the economist I. I. Ianzhul, in an article entitled "The Schoolteacher Has Conquered," pointed out that Germany's recent industrial upsurge and successful competition for world markets owed much to her school system.[7] Nothing less than Russia's future as a great power hinged on the collective efforts of these men and women. So too did Russia's social stability and internal progress. Commenting on an incident in which a suspected sorceress was nearly torn to pieces by an enraged crowd at the height of the cholera, the educator V. P. Ostrogorskii wrote: "Schoolteacher, where are you? Answer!"[8] Behind this *cri de coeur* (which would be repeated again in 1905) lay not only the practical requirements of schools, but also recognition on the part of educated society of the chasm separating it from the narod and the realization that in any attempt to approach the village or to influence peasant behavior and attitudes the rural teacher occupied a strategic position.

But who was teaching in rural schools? What kind of cultural credentials did they possess? How long did they remain in the profession, and what tended to hamper their work? Prior to the 1890s, answers to these questions simply could not be formulated. Zemstvo education statistics were in their infancy, there was little up-to-date literature on the status of teachers, and during the 1880s there had been few regular points of contact between teachers and educated society.[9] In effect, the schoolteacher, upon whom the success of any enlightenment project in the countryside might well depend, remained an enigma.

The Teachers' Question: Profile, Status, and Crisis

The first comprehensive attempt to provide information on Russia's teachers was undertaken by the Moscow Literacy Committee (MKG) in 1894–95. The Commission for the Investigation of Teachers' Status, chaired by I. M. Chuprov, received some five thousand replies to its questionnaire from teachers all over the empire.[10] The committee's data was soon supplemented by other materials: studies conducted by individual provincial zemstvos,[11] teachers' mutual aid societies, as well as discussion of the "teachers' question" in the press, in learned societies, and at professional gatherings.[12] From these sundry materials emerges a collective profile of teachers on the threshold of the new century. In general this profile is familiar to readers of Russian literature and recent studies of Russian education. Here we would like to highlight those features relating to teachers' potential as a strategic link between educated society and the peasantry, as well as those that reinforced fundamental contradictions in Russian teachers' professional status and which in a dialectical sense both hindered the growth of a movement and fostered organized militancy. From a welter of statistical materials and studies of teachers' status three images of the rural teacher stand out and define teachers' relations with educated society and its culture, with the peasantry, and traditional authority structures: the teacher as "civilized savage," "outsider," and "zemstvo rabbit," respectively. For educated society, now urgently committed to popular enlightenment, this evidence pointed to a profession of still unrealized potential, but also one in profound crisis.

Since 1880 the number of teachers in zemstvo schools had increased from 10,300 (in 9,138 schools) to over 18,000 in 1898. These accounted for most of the schools under the jurisdiction of the Ministry of Education in the provinces of European Russia with zemstvo institutions, although these schools now faced stiff competition from church-run schools under the Holy Synod.[13] Data gathered by the MKG and zemstvos showed that the intellectual background that teachers brought to the rural school was often meager. Drawn from myriad educational backgrounds, many teachers not only lacked adequate pedagogical training, but the general education backgrounds of many were suspect. Moreover, as schools increased in number, standards dropped.

We will deal more fully with this issue in the following chapter, but it seems clear that the question of teachers' cultural level involved several related issues and helped define their status. At the most basic level teachers' low qualifications (many lacked any formal certification) called into question their ability to teach basic literacy. Beyond this, after the famine of the early 1890s teachers were called upon to act as a more potent cultural force within peasant society. The evidence at hand casts doubt on their preparedness, particularly when to poor formal qualifications one adds their lack of access to reading material and the absence of other cultural resources in the village. As we will see, cultural deprivation and isolation from educated society threatened teachers' fulfillment of the role of "cultural pioneers" in rural society, severely damaged professional morale, and lowered their prestige in the eyes of society. Memoirs of this period amply demonstrate the Russian intelligentsia's disdain and pity for these "civilized savages," who were equipped with only the most rudimentary and spotty educations and then cut off from cultural amenities.[14]

If this savage was not a member of educated society, neither was he or she a member of the rural community. Indeed, rural teachers found themselves suspended between two worlds, a source of potential influence, but also much frustration. Within the rural community the teacher was an "outsider," legally, socially, and culturally. With few exceptions, teachers were not members of the rural communes where they served and thus lacked the right to participate in communal affairs.[15] Yet statistics gathered before the turn of the century evidenced a democratization of the teaching profession. In absolute terms the number of teachers of peasant origin had increased in recent decades. Most of these were men, which owed in no small degree to official policy. Since Count D. A. Tolstoi's tenure as minister of education, that agency had viewed male teachers from the peasant estate as a stable and reliable element and had opened teachers' training schools (seminaries) mainly for men. The government, aided by the zemstvos, offered substantial stipends to peasant sons wishing to study in teachers' seminaries.[16] Here official policy combined with peasant prejudice and calculation of opportunity costs to limit the number of female teachers of peasant background; fewer peasant girls received the primary, let alone secondary, educations that might lead to a teaching career. Therefore, throughout the Tsarist period, women teachers were drawn from other social backgrounds; many were daughters of the clergy.[17]

Although men of peasant origin comprised a significant contingent of teachers, the salient characteristic of the profession was feminization, which was proceeding steadily in most provinces by the 1890s. Whereas the 1880 school census had determined that only 20 percent of the teachers in rural schools were women, ministry data for 1898 showed the gap between the sexes closing: 56 percent men and 44 percent women (for all primary schools under MNP jurisdiction).[18] Feminization was even more pronounced in zemstvo rural schools, although the process varied from region to region and was slower in the South, where salaries were higher.[19]

The reasons for this trend are fairly straightforward. Russia offered relatively few opportunities to women with an education, and female teachers commanded lower salaries than their male counterparts. With the rapid expansion of the school system after the mid-1890s, it was natural that personnel would be drawn increasingly from this pool.[20] Concerning the question of who made better teachers—men or women—there was little consensus. Women appeared to be more committed to their vocation, as reflected in somewhat lower rates of turnover, but contemporaries questioned their ability to exert "authority" within the patriarchal commune. N. Lozanov, based on his experience as a school inspector in Saratov province, noted that peasants generally preferred male teachers, as evidenced by communal petitions to open new schools. According to Lozanov, women had less success conducting adult education programs, and "aside from this, peasants do not go to women teachers for advice on the puzzling questions of rural life; and she does not attend the village assembly when questions of school upkeep are discussed. All of this can be accomplished by a man, provided he serves in one school for a long time and adapts to local conditions."[21] Given the male-dominated structure of rural society, a male teacher was more likely to exert an influence outside the classroom, within peasant society at large. In a world that owed deference to age and male sex, however, increasing numbers of teachers were young, unmarried, and female. Feminization also reinforced teachers' low professional status with regard to competence and autonomy vis-à-vis their zemstvo employers and school officials and would thus pose problems in organizing a professional movement. In any case, the trend was steady, continuing up to World War I, when it was further accelerated by military conscription.[22]

Turnover, as Lozanov implied, reinforced the teacher's status as "outsider" in the village and did little to enhance professional status. Longevity in a given locale, crucial in acquiring a measure of influence, was the exception not the rule. Given flight from the profession (to other occupations, continued education, or marriage), as well as the rapid growth of schools after 1895, it is scarcely surprising that many teachers had been employed for a short time. In Saratov province, for example, 53.7 percent of the men, and 62.4 percent of the women had been teaching for three years or less; 72.3 percent of the men and 79.3 percent of the women had been teaching for five or less years. In Kursk province 49.9 percent of the teachers in zemstvo schools in 1900 had been teaching less than five years.[23] Aside from those who abandoned the profession, rural teaching was plagued by frequent transfers from school to school, initiated either by teachers seeking better working conditions or by local authorities. In Kursk province over a five-year period 60 percent of the teachers moved from one school to another at least once.[24] Lack of firm roots in the locale made it difficult for teachers to shed their status as "outsiders."

Moreover, as an occupation teaching did not automatically command prestige. Peasants were still ambivalent about the value of schooling, and intellectual labor was not held in high regard. In addition, teachers' dependence on the commune for fuel and other necessities often bred contempt and resentment among peasants who felt that zemstvo taxes, which supported schools, fell disproportionately on their shoulders. Dependence on communal officials was a common complaint of teachers who responded to the Literacy Committee survey, and zemstvos gradually moved to alleviate the situation by directly assuming such expenditures.[25] In addition, as the most visible agent of zemstvo policy, peasants often held the teacher responsible for unpopular zemstvo decisions, for example, an enrollment ceiling of eighty pupils per teacher.[26] At the same time, aside from petty control over school building maintenance, there was little community input into school management. Important decisions were made by the zemstvo, the state inspector, and the local school board, none of which was truly representative of the rural population. These were the institutions that appointed, confirmed, transferred, or dismissed the teacher, without the concurrence and sometimes against the wishes of the local community. Just as peasants would not view the teacher as "ours" in a social sense, the rural teacher was hardly *nash* in terms of school management. Indeed, peasants had a keen appreciation for the realities of power and privilege in the Russian countryside, and the teacher's extremely subordinate position did nothing to enhance authority. All of these factors would seem to militate against teachers achieving significant influence, the status of "notables" within the village, authority figures capable of assuming the protean tasks Russian society was now projecting for them in the wake of the famine and cholera.[27]

Uplifting teachers' level of culture and enhancing their status in the countryside were difficult problems which would be addressed by the Russian teachers' movement and educated society in subsequent years and which we will describe in the following chapters. Of more immediate urgency for this study, the information gathered by the MKG and others pointed to a profession in crisis, a malaise that threatened to undermine even the most modest plans to spread popular literacy.

Many of the problems of status that plagued the nascent profession, as well as the high turnover, were connected with material conditions. Studies indicated that the material situation of rural teachers was difficult at best. In reply to the MKG survey, all teachers complained of inadequate salaries (from two hundred to three hundred rubles a year, and often less), overcrowded classrooms, and the like.[28] Zemstvo studies showed that sanitary conditions in the schools and in teachers' living quarters were poor and that rural teachers were highly susceptible to a number of physical maladies, especially nervous and respiratory disorders.[29] Many respondents to the MKG survey declared that such circumstances drove their predecessors from the teaching profession and candidly admitted that they might also leave if a better opportunity arose.

It was also apparent that material conditions were not alone in dampening teacher morale. Particularly vexing was the problem of "legal status" *(pravovoe polozhenie),* a term conveying teachers' subordinate professional, administrative, and social status. Teachers' lack of rights *(bespravie)* was most evident in the administration of education, particularly in matters of transfers and dismissals, where teachers lacked the right of self-defense before local school boards and even of being informed of the motives behind disciplinary action.[30] The state school inspector could play a significant role in the teacher's life. The large territories under their jurisdiction and their broad responsibilities often made inspectors' control over schools tenuous, but existing legislation still gave school officials considerable powers over teaching personnel and cast the inspector in the ambiguous role of both preceptor and policeman, responsible for the "moral" and "political" reliability of teachers. Some inspectors, like the notorious M. T. Iablochkov of Tambov, tyrannized teachers, interfering in every aspect of their private lives; they controlled teachers' passports, right to marry, and issued special "rules" governing teachers' social relations. Others, like Lenin's celebrated father, I. N. Ul'ianov, acted as selfless mentors. For teachers, in any case, the inspector's authority was often arbitrary, and we will argue that from the 1890s, with the politicization of public education and increased government concern over control of schools, greater emphasis was placed on security.[31]

More broadly, low legal status connoted teachers' vulnerability before a phalanx of "authorities" *(nachal'stva)*—from police to local peasant officials—who held arbitrary power over the teacher and had a penchant for meddling in the affairs of the school. Numerous accounts testify that petty conflicts with rural officials or anonymous denunciations sufficed to trigger dismissal or transfer. As one zemstvo man put it, "it is enough for the teacher to be at odds with some local bigwig for the latter to obtain the teacher's removal." This phenomenon speaks volumes about the depressed professional status of teachers and surely affected their status within the local community. A teacher from Penza later remarked that most teachers were little interested in "public activity" and stood in constant fear of being suspected of "sedition" and of losing their pitiful positions, and for this reason earned the nickname "zemstvo rabbits."[32]

All of this made for a depressing picture. As V. A. Gol'tsev, who helped compile the MKG data, put it:

> The conclusions of many teachers attest to the fact that unsavory conditions, of both school buildings and teachers' lodgings, lack of books and teaching aids, the pitiful material status of teachers, all conspire to sap his energy, to prevent him from rising to the height of his calling and rendering to the population the benefits which could be achieved under better conditions.[33]

The "teachers' question," as N. A. Skvortsov wrote in 1897, could no longer be avoided:

> After heated articles and reports concerning the universal importance of public education, after repeated assertions that the might of Prussia was consolidated not by the army, but by the modest labors of the inconspicuous schoolteacher, that the future belongs to that state which possesses the best schools, it has become impossible to ignore the half-starved existence of the teacher, his nearly complete estrangement from the intelligentsia and extremely precarious legal status.[34]

It was clear, reasoned Skvortsov, that the "soul" of the school was the teacher and that this soul was ailing. By 1900 the press was full of ominous reports of a "teachers' crisis," reflected in a mass exodus from the profession into other endeavors, mostly by male teachers who left to assume posts in the state liquor monopoly, introduced between 1895 and 1901 under Count Sergei Witte's Ministry of Finance.[35] The Ministry of Education in 1900 reported that teachers were abandoning "en masse" their chosen vocation to serve as *sidel'tsy* in the new liquor stores.[36] The causes of this development were not difficult to divine. The minimum salary of a liquor manager was 248 rubles and most earned 300 rubles. Teachers' salaries in most parts of the country were lower and working conditions, arguably, more difficult. Add to this the teacher's low juridical status, extremely subordinate and vulnerable position within the school system and within rural society and it is not surprising that the liquor monopoly could successfully compete with teaching for scarce human resources.

Upon close examination it was clear that the teacher's position was compromised and failed to support the goals educated society had set for Russia after the calamities of the early 1890s and threatened the very processes of modernization and development that were central to the thinking of many state officials as well. The information that teachers provided concerning their educational qualifications, access to cultural commodities, material and legal status must have been disturbing to those who saw education as the path to Russia's salvation. These myriad problems made difficult the task of finding the necessary personnel to staff Russia's rural schools, and, perhaps more importantly, of keeping qualified teachers in the profession and in the countryside. In general, the findings of the Moscow Literacy Committee and zemstvos cast considerable doubt on the teacher's potential to act as a cultural force in the village. Teachers were, indeed, improbable activists, and the obstacles standing in the way of their mobilization seemed insurmountable.

The Zemstvos and the Politics of Public Education

The imperatives of economic modernization combined with the ethical imperatives of service to the long-suffering masses to make public education one of the most important issues of the postfamine decade. Within this context the zemstvos acquired considerable significance. Given the direct responsibilities of the zemstvos in the field of education, as mandated by statute, much of the energy directed toward enlightenment during the 1890s centered around local self-government. The postfamine era witnessed the first intensive efforts by the zemstvos in education since the Great Reforms, and this campaign had important consequences for Russia's schoolteachers. Any resolution of the contradictions in teachers' status or successful efforts at professional mobilization would, by necessity, be closely related to zemstvo initiatives. Further, the sharp politicization of the Russian teachers' movement has to be evaluated in the context of a spiraling conflict between state and society on the battlefield of peasant schooling beginning in the 1890s. To contest the autocratic institutions overseeing Russia's schools, teachers needed allies; to implement their plans and visions zemstvo activists required rural cadres. As it evolved in the 1890s, the partnership between teachers and liberal zemstvo men exemplified the broader left-liberal alliance between third element and zemstvo men which helped define provincial politics in 1905. Since the relationship between teacher and zemstvo proved central to the unfolding of a teachers' movement, the new zemstvo campaign in education merits closer attention.

But zemstvo efforts in education and the relationship between zemstvos and teachers carried wider implications. Russian liberalism, as is well known, was born and nurtured within the zemstvo milieu. Representing the principles of local autonomy, public initiative, and elective representation against the bureaucratic state, the zemstvos not only provided society with the experience of "public activity," but also led to demands that this experience be carried over to national politics. Nowhere was this logic more apparent than in zemstvo efforts in the field of public education, particularly when compared with those of the government. But the zemstvo record in education, particularly the relationship between teachers and zemstvos, also highlights some of the limitations of these institutions, both in furthering national progress benefiting all classes of the population and in serving as vehicles of democratization.

Boris Veselovskii succeeded in dispelling the notion that during the postreform era the zemstvos demonstrated full commitment to mass education. In fact, prior to the 1890s the record was spotty. Provincial zemstvos took little initiative, except for teacher training (funding teachers' seminaries and sponsoring summer courses). Activity at the district level was extremely uneven. For the most part gentry landowners, who dominated the elections to the zemstvos and controlled zemstvo policy, viewed primary schooling as first and foremost the concern of the peasants whose children would directly benefit.

The notion of universal education ran against the grain of such traditional views, and it was not generally accepted that the opening of schools was primarily the responsibility of the zemstvos.[37] In this light Allen Sinel has argued that the efforts of the government under the ministry of D. A. Tolstoi (1866–80) to limit the jurisdiction of zemstvos in the field of education should not be viewed solely as obscurantist attacks on the prerogatives of local self-government by a jealous bureaucracy.[38] Zemstvos were simply not living up to their obligations. Although exceptions did exist, notably the pioneering Moscow zemstvo, before the 1890s public education was not viewed as a national task, one that transcended narrow *soslovie* interests.

All of this changed in the decade before 1905. In quantitative terms the zemstvos' renewed commitment to education can be seen in the number of schools built during this period and increases in zemstvo budgets for public education, compared with the years before the famine. In the period 1894–1902 the number of zemstvo primary schools increased from 13,146 to 18,714; during the preceding eighteen years an increase of 3,046 had been registered.[39] Funding increased dramatically.[40] Zemstvos in the 1890s also began to assume many of the obligations for constructing schools and providing school supplies that were previously borne directly by peasant communities. Only gradually, however, did zemstvos take over the burden of teachers' salaries. This was an issue of crucial importance to teachers, for it freed them of excessive dependence on local peasant officials. Already in the 1880s the zemstvos began to assume this obligation, and by 1902 only in 24 percent of all districts in zemstvo Russia did communes still issue any part of teachers' salaries.[41]

The 1890s also saw expansion of zemstvo activity into the nearly virgin field of adult education *(vneshkol'noe obrazovanie)*.[42] Zemstvos began to seriously discuss the issue of universal schooling in Russia and the various problems attendant on any attempt to make the school accessible to all peasant children.[43] Many zemstvos conducted the first comprehensive statistical surveys of education in their respective provinces. A more committed and sophisticated approach to public education, especially by the provincial zemstvos, was also reflected in the growth of expert commissions and bureaus attached to zemstvo executive boards and staffed by third element specialists, who assumed increased responsibility over the day-to-day management of zemstvo enlightenment efforts.[44]

What is remarkable is that these new zemstvo initiatives to educate the peasantry followed close on the heels of a revision of the Zemstvo Statute in 1890, which was aimed at strengthening the position of the gentry, threatened by loss of landholdings since the Emancipation, as well as increasing state control. Peasant representation in the zemstvos, in fact, dropped fairly significantly between the mid-1880s and 1897: in the district zemstvos from 38 percent to 31 percent and in the provincial zemstvos from 11 percent to 2 percent.[45] What accounted for this shift within the gentry-dominated zemstvo milieu, and what tasks did zemstvo men envision for the rural school?

In the first place, the zemstvos were influenced by the new public interest in popular schooling. In the wake of the famine and cholera of the early 1890s and the general agricultural crisis of this period, zemstvo men were becoming increasingly aware, for both altruistic and pragmatic reasons, that education would play an important part in a rural modernization that would benefit all classes. Beyond that, important changes in the leadership of these institutions were also occurring in the mid-1890s, leading in many places to the ascendancy of a rather distinct group of zemstvo activists for whom the education of the peasantry occupied a pivotal place in a wider program of reform.

Voices continued to be raised within the zemstvos about the dangers of education for the masses; many argued that any schooling should be strictly limited and a heavy dose of religious and moral instruction enforced. Nevertheless, the value of public education was increasingly endorsed, and schooling assumed an increasingly important place within the zemstvos' overall program to modernize the countryside, to bring "culture" to the rural masses. For many the spread of literacy was the key to combatting rural backwardness and poverty. As the zemstvos intensified medical, agronomic, veterinary, and other programs in the countryside it became increasingly apparent that the ultimate success of zemstvo programs depended on the comprehension and receptivity of the peasantry. "Either ignorance or rational economy—these are two mutually exclusive notions," the Voronezh zemstvo responded to a query from the Ministry of Agriculture in 1895.[46]

The link between education and the agrarian question was also underscored during the deliberations of the Local Committees on the Needs of Agriculture, which met throughout the country in 1902 under the auspices of Finance Minister Witte.[47] Committee members stressed the role of literacy in transforming traditional peasant values and prejudices. In the Malmyzh committee (Viatka) a zemstvo agronomist remarked that his intentions were comprehended and he got results in those villages where there were literate peasants who read *Sel'skii vestnik*. In Khvalynsk (Saratov) the local gentry marshal, P. N. Davydov, remembered the cholera riots of 1892 and peasant disregard of zemstvo instructions during that crisis; he also recalled the disaster of the previous year when a dry spell put a premium on completion of the sowing during the traditional Easter holidays; the local peasants celebrated for eight days and then sowed on dry earth with the result that by Christmas hunger and scurvy had visited the district. Others alluded to the necessity of enlightenment in global terms: on a somewhat prophetic note the Glazov (Viatka) committee warned that "even in the Far East, Japan has begun to outstrip us in terms of culture."[48]

Some viewed primary education in vocational terms. For others schooling was the cornerstone of Russia's social, economic, and perhaps political rebuilding by moderate reformers. Only mass education, as N. A. Korf wrote, could in the long run assure the preservation of private property and public order. "Hasn't Russia already suffered enough from the ignorance of the masses? In what measure has Russia been forced to pay for the Pugachevshchina, cholera riots, and [the peasantry's] belief in a second freedom?"[49] Whatever the case—and considerable confusion still reigned regarding the role of school and teacher in Russia's immediate future—in the years after the disaster of 1891–92 there was some consensus within the zemstvos that education was important.

Nevertheless, as Veselovskii noted, the single most important factor in a given zemstvo's commitment to popular enlightenment was the physiognomy of that institution: the composition of zemstvo executive boards *(upravy)* and assemblies, specifically the presence of a dynamic and progressive element.[50] This Menshevik scholar and former zemstvo specialist demonstrated that the major impetus in the shift by zemstvos during the 1890s to a more activist stance, in nearly each case, was provided by a rather small nucleus of progressive zemstvo men.

Ultimate responsibility for schools lay with zemstvos at the district level, but much of the new dynamism of the 1890s owed to increased funding and activity by the provincial zemstvos, which issued funds to district zemstvos and peasant communities. Zemstvo activists at the provincial level attempted to use this funding mechanism to influence the activity of district zemstvos in public education, coordinate efforts, and ultimately unify educational opportunities and standards throughout the province.[51] Naturally, the degree and tempo of this new commitment to popular enlightenment during the postfamine years varied from province to province, but as one surveys the history of educational activity by individual zemstvos around the turn of the century a key ingredient in the shift toward popular enlightenment was the presence of a progressive zemstvo leadership with a special commitment to education. A brief look at several zemstvos illustrates this point.

The Kursk zemstvo had been among the most conservative in the country during the 1880s. Some idea of its commitment to education can be gathered from the fact that it closed the teachers' seminary which it had operated since the early 1870s. The zemstvo elections of 1894, as Veselovskii notes, signaled the beginning of the progressives' "hegemony" in the Kursk zemstvo: from this date the leadership included such liberals as Petr D. Dolgorukov, K. P. Arnol'di, V. E. Iakushkin, A. N. von-Ruttsen, and others. A provincial school commission, staffed largely by third element experts, was formed the same year. A statistical study of education in the province was undertaken under the supervision of the zemstvo statistician I. P. Belokonskii (in general the Kursk zemstvo pioneered in the field of school statistics), and during the ensuing period zemstvo allocations for public education increased dramatically, much of it provided from the coffers of the provincial zemstvo.[52]

During the period between 1894 and 1903, when a conservative backlash against the liberal leadership occurred, the Kursk zemstvo initiated new programs in the field of adult education, one of the most innovative of which was an experiment with special roving teachers who gave evening classes in different villages. The Kursk liberals also evidenced concern for teaching personnel: summer teachers' courses were held each year between 1897 and 1903, Dolgorukov and others helped establish a teachers' mutual aid society, and the zemstvo gave considerable financial support to a women's teacher training school founded by von-Ruttsen's sister Liudmilla.[53]

The Saratov provincial zemstvo presents a similar picture. Even during the mid-1890s the Saratov zemstvo remained relatively inactive, which prompted the local governor to urge the zemstvo to give greater attention to the needs of education. With the exception of Balashov, the district assemblies were also lethargic. A turnabout occurred at the end of the decade when provincial elections gave progressive *zemtsy* the edge. The new zemstvo board wasted little time in initiating a series of measures aimed at unifying and expanding zemstvo activity throughout the province: setting up a storehouse for distribution of books, organizing various commissions to manage the different spheres of zemstvo activity, reorganizing the nationally important zemstvo journal *Saratovskaia zemskaia nedelia,* and undertaking extensive statistical studies of education in the province. In 1901, in the face of strong opposition from conservatives, the zemstvo accepted a resolution to cease funding church schools.[54]

Among the leadership of the Ekaterinoslav provincial zemstvo there were few progressives during this period, and little was done to promote education. Thanks to a favorable tax base, however, certain district zemstvos in the province were able to divert large funds to education. In Slavianoserbsk, for example, the gentry, because of overrepresentation in the zemstvo assembly resulting from the Zemstvo Statute of 1890, were able to shift much of the burden for zemstvo projects onto the shoulders of industrial interests.[55] Still, it took the election of an energetic zemstvo board, under the chairmanship of V. N. Radakov, in 1897 to really get things moving. During Radakov's tenure, the zemstvo assembly accepted a project for universal schooling in the district and there was a dramatic increase in zemstvo allocations on public education, from 14,730 rubles in 1898 to 61,336 rubles in 1899. The Zemstvo also resolved to take over school construction and maintenance costs from peasant communes. Adult education programs were set up, teachers' salaries were raised to a minimum of 300 rubles, and, of course, the number of schools was increased. During the first thirty-four years of the Slavianoserbsk zemstvo's existence twenty-one schools were opened under its auspices; between 1897 and 1902, twenty-five new schools were opened, and another seventeen added by 1907.[56]

Roberta Manning and Natalia Pirumova have done much to provide a social and political profile of liberal zemstvo activists responsible for these changes and have explored the bases of their ascendancy within local self-government after the early 1890s, particularly in articulating zemstvo opposition to the government. The liberals constituted a relatively small group within the essentially moderate to conservative zemstvo rank and file. Their leadership before 1905 owed to apathy on the part of much of the zemstvo electorate, their own demonstrated expertise, managerial skills, and energy at a time when zemstvo programs were expanding, and finally their ability to tap a diffuse opposition among the gentry, whose traditional position seemed threatened by a growing agrarian crisis, aggravated by the state's economic policies under Witte and by what was seen as increased bureaucratic intrusion into local affairs and encroachment on zemstvo prerogatives. On this basis the zemstvo liberals were increasingly successful in politicizing the zemstvos, a process that reached a peak in 1905.[57]

Zemstvo liberals also succeeded in forging solid links with the non-zemstvo intelligentsia and third element. These liberals were relatively less involved in management of their estates; a high percentage were university educated and during their careers pursued a profession. In many cases, as Manning and Veselovskii have shown, the liberals served both as elected members (deputies of the zemstvo assemblies or members of the *upravy*) and third element specialists, usually doctors or other high-level personnel. Pirumova sees "social activism" *(obshchestvennaia aktivnost')* as the common denominator for this group: they often combined service as zemstvo deputies with other professional activity, journalism, and participation in learned societies and professional congresses. As Manning notes, the zemstvo liberals were, in fact, a kind of hybrid stratum, a "gentry intelligentsia."[58]

As such, the zemstvo liberals shared the intelligentsia's ethic of service to the narod. There was a considerable populist strain within Russian liberalism, and many zemstvo leaders of the 1890s and 1900s had, during their youth or university days, flirted with revolutionary populism. V. M. Chernov, the Socialist Revolutionary leader, who during the 1890s was employed by the Tambov zemstvo, described local liberals as "populist cultural activists" *(narodoliubivye kul'turniki)* whose liberalism was infused with the "spirit," if not the "ideology," of populism.[59] Their own backgrounds and ethical motivations, combined with their practical work, served to foster cooperation with the third element, particularly in the field of education.

Popular education was central to the liberals' vision of Russia's future—the establishment of a "legal," "cultured," and "enlightened" order—a vision not necessarily shared by the peasantry. Naturally, they reasoned that it was the peasant and his values that had to be transformed. In their blueprint only public education and literacy could assure the popular basis for a constitutionalist order, whenever that might prove feasible; only education could insure the integration of the peasantry into a national European-style legal order; only enlightenment could narrow the dangerous gulf between society and the narod, assure a modicum of social peace and economic progress; only enlightenment could efface such traditional and debilitating peasant practices as mothers giving vodka to infants in order to induce sleep while peasant women went out to work in the fields.

Of course, many of these considerations were shared by much of the nonzemstvo intelligentsia, which embraced the enlightenment ethos, particularly after the great famine. In this context it is worth noting that many zemstvo activists passed through a kind of apprenticeship in the Committees of Literacy during the late 1880s and early 1890s. Zemstvo men like D. I. Shakhovskoi, F. F. Oldenburg (Tver), I. T. Alisov (Voronezh), A. A. Savel'ev (Nizhegorod), A. P. Batuev (Viatka), N. A. Vargunin, and others participated in committee debates on universal schooling and other issues. As such they provided a link between the most current theoretical discussions in the capitals and zemstvo practice in the locales.[60] More important, the zemstvo education drive of the 1890s helped foster a close working relationship between zemstvo activists and third element intelligentsia, which by the turn of the century was developing into a liberal-radical alliance in provincial Russia. The realities of provincial politics and the potency of popular education as a "battle cry" for the autocracy's opposition, as we will see, strongly influenced the growth of the nascent teachers' movement.[61]

That the school question became politically charged should come as no surprise. The zemstvo men, particularly the liberals, clearly aspired to a position of greater influence in the affairs of state, if only in claims that the central government consult the zemstvos on important issues of local significance. Public education was one area in which the zemstvos could demonstrate their greater commitment to the population's welfare and, at the same time, demonstrate the efficacy of representative government and the competence of local zemstvo activists. It was also an area in which the government's record could easily be attacked (the zemstvos' own less than sterling record before the 1890s was not examined). Success in promoting public education provided zemstvo activists with a certain sense of legitimacy—grounds for considering themselves the natural spokesmen and leaders of the nation at large. Despite their domination by the gentry, the zemstvos were, it could be argued, transcending narrow soslovie interests and demonstrating commitment to the welfare of the masses, something the bureaucracy had failed to do.

There was some substance behind such assertions. Although somewhat belated, zemstvo activism contrasted sharply with the government's apparent lack of concern over popular enlightenment (with the exception of heavy subsidization of church schools). In fact, much of the government's activity in this field during the postfamine period was interpreted by zemstvo men, both liberals and conservatives, as bureaucratic interference in zemstvo activities. As zemstvos became more interested in schools they also became more critical of the administrative framework of primary education, dating from the 1870s, which seemed to restrict zemstvo initiative and control, especially the role of the government inspector in monitoring instruction and other aspects of school management, as well as the prerogatives of the local school board *(uchilishchnyi sovet)*, on which zemstvos were weakly represented.[62]

The regime countered on a battlefield chosen by zemstvo activists. The postfamine decade saw the government enact a series of measures that further impinged upon the zemstvos' competency in education and threatened teachers' professional position. In 1892 zemstvos forfeited to the church the right to open "literacy schools" *(shkoly gramotnosti)*. A February 7, 1894 law subjected zemstvo representatives on local school boards (the zemstvos were allowed to elect two members) to confirmation by the provincial administration. Zemstvo representation was further diluted in 1896 when land captains *(zemskie nachal'niki)* were made ex-officio members of the school boards.[63] It is questionable whether these measures actually had much impact on zemstvo activities; they did serve, however, to exacerbate zemstvo-government relations.

More serious was the law of June 12, 1900, which limited annual increases in zemstvo budgets to 3 percent, without special government sanction. In large part, this law was a response to increased zemstvo expenditures on public education during previous years, which competed with the state's industrialization drive for scarce resources in the countryside. Government officials had voiced concern over the financial burden that ambitious zemstvo programs might place on the population.[64] N. V. Chekhov considered the law of 1900 to have severely affected the continued growth of zemstvo expenditures on education, especially in the case of those zemstvos which had not significantly increased their education budgets prior to the law's enactment.[65]

As rural schooling became a battleground between state and zemstvos, government concern over supervision of these schools, and teachers, increased. Yet the number of state school inspectors was clearly inadequate: the staff of inspectors had remained nearly constant in the zemstvo provinces as of 1876. During the 1890s local officials complained about the lack of surveillance *(nadzor)* over zemstvo schools, and not only in a pedagogical sense. In 1900, and again in 1904, the inspectorate was beefed up in the zemstvo provinces.[66]

Finally, the government began discussions concerning revision of the 1874 School Statute and diminution of zemstvo prerogatives in public education. One commission, chaired by V. K. Pleve, met in 1892 and apparently considered revision of school legislation. A more serious threat to zemstvo prerogatives was contained in a project compiled by the Ministry of Education in 1900, the so-called Draft Instruction to School Boards, which would have drastically reduced the role of both local school boards and zemstvos in education in favor of the state inspectorate. With the implementation of this project, inspectors would be allowed to veto any decision by a zemstvo to open a new school, and zemstvos would be completely removed from the process of selecting candidates to teaching posts, a crucial issue, since candidate nomination provided zemstvos with one of the only available means to influence instruction in zemstvo schools.[67] Little came of these discussions, but throughout the postfamine decade a strong current within government circles continued to regard zemstvo educational efforts with grave suspicion. The church, in particular, adopted a militant attitude to the zemstvo school, its main competitor in the field of primary schooling. As zemstvos became more interested in their own schools they began to curtail grants to church schools, which had been substantial: as late as 1901, 265 out of 359 district zemstvos continued to provide some financial aid to church schools to the tune of 434,000 rubles.[68] By the end of the 1890s the issue of church versus zemstvo schools had become highly charged. Priests were instructed by their superiors to agitate among the peasantry against zemstvo schools, often adding to animosity between clerics and local teachers. Many zemstvo men had done a complete volte face in their attitude to church schools; whereas during the 1880s even zemstvo radicals like F. I. Rodichev and I. I. Petrunkevich had considered providing zemstvo support for church schools, during the next decade zemstvo men increasingly came to look upon the church schools as competitors for the minds and hearts of the population. This was also how the struggle was depicted in the rightist press: the influential *Moskovskiia vedomosti* mounted a vociferous campaign against the "antireligious" and "antistate" zemstvo school.[69]

These conflicts had important consequences for teachers. The zemstvo activists' critique of the bureaucracy held considerable appeal for teachers and, as we will see, influenced teachers' own professional and political program. No doubt, zemstvo conflict with the church seemed to mirror, and at the same time intensify, teachers' own local struggles with rural clerics and officials to achieve authority and autonomy. Moreover, as education became caught up in the wider zemstvo-state struggle, teachers acquired space in which to maneuver, room in which a movement could flourish. This owed much to the ambivalence of the government's policies in the field of popular education.

The Ministry of Education did not wholly deserve the appellation "Ministry of Popular Ignorance" attached to it by liberal society. In fact, the ministry did contain many enlightened officials, experts who understood the importance of a general, largely secular education for national progress. Such views were shared by others in government, within Witte's Ministry of Finance, for instance. The tsar himself, though he urged caution, also generally endorsed the spread of literacy among the masses. In fact, on the eve of 1905 the MNP was at work on projects of universal schooling in Russia (it is true that one of these would have limited the further growth of zemstvo schools and was interpreted by educated society as a veiled attack on the zemstvo school). In light of these plans, increased government funding for schools was included in the state budget for 1904 but was then suspended by the Council of Ministers with the onset of war with Japan at the start of that year.[70] These projects were continued and more state funds committed to education after the Revolution of 1905. One could argue that the government was making a commitment, haltingly of course, to public enlightenment. But its approach was marked by extreme ambivalence.

To a significant degree the government's commitment to enlightenment was offset by its traditional preoccupation with security and maintenance of the social order in the countryside. This concern was perhaps best expressed in the Ministry of Interior (MVD) and in the provincial administration. Aside from facilitating the collection of taxes, the primary function of the provincial administration, which had a rural administrative and police network stretching down to the *volost'* (a unit of rural administration encompassing several villages) and village level, was security. Invoking the image of "two societies" coexisting in Russia, one can perhaps best describe the function of the MVD and its apparatus as standing guard over the border separating rural from urban Russia, checking passports (literally, in the case of peasants seeking earnings outside of their villages), and regulating the contacts between the rural and urban societies. Such activities underscored government solicitude for the rural commune, especially in the face of increased peasant contacts with the city and the quickening tempo of industrialization in the later 1880s and early 1890s.

Rural schooling confronted the government with a similar problem. Nicholas II and his advisors recognized the imperatives behind literacy but were wary of the possible effects that rapid and uncontrolled diffusion of enlightenment, particularly a campaign initiated by educated society and the zemstvos, might have on the rural social order and upon traditional peasant attitudes, which government conservatives believed still included firm allegiance to the person of the tsar, religious faith, and a healthy suspicion of outsiders: hence the tsar's admonition that there was no need to hurry with the task of educating the masses and pleas from provincial officials for increased *nadzor* over the school.[71]

Official attitudes toward the teacher were, likewise, ambivalent. On the one hand the village pedagogue served as the Ministry of Education's (and often the zemstvo's) primary agent in the task of enlightening the peasantry, and as such it was logical to assume that the government would do all in its power to support and encourage the teacher in this work. But, on the other hand, since the Emancipation the government, particularly those responsible for security, harbored a strong suspicion of attempts by "outsiders"—whether revolutionary populists or the zemstvo third element—to intrude into the countryside, to cross the border between urban and rural Russia unchecked. The rural teacher, who was resident in the village at least eight months of the year, presented a special problem. Many agents of the zemstvos were dispatched into the countryside to fulfill very limited objectives, such as evaluation of property by statisticians for tax assessments. The government was extremely suspicious of zemstvo statisticians, and their comings and goings were a matter of great concern to rural police. Given their small numbers and limited assignments, however, the activities of zemstvo statisticians, veterinarians, and agronomists could be monitored. If need be they could simply be prohibited from working in the countryside. Some zemstvo doctors, it is true, did reside in the larger settlements, from which medical services were dispensed, but they too were spread rather thinly.

But for rural teachers, who numbered in the tens of thousands, a different solution was required. L. D. Briukhatov, the Tambov zemstvo activist, described the government's prescription for the rural teacher as one of "freezing" the teacher at the level of intellectual development provided by the teachers' seminary or other limited educational institution.[72] The teacher was then sent to the rural school where natural conditions conspired to isolate him from further access to "culture" and from intercourse with educated society. In this context the school inspector fulfilled a dual role, assuming both pedagogical and police functions: he not only provided the teacher with helpful advice on teaching methods and examinations, but also stood between teacher and society, including the zemstvos, mediating and monitoring the relations between teacher and society. Both functions, that of policeman and pedagogue, were built into existing school legislation. Where the balance was struck depended upon personalities and local conditions.

As zemstvos became more involved in education and as public enlightenment became a political issue, school authorities were increasingly thrust into the role of policeman, monitoring and even blocking contacts between the zemstvo and school—even contacts which, as we will see in subsequent chapters, had as their ostensible purpose improvement of the quality of teaching personnel. The school inspector, of course, was responsible for disciplining teachers, and in cases of conflict between teachers and other local authorities, particularly when the issue of security was raised, school officials were under considerable pressure to support the authorities. Officials in the Ministry of Education admitted as much, arguing that it was very difficult for an inspector to defend teachers who ran afoul of local land captains, gentry marshals, or even priests, in matters relating to the classroom, let alone in cases where the "political reliability" of a teacher was in question.[73] The reality of power in the countryside only reinforced a tendency on the part of teachers to rely on a rival source of authority such as the zemstvos.

The government was attempting to pursue two irreconcilable aims: to educate the peasantry, within limits to be sure, and also to isolate and protect school and teacher from what were viewed as dangerous and unsettling currents within educated society. Such a strategy only nurtured the isolation and cultural deprivation that characterized the teaching profession in Russia. If the school was to serve as an oasis of culture in the dark countryside, if the teacher was to play the role of cultural agent among the peasantry, neither could reasonably be cut off from the higher culture. Neither educated society, the zemstvos, nor the government could be content with simply arming teachers with a modest training, sending them to village schools, and then leaving them to incubate a generation of literate peasant citizens.

This situation made it difficult for teachers to play a positive role as cultural agents in rural society (the dangers of professional regression and vegetation were real) and, more immediately, tended to thwart efforts to both attract and keep qualified personnel in the rural schools. The government was fundamentally unable or unwilling to deal with the problem of the teacher's status, in part because it was still not prepared to make a substantial financial commitment to primary education (and thus help ease teachers' material status). But more importantly the government, or at least influential elements within it, was still wedded to the notion that maintenance of the traditional social order took precedence over other considerations and that the primary threat to that order lay in the intrusion of urban Russia's values and ideas in anything but cautious, measured doses. Riven with contradictions, official policy, as we will see, contributed mightily to the politicization of the Russian teachers' movement, compelling teachers to seek resolution of their ambiguous status in opposition to the regime.

In equal measure educated Russian society's campaign to enlighten the rural masses helped shape teachers' emerging professional identity. For those in educated society, including many in the zemstvos, the threat to national progress, however defined, lay in the fact that rural society was a world with which they had few links. The benighted masses *(temnyi narod)* it was reasoned, did not share their vision of progress, not because its interests were irreconcilably opposed to those of educated society, but because it had been bound in chains of poverty, ignorance, and bureaucratic tutelage. Enlightenment was seen as the crucible in which these bonds would be melted down.

It was within this climate that public interest in education and the teacher revived. Teachers provided society not only with a sympathetic cause, but also an eminently practical one. Their significance in any campaign to enlighten the rural masses was incontestable; during the decade after the great famine Russians frequently cited the example of the German teacher and the "lesson of Sedan" as proof that national progress could only be built upon a bedrock of literacy and universal schooling. But the reality of the teacher's existence clashed sharply with the image of the teacher as a key cultural force in the countryside. The "teachers' question" was one with which society, and particularly the zemstvos, had to be concerned. It was logical that as the zemstvos displayed more interest in their schools, as was the case from the mid–1890s, zemstvo men would show increased concern with the personnel that staffed these schools—with their educational qualifications and intellectual background, as well as the factors hindering the teacher's work and often driving him out of the profession.

From the 1890s, therefore, zemstvos came to provide material and moral support to the teachers' professional movement. Naturally, the zemstvo liberals played a central role in the teachers' movement, since these were the people who tended to direct the zemstvos' shift toward activism during the postfamine period. Indeed, involvement of zemstvo men in teachers' summer courses and congresses, and in attempts to build professional organizations, was generally restricted to the fairly distinct group of progressive zemstvo representatives for whom public education held special importance within a broader program of rural modernization, reform, and political opposition. Not only did they interpret the teacher's potential as a cultural agent broadly, but they also came to see teachers as potential allies in opposition to the government and cadres for political mobilization in the countryside. The emergence of the teachers' movement thus necessarily ran parallel to that of the zemstvo opposition. There would be clashes between these groups, to be sure, but before 1905 teacher activists would depend heavily on the zemstvos for financial, organizational, and moral support, especially in the face of the government's policy of benign neglect and resistance to teachers' efforts.

That teachers should view the zemstvos as benefactors was quite natural, but there was an element of illusion here. Prior to 1905 much of the so-called democratic intelligentsia tended to pin excessive hopes on these institutions. The zemstvo gentry, as it turned out, was not very liberal, and certainly not democratic. Their commitment to political opposition was provisional and their understanding of enlightenment (and the role of the teacher) rather limited. Faced with the specter or revolutionary political and social change, zemstvo men might embrace the government's view that the teacher posed a threat to the social order and thus had to be isolated and controlled. Teachers could be caught in a wicked crossfire between government and zemstvo reaction, an aroused and suspicious peasantry, and a liberal opposition too weak to carry the day.

The ephemeral quality of zemstvo liberalism was only dimly perceived before 1905. Given their position, teachers would have been among the last to divine this weakness and its consequences. As for the period before 1905 it was one of optimism and rising expectations for rural teachers, as for Russian society in general. That the "public movement" of this period could sweep up the humble rural teacher says something about its intensity and depth. For here was a would-be "enlightener" of the narod who shared with that population various disabilities: poverty, bureaucratic constraints, *bespravie*, cultural deprivation, and isolation.

3. Cultural Impoverishment and the Impulse to Associate

Many teachers at the turn of the century were ill-equipped, both in terms of pedagogical training and general education, to spearhead an enlightenment campaign in the countryside. Qualifications were extremely varied. Much depended on local conditions, such as the existence of a teachers' seminary in a given province, but some generalizations can be made. Men were increasingly drawn from normal schools; in some provinces teachers' seminaries provided 60 percent of the men teaching in primary schools. The remainder were graduates (or dropouts) of theological seminaries, advanced primary schools (the six-year *gorodskie uchilishcha* established for lower-class urban children), or various elementary schools. Given the opportunities for employment elsewhere and in higher education, few graduates of men's secondary schools entered the profession.

The opposite was true of women, who were coming to dominate the profession in many provinces. Women were recruited from various secondary institutions: gymnasiums, the more limited, in terms of instruction, diocesan *(eparkhial'nye)* schools run by the church, or progymnasiums (incomplete secondary schools). In many provinces at the turn of the century *eparkhial'ki* constituted 40 percent of women in zemstvo schools. Given the existence of only a handful of zemstvo and private women's normal schools, females with specialized qualifications comprised a small percentage of teachers in most provinces.[1]

Confronted with this mélange, and with little evidence as to performance in the classroom, experts disagreed as to who made the best teachers. Seminary graduates, it was granted, seemed best prepared in terms of methodology, especially the "pedagogical tightrope walking" *(ekvilibristika)* demanded by simultaneous work with three groups of pupils.[2] On the other hand, graduates of state normal schools often suffered from basic deficiencies in general knowledge.[3] As for products of the diocesan schools, to say nothing of those with lesser backgrounds, the situation was generally worse.

At the same time qualifications were declining, particularly after 1895. Zemstvo statistics demonstrate that the percentage of teachers with "satisfactory" backgrounds (those with higher education, of which there had always been few, complete secondary, or specialized) was declining in many provinces.[4] The rapidly expanding school network placed considerable strain on existing sources of recruitment, such as the teachers' seminaries, the number of which remained nearly constant since the 1870s. At the same time the booming urban sector of the 1890s offered attractive alternatives to the literate sons, and sometimes daughters, of the lower classes. A young peasant with some education could just as easily find employment as a commercial clerk in the city as become a rural teacher.[5]

If one did choose teaching there were few means to augment a rough formal education. Summer refresher courses provided one answer. Continued independent study, or "self-education," was just as vital. Reading could supplement a meager education, and, perhaps more important, it could keep the teacher's head above the uncultured morass of rural life. Recidivism posed a danger not only to graduates of the modest three-year rural school, but to their teachers as well. As teachers constantly pointed out, reading material was indispensable for both classroom effectiveness and teachers' well-being: "For no other person does the book have such significance as for the rural teacher. Others may substitute intelligent society for reading material, but for the teacher the book is irreplaceable." If teachers were to be in a position to answer the varied questions posed by the peasantry and perhaps disseminate new and useful ideas—to acquire, as teachers put it, the necessary "authority" and status of "notables" within the local community—reading was essential. This was increasingly the case as peasants experienced more contact with the outside world and became more curious about affairs beyond the village. As one teacher wrote:

> Among the peasantry are some reasonably literate people who are eager to find out something novel about politics and other affairs. Quite often one encounters such persons and hears from them: "Well, how are things going (for example) in Greece? You know, they say that the Turks are abusing the Greeks." Or else: "What is this about France being destroyed on the market?" You don't understand what they are talking about.[6]

This remark was made at the end of the 1890s. Peasant interest in extravillage affairs rose appreciably in subsequent years. Teachers who gathered in Riazan province in 1904 argued that access to periodical literature was essential if teachers were to fulfill their function as enlighteners. Often the sole *intelligent* in the village, if the teacher was unable to answer peasant queries or offer sound advice, his or her authority suffered.[7] Liberal zemstvo activists concurred. That same year the Viatka zemstvo recognized that "the zemstvo school must not only impart simple literacy, but also widen the intellectual horizons of its pupils so that, upon graduation, they will seek to continue acquiring knowledge." This, the zemstvo reasoned, required that teachers possess a good education (those with primary or so-called "lower" backgrounds, like the *gorodskie uchilishcha,* were clearly inadequate) and be able to explain "important natural phenomena as well as major public events." Only through reading and "intensive intellectual labor," the zemstvo argued, could teachers expand their own awareness and then help raise the cultural level of the masses.[8] Teachers, educators, and zemstvo men all agreed that if teachers were to properly fulfill their function in the school and serve as multipurpose "cultural agents" in the countryside, access to books, journals, and newspapers was essential. How accessible were such cultural commodies?

Here lay a basic contradiction in the teacher's status, that of a culture-bearer cut off from the well-springs of culture. Here the teacher's status as a "civilized savage," to quote one observer, was most apparent.[9] The teacher's world was materially insecure, arbitrary, and precarious; not surprisingly, it was also poor in cultural amenities. With the exception of pulp *(lubochnye)* literature, distributed by itinerant peddlers or sold at rural markets, books were not a regular feature of rural life. Newspapers did not find their way into the village in any quantity until the Russo-Japanese War and 1905 revolution sparked popular interest in national events.[10] This is not to say that the countryside was entirely devoid of reading material. Some landowners maintained libraries and teachers could sometimes borrow books. A teacher from Ekaterinoslav province recalled that on his salary of twenty-five rubles he had to support a wife, two children, and younger sister and could only dream of subscribing to a newspaper. He was able, however, to borrow newspapers from a local estate, having promised the *barinia* not to read *Russkoe slovo* to the peasants.[11]

The teacher was not readily accepted into the society of *pomeshchiki* and other notables. A 1904 survey in Novgorod that attempted to assess relations between teachers and school trustees *(popechiteli)*, posts often held by landowners, found that relations between teacher and trustee were not close.[12] The relationship was often strained, teachers viewing the trustee as simply one more "authority" meddling in the affairs of the school. Add to this the fact that many gentry barely stood above the general cultural level of the rural milieu, and it can be seen that the teacher's thirst for reading material could hardly be met from this quarter.

Some district towns did offer various cultural amenities. Most zemstvos kept small libraries for their employees (a few specifically for teachers), and newspapers were generally available. Ten versts or less was considered accessible, since it could be covered on foot and did not entail the expense of hiring a horse and wagon (as one teacher remarked, "I could only walk, and on foot only the apostles ever got very far.").[13] Of 599 teachers who replied to the Novgorod survey, however, only 17 lived within a ten-verst radius of town. One hundred and two teachers resided 10 to 25 versts from town; 176 at 25 to 50 versts; 206 at 50 to 100 versts; and 96 at over 100 versts from town.[14]

Postal services, either those provided by the government or zemstvos, could be important to teachers who wished to subscribe to a periodical, borrow books from the zemstvo *uprava* library, or serve as a rural correspondent for a provincial newspaper, a practice not uncommon among teachers, particularly in 1905. The same survey, however, concluded that many rural teachers did not enjoy access to the postal network. This was also an impediment for those who sought to organize mutual aid societies among scattered teachers. To these communications problems must be added other, no less characteristic aspects of life in rural Russia. Teachers could have their correspondence addressed to the volost board, the basic rural agency of the Ministry of Interior. One teacher described the situation there to the zemstvo statistician Belokonskii: "I receive my mail from the volost. It is ludicrous, but a fact, that long before I get my letters I already know their contents, and the newspaper I subscribe to never reaches me until at least a week after it arrives at the volost. The situation here regarding correspondence is Gogolesque." Another teacher concurred: "From the volost not only private but even official correspondence is received opened."[15]

For these reasons, many teachers were unable to utilize libraries set up by many zemstvos. The Moscow provincial zemstvo found that 56 percent of the teachers had used libraries at local zemstvo boards during the school year 1896–97 (frequency is not indicated). Some replied that this was because of the poor selection of material, but more often lack of access was cited. Many respondents argued that zemstvo libraries should be decentralized among centrally located schools at the volost level, with circulation between schools, but zemstvos took little initiative here before 1905.[16]

The major impediment to satisfaction of teachers' intellectual needs was poverty. For the teacher, especially one supporting a family, it was often difficult to squeeze the few rubles necessary to buy books out of a salary of at most 200 to 300 rubles a year. A former rural teacher described the situation in the 1880s:

> What could I do in my isolated backwater? What could fill the free time? Turn to a book, but where could one get hold of one? Teachers' libraries did not exist at that time, and subscribing to books from town was not easy, and in any case not within the means of a teacher receiving 16 rubles, 65 kopecks a month with a family. Even materials like instructional aids were lacking and we did not even know about many of these. For lack of more useful diversion, the teacher was forced to spend this free time at card games like "fools," blindman's bluff, or drinking. Most of us first approached teaching with zeal, but these good intentions, due to the conditions in which we were forced to live, soon shattered. Even those teachers most dedicated to the school, having lost their health, endured so many spiritual trials and not seeing any recompense for their difficult work, finally abandoned the school and sought more gratifying employment.[17]

Teachers' salaries did increase slightly during the next decade, as some zemstvos began issuing periodic supplements to salaries, for example, fifty ruble increments at five-year intervals. Nevertheless, before 1905 there continued to be wide differences between salary levels in different districts, and many zemstvos failed to adopt supplements. The teacher's world thus remained culturally impoverished.

The Moscow Literacy Committee survey provides an indication of teachers' access to reading material during the mid-1890s, though the results are probably skewed in favor of the more "activist" personnel and therefore underestimate the problem.[18] Of 109 teachers responding in Vladimir province, 27 reported that they had their own small libraries *(uchitel'skie biblioteki)* attached to the schools. These held from 10 to 508 volumes (in one case), but in most instances their content was meager, often limited to classroom texts and weak in belles-lettres and general subjects. As for other sources, 27 teachers indicated that they were able to borrow books without charge from zemstvo libraries since they lived close to the district town; 36 occasionally borrowed books from private sources but reported that the quality of such material was low; 23 reported that they had no access whatsoever to reading material. A handful subscribed to a periodical, usually with the help of the trustee.[19] The situation in Kazan was similar: 36 percent reported spending something out of pocket for reading. In one district (Chistopol) the zemstvo set up five regional libraries for teachers. The Laishev zemstvo allocated 120 rubles per year to cover fees for teachers at the town public library. Elsewhere the issue was "left to chance." In Kostroma, Penza, Smolensk, and Kaluga provinces the situation was much the same.[20]

Conditions were somewhat better in the South, where salaries tended to be higher. Of 128 respondents from Samara, 59 subscribed to periodicals at their own expense; salaries ranged on average 300 to 350 rubles. In Ekaterinoslav, where the yearly rate was around 350 rubles, 60 percent reported holding subscriptions at their own expense (spending on average 16 rubles per year).[21] In Tauride many zemstvos apparently subsidized subscriptions to journals like *Obrazovanie, Russkii nachal'nyi uchitel', Sel'skii vestnik, Plodovodstvo,* and *Russkaia shkola.* Salaries were exceptionally high in this Black Sea province, averaging 400 rubles, and it is not surprising that 63 of 79 respondents spent on average 15 rubles per year on subscriptions.[22] There was strong correlation between salaries and teachers' outlays for reading material, as was clearly demonstrated in a later survey conducted by the journal *Vestnik znaniia.* Food, clothing, light, and fuel accounted for most of the teacher's monthly wage, especially where it was low.[23] One poor soul, receiving 163 rubles a year and living forty versts from town, wrote: "For the past eight years I have read nothing besides classroom texts and have read over and over again 'Ruslan Lazarevich' " (a popular lubok tale).[24]

Many rural teachers read little or nothing. Of 602 schools surveyed in Tambov province in 1901–2, 109 teachers declared that they "had no access to books" *(ni otkuda knig ne dostaiut).* In Moscow in 1899, of 478 teachers replying to a zemstvo survey, 150 claimed that they owned no books or subscriptions; 38 of these replied that they never read anything but classroom materials. Similar information is available from other zemstvo provinces.[25] Of course, as zemstvos and other agencies attempted to disseminate reading material among the rural population, teachers had access to various "popular libraries" intended for the adult peasant and reading rooms managed by "societies for popular sobriety." These were geared toward a mass audience; the quality was low and selection sparse, in part because they were restricted until December 1905 by ministry catalogs. For the rural teacher, who was supposed to stand above the general cultural level of the village, these were hardly satisfactory, and teachers of all educational backgrounds—lower, secondary, and specialized—expressed a desperate need to supplement their formal training.[26] To alleviate teachers' cultural deprivation assistance was necessary from other quarters.

Zemstvo activists recognized the dangers inherent in teachers' cultural deprivation: ineffectiveness, recidivism, despair. For those who saw the teacher as an agent of rural modernization the situation seemed urgent, and some zemstvos before 1905 made an effort to quench teachers' thirst for reading material. In 1901 the Saratov zemstvo voted 1,000 rubles to help teachers purchase books and periodicals and offered discounts on materials from the zemstvo's bookstore *(knizhnyi sklad),* noting that only single teachers were able to devote a portion of their budget to such purchases.[27] The first systematic attempt to aid teachers in subscriptions was made by the Iaroslavl zemstvo in 1901; teachers were given up to five rubles a year, having to provide the rest of the cost out of pocket. The plan met with great success and was expanded in subsequent years. With the zemstvo subsidy nearly all the 536 zemstvo teachers in the province (94.8 percent) received at least one journal or newspaper; by contrast, only 26 percent of the teachers in church schools carried any subscriptions.[28]

On the basis of material from Iaroslavl and other provinces, several things can be said about teachers' reading habits. There was little interest in pedagogical journals, either liberal organs like *Russkaia shkola* and *Vestnik vospitaniia* (which cost eight rubles) or the semi-official *Russkii nachal'nyi uchitel'* (three rubles). Given that teaching was exhausting labor pursued in relative isolation from educated society, teachers preferred "general education" journals: "Reading them the rural teacher could experience that which was experienced by the advanced intelligentsia, feel that he was not cut off from the world . . . and could forget for a time the harshness of reality."[29] The most popular periodical among teachers was undoubtedly the illustrated weekly *Niva* (The Wheatfield). *Niva* was a good deal less scholarly and highbrow than the standard "thick journals" of the Russian intelligentsia.[30] More space was devoted to literature, including translations of foreign authors like Jules Verne; in 1903–4 a full subscription to *Niva* (eleven rubles) included the complete works of Chekhov. Many of the stories in *Niva* had less literary merit, but adventure tales of "darkest" Africa and the like did provide an opportunity to escape from the monotony of rural life, if only vicariously, and this probably explains the hegemony of *Niva* in all studies of teachers' subscriptions. It carried less commentary on politics and other issues with which society was so involved. The educator N. Bratchikov remarked that "*Niva* stands far from the questions of public life, from current trends in the realm of science and scholarship." Only a person in a state of "intellectual somnolence" could be satisfied with this journal.[31]

As critics pointed out, the teacher's affection for *Niva* certainly attested to his "lack of culture" and the fact that he was not a full-fledged member of the intelligentsia. Yet in their reading teachers compared favorably with other professional groups, for example, white-collar railway employees *(sluzhashchie),* who by virtue of their work generally had greater access to reading material. A study conducted among employees on the Riazan-Ural Railway in 1905 showed that, among journals, *Niva* was by far the most popular (1,697 subscriptions, followed by *Rodina* with 949). *Vokrug sveta,* a journal similar to *Niva,* registered 425 subscriptions among railwaymen, five times greater than the demand for *Mir bozhii* and six times greater than that for *Russkoe bogatstvo,* two respected thick journals.[32] In any case, looking at the Iaroslavl data one can see improvement over time in the quality of teachers' subscriptions, as well as greater interest in newspapers. With aid from the zemstvo, periodical literature had overall become much more accessible to Iaroslavl teachers (in 1897 total subscriptions failed to exceed one hundred), and other zemstvos followed its lead.[33]

Official policy was more cautious. Given its ambivalent view of teachers, it is hardly surprising that the government sought to monitor what they read. Ministry of Education catalogs permitted only 3 percent of the books and 17 percent of the periodicals passed by the censor for general circulation to appear in libraries and reading rooms, which zemstvos began to open for a lower-class clientele in the 1890s.[34] The content of teachers' libraries, which existed at many schools, was similarly restricted, in this case to material permitted in secondary schools. In other words, teachers (and by extension peasants) were not deemed fit to read all literature passed by the censor for the general consumption of educated adults in urban Russia and available in public libraries in town. A. A. Stakhovich, who analyzed the catalogs regulating teachers' libraries, found that they excluded countless works of interest to teachers: studies on adult education by A. S. Prugavin and Vakhterov, leading educational journals, and major contemporary Russian writers. "Why are teachers equated with children?" asked Stakhovich.[35] The answer was obvious to anyone familiar with the government's attitude toward the rural teacher and the potential risks he posed for a security-conscious administration. To what extent these restrictions were enforced is unclear; much depended on local school officials, who during their periodic visits would, presumably, inspect these libraries. In any case, the content of "teachers' libraries" (when they existed at all) was generally poor: a teacher from Vladimir referred to them as "rubbish" *(khlam).* Only in 1905 was the teacher's right to read equalized with that of the population at large.[36]

Some school officials attempted to restrict subscriptions to periodicals they judged excessively liberal. After the Iaroslavl zemstvo initiated aid to teachers, the provincial school director banned certain journals and periodicals: *Obrazovanie* and *Mir bozhii,* which devoted considerable space to social issues within a Legal Marxist framework, and the liberal newspapers *Russkiia vedomosti* and *Severnyi krai.*[37] This ban was never strictly enforced; perhaps a warning was deemed sufficient to persuade all but the most daring teachers to steer clear of such fare. Official concern over teachers' reading was also reflected in policy toward legal professional organizations. According to the "normal statute" governing teachers' mutual aid societies, many of these lacked the right to provide for the cultural needs of members, including bringing reading material closer to rural teachers. In 1903 the Kaluga Teachers' Society adopted a project to set up a system of twenty-five regional libraries which would circulate materials to teachers throughout the province. With financial assistance from urban intellectuals, lawyers, and "influential *Kaluzhane,*" the society planned to stock these libraries with legal literature of high quality and in accord with teacher demand. School officials, fearing that "tendentious" material might be included, confiscated the libraries and the experiment collapsed.[38] As critics of the government pointed out, there was a fundamental contradiction in the policy of a state which, on the one hand, set as its goal mass education, and, on the other hand, restricted teachers' access to legal reading material.

To summarize, the general cultural poverty of the Russian countryside, teachers' own isolation and penury, and official suspicion all conspired to limit access to the most basic of cultural commodities. It was clear that for the teacher, as "cultural pioneer," reading material had immeasurable significance. Self-education was essential to supplement the often inadequate qualifications that many teachers possessed, to perform satisfactorily in the classroom, and perhaps to play a wider role within the community. Otherwise, as one teacher wrote, one faced the danger of "moving backward, sinking to the level of the peasant *(priblizhat'sia k krest'ianinu).*"[39]

Neither can the psychological importance of this question be discounted. As a teacher from Moscow district, M. N. Sollogub, argued, "a good book with literary content affords the teacher spiritual relaxation *(nravstvennyi otdykh)* and serves as a substitute for society."[40] Even the modest *Niva* provided the rural teacher a vital link with educated Russian society. A subscription to a journal could well spell the difference between continued dedication to teaching in the village and abandonment of the profession out of despair. Turnover among teachers was perilously high. Economic factors played a major role, but the evidence suggests that for many cultural deprivation was no less significant. For the dedicated and idealistic professional rural isolation for much of the year and harsh living and working conditions could be rationalized and endured; the threat of slipping into the morass of rural ignorance *(temnota),* however, of becoming "wild" *(dichat')* in a cultural sense, could in no sense be justified. Only by recognizing this can one appreciate the significance of issues like self-education and access to reading material within the Russian teachers' movement and comprehend the degree of passion and militancy that these questions would generate.

Books and newspapers, however, were no substitute for regular contact with educated society. A former teacher, writing in the 1920s, somewhat apologetically explained this affinity for polite society.

> The city stirred our brains. Kaluga was not a town where the workers' movement was prominent, and I, for a long time, did not even notice it. Perhaps this can be explained by the fact that, like a plant reaching toward the light, I was drawn toward the educated, the intelligentsia. The pull was observable among all teachers. Can one blame us for this? Comrades of today, do not cast stones at us; we sought something better in life and this was only natural.[41]

Nor was reading a surrogate for contact with other teachers, so important in fostering a corporate identity shaped by shared experience, frustrations, and aspirations. The framework for such teachers' association, and for contacts with society, was set up during the zemstvo school's first decade in the form of short-term courses and local congresses. In the tortuous history of these gatherings one can trace the beginnings of teacher mobilization, the contours of future political alliances, as well as discern the relative flexibility of the Russian autocracy when faced with demands for social and professional autonomy from new groups in a rapidly changing society.

Teachers' Gatherings before the 1890s: The Imperatives of Enlightenment and Order

Summer courses *(kursy)* and local teachers' congresses *(s"ezdy)* were organized during the late 1860s and early 1870s, mainly by provincial zemstvos, in order to grapple with a shortage of trained teachers. Specialized training schools, both state and zemstvo teachers' seminaries, were few in number and had small graduating classes.[42] Zemstvos, which were primarily responsible for nominating candidates—with inspectoral sanction—to vacant posts sponsored a wide range of meetings aimed at upgrading and standardizing skills. In theory, the courses and congresses dealt with complementary aspects of the teacher's experience. Summer courses, in which teachers were passive auditors, concentrated on teaching methods; congresses dealt with general problems of operating the school, the relationship of school and teacher to the peasant community, the demands placed upon the school by the local population (which before the 1890s shouldered much of the cost of school maintenance), and even with questions of teacher's status. Here teachers took an active part. Joint discussions involving teachers, zemstvo men, school officials, and educators constituted an invaluable source of information on the state of affairs in zemstvo schools.[43]

For teachers the courses and congresses provided an opportunity to exchange experiences with their fellows, as well as to meet with members of educated society. Teachers cited the ever-present danger of sinking into the uncultured morass of rural life, where, in the words of a participant at a teachers' congress held in Novgorod in 1883, "the teacher is condemned to grow ignorant and obtuse" *(prikhoditsia glupet' i tupet')*.[44] A contemporary described the congresses of the early 1870s in Simbirsk as "a kind of holiday, bright points amidst the endless twilight of a colorless, much too isolated existence in remote rural settlements."[45] The term "holiday" *(prazdnik)* figures prominently in descriptions of these meetings and connotes not a summer's respite from labor in the rural school, but a chance to enjoy intellectual contact with educated, urban society and to replenish oneself, both intellectually and spiritually.

Estimates vary, but it is clear that at least two hundred teachers' gatherings were held in provincial and district towns during the period 1867–74.[46] Some provincial zemstvos were especially active in this area; others did not sponsor a single meeting during the entire period 1869–1903.[47] Overall, as the memoirs of participants indicate, this formative period was a kind of "golden age" in the history of teachers' association in Russia.[48] Selection of lecturers, number of participants, formulation of program were determined by local sponsors with only minimal supervision by school authorities.[49] Teachers' congresses of the early 1870s elicited wide interest in provincial society, and the issue of teacher preparation and association managed to generate some of the enthusiasm that had characterized the period of Great Reforms.[50]

Yet the Ministry of Education under Dmitri Tolstoi, eager to extend state control over elementary schooling in general and teacher preparation in particular, soon intervened. Faced in 1873 with initial attempts by radical youth to go "to the people," Alexander II and his advisors proved increasingly responsive to Tolstoi's arguments for a larger state role in education, with increased supervision over instruction through the ministry inspectorate. As Allen Sinel has noted, fear of radical influence in the school was an important motive in framing the new School Statute of 1874, which magnified the role of both gentry and inspectors in school management at the expense of local forces in the zemstvos and school boards.[51] It was in this climate that the government moved to limit zemstvo initiative in organizing teachers' gatherings. By rules of August 5, 1875, issued by the MNP, zemstvo summer courses were placed under the direct supervision of the inspectorate, which had recently been significantly expanded at Tolstoi's prompting. Zemstvos retained the right, or rather obligation, to fund courses but forfeited control over their organization. The content of courses was strictly regulated, the ministry intending to impart to them a narrowly practical aim of providing teachers with rudimentary skills.[52] The result, as most observers agree, was a sharp decline in zemstvo activity in this sphere.

In addition, the rules of 1875 had a stifling effect on the more lively teachers' congresses which had held such promise, since local authorities were loath to sanction public meetings that had no basis in statute.[53] Except for a brief period of relaxation in 1882–83, zemstvo petitions to hold teachers' congresses were routinely turned down in ensuing years.[54] On July 18, 1885, the ministry issued a directive banning congresses altogether, a decision not superseded until 1899.[55]

The strait jacket was put on teacher association largely because of political considerations. During the 1870s, teachers were conspicuous participants in the Populist movement; in some cases young radicals became rural teachers, calculating that this was a sure way to make contact with the peasantry without incurring the suspicion of the authorities. Police organs' assumption that rural teachers represented a potential conduit for revolutionary agitation in the village dates from this time, when more than three hundred fifty zemstvo teachers were implicated in radical movements.[56] Lists of teachers who planned to attend congresses had to be checked out by the police during the early 1880s, and finally the congresses were banned.[57] Clearly, the government intended to isolate rural teachers from society.

Combined with the zemstvos' relative inactivity in public education during the 1880s, official intervention guaranteed teachers' isolation.[58] According to one teacher, the general sense of malaise was reinforced by rumors that zemstvo schools would be transferred to the Holy Synod, and he noted that at the end of the 1880s many teachers left the profession at the first chance of alternate employment.[59] The Populist writer Gleb Uspenskii described the "quiet" decade's impact:

> Now the teacher is left to pine alone with his textbook. He notes down the pupil's absence from class, but to state that the boy was absent because of his father's drunkenness, and further to explain why he became a drunkard (as transpired at the previous congresses), now there is none of this. A lively observation of popular needs, which is instructive for public activists and ties them together, is now absent.[60]

An expert from the ministry later concurred that after the first decade of the zemstvo school's existence "came years of complete dissociation *(razobshchennost')* for zemstvo teachers."[61]

The extent of this isolation was evident from the Moscow Literacy Committee survey of 1894–95. Given chronic turnover in the profession, its results are not surprising. Of 115 teachers responding from Vladimir province, only one had ever attended a congress, though all agreed that such gatherings would prove useful. From Kostroma 8 teachers had participated in teachers' assemblies during the period 1873–76. Of 85 respondents from Ekaterinoslav, only 3 had attended courses and 1 a congress. Similar results came from Tauride, Smolensk, and other provinces for which the survey results were published. All respondents believed that teachers' congresses and broad "general education" courses (as opposed to those that taught applied vocational skills) would be useful.[62]

However one evaluates the teachers' assemblies of the 1870s and early 1880s, there is little doubt that professional association, particularly in the form of local congresses with a consultative character, held considerable promise for the development of zemstvo education and for teachers.[63] A useful comparison can be drawn with zemstvo medicine, where regular congresses of doctors evolved into an indispensable component in the formulation and implementation of policy, particularly measures geared toward making medical services more accessible to the population at large. The result was that, after five decades, zemstvo medicine had developed into a unique internationally recognized system. Doctors' congresses were sanctioned, often grudgingly, by the "second element" in the zemstvos and by the government. Zemstvo assemblies did not always accede to the recommendations of physician-employees, for the reaction of the 1880s also affected medicine. But medical congresses were held fairly frequently, thus ensuring a significant degree of third element input and aiding the growth of a corporate ethos among the medical profession.[64] Teachers remained virtually isolated and silent. And yet, paradoxically, within a few years a militant teachers' movement, armed with concrete demands, shattered this stillness. Contemporaries discerned a leap in the collective consciousness of Russia's teachers, spurred on by the public resurgence of this period and new developments in teachers' association after 1895.

Rising Expectations: Teachers' Courses, 1895–1903

Only eight pedagogical courses for zemstvo teachers were held in the period 1890–96, but after that the situation began to change.[65] With renewed zemstvo interest in public education, particularly at the provincial level, summer courses were again viewed as a practical means of providing qualified personnel in as short a time as possible.[66] The 1890s witnessed a rapid growth of zemstvo schools, while the number of normal schools remained nearly constant, threatening a relative decline in qualified teachers, soon borne out by zemstvo statistics. Some zemstvo men also recognized the insidious effect of isolation and cultural deprivation on teachers' morale and effectiveness.[67]

Another factor was a relaxation in the posture of the government. The Ministry of Education admitted that teachers' skills were weak and not standardized given the myriad backgrounds from which they were drawn and further owned that it lacked the funds to substantially augment the number of candidates trained in specialized institutions.[68] Moreover, in light of high turnover rates and reports of teachers fleeing to the new state liquour monopoly, the government became convinced that the profession was in crisis. Unwilling to allocate funds to increase teachers' salaries at a time when the state's industrialization drive took priority, the government was apparently ready to make other concessions to ameliorate their status. Finally, the regime felt reasonably confident concerning the rural social order and the unlikelihood that teachers would disrupt it. Commenting that the administration had never doubted the merit of teachers' assemblies, an authoritative ministry spokesman noted that the "anarchist movement" of the 1870s and 1880s had forced limitation of this kind of association. Happily, the situation was now different (this was a rather quiet period in the countryside, though not in the industrial centers). In addition, he pointed out, teachers now constituted a more "reliable and steady professional *soslovie*" than in previous decades, when "dropouts, *raznochintsy,* and casual elements" had entered the profession.[69]

Thus, the climate was favorable to renewed zemstvo efforts, and in 1897 nine provincial zemstvos sponsored summer courses, generally lasting from four to six weeks, a marked increase over recent years. Teachers responded favorably to the resurrected courses. In Tambov, courses had not been held for twenty-three years, and only one teacher, now sixty years old, had ever attended such a gathering. When in 1897 the local zemstvo nominated 80 teachers to take part in the courses, 168 showed up, many of whom had traveled to Tambov without financial support from zemstvos and some of whom journeyed from other provinces.[70]

The courses of this period were organized on the basis of the rules of 1875, and school officials retained supervisory functions. Not all petitions to hold courses were approved, often because ministry officials refused to sanction lecturers invited by the zemstvos. The composition and number of auditors was likewise a touchy issue, as was the question of subject matter and program. Zemstvo representatives frequently found themselves in last-minute negotiations with school officials in order to salvage scheduled courses. Often compromises were hammered out; for example, in one instance progressive zemstvo men agreed to include subjects like choral singing and religious instruction in return for the inclusion of history and natural sciences.[71] Zemstvo activists and the liberal press complained bitterly about the red tape and arbitrariness attendant to the petition process.

Nevertheless, teachers' courses were sanctioned and held with increasing frequency after the mid-1890s: provincial zemstvos sponsored eleven courses in 1898, twelve in 1899, eighteen in 1900, while in the summer of 1901, twenty-two zemstvos organized courses. The number of provincial courses then tapered off in 1902 (eighteen) and 1903 (seventeen). At least twenty courses were held by district zemstvos during this period.[72] Zemstvos shouldered much of the cost, covering travel expenses (a key item for rural teachers) and housing in the provincial capital. Even though lecturers often refused remuneration, for leading educators and university faculty viewed their appearance as "public service," a zemstvo could spend as much as 5,000 rubles per course.

Despite the arbitrary character of the 1875 rules and official supervision, the courses held after 1896 did not always adhere to ministerial script. According to A. S. Prugavin, some school officials clearly recognized their obsolescence. The Kursk zemstvo annually sponsored courses that diverged from the rules, owing to "the absence of formalism on the part of the provincial school directorate and its enlightened aid to zemstvo efforts."[73] N. F. Bunakov and other lecturers were able to hold discussions with teacher-auditors in a manner reminiscent of the earlier teachers' congresses. At courses held in Tambov in 1901 the zemstvo board arranged conferences with teachers to discuss various school issues; these were attended by the inspector.[74] In some cases local school officials allowed sponsors to open the doors to all wishing to attend, including nonteachers. Much depended on local conditions and timing. For example, after Tambov Bunakov was prohibited from appearing at courses, the government citing previous departures from the 1875 rules, diversions which had previously been duly scrutinized and approved by local authorities.[75] Furthermore, and more significant, from 1899 the scope and content of the courses was expanded to include a wide range of general education subjects: natural science, hygiene, history, elementary psychology, Russian literature, paralegal skills. The intent of such courses was not so much to sharpen teaching skills as to expand teachers' general fund of knowledge. Zemstvo activists and educators argued that the intellectual profile of teachers had changed considerably since the 1870s; courses should no longer be limited to imparting pedagogical methods in reading, writing, and arithmetic. Most teachers had a good grasp of method.[76] Discussing projected teachers' courses in 1902, the Vladimir zemstvo assembly concluded that "today most teachers possess satisfactory preparation and are little interested in narrow pedagogical courses."[77]

Given the requirements of the three-class zemstvo school and the recent rapid increase in the number of schools, the teacher's grasp of method is open to question, but there is little doubt that the general education courses were useful and attractive to teachers. In this respect teachers' own cultural concerns corresponded with the wider role that many zemstvo activists, educators, and teachers were projecting for the school within the peasant community. Success in adult education *(vneshkol'noe obrazovanie),* possibly the whole mission of the zemstvos in the village, could well hinge upon the expansion of the intellectual horizons of the teacher. How could the teacher assume a position of authority in the community if he or she was unable to respond to a variety of peasant queries, progressive zemstvo men reasoned? The teacher was a primary (perhaps the key) agent of zemstvo policy in the village. Teachers who aspired to a wider role of "public activist" concurred, and for these the zemstvo summer courses compared favorably with the stale curriculum of state teachers' seminaries, which, to quote a report submitted by teachers in 1899 to the Novotorzhok (Tver) zemstvo assembly, could not yield a "genuine zemstvo worker."[78] The latter term conveyed a strong ideological, idealist element and was commonly juxtaposed with the teacher as a "craftsman" *(remeslennik),* who limited his activity to teaching the three "R's" and did not aspire to a wider role in the community.

Predictably, conservatives argued against the courses. Not only did they doubt the basic premise of educating the masses, they were also uneasy over the mounting opposition to the Old Regime and, from spring 1902, over social unrest in the countryside. At the 1900 Saratov zemstvo assembly the archconservative deputy P. A. Krivskii vehemently opposed the board's proposal to organize courses the following summer at a cost of 3,000 rubles. The zemstvo, he argued, was not a tourist bureau in the business of providing teachers free passes to gaze at the "wonders" of Saratov, the "Athens of the Volga." More to the point were his reservations about the inclusion of subjects like psychology in the courses' curriculum:

> And what is so surprising if our teachers, having heard such lectures, disperse to their villages and begin to preach that we do not have souls, but only an empty cavity, that immortality and life beyond the grave is all nonsense. They will deprive the peasant of his last faith, his final comfort . . . this is unforgivable and cannot be tolerated.

A majority of the zemstvo assembly was not swayed by these arguments and funds were allocated.[79] When in 1902 general education courses were discussed in the Moscow zemstvo, F. D. Samarin questioned the premise behind such meetings: to make the teacher an "enlightenment agent" *(prosvetitel')* among the population, a "purveyor of ideas" *(propovednik idei).* It was the teacher's task, insisted Samarin, to teach children the ABC's, "not to enlighten the surrounding milieu." The zemstvo voted to fund the courses, but MVD officials who conducted an audit of the Moscow zemstvo in 1904 concurred with Samarin, commenting that the notion of utilizing teachers as *prosvetiteli* among the rural masses showed again that the zemstvos refused to limit their activity in public education to that prescribed by law. Besides, teachers were much too immature to assume such a sensitive role and "would merely serve as the mouthpieces of the vacillating [oppositional] views which at present reign in our society."[80]

Despite such reservations, zemstvo interest in the courses was on the rise, and teachers' response to these ventures, particularly general education courses, was overwhelming. Initiative in setting up such courses was taken by, among others, the Kursk, Saratov, Viatka, and Tambov zemstvos, each of which was spurred on by an activist core of liberal deputies with a special interest in education. N. V. Chekhov credits Petr Dolgorukov and the school commission of the Kursk zemstvo with formulating the first program for general education courses.[81] The Kursk zemstvo was among the most active in education in this period, and the Kursk courses were immensely popular among teachers. A. P. Nechaev, a frequent lecturer, wrote that the first expanded courses held in Kursk in 1899 attracted more than three hundred teachers from twenty-three provinces, in addition to the auditors from Kursk province. Many of these arrived, in Nechaev's words, "on their own responsibility" *(na svoi risk i strakh).* General education courses were also held in Pavlovsk, on the initiative of the local school director with zemstvo funding. Lectures were read by faculty from St. Petersburg University (for example, by Platonov on history) and drew teachers from as far away as the Caucasus and Siberia.[82]

The Saratov zemstvo sponsored teachers' courses during the summers of 1897 through 1902, and from 1899 these included natural sciences, psychology, hygiene, ethnography, pedagogical theory, and Russian literature. The zemstvo later solicited responses from participants. The majority clearly recognized the benefits received from the skills and knowledge provided: of 225 responses concerning the value of general education subjects, only two were negative; 214 (95 percent) gave unqualified support.[83] On this basis the zemstvo planned to further expand the program for 1902–3. Significantly, many of the Saratov teachers lauded the courses as an invaluable opportunity to gather and exchange experiences with their colleagues. As one *kursant* replied, the "courses raised the energy of teachers through contact with their comrades, reinvigorating them after a long winter of solitary labor and isolation." Another remarked that "those who live in town cannot comprehend what these courses mean to us, denizens of bears' corners." Still others replied that the courses instilled a consciousness of teachers' ideological ties with "society," with the "zemstvo's mission," and with "zemstvo people" and underscored how crucial contact with educated society was for the profession.

> I see great value in mutual intercourse among so many teachers and in the sympathy evidenced by zemstvo activists and lecturers toward the teacher and school. Seeing such a multitude of people who have sacrificed themselves for the sake of education, seeing the concern of zemstvo activists for the school, the teacher is renewed and departs for his village reinstilled and reinvigorated. Only since 1897 (the first year courses were held in Saratov) has the teacher of Saratov province looked upon himself as a personality, who possesses a tie with the government and the zemstvo, and only since then has he understood that the enlightened stratum of Russia is concerned about him, and this fact has contributed greatly to an uplifting of his moral spirit.

Similar responses came from teachers who took part in the Kursk courses of 1899.[84] A survey in Nizhegorod district (1905) elicited a decided preference for the broader courses, as did a poll taken in Novgorod province by the local mutual aid society in 1904. Only a small number of respondents to

Teachers and lecturers at summer general education courses held at Pavlovsk, August 8–September 9, 1900. Source: *Niva*, No. 42, October 14, 1900, p. 844.

the latter (42) had actually attended general education courses (in Pavlovsk), since school officials had rejected local zemstvo petitions to hold them. Nevertheless, the vast majority (686 of 741) expressed a need for supplementary knowledge and the desirability of courses.[85]

No doubt, such responses reflect the views of the more activist teachers who aspired to a wider role as "public activists." Still, the courses were potentially significant for all teachers, not least in terms of professional solidarity. The summer courses provided a point of contact with other teachers; with "zemstvo people," including the third element; and with educators of national repute (lecturers like Vakhterov, Ia. I. Dushechkin, and the young historian N. A. Rozhkov, who would play key roles in the teachers' movement of 1905).[86] Many teachers were also painfully aware of their own intellectual shortcomings, a condition in which they appeared frozen, given their isolation. The zemstvo courses were thus an important step in bridging the gap that separated the rural teacher from educated society, affirmation that this "civilized savage" belonged to that society. When the movement to organize courses stalled after 1903, teachers were understandably bitter. A respondent to the Nizhegorod survey remarked: "If it is now considered feasible to organize popular universities, where simple workers will be auditors, then it is all the more imperative that schoolteachers be given the opportunity to expand their knowledge."[87] The realities were depressingly clear: the cultural opportunities afforded by the city, even to workers and shop clerks, were often inaccessible to the rural teacher.

Third Element Influence and Security: Teachers' Congresses before 1905

The summer courses played a crucial role in forging a professional movement among Russian teachers. Not only did teachers first establish links when they came together in dusty provincial towns and future leaders first addressed their colleagues, but rural teachers found valuable allies in educated society, most notably among progressive zemstvo men. In this sense the courses served to channel activist teachers into the emerging zemstvo–third element alliance then beginning to transform and enliven provincial politics. This would soon find firmer organizational expression, as we will see, in the formation of mutual aid societies. That the zemstvo-teacher partnership was still characterized by paternalism there is little doubt, but also evident was a growing impulse among more activist teachers to restructure the relationship in the direction of greater autonomy by gaining for teachers a stronger voice in discussion of professional needs and by institutionalizing teacher input into the formulation of zemstvo educational policy. Teachers had a model in the organization of zemstvo medicine and a precedent in teachers' congresses of the 1870s.[88] Despite the official ban of 1885, teachers' support for resurrection of the congresses was evident in the Moscow Literacy Committee survey and at summer courses.[89] The issue sparked a debate within zemstvo circles, which pointed up both the strengths and limitations of the emerging zemstvo-teacher alliance.

The first substantive discussion of teachers' congresses in many years took place in early 1898 in the Moscow provincial zemstvo, which was among the most progressive in the field of education, having adopted a project for universal schooling two years earlier. Proponents of teachers' congresses pointed out that rational management of schools dictated greater teacher involvement in policymaking. M. P. Shchepkin, M. V. Chelnokov, and other zemtsy argued that teachers, by virtue of their daily experience in the schools and contact with the community, were often the most competent persons available to speak on various issues. The inspector, often responsible for more than one hundred schools, could not adequately supervise education or provide zemstvos with necessary information, and the task was beyond the powers of the zemstvo and school boards. They recalled the success of teachers' congresses held in Moscow province before the 1885 ban and underscored the value of meetings of doctors, veterinarians, and agronomists. Shchepkin pointed to

Germany, where teachers' congresses were held regularly and, paraphrasing Bismarck, averred that the Prussian schoolteacher had made a sizeable contribution to Prussia's victory over France in 1870 and to German unification. The "lesson of Sedan" was frequently invoked by Russians to dramatize the link between schooling and broader national imperatives.

Still there was considerable resistance in Moscow to teachers' congresses. Opponents charged that, given their "low cultural level" *(nizkokul'turnost')*, most teachers were not prepared to participate in meaningful discussion of school affairs. Many zemstvo men clearly were unwilling to accept teaching as an "expert" field, certainly not in the sense that medicine or statistical work were. Such bias was reinforced by the social and, increasingly, sexual distance that separated zemstvo men from teachers. Nevertheless, by a narrow margin the Moscow zemstvo voted to petition the government to revoke the 1885 circular, and this action was soon followed by other zemstvos.[90]

Aware that the "teachers' crisis" had reached alarming proportions, some in the government met these with sympathy. On November 26, 1899, the MNP, under N. P. Bogolepov, issued "temporary rules" on teachers' congresses. This was not the surgical operation excising the 1885 circular recommended in zemstvo petitions. Hoping to impart to the meetings a "purely businesslike character," the ministry placed considerable restrictions on their organization, limiting the initiative of zemstvos and teachers.[91] Zemstvos could now petition to sponsor teachers' congresses, which would be limited in scope to the inspector's circuit (*raion,* one or two districts), thus precluding provincial assemblies or attendance by teachers from neighboring districts. Congresses could not be held concurrently in more than one circuit of a province, a security precaution that ruled out frequent meetings. Congresses would last no more than seven days, which, as critics suggested, gave the discussions a hurried character. Programs and lists of participants had to be submitted to the regional school officials well in advance, and deliberations would be limited to issues directly relating to the teacher's experience in the school and in no case touch upon "the conduct of the school administration or other government and public institutions."

The local inspector would chair the meeting and, "in case of disturbance," remove any participant from the hall or close the congress. The mere presence of their direct superior could inhibit open discussion among teachers.[92] Some officials apparently used their considerable leverage over teachers to sabotage the experiment. In Kazan district in 1903, 150 zemstvo teachers had registered for a projected congress; then, inexplicably, 70 sent word to the zemstvo that they would not be able to attend owing to illness.[93] Given Russian conditions any form of voluntary association had political implications, especially during this period when meetings of professional and other groups were utilized to voice criticism of the bureaucracy and to organize "public opinion" against the autocracy. Officials were clearly concerned that rural teachers might be swept up in this movement and feared the repercussions this might have in the countryside. Accordingly, teachers would not even be permitted to vote and adopt resolutions on the issues discussed at the congresses.[94] V. V. Kir'iakov, a former teacher, summed up the situation: before publication of the 1899 rules teachers lacked completely the right to voice their opinions; now they had the "right to half-a-voice" *(pravo na polgolosu).*[95]

All of these restrictions came in for sharp criticism from the press and zemstvos, particularly the subordinate role to which self-government had been relegated. A. A. Stakhovich, from the Elets zemstvo (Orel), contended that the bureaucracy had adopted a posture of overkill in the screening of teacher-participants and had needlessly complicated the petition process. Teachers' reliability should be assumed, given the fact that they had already been nominated, sanctioned, and confirmed in their posts by zemstvo, inspector, and local school board respectively.[96] Such objections were echoed at a conference held in March 1901 at the Moscow *okrug* and attended by ministry officials and chairmen of school boards (that is, gentry marshals, many with strong zemstvo connections). Here it was suggested that voting take place at the congresses and that school board chairmen lead the discussions.[97] Such proposals indicate general dissatisfaction with the 1899 rules, while their provenance merely underscores the dilemmas confronting the government in the matter of mass education.

Despite the restrictions, a number of zemstvos petitioned to hold teachers' congresses. The first and most publicized was held in Moscow in August 1901.[98] More than two hundred teachers came from Moscow and Podolsk districts (constituting an inspector's *raion*). Ninety percent were women; only three of the participants had taken part in congresses during the 1880s. Leading zemstvo representatives were present, and the sessions were chaired by the provincial director of schools, assisted by two inspectors.

The program included twenty points, most having to do with teaching methods, curricula, teacher-pupil relations, and professional status. Some questions, notably in adult education, had been deleted by the ministry. Teachers presented reports, which on the whole were substantive, drawn as they were from personal experience. Considerable attention was focused on curricula. Teachers pointed to the excessive weight given to grammar and orthography in the ministry's "model programs"; since most peasant children did not continue their schooling beyond the three-year primary level, it made more sense to channel teachers' energies toward imparting knowledge about nature, history, and geography rather than the complexities of Russian grammar. Literacy and acquiring a taste for further reading were more important than formal polish. Teachers also evidenced a strong bias against applied subjects. Instruction in singing drew considerable fire: "teachers are burdened with this obligation, but all the same they sing out of fear of incurring the wrath of school authorities, who with particular insistence recommend that teachers conduct singing classes."[99]

Issues of vital concern to teachers were raised in a report by V. A. Sokolova: "The Rights and Obligations of Public School Teachers according to Existing Laws." In a surprisingly frank exposition Sokolova touched upon the question of "legal status," an emotionally charged issue that would serve as the rallying point for the teachers' movement. The issue had broader implications, since the "lawlessness" *(bespravie)* which permeated the teacher's condition was symptomatic of the general *bespravie* plaguing rural society. The connection between teachers' status and that of the peasantry was not explicit in her report (it would be later), but nevertheless she delivered a wide-ranging discourse on the status of teachers, which paid particular attention to their vulnerability vis-à-vis various "authorities." Sokolova hinted at the hypocrisy inherent in a situation in which the mantle of "enlightener of the people" was placed upon the teacher, who was then "left to languish in a state of semistarvation, confined in an isolated wasteland without newspapers or books." She noted that teachers' courses and congresses were at present barely tolerated, a paradox that teachers found difficult to fathom.

Sokolova concluded her report with nineteen "recommendations." These included the right of self-defense in cases of disciplinary action at school boards; participation in zemstvo sessions as "experts" in matters of school policy, and the right of teachers to nominate candidates to vacant posts, similar to the rights of zemstvo doctors on the medical councils; improved material status; greater rights for teachers at the congresses; subscriptions to journals and newspapers at zemstvo expense and increased cultural opportunities in general. Sokolova's report met with sustained applause, though no vote was taken on the "wishes" expressed.[100]

In seven short days the congress covered much ground. Only a minority of teachers took an active part in the discussions; the presence of their direct superiors, the inspectors, certainly inhibited open dialogue. Teachers were likewise silent when it came to questions like the condition of school buildings and hygiene, according to Kir'iakov in deference to their zemstvo *khoziain* (master), N. F. Rikhter, chairman of the district board. The congresses were a new experience for teachers, and educators argued that their timidity not be misconstrued to reinforce stereotypes concerning their lack of competence. The congress held in Moscow appeared to be a hopeful beginning. One of the older teachers in Moscow district, A. P. Potapov, concluded his report with the plea: "Trust, let us have more trust in the schoolteacher."[101]

Other congresses followed. Rural teachers gathered in December 1901 in Aleksandrov district (Vladimir).[102] The Balashov zemstvo (Saratov), like Moscow a liberal stronghold and active in education, sponsored a congress in June 1902. The petition process was lengthy, and of forty-three issues included in the zemstvo's program, eleven were excluded by school officials: causes for frequent teacher transfers, introduction of collegial school trusteeships *(popechitel'stva)* aimed at involving the community more closely in the schools, adult repeater classes for primary school graduates, and other issues dealing with *vneshkol'noe obrazovanie.*[103] The Balashov zemstvo supported the notion of the teacher as "public activist" in the local community, a concept of which school officials remained wary.

One of the more successful teachers' congresses was held in May 1903, in Nizhegorod district, the result of close cooperation between the zemstvo and liberal inspector N. N. Iordanskii. The situation was novel in that Iordanskii organized preliminary meetings of teachers throughout the district at which the issues to be aired at the congress in May were hammered out. A zemstvo teacher N. N. Nardov read a report urging greater involvement by teachers in the formulation of policy: representation on local school boards, organization of zemstvo school *sovety* patterned after the medical councils, and teacher participation in a future "small zemstvo unit," a decentralization scheme widely discussed at the time in the press and zemstvos. The results of the congress were discussed by the zemstvo assembly in autumn 1903 and resulted in the formation of a school commission in which teachers and zemstvo men reviewed textbooks and classroom materials. One participant, writing thirty years after the event, recalled that teachers hailed this experiment as the dawn of a "new era," and some spent their last kopecks to attend.[104]

Despite the intense interest of teachers in the congresses and the fanfare surrounding them, few were ever held. According to one estimate, no more than three zemstvo-sponsored congresses were held annually for all of Russia between 1901 and 1905. This writer has counted only nineteen district congresses between August 1901 (Moscow) and January 1905 (Yalta).[105] In the vast majority of districts teachers' congresses were never organized during the reigns of Alexander III and Nicholas II, a fact that speaks volumes about teachers' isolation. The rules of 1899 remained in effect until the end of the Old Regime, when a ministry spokesman admitted that "the complexity of procedure for sanctioning the congresses, the limitations placed on zemstvos in their organization, their restriction to the inspector's circuit, and the fact that teachers were given a largely passive role, all of this resulted in the fact that in the fourteen years since their publication the rules have had exceedingly small application."[106] This was a rather damning statement from the government.

Liberals agreed, directly blaming the government for the fact that the congresses proved stillborn; as early as 1901 Dmitri Shakhovskoi declared that the rules were excessively restrictive and would remain a dead letter.[107] Certainly, some zemstvos were disinclined to fund teachers' congresses over which they exercised little control. In some cases (how many is unclear) zemstvo petitions to sponsor congresses were rejected by provincial authorities for security reasons.[108] Despite the restrictions and tortuous petition process, it is difficult to disagree with E. A. Zviagintsev's assessment that the failure to utilize even these poor regulations had been a mistake.[109] The rural teacher would surely have agreed with Kir'iakov that the "right to half-a-voice" was better than none at all.

In assessing the failure of this promising experiment teachers could not help but feel resentment toward the zemstvos, particularly the inert and conservative district assemblies, only a fraction of which ever endorsed the idea of congresses. According to MNP data for 1904, of 243 district zemstvos only 12 passed resolutions to fund congresses that year.[110] In Vladimir province in the course of ten years only one congress (that in Aleksandrov in 1901) was held. In the remaining 12 districts only one zemstvo, liberal Kovrov, ever voted funds to organize a congress.[111] Clearly, zemstvo apathy was a major factor. The attitude of rank-and-file zemstvo men was that teachers had little to contribute to discussion of public education, which was best left to their zemstvo "masters." Even in the Moscow provincial zemstvo, a pioneer in the field, doubts had been raised about the value of teachers' participation. The attitude of district zemstvo assemblies in Kazan or Penza can well be imagined. And it is worth pointing out that even in their relations with higher level, male-dominated professions, zemstvo deputies jealously guarded their prerogatives against encroachment by third element specialists, as is reflected in the well-publicized "statistical conflicts" around 1900 and widespread warnings of a "zemstvo bureaucracy" usurping the rights of the elected second element.[112]

Had the 1899 rules allowed for teachers' congresses at the provincial level, where liberal forces were concentrated, the situation might have been different, but petitions for provincial meetings were rejected.[113] By 1902 the Ministry of Education was considering changes in the 1899 rules. Even the Department of Police indicated that it had nothing against satisfaction of a petition from the Tauride provincial zemstvo: that voting be introduced to ascertain true consensus, that congresses not be restricted to the circuit, that zemstvo representatives be allowed to participate more fully, and that confirmation of lists of teacher-participants be facilitated.[114] How serious this discussion of reform actually was is unclear. As it turned out, the rules were not revised. Instead, as we will see, the government's position on teachers' association soon hardened, scuttling any plans for liberalization of the 1899 rules and crippling the summer courses.

Teachers' courses, and potentially the local congresses, had immense significance for rural teachers, in both a pedagogical and corporate sense. Teachers viewed these gatherings as means to supplement their often meager education and widen their intellectual horizons. That such meetings served a pressing need was recognized by the government, which acknowledged its own inability to grapple with the problem of educational qualifications and the demand for personnel without aid from the zemstvos. Summer courses gave teachers an opportunity to meet with representatives of educated society, with the intelligentsia, with which they increasingly identified. This was a far cry from the usual "society" of priest, tavern keeper, and handful of literate peasants which the countryside offered. No wonder teachers often referred to such assemblies as "holidays" or that they were grateful to zemstvo patrons who had made these wonderful events possible. The experiment with teachers' congresses, to be sure, revealed the underlying tension in teacher-zemstvo relations and indicated limitations to professional autonomy within the zemstvos. Official interference, however, tended to muddy the waters surrounding this venture and thus partially obscure deeper zemstvo prejudices. In any case, as the teachers' movement became more politicized, teachers' alliance with liberal zemstvo activists held firm, based as it was on a degree of programmatic consensus and common hostility to the bureaucracy.

Finally, these gatherings played an important role in unifying teachers, instilling a sense of common needs and interests. They did much to rekindle the populist commitment to the narod and to teaching as a form of service. As one teacher described the courses in a letter to V. P. Vakhterov, a frequent lecturer:

> Cast adrift and scattered, thinking alone, feeling alone, creating our ideals in isolation and in isolation losing them; with a feeling of deepfelt thanks we will remember your talks which were so filled with faith in the value of our labors in the field of education. You resurrected this faith in the souls of many of us who had either lost it or were on the verge of doing so . . . and it is this faith that is dearer to us than all the undoubtedly valuable and useful information that we received at the courses.[115]

Not only did the summer courses play a crucial role in the growth of professional consciousness among teachers in the decade before 1905,[116] they also helped forge more permanent organizational links.

4. Organization and Program

The Emergence of a Teachers' Movement

Forging a movement of rural teachers in late nineteenth-century Russia appeared to be a nearly impossible task. Indeed, after the turn of the century observers continued to point to the "timidity," "low culture," and "tendency to lose one's identity in the rural morass" that seemed to characterize many of these "zemstvo rabbits."[1] Nevertheless, from the mid-1890s a movement among teachers to overcome their isolation was clearly evident, reflected in an impulse toward "self-education," professional association, a growing consciousness of shared interests with other teachers, as well as a sense of partnership with society in the task of popular enlightenment. When rural teachers first came together at summer courses they searched for firmer institutional foundations and, like other social groups in late Imperial Russia, were willing to utilize whatever modest organizational means permitted by the regime.[2] A handful of teachers' mutual aid societies had been organized before 1890, mostly for teachers in the two capitals, graduates of specific institutions (for example, the teachers' *instituty,* which trained teachers for urban schools), or teachers in Jewish schools.[3] The first societies aimed primarily at a rural constituency were organized in Kazan, Petersburg, and Nizhegorod provinces in the early 1890s under the name "societies of mutual aid for teachers and former teachers" *(obshchestva vzaimopomoshchi uchashchim i uchivshim).* Most of these were set up on a province-wide basis, though in some locales district societies were formed.[4]

Teachers' mutual aid societies performed largely beneficent functions, providing loans or subsidies to members in time of crisis. Aid in the education of teachers' children, for instance, maintenance of dormitories in the provincial town for pupils studying in secondary schools, increasingly took a lion's share of these societies' budgets. For teachers with families this was an emotional issue, as they argued that they could not, with equanimity, teach others' children for salaries that failed to provide their own offspring with proper instruction.[5] Such aid was necessarily limited in its appeal, since the majority of rural teachers were young and unmarried, and activists demanded that these legal associations meet the varied and growing needs of all teachers.

Such plans, however, ran counter to official policy on the teachers' societies, which limited their functions to provision of material assistance. In July 1894 the Ministry of Education issued a "normal statute," which regulated all societies incorporated after that date. This statute diverged in important respects from those of the early 1890s which had stipulated that, in addition to various types of material aid, teachers' societies were "to assist in supplementing teachers' pedagogical knowledge" through the organization of libraries, pedagogical museums, and lectures. These provisions were not included in the 1894 guidelines. At a time of rising cultural aspirations among teachers the government intervened to circumscribe the activity of the mutual aid societies to material assistance and blocked any attempt to form societies not strictly adhering to ministry rules. Predictably, one of the major demands voiced within the societies, particularly after 1900, was for revision of the normal statute to allow societies to look after the intellectual and cultural interests of their members. The special poignancy of this issue is better conveyed by the Russian term employed by teachers themselves: *dukhovnye zaprosy,* or "spiritual needs."[6]

Despite the restrictions imposed by the ministry, teachers' societies mushroomed: forty-eight of seventy-one societies existing as of 1903 had been organized after 1895; in many cases plans to organize societies were initiated at the time of summer courses. By 1902 only nine zemstvo provinces lacked teachers' societies, and in two of these (Poltava and Kherson) several district organizations existed. Societies were also formed in the outlying areas of the empire, in Siberia and in the western borderlands.[7]

The poverty of teachers was a major stimulus, for the mutual aid societies at least held out some hope of receiving emergency aid. By the late 1890s many provincial zemstvos had established pension funds for teachers and other employees, with eligibility based on twelve years of service.[8] The tenure of most rural teachers was shorter, and, in any case, pensions did not cover teachers' needs during their career. Accordingly, many mutual aid societies attempted to expand material aid to members, providing lodging to those visiting the city, free medical services, and discounts on railway travel for teachers and their families. Given the teacher's strained budget, the significance of such assistance cannot be lightly dismissed. Other societies afforded legal aid (as with physicians, lawyers considered such aid "public service"), though in some places school authorities opposed such activity, arguing that it would lead to "malicious litigation" among teachers.[9]

Teachers and former teachers could become "active" members of the mutual aid societies simply by paying yearly dues of two to five rubles. Membership was generally limited to those in primary schools under the Ministry of Education—zemstvo, two-class ministry, city, factory, and railway schools—either by statute or disinclination on the part of teachers in church schools or secondary institutions. Since zemstvo schools comprised the largest share of "secular" schools in European Russia, zemstvo teachers dominated membership rosters. "Active" members had a claim to all aid provided by the society, could participate in the annual assemblies and hold office on the society's executive board.

Teachers' societies, including those based on the 1894 statute, provided for a second category, the "associate members" *(chleny-sorevnovateli).* Any interested party could, upon payment of a fee, become an associate. Often wealthy notables made substantial contributions to society coffers, and the rolls of many societies were graced with the names of aristocrats, high government officials, and churchmen (the reactionary mystic Ioann Kronshtadtskii was a member of several teachers' societies). The presence of such people underscored the largely beneficent nature of the societies as originally conceived, and their role in the day-to-day life of the societies was negligible. Zemstvo activists and the provincial intelligentsia played a more visible role in the teachers' societies, enjoying as associate members all rights of participation (voting and holding office) except for receipt of aid. During the decade between the great famine and the Revolution of 1905 the teachers' societies served as one of a handful of legal associations open to the provincial intelligentsia. They provided progressive society with a field for "public work" and involved a wide spectrum of interested outsiders: zemstvo deputies, third element personnel, and even political exiles in provinces like Viatka and Vologda. For educated Russians few causes were closer to hand or more sympathetic than the plight of the rural teacher, and few associations better combined the imperatives of practical cultural activity and the idealism of the period.

Many societies were, in fact, organized on the initiative of nonteachers, and zemstvo men, urban *intelligenty,* and, to a lesser extent, urban teachers tended to manage society affairs. Residing in towns, they possessed the requisite skills and leisure time for "public activity." Their prominence raises two questions. To what degree did rank-and-file teachers participate in these associations? What was the character of the societies: simply charitable institutions in which the teacher was merely the object of society's solicitude or viable corporate organizations which contributed to a sense of solidarity and professional identity?

Much of the rationale and activity of the societies suggested associations overseeing emergency insurance funds rather than corporate organizations formulating and defending professional interests. The participation of teachers was often limited to payment of membership fees, and zemstvos sometimes covered even these, in addition to annual block grants to societies.[10] It was argued, particularly after 1905, that zemstvo aid constituted patronage and hindered the growth of professional solidarity. What was needed were teachers' societies based on genuine mutual aid among teachers, supported by their own resources, no matter how modest.[11] This argument, born of the bitter experience of reaction, seems slightly off the mark. Teachers' apathy resulted from poverty, dissociation, and a nearly complete absence of rights within the administration of schools. The notion of solidarity took root slowly among "zemstvo rabbits," who required outside assistance to break out of this debilitating cycle. With this assistance, the societies, as the only legal teachers' associations in Russia, held out some potential for professional mobilization and provided a rudimentary framework for more vibrant corporate activity.

The movement to organize teachers' societies gathered momentum, especially after 1895, but the majority remained outside the societies; by 1903 they encompassed nearly 25,000 teachers, one-third of the primary teachers under the ministry.[12] Before 1905 provincial societies attracted one-third, rarely half, of those in zemstvo and other "secular" schools. In Novgorod in 1904, of nearly one thousand teachers in zemstvo and ministry schools, only 275 were members of the local society; in Chernigov 445 out of 1,045.[13] Membership in these instances encompassed mainly rural teachers, but the situation was not much better among city teachers. The Society to Aid Primary Schoolteachers in the City of Moscow had been established in 1895, with a statute providing for wider activities than the ministry's "normal statute." In 1896 membership comprised 27 percent of those teaching in city schools; in 1901 it reached 35 percent (451 of 1,285). One might think that the better paid, better educated, and less culturally disadvantaged urban teachers had less need for a professional association, but the Moscow Society itself reached a different conclusion: "All around us is being completed a mighty, principled process of people uniting into corporations, but among teachers the striving toward unification develops in extremely weak fashion."[14]

Was there a weakness of "corporate spirit" among teachers? This was the subject of much discussion within the societies before 1905. Various factors were cited as inhibiting solidarity. Many rural teachers were not even aware of the existence of a provincial society, and for those who were and did join, attendance at society assemblies which discussed professional concerns and elected the executive board, was often sporadic.[15] As one teacher complained, for many colleagues the society more closely approximated a "charitable committee for the care of orphans and widows than a living teachers' organization, experiencing the difficult and joyful moments in the teacher's existence."[16] Formation of district sections of provincial societies would bring the organization closer to teachers in the villages, but only a handful of district societies existed before 1903, and even in these, given traveling costs, teachers' participation in meetings was not extensive.[17] Official sanction for the formation of district "filial" sections came in 1903, but even then the movement stalled, owing in part to opposition by local authorities who charged that decentralization would subvert supervision over society activities.[18]

Activists within the societies also ascribed teachers' apathy to the limited aims of most societies. At its annual meeting in June 1904 the Chernigov Teachers' Society found that its activity had been excessively one sided. Only one issue had been seriously tackled: children's education. "But teachers without families are also members, and other material and moral needs exist which must be satisfied." Self-education and other cultural demands had not been addressed, the society's annual report concluded, "not because they were unknown to the society," an oblique reference to administrative constraints.[19]

Such criticism was voiced by the more activist elements in the profession. Material concerns held secondary importance for this "idealistic" minority. Those teachers who showed greater interest in cultural concerns (measured by book and journal purchases, participation in summer courses) were also more active in the mutual aid societies: more often they were male teachers without families.[20] At first glance this may seem paradoxical, since the existing societies were not in a position to satisfy their wider interests. Nevertheless, these organizations provided teachers with some basis for contact with other teachers, and with society. For activist teachers the formation of a teachers' society—the only form of permanent professional association tolerated by the government—constituted a first, though modest, step toward a viable corporate movement. As with the summer courses, the societies offered psychological support through contact with zemstvo men, third element and educated society at large. Influential zemstvo activists and others who entered the societies as "associate members" provided valuable services. As a teacher and member of the Nizhegorod Society recalled, "persons with weight" were frequently elected as officers; people who could intercede on behalf of the society before the zemstvo, local officials, and other institutions.[21] For nonteachers the mutual aid societies afforded a link with teachers, which, given the administrative framework of public education in Russia and official suspicion of contacts between teachers and educated society had often been tenuous. By 1905, as we will see, both liberal zemstvo activists and radical intelligenty attempted to exert political influence on teachers through the mutual aid societies. By most accounts, such "associate members" played a positive role in encouraging professional activism among teachers.[22]

School officials were alert to the potential dangers of contact between teachers and educated society in the societies. Thus, the "normal statute" of 1894 stipulated that societies' executive boards contain at least one "permanent" member appointed by the ministry, usually a school director or inspector, occasionally from among the generally conservative teachers of local secondary schools or "urban schools" established according to the statute of May 31, 1872, as advanced elementary (but terminal) schools for children of the urban lower classes.[23] Surprisingly, the permanent members lacked clout; they did not have veto power over decisions of the board or assembly, and their function appears to have been to keep authorities informed of society activities.

By 1903 there existed some consensus in government circles that the "associate members" constituted an "unreliable" and potentially unsettling element within the teachers' societies, which should be excised by revising the normal statute to remove nonteachers. Homogeneous teachers' associations, dominated directly by local school authorities, could display little independence. In 1899 punitive action was taken against the Tula Society, when, in contravention of the statute, "associate members" were prohibited from holding office. Only after lengthy petition to the Senate was the right restored.[24] The curator of the Odessa school district suggested that teachers in secondary schools be encouraged to join the societies, where, "as a reliable element. . .they would act as a counterweight to those associate members who involve themselves in the teachers' societies only to propagate their own ideas among teachers, while having nothing in common with the true tasks and goals of teachers."[25] Despite concessions and vacillation, ministry officials continued to jealously guard the frontier that separated the rural teacher from educated society.

In order to sketch out the main lines of development and summarize the issues connected with the formation of teachers' societies, it is worthwhile to examine the history of one society before 1905. The Iaroslavl Teachers' Society was typical of teachers' societies at this time. Plans for the formation of a mutual aid society in Iaroslavl were laid at summer courses held by the zemstvo in 1898. The initiative came from liberal zemstvo deputies D. I. Shakhovskoi and S. A. Musin-Pushkin; the editor of the liberal *Severnyi krai,* V. M. Mikheev; zemstvo employees and a small group of activist teachers, including G. A. Sokolov, who taught at a zemstvo school; P. A. Kritskii, at a city school; and V. K. Burtsev, who taught at a railway school.[26] The courses struck a responsive chord among teachers, and many enthusiastically embraced the idea that a mutual aid society could serve as a more permanent organization for those who would disband after the courses ended. Many Iaroslavl teachers had attended the 1896 Nizhnii-Novgorod Industrial Exhibition and had familiarized themselves with the organization of the local teachers' society. After the 1898 courses in Iaroslavl the zemstvo submitted a petition to establish a similar society in Iaroslavl. The MNP rejected the zemstvo's project, which made provision for teachers' cultural and intellectual needs, as excessively liberal.

Two hundred teachers took part in courses in 1900. According to Burtsev, the mood was more oppositional than in 1898; those attending were generally younger and more susceptible to liberal and "red" influences. Discussion centered on expansion of the school's course to four years and development of adult education programs.[27] A new petition was submitted to the MNP, and in 1901 the Iaroslavl Society was founded on the basis of the normal statute, with monetary support from the zemstvo and the apparent blessing of school officials.

The first membership assembly met in early 1901 and elected a fairly radical board: third element members of the provincial zemstvo's school commission[28] (its secretary Minaev and the statisticians Sadikov and Didrikil') and the teachers Burtsev and Kritskii. According to Burtsev, all of the recently elected board members, with the exception of Kritskii, were members or sympathizers of the socialist parties. Governor B. V. Sturmer moved quickly to crush the new board, ordering the zemstvo to dismiss Minaev and Sadikov and threatening the dismissal of Burtsev and Kritskii if they refused to step down. As teachers, these two were vulnerable, and so they resigned. This episode underscored the advantage of having independent nonteachers as board members.[29] A second assembly met in December and under official pressure (aided by selective invitations) elected a new board with the school inspector F. I. Nasilov as chairman and passed a resolution to exclude many of the associate members. This was in clear violation of the society's statute and was subsequently overturned by the ministry. Under the new board the society lay dormant, and no meetings were held during the next two years.

In 1903 fortuitous circumstances again made possible revitalization of the Iaroslavl Society. In 1902, Sturmer had been promoted to the post of director of the Department of General Affairs of the MVD, where he achieved notoriety for his investigation of the Tver zemstvo. His replacement in Iaroslavl, A. A. Rogovich, was reportedly on bad terms with Pleve and was not as uncompromising as Sturmer.[30] Also, though the reason for his action is unclear, Nasilov stepped down as chairman, remaining as "permanent" MNP representative. The stage was set for the "democrats," to use Burtsev's characterization, in their attempt to recapture the society and address the growing demands among teachers that the organization respond to their professional concerns.

After a two-year hiatus the Iaroslavl Society's membership convened in December 1903 and chose (this time by secret ballot) a new board. Mikheev became chairman. His role in local society was large; official reports characterized him as the "creature of Shakhovskoi," but he also had close ties with revolutionary groups, particularly the SDs, many of whom worked on his newspaper.[31] Burtsev, who was close to the SDs, and Kritskii were again elected, as were Didrikil' and A. V. Kudriavtseva (an SR and wife of a zemstvo doctor). Also elected to the board was Musin-Pushkin, a member of the provincial zemstvo board. Musin-Pushkin was a radical zemstvo man (police reports pointed out that he was married to a peasant) who was immensely popular among teachers, having served many years as zemstvo representative on the Mologa district school board and having personally toured the schools. Also active in the society were A. A. Loktin, a zemstvo employee, and Ol'ga Florovskaia, wife of a doctor and sister of the revolutionary populist Vera Figner.[32]

This constellation of forces is similar to that in other teachers' societies: the more activist teachers, liberal and radical intelligenty, and liberal zemstvo men who stood considerably to the left of the majority of zemstvo gentry. In Iaroslavl this liberal minority was quite small.[33] But, as elsewhere prior to 1905, acting in close cooperation with the third element, it was largely responsible for the gains made in public education. The alliance between liberal zemtsy and radical third element was evident in the activity of various institutions: zemstvo school commission, the local Society to Encourage the Spread of Public Education (led by Shakhovskoi's wife), and the Teachers' Society. As with enlightenment societies at the national level, examined by Pirumova, Emmons, and others, such associations played an important role in political mobilization in the provinces before the formation of legal political parties.[34]

Politicization, as we will see, went hand in hand with rising professional activism, and in this regard the Iaroslavl Teachers' Society registered some tangible gains by 1905: response from local zemstvos on the issue of salaries and an increase in membership as the society sought to expand its services, including aid to teachers in periodical subscriptions. The significance of these modest gains for the rural teacher and of the role played by progressive nonteachers in the mutual aid societies is clear when one considers those societies in which such influence was lacking. Active membership in the Ekaterinoslav Society, for example, steadily declined during the five years prior to 1905. The board was completely dominated by conservative school officials and instructors in secondary institutions; liberal zemstvo activists and urban intelligenty were conspicuous by their absence. By the standard of teachers' societies, the Ekaterinoslav Society accumulated a huge treasury of 15,000 rubles, but, despite stubborn opposition from an activist minority of teachers, the board refused to expand the society's activity beyond issuing loans.[35]

What the teachers' societies represented was an alliance of nonteachers interested in education and in general political reform (especially from the zemstvo milieu) and a growing minority of the more active teachers. Before 1905, rank-and-file teachers tended to be passive members of the societies, or they remained outside of them, oblivious to the notion of corporate activity. Frequently, a leading role was played by specific categories of teachers in particular locales: teachers of zemstvo "repeater" courses for adults (Saratov, Kursk, Chernigov), railway schoolteachers (Ekaterinoslav), and those in city primary schools (Nizhnii-Novgorod, Perm, Ekaterinoslav, and the two capitals). Former teachers, in particular, occupied a commanding position in many societies. Many of these had been dismissed for "political unreliability" and subsequently gravitated to employment with zemstvos and city governments. As former teachers they enjoyed all rights of active membership and were sensitive to teachers' needs. Further, as people who had "suffered for their convictions" they symbolized the teachers' difficult legal status and enjoyed considerable prestige among their fellows. Finally, they were no longer subject to disciplinary action from school authorities and so, like the "associate members," constituted an independent element within the societies.

Much about the teachers' societies—their limited functions and the role played by nonteachers—characterizes them as charitable associations. Still, they contained elements of corporate activity, providing a forum where teachers' professional interests were aired, popularized, and pressed. Just as the teacher had received "half-a-voice" by virtue of government concessions on local congresses and courses, the mutual aid societies contained the germ of a more vital professional movement. What is remarkable to the historian is not their degree of dependence on outside forces, but the rapidity with which teachers moved to expand the parameters of the societies from narrow concern with mutual aid and utilize these organizations to struggle openly for professional and political demands. In the process they began to forge links between teachers' organizations at the national level and, just as important, hammered out a program, a "teachers' bill of rights," which would help guide the nascent movement through the turbulent social and political conflicts that swept Russia with the dawn of the new century.

From Nizhnii-Novgorod to Kursk: A Movement Emerges

If one had to identify the birth of the Russian teachers' movement, he or she could do no better than to choose the Industrial Exhibition sponsored by Witte's Finance Ministry as a showcase for Russian achievements in industry and other fields (including education), held in the summer of 1896 in the old trading center of Nizhnii-Novgorod on the upper Volga. With official sponsorship and free travel, nearly 6,000 teachers visited the exhibition before summer's end. The Nizhegorod Teachers' Society, acting as midwife, played an important role in popularizing the idea of teacher unification. The society, founded in 1893–94 according to a liberal statute providing for cultural services as well as "filial" sections, dramatized the possibilities of corporate activity. Aside from 262 teachers from Nizhegorod province, 4,518 visitors from eighty provinces and regions of the empire took advantage of cheap lodgings provided by the society. Of these, 1,843 were male teachers and 2,266 female teachers.[36] A teacher from Chernigov wrote to the Nizhegorod Society's organizing committee that he was willing to sleep in any "dog's hovel" only to visit the exhibition. Those who attended concurred that this "event" lent a decided impetus to the teachers' movement. One account compared the teachers of Nizhegorod province to the seventeenth-century national hero Kuzma Minin, leading Russia's teachers out of their own "time of troubles."[37]

Teachers viewed the exhibits but, more importantly, met and exchanged experiences with teachers from other parts of the country, "each feeling that thousands lived his grief and joy."[38] The local society organized informal meetings during which prominent educators like Bunakov and Vahkterov helped instill idealism and renewed dedication.[39] Teachers' attendance was fluid and unstable, but participants later referred to it as the first "All-Russian Teachers' Congress." It was here, recalled the veteran populist N. A. Malinovskii, that teachers first came to understand the significance of unification and where links were forged among revolutionary teachers who formed a loose organization of "touring artists" *(gastrolery)* and subsequently agitated at summer courses and mutual aid societies.[40] Most important, the potential of teachers' association, as demonstrated by the exhibition and activity of the Nizhegorod Society, helped spur the formation of mutual aid societies, most of which were incorporated after 1896. An issue raised in Nizhnii was the need for a sanatorium for ailing teachers. Such a project would require a pooling of resources, and in 1900 the Kaluga Society proposed a national congress of societies to discuss the issue. In light of the upsurge in professional activity and heightened expectations of recent years, the effectiveness of restricting such a gathering to issues of material security and "charity" was highly problematical.

The Moscow Teachers' Society assumed responsibility for organizing a congress, canvassed the idea among provincial societies, and then began the tortuous petition process, first before the archreactionary Governor-General of Moscow, Grand Duke Sergei, and then the Ministries of Interior and Education. From the preliminary program it was clear that the organizers intended to air all questions connected with teachers' mutual aid: material insecurity, cultural needs, *and* "legal status."[41]

A favorable official response was by no means assured, since the Ministry of Education had recently turned down two petitions for large meetings of educators. The petition was stalled for three months in the chancellery of Grand Duke Sergei. After a personal meeting with Prince Pavel D. Dolgorukov, chairman of the Moscow Society, who reassured the governor-general that a congress of mutual aid societies would be small (five delegates per society) and pose no security threat, Sergei gave his blessing, a decision he would bitterly regret. Officials later claimed that Dolgorukov had deviously created the impression that the congress would limit itself to questions that fell within the scope of the 1894 normal statute, in other words material status, while intending that "internal politics" should occupy a prominent place.[42]

Why official circles placed such "great trust" in Dolgorukov is unclear, for this wealthy aristocrat and gentry marshal from Ruza district (Moscow) was a leader of the liberal opposition. What seems clear is that influential circles within the government, particularly in the MNP, were willing to make concessions in the area of public education. The spirit of relative toleration of teachers' association, which had helped foster professional activity after 1895, still claimed adherents at the highest levels. Senator E. A. Turau, who later investigated the whole affair, ascribed great significance to the "timeliness" of the Moscow Society's petition, which struck a responsive chord because of the "general mood" of the MNP under P. S. Vannovskii, at that time guided by a "credulous desire to establish amicable cooperation between government and public with the aim of improving the lot of the schoolteacher with the aid of beneficent societies."[43] By 1900 ministry officials had acknowledged the existence of a "teachers' crisis":

> The meager salaries of teachers (50, 100, 150, 200, 300, 400 rubles a year) result in the fact that many teachers place little value on their posts, and at the first opportunity leave them for other, more remunerative occupations. This is not surprising if one considers the conditions of life of both men and women teachers: cast into the remote countryside and barely receiving maintenance sufficient for basic sustenance, they are condemned to endure all the inconveniences of rural life—at times housed in a smoky, filthy peasant house, nearly subsisting on bread alone, bereft of contact with people who have even a modicum of education, etc.—and finally, serving in the school until loss of health and then left without a position and without means to exist.[44]

The emphasis was on material conditions, but with an admission that other issues, such as cultural contacts, were important. Ministry experts concurred with zemstvo men that measures had to be taken to ameliorate teachers' position and check the drift from the profession at a time when both groups were beginning to seriously discuss the prospect of universal schooling in Russia. Viewing the projected congress of mutual aid societies as a way to air proposals to that end, the ministry gave its assent in November 1901. In view of the late date—the congress had been scheduled for Christmas recess in 1901–2—the Moscow Society postponed the gathering for another year to allow local societies to elect delegates, discuss the agenda drawn up in Moscow, and prepare formal reports for the sessions. By the close of 1901 more than fifty societies had responded, and, as the Turau report later noted, efforts of the Moscow Society to popularize the congress led to "unprecedented activity" in many provincial organizations. This was especially so in Kursk.[45]

Since 1894 the Kursk zemstvo had been among the pioneers in popular enlightenment. As elsewhere, much of the impetus came from a core group of liberal deputies who dominated zemstvo affairs during the postfamine era: V. E. Iakushkin, A. N. von-Ruttsen, A. V. Evreinov, N. V. Shirkov, N. V. Raevskii, and Petr D. Dolgorukov, twin brother of Pavel and Sudzha gentry marshal. The Kursk zemstvo provides a classic example of the influence which a liberal minority was often able to wield in zemstvo affairs before 1905. This resulted from general apathy among the zemstvo gentry electorate and the fact that Witte's economic policies had engendered gentry opposition ("fronde"), thereby facilitating a tenuous "compromise" between liberals and conservatives.[46] Third element influence was also considerable in Kursk, where employees sat on various collegial bodies and the recommendations of hired specialists often weighed heavily in zemstvo decisions. One of the most important of these organs was the zemstvo's educational commission, which until 1904 served as a kind of general staff overseeing the education campaign. The Kursk commission, established in 1894 (only Moscow preceded it) consisted of *uprava* members, elected zemstvo deputies and third element personnel. In concert with the zemstvo board, it formulated and executed plans for universal schooling, adult education experiments, innovations in zemstvo statistics, and organization of summer teachers' courses.[47]

Courses had been held annually in Kursk since 1897 and were again planned for the summer of 1902 in conjunction with Russia's first national exhibition of zemstvo achievements in education. The Kursk Exhibition played an important role in the zemstvo opposition movement, specifically in organizing liberal forces in advance of Witte's Local Committees on the Needs of Agriculture.[48] It was also a landmark in the history of the teachers' movement, particularly in preparation for the upcoming Moscow Congress of Teachers' Mutual Aid Societies, which centered around the local teachers' society. The Kursk Society had been established quite recently, in late 1901. In a short time, under Dolgorukov's chairmanship, it became very active. The society played host to teachers attending the courses and the Kursk Education Exhibition, which opened on June 23, 1902.

That many of the 5,000 visitors were teachers from other provinces (two teachers traveled on foot from Tver) suggests that the thirst for culture among rural teachers was enormous. At Kursk they were not disappointed, hearing lectures by P. F. Kapterev, A. P. Nechaev, and the historian N. A. Rozhkov, all scholars of national repute.[49] Moreover, Nikolai Chekhov noted a new assertiveness in those who journeyed to Kursk in 1902, as compared with those in attendance at Nizhnii-Novgorod six years earlier; they arrived with more clearly defined aspirations and demands and took a more active part in discussions.[50] No doubt, this reflected the recent upsurge in teachers' association and the internalization of a new professional ethos, that of confident cultural activists.

More important, the movement's maturation was reflected in the rudimentary program worked out at Kursk by teachers and their supporters. At unofficial meetings Petr Dolgorukov and E. A. Zviagintsev, a third element education expert and Socialist Revolutionary, indicted the government's record in education and assured teachers that in a reformed, zemstvo-controlled school system they would receive greater autonomy. At sessions of the Kursk Teachers' Society delegates aired reports for the upcoming Moscow Congress which went well beyond prosaic concerns of mutual aid to include teachers' participation in a future "small zemstvo unit" (a plan widely discussed in liberal circles), legal status, a "court of honor," through which teachers would police their profession, and diminution of inspectoral power. These deliberations assumed final form in a set of nineteen "theses" adopted by the Kursk Society on October 21, 1902. This "bill of rights" covered: (1) salary improvements and other material issues; (2) cultural demands and removal of limitations on teachers' association; (3) normalization of teachers' administrative status aimed at providing greater security in disciplinary matters and protection from arbitrary actions of various *nachal'stva;* (4) greater autonomy in managing the internal life of the school; (5) the small zemstvo unit aimed at enhancing teachers' authority within peasant communities; (6) a measure of input into zemstvo policy through teacher representation on zemstvo school commissions, modeled after existing medical councils.[51]

Though never published, the Kursk theses marked an important stage in the rise of the Russian teachers' movement. The demands voiced in Kursk would be sharpened a year later in Moscow, particularly in criticism of the inspectorate and in their general oppositional tone, but the basic program was in place. How different this was when compared with the last major national meeting that dealt with education! Held in Moscow in 1895–96, the Second Congress on Technical Education was attended by only a handful of teachers, who remained silent, and the meeting had only the slightest echo in the rural school.[52] Although the Kursk program reflected the demands of the more activist teachers and their allies among zemstvo liberals and third element specialists, the gains in teachers' association in recent years suggested its potential for rallying a mass professional movement. As a byproduct of deliberations between teachers and zemstvo men, the Kursk program also underscored teachers' evolving alliance with the zemstvo left; at the same time it pointed to tensions inherent in the teacher-zemstvo relationship. Moderate zemstvo men like D. N. Shipov and P. A. Geiden (present at Kursk), let alone the rank and file, were less than enthusiastic about plans for a "small zemstvo unit" at the volost level, dominated by peasants and third element intelligenty. Furthermore, the idea of direct teacher representation on zemstvo school commissions met with considerable resistance. Zemstvo men gathered in Kursk agreed that zemstvo representation on district school boards should be increased beyond the two deputies stipulated by the 1874 School Statute, on the assumption that they themselves best represented popular education. Teacher activists, while acknowledging a large debt to zemstvo progressives in their common struggle against the bureaucracy, nevertheless searched for firmer guarantees, in a larger voice within zemstvo institutions.[53]

Participants later described the Kursk Exhibition as a "celebration of the teacher," "dress rehearsal" for the Moscow Congress, and, more importantly, the organizational seedbed of the teachers' movement of 1905. The government concurred, ascribing "decisive significance" to Kursk in mobilizing teachers and zemstvo men against the government, which continued during the following months as local mutual aid societies selected delegates and drew up reports echoing the Kursk discussions.[54] Fresh winds ventilated the drab meeting halls of teachers' societies from Chernigov to Perm where it was already apparent that any discussion of teachers' professional interests, bound up as they were with the wider social and political realities of Russian life, might in the charged atmosphere of Moscow touch off an explosion of indignation against the regime which would then like an electric current be communicated to teachers in the hinterland.

The Moscow Congress: Organization and Issues

The All-Russian Congress of Representatives of Teachers' Mutual Aid Societies opened on December 28, 1902, in the spacious quarters of the Moscow Gentry Assembly, with subsequent sessions scheduled for the Historical Museum off Red Square and Moscow University. Some three hundred fifty delegates represented seventy-six societies, of whom half were teachers and the remainder zemstvo men and other associate members. In addition, seventy-one "experts" took part in the deliberations, including such well-known zemstvo activists as Shipov, D. I. Shakhovskoi, A. A. Stakhovich, specialists like V. I. Charnoluskii and G. A. Fal'bork, as well as teachers.[55] Assembled in Moscow was a broad cross section of people involved in popular enlightenment and nearly all leading activists of the nascent teachers' movement. The government subsequently explained the oppositional character of the congress by its "heterogeneous" composition and the fact that so many delegates stood outside the MNP's jurisdiction and hence were not susceptible to "pressure."[56] According to I. L. Tsvetkov, the gathering reflected the relative strength of various currents among organized teachers: a conservative minority (for example, the Samara, Ekaterinoslav, Penza and Iaroslavl delegations), a majority under liberal zemstvo influence, and a substantial "revolutionary" group.[57]

Most sessions were open to the public, since the ministry, hoping to defuse mounting opposition, intended to "widely open the doors of the congress and permit it to work under the widest publicity." Several large groups of teachers from the provinces came to Moscow. The congress also attracted a large number of interested outsiders from local society, the press, and, as police reports stressed, student youth. Local committees of the Social Democratic and Socialist Revolutionary parties issued proclamations to the arriving delegates, and, according to the ubiquitous N. A. Malinovskii, most of the revolutionary teachers' organizers who had met at the Nizhnii-Novgorod Exhibition in 1896 were present.[58]

At the same time, the government took precautions. The Moscow school director V. S. Novitskii and five inspectors, appointed as "supervisors," were vested with considerable powers to control the proceedings. Nevertheless, it is hard to disagree with critics from the Ministry of Interior who charged that during the nine days of sessions MNP officials allowed discussion of a broad spectrum of questions transcending teachers' material needs. Indeed, Section One of the congress, dealing with "general questions on the improvement of teachers' life," was the most well attended, since it reviewed the crucial problems of legal status and association.[59]

The Moscow Congress opened in an atmosphere of excitement, reflecting heightened expectations among teachers in recent years. The Moscow daily *Russkiia vedomosti* on December 28 carried an article by E. E. Mattern of the Moscow Society expressing the hope that the congress would lay the basis for a national union of teachers' societies in Russia that would rival the

Congress of Teachers' Mutual Aid Societies' Representatives held in Moscow during the Christmas holidays, 1902–1903 (Prince Pavel D. Dolgorukov, first row, third from left). Source: *Niva,* No. 4, January 25, 1903, p. 76.

German Teachers' Union with its 100,000 members. The meeting commenced with greetings from spokesmen for the MNP, zemstvos, city government, and the Moscow gentry. All asserted that the humble teacher was destined to play a pivotal role in the enlightenment of Russia's masses and in national progress. Director Novitskii declared that the government highly valued the teacher's labor, adding that it must be pursued "in a spirit of faith, love and loyalty to church, throne, and fatherland." According to police reports, his assertion that the government was sympathetic to teachers' plight (as evidence he cited establishment of the state pension fund in 1900) "elicited sarcasm" among the "unreliable element" of the congress.[60]

Pavel Dolgorukov, who was elected chairman of the gathering, assured the delegates that "Russian society will bend every effort to realize the proposals of the congress," since it recognizes that "the success of education depends on improvement in teachers' status," not only in a material sense, but also in terms of legal status, cultural needs, and association. His statement that teachers should look to "public organizations" like the zemstvos, rather than the government, struck a responsive chord among the delegates, according to the Okhrana. A zemstvo teacher from Balashov district (Saratov), V. S. Dokunin, voiced the conviction that if the government failed to respond to teachers' needs, educated society would come to their aid.[61] These statements tended to set the tone for the remainder of the congress and, indeed, for the teachers' movement as a whole during this period: antipathy toward the government, MNP officials in particular, and a fervent belief that the interests and ideals of teachers were shared by educated society, especially the zemstvos. In time teachers' professional agenda would come into conflict with the social and political bases of zemstvo rule. But for now the zemstvo-third element alliance was emphasized. And with good reason, for since the bleak 1880s zemstvos and educated society had shown a new commitment to school and teacher which had translated into real gains: a slight improvement in salaries and working conditions, greater access to cultural commodities and professional association, and, above all perhaps, an enhanced self-image and professional ethos.

This identity certainly contained a strong idealist strain, which helps explain why questions of material status did not occupy the central place at the congress envisioned by the Ministry of Education. In fact, N. V. Tulupov claimed that the majority of teachers, in contrast to other professions, viewed their vocation as discharging a "debt," as "service" to the narod.[62] Still, teachers' economic plight could not be discounted; during the previous year the case of a teacher in Novgorod province who had died of starvation received national notoriety.[63] The delegates felt compelled to grapple with the issues of teachers' penury, overcrowded classrooms, and unhealthy working conditions. But they did so somewhat reluctantly, evincing fears of cooptation by the regime and populist concerns for teachers' position in the village as well as their professional identity, seemingly conscious that the self-image they were defining in Moscow might affect the profession's claims to autonomy and authority.

Discussion of salaries highlighted these concerns. A report by S. V. Anikin (from the Saratov Society and close to the SRs) pointed to the low wages in Russian schools; salaries averaged 270 rubles for men and 252 for women, which compared unfavorably with "civilized countries." Delegates suggested that salaries be raised to a minimum of 500 rubles with 20 percent increases at five-year intervals. Surprisingly, this proposal encountered some opposition. A rural teacher (and SR) from Kursk, Fedor Lozovoi, argued that such a scheme would make teaching positions "cushy sinecures" *(teplen'ki)* and attract less dedicated candidates, "people of little use to education." Most delegates dismissed this warning and decided to petition zemstvos and city governments to raise salaries. They requested that the government help subsidize the plan, with the stipulation that state aid would in no way diminish zemstvo competence in the field of education, since they feared increased bureaucratic control over schools.[64]

In keeping with the spirit of zemstvo-teacher solidarity, delegates ascribed the lack of more substantial progress to the fact that zemstvos were hamstrung by a suspicious government: the 1900 law fixing zemstvo tax rates was frequently cited as an obstacle to salary improvements.[65] Disaffection with local self-government surfaced, however, during heated debate on the question of teacher-pupil ratios. The issue was raised in a report by Dr. D. D. Bekariukov, an expert on school hygiene who cited Western studies to demonstrate a positive correlation between overcrowding in poorly ventilated classrooms and nervous and respiratory disorders among teaching personnel, and zemstvo studies were used to show a disturbing incidence of such maladies among teachers in Russian schools where teacher-pupil ratios often approached, and sometimes exceeded, 1 to 100.[66]

The Congress's Second Section recommended a 1 to 40 ratio, a norm well below that in most rural schools. Some delegates, led by Liudmilla von-Ruttsen, founder of a women's teacher training school in Kursk, ardently opposed such a norm, arguing that it would severely impede the country's advance toward universal schooling and condemn at least half of school-age children to illiteracy. She pointed out that in Kursk province, where a ratio of 1 to 60 was common, only one-half of the boys of school age were in school, and two-thirds of the girls remained illiterate. She and I. Iakhontov, a zemstvo man from Novgorod, saw the dilemma as one in which the interests of the population should supersede the "selfish concerns" of teachers.

But these arguments, voiced mainly by nonteachers, met with loud protest from other delgates. A. N. Rumiantsev from the Mozhaisk Society insisted that the forty-pupil norm was absolutely essential to protect teachers' health and insure their productivity. Dokunin from Saratov and Ia. I. Tikhov of the Nizhegorod Society protested against shifting the burden of universal schooling onto the teacher's shoulders, while the state earmarked only 0.9 percent and the zemstvos 17.5 percent of their budgets for primary education, and they accused von-Ruttsen and her supporters of trying to "pursue the task of public schooling over the corpses of teachers." A majority of the congress endorsed the forty-pupil norm.[67]

Many reports contained graphic descriptions of teachers' living conditions. As a rule teachers' quarters were located in school buildings, described in one report as follows: "There is not a single peasant *izba* in such a woeful sanitary condition as the school, since the school has social intercourse with the whole village, even several villages, and is considered by experienced zemstvo physicians as a barometer of infectious disease."[68] A series of proposals followed to protect teachers' health. Aside from improving conditions in the village, these included support for teachers' courses and congresses held during the summer, which, in addition to their educational benefits, would have a salutary impact on teachers' mental health.

Other proposals regarding teachers' economic position, seemingly in conflict with teachers' new professional ethos, occasioned considerable soul-searching. It was suggested that the law of 1897, according to which schools could receive three desiatins of land, be applied more extensively to provide teachers with an additional source of income and food, as long as teachers were not turned into purveyors of agronomic skills. Some delegates saw a danger here. E. A. Solov'eva argued that this plan would deflect teachers from the important tasks of self-education and association. Rumiantsev predicted that teachers who in summer were drawn to the culture of the town "will not plant cabbages," and V. D. Shcheglov from Moscow warned that peasants would be hostile to any allotment of land for the school given their own land hunger. Nevertheless, the proposal was finally accepted.[69]

With barely concealed embarrassment the congress took up the question of state subsidies for the education of teachers' children and a 50 percent discount on railway travel. For militant activists, who had already begun to define the movement's ideological axis in opposition to the state, such proposals seemed to invite the danger of cooptation.[70] As for the majority, the government, through material and other incentives, might have been able to contain their opposition and enforce a measure of conformity. Such a strategy, as we will see, was entertained in official circles on the eve of 1905, but little came of these discussions. Even the petition for aid to teachers' children remained unanswered.

While the congress eventually accepted petitions for railway discounts and other subsidies, proposals that seemed to adversely affect relations with the peasantry were soundly rejected. In a report "On the Social Position of Teachers of Peasant Origin," I. M. Shigin, a Moscow city teacher, argued that teachers should enjoy all the rights and perquisites of state service, complete with official ranks *(klassnye chiny),* pensions, and service medals. Shigin argued that this would not only result in material benefits, but enhance the teacher's status within the community as well as place him in a more enviable position vis-à-vis the officials with whom he had to deal, thus improving teachers' legal status. With the exception of a handful of delegates from Poland and other borderlands, Shigin's proposals were roundly condemned by members of the congress's First Section, where they were first aired. By transforming the rural teacher into a "bureaucrat," Shigin's plan would merely erect an artificial barrier between the teacher and the local community. Given existing cultural and often social differences, it was difficult enough for teachers to win the hearts and minds of the peasantry, to induce the village to accept the teacher as *nash.* V. F. Glavatchuk, from the Slavianoserbsk (Ekaterinoslav) Society, predicted that such measures would not raise teachers' "moral authority": "I am afraid that the authority of a teacher-*chinovnik,* with shining buttons and cockade, would without fail wither." Peasants would simply come to view such a teacher as another representative of *nachal'stvo.* V. P. Kondrat'eva, of the same society, assured the delegates that "the teacher prefers membership in a hungry, but free profession to the rights of state service," and the delegate Filatov exclaimed "if we make a *chinovnik* out of the teacher this will only serve to fill the ranks of the bureaucracy, which are already overstocked." S. A. Spasskii from Tver remarked that as a priest's son it was already more difficult for him to gain acceptance by the narod than if he were of peasant origin. Shigin's proposals would make acceptance impossible. If the peasants would accept him as "their own," professed Spasskii, then he "would readily submit to corporal punishment and two days in the lock-up, to which a teacher of peasant origin is subject, since for me this physical punishment would be easier to endure than the moral agony of alienation from the narod."[71]

Teachers clearly recognized that they were "stranger-outsiders" within the peasant community (to borrow the typology of Teodor Shanin), the advance guard of an essentially alien culture, and that they would have to work to gain a degree of acceptance. The trappings of state service might well transform the teacher into a "plenipotentiary-outsider," in the eyes of peasants an official representing an equally alien, and coercive, state power.[72] This the overwhelming majority of delegates was unwilling to accept, both because it clashed so sharply with their idealist, populist ethos and would erect obstacles in the way of popular enlightenment.

As much as the delegates feared cooptation into the bureaucracy, they were alert to another danger faced by teachers: sinking into the uncultured rural morass. The issue of access to culture held a central place in the deliberations in Moscow and generated demands for liberalization of the statute for mutual aid societies, radical revision of the rules on teachers' courses and congresses, as well as redoubled zemstvo efforts to bring culture to rural teachers.[73] Most delegates expected that aid would be forthcoming. Zemstvo men were viewed as allies in the protean task of enlightening the rural masses; it was the bureaucracy, suspicious of the rural teacher, monitoring and limiting his access to culture and educated society, that was viewed as the main culprit.

This was the message conveyed in the report of Emilia O. Vakhterova, "The Teacher's Intellectual Needs and Their Satisfaction," which attracted a throng of delegates and a large public audience that packed one of the largest auditoriums of Moscow University and which had drawn fire from the MNP before the congress even opened.[74] Vakhterova's report contained a wealth of material on teachers' access to books, much of it gleaned from correspondence with teachers she and her husband had met at summer courses. She concluded that the government had contrived through the police powers of the inspectorate and restrictive catalogs to deny teachers a whole range of reading material permitted by the censor for the adult population of urban Russia. In a series of resolutions, unanimously accepted by the congress, Vakhterova suggested that general censorship be applied to teachers' libraries (both at schools and zemstvo boards) and that zemstvos make every effort to bring quality books and periodicals within reach, through subscription aid (she cited the Iaroslavl experiment), discounts at zemstvo book stores, mobile teachers' libraries, and so on.[75]

Despite a request by the Moscow curator Nekrasov that Vakhterova's "tendentious" report be amended, it was read in full at the congress. Vasilii

Vakhterov set the tone for the ensuing discussion when, paraphrasing a letter from Voltaire to Catherine II, he opined that "only thick heads and mean people can fear an educated teacher." (Okhrana agents in the auditorium recorded his words as "putrid heads"—*gnilye* rather than simply *tupye golovy.*)[76] Similar exposés of bureaucratic "stupidity" or "putrefaction" were contained in other reports. After a report on "pedagogical museums," which in theory would make pedagogical literature and teaching aids available to teachers, A. A. Stakhovich remarked that these were not easy to set up given myriad administrative hurdles. A ministry spokesman, E. P. Kovalevskii, taking offense at this remark, pointed out that the Russian museum at an exhibition in Philadelphia had received international acclaim, to which a delegate, Lavrov, shouted, "Gogol also knew one mayor who did not take bribes, so one museum is not worth talking about."[77]

For teachers the issue of culture was vitally connected with that of unification. All delegates agreed that for the teacher, especially in the village, contact with their fellows was crucial, both in a pedagogical sense—sharing information and experience—and in a broader social and cultural sense—as a source of moral support. In a report, "On Private Gatherings of Teachers," S. A. Sokolova from Moscow district, described teachers' isolation:

> Our peasants are not yet sufficiently developed so that one could discuss with them things one has read. Neighbors with whom you can bare your soul, as you know, barely exist. And really, to visit such neighbors as *pomeshchiki,* requires both time and a suit, to say nothing of that humiliation which the teacher must experience in visits to people who look at you condescendingly.

What kind of "society" can the teacher find, Sokolova asked, particularly a woman: "a male teacher can at least visit the village tavern," but, given the social taboos of rural Russia, even this form of social intercourse was closed to a woman. Small, informal gatherings of teachers could help fill the void; teachers could pool money for journal subscriptions and school supplies, such as projectors used in adult education classes, and the advice of older teachers would prove invaluable to new recruits who had trouble adapting to the rigors of the rural school, with its three sections.

As Sokolova noted, school officials rarely visited the village to provide such guidance and, ironically, were often not sympathetic to teachers meeting among themselves. During the previous spring she and her fellows had received notice from the inspector prohibiting any "assemblies" without his sanction; the size of such meetings was not stipulated, and Sokolova could only query, "are small gatherings, say three teachers, illegal?" This was in no way a frivolous question. School officials possessed wide discretionary powers over teachers—even the enactment of dress and moral codes and blanket prohibitions on social intercourse among teachers were not unknown.[78]

Throughout the proceedings delegates remained alive to the possibilities of firmer organization and greater autonomy. Some marveled at the situation in Germany where state and teachers' unions cooperated to send teachers to summer courses at universities. Others, selecting native models, pointed to the gains made by other Russian professions which held regular meetings: "only we," lamented a teacher from Ruza district (Moscow), "are deprived of professional contacts."[79] Within this context, several reports pointed out that in fields like zemstvo medicine and agronomy mixed collegial organs, consisting of zemstvo men and third element professionals, had considerable influence on zemstvo policy. Although not binding on the zemstvo assembly, the recommendations of these councils were often accepted by the deputies as expert opinion. Furthermore, these consultative organs, especially in medicine, had become institutionalized. As a teacher M. K. Chernogubova put it, "not one decision to open a hospital or appoint a doctor is made without the participation of the physicians."[80]

A few zemstvos had recently begun to experiment with such advisory bodies in education, but teacher involvement had met with opposition from authorities who viewed the teacher as a special case among third element employees and regarded free discourse between teachers and zemstvos with suspicion. And zemstvo opinion itself was not automatically receptive, cautioned S. I. Akramovskii. The "best" zemstvos, he noted, looked upon the teacher not as a "hireling" *(naimit),* but as a coworker; many others, however, did not. According to the Zemstvo Statute (articles 72 and 105), zemstvo boards had the right to involve third element employees in joint discussions, yet the Saratov delegate and SR activist suggested that the congress petition that the statute be amended to make such participation mandatory. The delegates heartily endorsed the idea of zemstvo school *sovety,* yet, apparently placing greater faith than Akramovskii in a positive response from zemstvos, resolved to petition the latter to implement the idea.[81]

Delegates in Moscow also drew up a project for a national union of teachers' societies and empowered the Moscow Society to petition the government on its behalf and, in the meantime, act as an informational center for provincial societies.[82] Here teachers drew inspiration from the Pirogov Society of doctors (established 1885), which coordinated medical congresses and published professional literature for zemstvo physicians. But, as delegates recognized, the decisive struggle for professional unification would have to be waged at the grass roots. It was in the countryside where the social and cultural impediments to association were most pronounced, where teacher timidity and "cowardliness" *(trusost')* impeded efforts to mobilize Russia's "zemstvo rabbits," and where *bespravie* was most in evidence. This simple truth prompted a delegate from Saratov to ask the chairman Dolgorukov whether there were any guarantees that teacher-delegates would not suffer reprisals when they returned home if they expressed their honest opinions in Moscow.[83] Prince Dolgorukov's assurances notwithstanding, there really were no guarantees. For this reason, and because legal status was bound up with every other facet of the teacher's existence, this question dominated the proceedings.

No single issue at the Moscow Congress occasioned such heated discussion and official discomfort as teachers' legal status. It was the rural teacher's subordinate status before an imposing phalanx of "authorities"—from rural officials to the school administration—that hindered corporate activity and reinforced isolation. Report after report hammered away at the theme that dissociation *(razobshchennost')* was enforced by a mean and suspicious bureaucracy.[84] In addition to economic insecurity, the teachers' lack of rights compelled many to abandon the profession. The fact that nobody, not even the drunken peasant who served as school guard, stood lower in the hierarchy of school administration, weighed heavily on the teacher's personality.[85] Thus, despite the intention of the Ministry of Education, its officials and the entire administrative framework of primary education in Russia came under intense fire at the congress.

Delegates sharply criticized the police functions performed by many school officials. The fiery Kursk delegate, Lozovoi, who would be in Siberian exile before the year was out, read from the "instructions" *(nakazy)* issued by officials in Kursk and elsewhere regulating teachers' personal lives: their dress should at all times be modest and they should limit their social contacts to "good, religious people, priests, etc."[86] Much attention was devoted to teachers' precarious position regarding dismissals and transfers. According to Anikin, transfers were common occurrences in the teacher's career. In a five-year period 60 percent of the personnel in Kursk province had moved from one school to another at least once, and during the school year 1900–1, 23.4 percent of teachers in Saratov transferred, most of these transfers resulting from administrative fiat rather than teacher request.[87] For the rural teacher who lacked the right of self-defense before local school boards, the specter of the charge of "unreliability" was a constant companion. Ekaterina Vagner, a veteran teacher from the Kuban Society, remarked that "as in the case of train wrecks it is always the switchman who is found guilty, so in the village it is the teacher. Even a hardened criminal is allowed a 'final word.'" She then recited cases of arbitrary dismissals and persecution gleaned from the press: "Here a teacher was dismissed simply because she resembled [the revolutionary Sofia] Perovskaia; in Tver province a teacher was sacked because he arranged a party *(vecherinka)* at his place, and in Viatka another for corresponding with a newspaper; here a teacher in Kursk was driven out of the school by the trustee who tossed her things out on the street." Calculating that these cases represented only an infinitesimal fraction of such dismissals, Vanger threw her press clippings into the air, to the thunderous applause of the delegates and the embarrassed confusion of the official supervisor.[88]

Many reports, as it turned out, touched on the question of teacher *bespravie*, and to systematize these materials a special "Commission to Elucidate the Legal Status of Teachers" was hastily put together and attached to the congress's First Section. I. N. Sakharov, a radical Moscow lawyer and delegate from the Moscow Pedagogical Society, chaired the Legal Commission's sessions; seven of its fifteen members were identified as being under police surveillance. Its radical complexion closely corresponded to the sentiment of the majority of delegates on this sensitive issue and, as the government later remarked, virtually insured that the commission produced an incendiary document.[89]

Sakharov read the final report at the January 4 evening session of the First Section before a packed auditorium. With a force that must have literally shaken the MNP supervisor, inspector M. P. Bulygin, the Moscow lawyer launched into a lengthy indictment of the school administration. Inspectoral supervision over the moral and political reliability of teachers, based on a long chain of circulars from the ministry and regional curators, the report asserted, contradicted the intent of the 1874 School Statute, that the inspector's task was to oversee instruction in the classroom *(uchebnaia chast')*. Instead of receiving solicitous concern and guidance from his superiors, the teacher was thrust into an "atmosphere of criminal investigation". If the teacher ran afoul of a priest or communal officials, the latter, cognizant of school authorities' own suspicions, would readily resort to denunciations in order to secure the teacher's dismissal. The Legal Commission suggested that even in the area of instruction official interference often caused considerable harm because many inspectors possessed inadequate pedagogical training. Much of this arbitrary behavior could be eliminated if all inspectoral directives were made through the zemstvo boards, "serving as mediators between the inspectorate and teachers."[90] Such reform, of course, would signal a complete reversal of government school policy, for it was the inspector's role, after all, to stand between teacher and educated society, the zemstvo included.

Not surprisingly, the commission had little favorable to say about district school boards, which were composed largely of persons "alien to the tasks of public education" and, in any case, overburdened with other duties and unable to devote much time or energy to board affairs. The role of land captains drew particularly sharp fire. Board sessions were removed from "public control," and, of course, teachers were not represented, even when their own fates were being decided. As Sakharov noted, participation of board members in the annual school examinations was often limited to meddling and imposition of unreasonable, and often conflicting, demands on the teacher, again by persons who lacked competence in this area. As for school trustees, the commission condemned their involvement in "pedagogical and moral-political control over teachers, as well as their influence on appointments and dismissals" and favored their replacement by collegial trusteeships on which teachers would be represented.[91]

In keeping with the third element-zemstvo alliance, the commission pointed out that real improvement in teachers' legal status depended on an enlargement of zemstvo prerogatives in education (only one, possibly two, of the commission's members were zemstvo men). The report did not call for any overhaul of local self-government; only amid the flush of excitement and disillusionment of 1905 would teachers insist on zemstvo democratization. Instead, the delegates in Moscow called for increased zemstvo competence in school management, not restricted to the "economic" *(khoziaistvennaia)* side. "The *bespravie* of zemstvo and municipal institutions in matters of instruction" resulted in hypertrophied inspectoral power. Zemstvos were hamstrung by existing legislation and administrative practice and were thus unable to effectively meet teachers' needs and intervene on their behalf.[92]

The Legal Commission also felt compelled to address the question of peasant rights, inasmuch as these contradicted teachers' "enlightenment ethos" and populist sympathies. Several reports had asked whether teachers of peasant origin, like peasants, were subject to corporal punishment by rural authorities, which generally took the form of beating with rods. In fact, teachers were immune to such punishment, at least during active service. Still the commission demanded abolition of this degrading vestige of serfdom and found that it could not "silently countenance the privileged position of the teacher."

> Can the teacher consider himself a citizen with full rights if this disgraceful punishment can be meted out to members of his own family; can he without shame fulfill the task laid on him by the state to nurture in his pupils a sense of human dignity when it is so cruelly assaulted upon their exit from the school, in complete contradiction with the best precepts of the school?[93]

The commission ended its report with thirty-two theses considered essential for any resolution of teachers' legal status and reform of public education in Russia. These called for strict legal guarantees for teachers, sharp diminution of inspectoral power, and enhanced zemstvo control over schools, on condition that teachers be accorded institutionalized input into zemstvo management and a measure of control over their own profession. Chekhov described this document as a "declaration of rights of the Russian teacher," and at a banquet held after the congress the populist writer N. K. Mikhailovskii went so far as to declare that "in these thirty-two theses the teacher has exposed the lack of rights and slavery not only of the teacher, but of the whole Russian narod." Mikhailovskii remarked that the congress had still not articulated the thirty-third thesis, but, as one of his listeners later wrote, "it was clear to all that this thesis could only be 'Down with the autocracy.' "[94] Whether the majority of delegates had come that far is a moot point, but the Legal Commission's statement did challenge the autocratic institutions and social relations governing education and thus, implicitly, the political culture of Tsarist Russia.

According to the Okhrana, "dead silence" reigned in the crowded auditorium as Sakharov read the Legal Commission's report, after which those in attendance burst into sustained applause, accompanied by a "deafening stamping of feet and cries of 'bravo.' " Supervisor Bulygin whispered something to the chairman of the First Section, K. K. Mazing, who hurriedly called a ten-minute recess; both then rushed from the hall to confer with ministry officials. Mazing finally emerged in an "agitated state" and confessed that he had erred in allowing the complete theses to be read before the congress without official review.[95]

The delegates openly accused Mazing of cowardice and duplicity. One delegate read a revolutionary statement calling for an end to autocracy. The luckless chairman, who on quieter days was director of a Moscow secondary school, was clearly losing control of the proceedings. Mazing had never held the delegates' trust; he had received a paltry twelve votes in balloting for officers and assumed the chairmanship of the pivotal First Section when P. S. Uvarov, the congress's choice, declined the post—which they were only too happy to remind him now. Vakhterov and others argued that the theses constituted an integral whole and, if need be, should be removed altogether. Mazing tried to put the issue to a vote, but according to the police, pandemonium broke out. Revolutionary proclamations were read. When a delegate from the Kazan Society urged his colleagues to maintain order and stick to "legal grounds," Lopatin of the Pskov Society shouted, "the law is one thing, but its interpretation something else entirely." Declaring his conscience clear before "society," Sakharov grabbed his briefcase and, followed by nearly everyone else, marched out of the hall to the sound of taunts directed at Mazing: "For him this is a question of his own skin—they may close his school."[96]

The following morning the congress's Executive Committee received a letter of protest signed by more than one hundred delegates, which demanded that the commission's full report be tabled for discussion. Dolgorukov promised that the theses would be printed in the congress's official proceedings, and the protesters relented. Therefore, the final session was held according to plan on January 6, 1903. Fearing that this assembly might be exploited by the revolutionary parties, Dolgorukov requested that a squadron of police be posted outside the Historical Museum. The auditorium was crammed with delegates and interested outsiders, many of whom, according to the Okhrana, pushed their way in without tickets.[97]

Once inside they heard P. A. Nekrasov, curator of the Moscow school district *(okrug),* assure the delegates that his ministry would closely consider their resolutions and reiterate the hope that government and educated society could cooperate in promoting public education. Chekhov recalled that each word of the curator "fell upon the auditorium like sparks to gunpowder," and Vakhterova wrote that a wave of coughing afflicted the delegates during Nekrasov's speech.[98] Dolgorukov urged them to popularize the congress's resolutions upon their return home. M. D. Ershov remarked that teachers in Russia now stood at the threshold of a bright future and only by joining hands could they cross their Rubicon, while the ill-starred Mazing assured that there could no longer be any doubt as to the teacher's impulse toward unification: "our teacher refuses to be a narrow professional, but wants his efforts to be closely aligned with the needs of the popular masses, and to satisfy these needs teachers must participate in public activity."[99] Delegates, both teachers and zemstvo men, pledged fidelity to their partnership. Zemstvo activists N. N. Khmelev and A. A. Stakhovich called on local zemstvos to carefully consider the congress's resolutions and heartily endorsed a greater voice for teachers in zemstvo affairs. Teachers gathered in Moscow felt that they had powerful allies in a common struggle against peasant ignorance and a hostile bureaucracy.[100]

Official assessments were less sanguine. While MNP spokesmen concluded that the Moscow Congress had brought much valuable material to light, indicating needed reforms, security organs saw only a dark cloud in their postmortems and blamed MNP officials for losing control of the proceedings. D. F. Trepov, the Moscow police chief, and Grand Duke Sergei pointed out that local committees of the SD and SR parties openly agitated among the delegates.[101] The government moved to stymie publication of the results of the congress, particularly the report of the Legal Commission. The right of the Moscow Society to publish the official proceedings was rescinded. Book-length summaries of the congress, one by the liberal education specialists N. V. Tulupov and P. M. Shestakov and the other by the SRs and former teachers S. I. Akramovskii and V. V. Kir'iakov, were confiscated and destroyed at the printers.[102] Minister of Interior Pleve justified these actions in May 1904:

> No doubt, these books would elicit a tremendous response among teachers. But they can only engender hostile attitudes to the state, since from beginning to end they point out that the government is to blame in all the misfortunes and misadventures of the teacher. These works would also have an unsavory influence on the masses, since they insinuate that the government is not at all concerned about the development of the public school and is taking few measures to improve the situation. Books like these must be reckoned as especially harmful.[103]

Despite these measures, all sources agree that the period after the Moscow Congress saw increased ferment in local teachers' societies. No longer were teachers willing to settle for corporate organizations that offered little more than loans, burial insurance, or discounts on medicine. As the delegates in Moscow had determined, what was needed was a fundamental alteration in teachers' cultural, legal, and social status, and teachers demanded that mutual aid societies and zemstvos address these needs.

The aftermath of the congress was also marked by sharp hostility toward school officials, the "educational gendarmes" who served as permanent members of society executive boards.[104]

The Orenburg Society, for example, had existed for nine years but had shown little life. Under the impact of the Moscow discussions, and with a new energetic board led by the lawyer and Union of Liberation member, A. N. Kremlev, members in April 1903 insisted that the society satisfy the pressing cultural issues raised in the old capital. The provincial school director A. I. Tarnavskii protested that these proposals violated the organization's statute. Nevertheless, they were endorsed by a huge majority, after which the society's board waged a vociferous press campaign to expose the obscurantism of school officials. The latter remarked nervously that "everywhere among teachers there is talk of a new era," and the curator of the Orenburg school district noted that, given the current structure of teachers' societies, officials were powerless to stem the tide of growing militancy and, in fact, it was not safe for his deputies to show up at society meetings where they were openly reviled.[105]

Local officials also complained that zemstvo liberals and the radical third element had commandeered the leadership of several mutual aid societies in order to promote political agitation among teachers. This was true of the Vladimir Society, where a liberal-radical coalition of associate members and former teachers led a drive in 1903–4 to expand its activity, particularly by organizing local affiliates to reach teachers in the village.[106] The Saratov Society, organized in 1900, was headed by the zemstvo liberal A. D. Iumatov, but a major role in its affairs was played by third element personnel, some of whom were former teachers and most of whom were adherents of revolutionary parties. The Saratov Society sent a radical delegation to the Moscow Congress, and in elections of new officers in May 1903, S. V. Anikin, G. K. Ul'ianov, A. A. Bogdanov, and Z. A. Serebriakova joined the board, all members of the local Socialist Revolutionary organization. The police even viewed the society as a kind of legal appendage of the party, promoting and coordinating revolutionary work among rural teachers.[107]

Official alarm resulted in a secret circular of April 16, 1904, from the Department of Police to all governors ordering closer supervision of existing societies and a freeze on petitions to open new ones.[108] Meanwhile, the Ministry of Interior launched an investigation under Senator E. A. Turau to discover why the modest mutual aid societies had spawned such a militant congress and to recommend "reforms." Turau prescribed a two-pronged strategy to undercut teacher radicalism. On the one hand, he proposed that the societies' statutes be amended to remove nonteachers from an active role, specifically the zemstvo men and sundry intelligenty who crept in as associates. On the other hand, school officials would be granted wider authority. At the same time Turau recommended that the societies, and school officials, begin to address some of the wider issues that teachers had raised in Moscow. Like other perceptive Tsarist officials who analyzed sources of opposition (Sergei Zubatov's assessment of workers comes to mind), Turau concluded that the state should actively champion teachers' professional needs. This had been done in Western Europe, but "here [in Russia] the teacher, left to his own devices, is forced to seek defense in influential patrons who join the teachers' societies or seek aid from the zemstvos."[109]

What Senator Turau was suggesting was a rather abrupt turnabout from previous policy. He proposed that school officials add to their traditional police functions an active concern for teachers' professional needs, including association, thereby extirpating the roots of teacher radicalism. What effect this program might have had is difficult to say. It was again discussed within the Ministry of Education in 1905 in response to the open politicization of teachers' societies that year but was never implemented.

In the meantime Pleve's ministry adopted a very different strategy for containing the teachers' movement, one that threatened to roll back professional gains achieved during the past decade. Pleve had long been sensitive to the danger of intrusion into the countryside by "alien" elements of the intelligentsia. In response to the agrarian disturbances of 1902 he cancelled zemstvo statistical investigations and referred to the third element as a "microbe of social scandal." After the Moscow Congress he "became convinced that teaching personnel exert[ed] a harmful influence on the narod."[110] The gathering contributed substantially to a hardening of the traditional official view of teachers as a potential threat to the existing social order, and it called into question the policy of the Ministry of Education that had resulted in modest concessions to teachers' association in recent years. Just as the MNP representative at the congress was calling for cooperation between government and society to enlighten the peasantry and improve teachers' status, it was already evident that the era of "heartfelt concern" *(serdechnoe popechenie),* which had characterized recent policy, was over.[111] The scales had tipped. Security concerns were once again ascendant and, as we will see in the following chapter, only contributed to the cycle of raised expectations, repression, and inevitable politicization.

To summarize, the Moscow Congress capped a remarkable decade of professional development and mobilization for Russia's teachers. Much had changed since the doldrums of the 1880s. Solicitude on the part of educated society and zemstvos toward teachers and their needs; renewed commitment by the intelligentsia to popular enlightenment; government concessions in the area of teachers' association and professional activity—all affected teachers in a positive sense. Thousands took part in the summer courses, mutual aid societies, and in discussions of professional and educational issues. The cumulative experience worked a sea change in teachers' consciousness: it stimulated commitment to teaching, solidarity, and a militant embrace of the mission to transform peasant society. As in the 1870s, many idealistic young people entered the profession, lending the teachers' movement a strong idealistic bias, as well as a sharp political edge. Nevertheless, it was the contradictions in teachers' status and the tensions inherent in government policies which ultimately swept many of these "zemstvo rabbits" into a professional movement and then into political opposition. In Moscow teachers posited a professional self-image as public activists, destined to play an important role in Russia's cultural transformation, and hammered out a program which linked professional demands with broader political and social change. The Legal Commission's theses, in particular, foreshadowed many of the demands voiced in 1905. In Moscow delegates cemented the initial organizational ties upon which the 1905 Union of Teachers would be based. Indeed, the nascent movement was already launched into the gathering storms that were Russia's social and political conflicts on the eve of 1905.

5. The Turn to Activism

Teachers and Politics on the Eve of 1905

In mid-1903 Pleve told a gathering of marshals of the nobility in Moscow that the main conduit for sedition in the countryside and the implacable foe of gentry interests was the zemstvo teacher.[1] But disaffection among rural teachers could pose little threat to the regime if not for the presence of organized political movements seeking to enlist teachers as a link with the rural masses. Liberal, revolutionary, and in the borderlands of the empire, nationalist movements were all highly visible by 1902–3. Widening circles in educated society clamored for civil liberties, a constitutional order, and social reforms. Support for this Liberation Movement came from the so-called democratic intelligentsia, mostly members of the burgeoning professions, as well as a liberal minority among the zemstvo gentry. By 1902 this coalition had acquired an influential voice in Petr Struve's émigré journal *Osvobozhdenie,* and in the years before 1905 the "liberationists" succeeded in establishing loose organizational ties and attracting adherents through a series of professional congresses and conferences of zemstvo men. These developments culminated in the formation of a Union of Liberation, the avowed goal of which was a constitutional regime in Russia.[2]

Moderates and conservatives soon added their voices to those of the "liberationists." Upset over the government's agrarian policy, official attacks on local self-government, the conduct of the war with Japan, and the regime's apparent inability to deal with a rising tide of social unrest in city and countryside, on the eve of 1905, rank-and-file zemstvo gentry were calling for political reforms. The alienation of these traditional supporters of autocracy only served to highlight the government's isolation. For supporters of the Old Regime there was also clear and present danger to the left of the liberals. The growth of an industrial working class was soon followed by formation of a Social Democratic party characterized by considerable militancy, and by 1901 revolutionary populists had succeeded in launching the Socialist Revolutionary party (PSR), which combined propaganda and organization of the urban and rural masses with terrorism directed against government officials.[3]

Faced with mounting opposition in educated society, as well as the specter of popular unrest—a wave of industrial strikes in 1902 and 1903 and the most serious peasant disorders in decades in the Ukraine during spring

1902—the government was suddenly confronted with the surprisingly militant Moscow Teachers' Congress. From that moment it was apparent that a professional teachers' movement was likely to pursue radical political as well as professional aims. The prospect that the rural intelligentsia, teachers in particular, might be mobilized by urban-based opposition groups as a wedge into the countryside clearly alarmed Pleve and his colleagues and seemed to catch them off guard.

Their surprise is somewhat ironic, since the official view, dating from the 1870s, had been that the rural teacher posed a potential threat to the social order. Inspectoral supervision and policies on teacher association had more often than not been based on this assumption. Hiring procedures were designed to screen out candidates of suspect "moral" and political reliability, and once he or she arrived at the school the whole social and administrative order, as well as precarious economic status, tended to isolate the teacher. This system had deleterious effects on the profession, but for provincial security forces the teacher's potential as a radical influence in the countryside had apparently been neutralized. State policy on the teacher and rural school, was also ambivalent: it fluctuated, which set in motion a pattern of rising expectations, frustration, and radicalization and also provided a niche in which a movement committed to breaking this cycle of repression could develop. Given the basic contradictions in official policy, it is not hard to see how the government not only failed to contain the teachers' movement, but also failed to anticipate it.

As if to confirm impressions drawn from the Moscow Congress, Pleve had begun to receive disquieting reports from his subordinates in the provinces. With the agrarian disturbances of spring very much in mind, several governors in their annual reports for 1902 indicated the existence of antigovernment activity among teachers. The governor of Tambov noted that in the past year twelve teachers had been implicated in agitation among the peasant population. His counterpart in Saratov, where disorders had actually taken place, pointed to the involvement in revolutionary activity of male teachers who were most dissatisfied with conditions of "economic insecurity and isolation in semicultured settlements, in view of which they easily succumb to political propaganda." The governor of Pskov ascribed teachers' radicalism to frustrated attempts to overcome cultural isolation and identify with educated society: "having in the course of several years at the teachers' seminary tasted the fruits of contemporary provincial civilization, they return to the village to teach." Receiving a salary of less than three hundred rubles and unable to maintain intercourse with the city, they became increasingly discontented.[4] The implication was that some teachers might conclude that the government, which allocated few funds for public schools and erected a wall of administrative regulations and bureaucrats to stand between teacher and educated society, was to blame for their predicament.

Tsar Nicholas II read these reports and recommended that the Ministry of Education make special efforts to train women teachers, as it "seems desirable to replace male personnel with female."[5] The assumption was that women, whether by virtue of their supposed passivity or because they would be more easily reconciled to difficult conditions given the relative absence of other employment opportunity, would constitute a more reliable element. In any case, a natural process of feminization was already altering the profession's physiognomy. What is interesting is an apparent shift in official opinion as to who would make the best, most reliable rural teachers. During the 1870s, Count Tolstoi had considered the best candidates to be men of peasant origin, who would be able to adapt more readily to rural life and would presumably share the peasantry's loyalty to throne and church. In 1903 the ministry continued to endorse as teachers seminary graduates, overwhelmingly men of peasant background, as most suitable.[6] The seminary curriculum was carefully circumscribed and included a heavy dose of moral and religious instruction and correspondingly deemphasized general education subjects. Yet reports received in St. Petersburg at this time indicate that even these institutions, which many contended were run like military barracks, had become infected with radical politics. The governor of Novgorod complained bitterly in 1902 that most graduates of the Novgorod and Cherepovets seminaries could not be trusted to instill a sense of morality and religiosity in the younger peasant generation, to which the tsar replied: "It is necessary to eradicate this evil."[7]

Evident in these reports was a growing realization among officials that the time-honored methods of training, selecting, and monitoring teaching personnel had not been entirely effective. More perceptive observers recognized that the basic contradiction in the teacher's status, the cultural isolation of a *Kulturtrager,* was a source of radicalism. One can see the evolution in official opinion by comparing two reports from Chernigov province, one filed in 1896, the other in 1904. In the first the governor remarked that all was well in the schools, noting parenthetically that, "thanks to the involvement of land captains in school affairs, it is impossible to place a disloyal teacher in a rural school." Eight years later a police survey contended that "zemstvo teachers, both men and women, without exception, if not constantly waging open propaganda, undoubtedly exert a harmful influence on the peasantry by virtue of their negative attitude to the political and social order and criticism of any official act they deem insufficiently liberal."[8]

The role of teachers and other rural intelligenty in actually fomenting peasant disorders in 1902 is questionable; that some teachers helped engender a "critical attitude" to the existing order cannot be discounted. In any case, the government discerned a thread linking the urban opposition and agrarian movement in the behavior displayed by teachers in Moscow and moved to sever it. Evidence suggests that the 1902–3 school year was marked by considerable harassment and political arrests of teachers. A certain "Volosatyi," writing in *Osvobozhdenie,* enumerated a series of such cases throughout the empire and concluded that the government now viewed every teacher suspect by virtue of his profession. Arrests and disciplinary action against rural teachers would increase in 1903–4 and were liberally documented in *Osvobozhdenie* and the PSR's émigré *Revoliutsionnaia Rossiia,* which described repression of teachers in Kursk, Saratov, Tver, and elsewhere as a wholesale "pogrom." Among these were quite a few participants in the Moscow Congress of Teachers' Mutual Aid Societies who suffered reprisals upon their return home, Prince Dolgorukov's assurances of the government's good faith notwithstanding.[9]

This new climate, not surprisingly, adversely affected the government's recent toleration of teachers' association. Among other benefits, summer courses had provided teachers vital psychological support through association with their fellows and contact with educated society. But this was precisely why security officials took a jaundiced view of the zemstvo courses. In the wake of the agrarian disorders of spring 1902 in Kharkov and Poltava, when the third element came under a cloud, authorities were once again inclined to see the courses as a prime recruiting ground for urban radicals. After all, these were fairly populous gatherings where teachers came into contact with zemstvo liberals, third element, and members of revolutionary parties, many of whom were employed by local zemstvos. On May 21, 1902, Pleve and the head of the Department of Police issued a circular to governors. Commenting on the recent peasant disturbances, they stated that they fully expected revolutionary elements to redouble their efforts in the countryside and "in future strive to organize circles of rural teachers, making contact with them during the summer at congresses and pedagogical courses." Local officials took the threat seriously. Zemstvo courses in Tver were not sanctioned that summer. In Tambov, courses were cancelled by the governor for 1902, following the arrest of teachers who had participated in courses the previous summer.[10] General education courses were held in Kursk in 1902, as they had been since 1897, this time in conjunction with the zemstvo education exhibition. Participants judged them an unqualified success, but in his annual report to St. Petersburg the governor claimed that they had been the scene of illegal meetings and "harmful propaganda" and urged that tighter controls be placed over lecture content and particularly over teacher-auditors' free time. One incident in Kursk immediately caught Pleve's attention: Petr Dolgorukov's attempt to organize a deputation of 500 teachers to greet Leo Tolstoi as his train passed through Kursk from the Crimea. The minister interpreted this as a blatant attempt to involve teachers in an open antigovernment demonstration, because of the great writer's internationally known opposition to the regime and the Orthodox church. For a rural teacher, as one might imagine, a glimpse of Russia's greatest living writer had to be a memorable event. To the government it was a seditious act.[11]

Official reports for 1903 expressed even more apprehension about the summer courses. Some even predicted a "teachers' mutiny" *(uchitel'skii bunt).*[12] Accordingly, the number of summer courses sanctioned by the administration dropped off. In 1903 the government rejected petitions by eleven zemstvos to hold courses that summer, most of the general education type (Kazan, Iaroslavl, Ufa, Tambov, Vladimir, Saratov, Samara, Poltava, Perm, Novgorod, Voronezh).[13] Many of these zemstvos had held identical courses in 1901 and 1902. Zemstvos which held courses in 1903 reported increased supervision by both school and regular authorities as well as "strict constraints" on their organization.[14] By 1904, courses were held in only four provinces, in addition to the ministry's own courses in Tsarskoe Selo.[15] The program for the Kostroma courses of 1904 was sharply curtailed, and school officials did their best to maintain vigilance over the auditors. One teacher, a woman, later remarked that "the director did not even leave the lavatory in peace, but held watch even there." Still, by all accounts the Kostroma courses were a great success. Teachers even heard a supportive speech by the local governor, who cited the need for solidarity among teachers and greater "trust" in teachers from government and society.[16] But this was an exception. The governor of Kostroma was clearly out of step with his colleagues in other provinces and his superiors in St. Petersburg. A. A. Stakhovich remarked that the Ministry of Education had adopted a "new tactic" of simply not replying to zemstvo petitions to hold teachers' courses.[17] In early 1905 zemstvo courses were banned altogether.[18] Teachers in church schools under the Holy Synod did attend courses in summer 1905.[19] Yet parish schoolteachers were deemed politically reliable; certainly they had never displayed the militancy shown by teachers in secular schools at the Moscow Congress. And in this case the sponsoring agents were not the suspect zemstvos. For zemstvo teachers the years 1902–5 saw steady erosion of legal means for professional association, part of a futile attempt to quarantine the countryside from mounting opposition in the cities. Teachers came to see the state as helping perpetuate their isolation and cultural deprivation, and, in the light of the rising expectations and solidarity of recent years, the result for many was a high level of frustration, reflected in political opposition.

A Link with the Peasantry: Teachers and Revolutionaries

For Pleve the calculus of revolution in the countryside was clear. Because of his strategic position in the village the teacher could provide urban-based revolutionary groups a vital link with the rural masses. And where better to mobilize rural teachers than at large, legal gatherings such as summer courses? Not surprisingly, the revolutionary parties evaluated the teacher's significance in similar terms. This was especially true of the Socialist Revolutionary party (PSR), which, particularly after the peasant disorders of 1902, stepped up its efforts in the countryside.[20] Provincial society was by now much more complex than even ten years earlier. Political groups could recruit cadres among third element professionals, migrant peasant workers, and even a nascent stratum of "peasant intelligenty." But among these potential links, teachers were quite important. Despite their status as outsiders teachers resided in the village for much of the year and, with the rapid spread of schools from the mid-1890s, became much more common figures; zemstvo teachers alone increased from 10,300 in 1880 to 27,000 in 1902. Thus, the PSR saw teachers as a "natural conduit of revolutionary socialism in the countryside."[21]

At the same time the PSR conceded that because of their vulnerability, submissiveness to authority, and intellectual limitations, these "zemstvo rabbits" were often ill-prepared to aid in raising the revolutionary consciousness of the rural masses. An article in the party's émigré organ cautioned:

> Anyone familiar with teachers knows what a torpid lot they represent and must admit that first it is necessary to expand their own intellectual horizons to render them capable of revolutionary work. Admittedly, quite a few conscious, fully prepared teachers exist, but behind them lurks that average, grey mass which still needs to be made conscious of its debt [to the narod]. After all, many teachers have limited educations, teachers' or theological seminaries, and often much less. Once they enter the profession they can't get hold of a decent book.

Here was one void the party should attempt to fill, since the teacher's position offered "advantages for revolutionary work among the peasantry which other professionals lack." Many teachers were themselves of peasant origin, and for these "it is easy to find the road to the peasant heart and mind." Even a teacher of nonpeasant background, as the "lone representative of the intelligentsia in the village," could exert a "sustained influence on peasant affairs, communal decisions, and conflicts with officials, priests, and landowners." "All of this," reasoned *Revoliutsionnaia Rossia,* "compels us to pay special attention to teachers with the aim of making them conscious propagandists."[22] Teachers' courses (and to a lesser extent the mutual aid societies) provided a unique opportunity to mobilize teachers, and there is ample evidence that revolutionaries, particularly the SRs and their immediate populist forerunners, seized the chance to make contact and instill in teachers a sense of their "historic mission" to help deliver the peasantry out of social and political bondage.[23]

As early as summer 1896, at the Nizhnii-Novgorod Exhibition, a loose organization of populist teachers had coalesced. Many of these were former teachers, dismissed on political grounds and now banned from teaching anywhere in the empire. This organization of "touring artists" *(gastrolery)* made contacts among the teachers visiting the exhibition that summer, and after 1896 members of the group attended teachers' courses, congresses, and meetings of mutual aid societies throughout Russia.[24] The *gastrolery,* and other loosely affiliated populist groups which would join in the PSR in 1901, were able to forge links with teaching personnel. The summer courses played an important role in this process of political education and mobilization. SR activists (or proto-SRs) were present at teachers' courses held annually in Saratov between 1897 and 1901. Saratov was a party stronghold, and evidence of propaganda at the provincial courses contributed to the routine rejection of zemstvo petitions to continue them in subsequent years.[25] There is evidence of agitation at courses held in Perm in the summer of 1901. These courses were sponsored by the local zemstvo and supported financially by N. V. Meshkov, a wealthy merchant and zemstvo deputy who was close to revolutionary circles. According to *Osvobozhdenie,* Meshkov employed more than a thousand factory workers and owned the finest house in town—he was also arrested for his involvement in a "Ural Union of SRs and SDs" organized behind the scenes at the courses. Major figures representing the PSR, E. K. Breshkovskaia and G. A. Gershuni, were in Perm, as was the populist journalist N. K. Mikhailovskii. Local SRs—the zemstvo statistician V. A. Vladimirskii and the city teachers F. N. and A. N. Iagodnikov—along with Perm SDs organized illegal gatherings of teachers during the courses; police suspicions were aroused, in particular by excursions along the Kama River which Meshkov, who owned a steamboat line, arranged for the auditors.[26] According to police reports, the "state criminals" Gershuni and Breshkovskaia continued their work that summer at sessions of the Perm Teachers' Society, the board of which was dominated by a group of SRs led by the Iagodnikovs and A. G. Sobol'ev.[27]

Zemstvo teachers' courses were also exploited by SR organizers in Tambov: V. M. Chernov, A. N. Sletova (Chernov's future wife), and her brother S. N. Sletov, historian of these formative years and an important influence in the party with his contributions to its theory. Like many provincial radicals, Chernov and Sletov found work in the 1890s with the local zemstvo, where radical third element personnel had forged a working association with liberal zemstvo leaders. Various unofficial gatherings of teachers were held in Tambov at the summer courses of 1901. The zemstvo men M. P. Kolobov and L. D. Briukhatov, as well as the progressive school inspector T. E. Ostroumov, participated in conferences at which teachers discussed mainly educational issues. Other meetings had a more political character. At one of these Stepan Sletov, who would soon join Chernov in emigration, read the manuscript of his brochure "On the Question of Revolutionary Work among the Peasantry," which proved to be a seminal work since it presaged the shift toward greater SR activities in the countryside. That it was first aired before an assembly of rural teachers was no accident.[28]

What of the PSR's major revolutionary rival, the Social Democratic party? The SD press periodically carried appeals to teachers urging them to support the struggle of the Russian proletariat.[29] Local SDs took advantage of legal teachers' association in order to make their views known to rural teachers. They were present at the courses in Perm as well as at those organized by the Tver zemstvo in 1903 in the district town of Rzhev, which were attended by some three hundred teachers. The Tver RSDRP committee reported earlier in 1903 that it had been able to establish ties with teachers in only three districts. In one of these, Rzhev, the SRs enjoyed far more influence among teachers. Both parties had fairly strong teachers' groups in Novotorzhok, admittedly one of the most politicized of all districts in Russia and where the local zemstvo provided a kind of haven for radical teachers.[30]

The efforts of the Social Democrats among teachers, as with the party's overall commitment to the countryside, were no match for their rivals. Individual Marxists who offered their services as lecturers at teachers' courses did enjoy great popularity. Foremost among these was N. A. Rozhkov, a young historian and instructor at Moscow University and the Moscow Teachers' Institute, which trained teachers for primary schools in the old capital. Rozhkov, who did not join the Bolsheviks until 1905, gave lectures on Russian history at courses in Voronezh, Tambov, Ufa, Rzhev, Kursk in 1902 and 1903, and elsewhere. Police reports underscored his radicalizing influence on the *kursanty.* At courses in Ufa (1902) teachers drew up a petition to the zemstvo, containing various demands that would soon be aired at the Moscow Congress, including representation for teachers at zemstvo assemblies and the right to defend themselves before school boards against arbitrary actions by the school inspector and land captain. Local authorities ascribed a large role in the compilation of this document to zemstvo employees and to "associate professor Roshkov [sic]." Referring to unauthorized talks held after lecture hours, Rozhkov recalled "illegal discussions" with teachers on various "social issues." Finally, in 1903, after his participation in the last courses permitted in Kursk, which turned into an open antigovernment rally and prompted a purge of teaching personnel, all zemstvos were prohibited from inviting Rozhkov as a lecturer. In his memoir Rozhkov explained this ban as a direct result of his private talks with teachers and the historical materialist bias of his lectures.[31] Other Marxist academics, including the future dean of Soviet historians, M. N. Pokrovskii, also lectured at teachers' courses. An indication of their personal influence among teachers is that both Rozhkov and Pokrovskii occupied leading positions in the All-Russian Union of Teachers in early 1905. On the whole, however, SR activity among rural teachers before 1905 was much more intensive than that of any other revolutionary party. The importance attached to this arena soon led to the formation of a special SR Union of Teachers, the *Soiuz narodnykh uchitelei P.S.R.*

Both the origins and activity of this union are obscure. The sources do not agree when the organization was founded. Its activities and the composition of its leadership are difficult to determine not only because of the paucity of sources (even the PSR's Central Committee appeared ill-informed about it), but also because of the existence of a parallel illegal Union of Teachers that claimed to be *nonparty* yet had close ties to the SR organization.

The interest of the Socialist Revolutionaries in the countryside was underscored by the formation, in the wake of the 1902 agrarian movement, of a party-affiliated Peasant Union. Local union groups and armed peasant "brotherhoods" would, the PSR hoped, provide them with a mass base. According to Malinovskii, a similar organization, uniting teachers, was launched in 1902, the culmination of agitation by Breshkovskaia and others at summer courses in recent years; "in each province teachers' circles coalesced and united into a party teachers' union . . . the main directive to SR teachers being the organization of peasant unions and brotherhoods."[32] The official organ of the PSR confirms that a Union of Teachers was discussed during 1902.

> The idea of an organization uniting teachers for illegal work arose, as far as we know, among teachers themselves in the later months of 1902. With this in mind, organizers took advantage of all courses and teachers' meetings. With the help of certain prominent SR activists [Breshkovskaia, Gershuni?], links were forged with distant parts of Russia and the most revolutionary teachers identified. Teachers were exhorted to struggle not only for their own demands, but in the interest of all the laboring masses against the tsarist autocracy.[33]

Agitation for an illegal teachers' union no doubt carried over to the mutual aid societies and the Moscow Congress. The Moscow committees of both the Social Democratic Party and PSR expended considerable efforts to influence the 350 delegates, and a revolutionary Union of Teachers *(Soiuz narodnykh uchitelei)* was established behind the scenes. It is impossible to determine how many delegates took part in the formation of this union. One thing is certain: the Union of Teachers adopted a *nonparty* character, as evident from the composition of its "bureau" and an appeal issued by it in 1903.[34] The members of the Union of Teachers declared themselves to be "revolutionary socialists" but refused to affiliate with any existing group, noting that current polemics between the socialist parties were counterproductive, posing a "serious obstacle to the unification of new political activists, sowing confusion in their youthful minds, and complicating practical work among the masses." The union saw as its immediate task the overthrow of autocracy in favor of a democratic republic (a "socialist order" was teachers' final goal), and to this end urged cooperation of all progressive forces: SRs, SDs, *and* "constitutional democrats." This, in substance, was the strategy that would underlie the Union of Liberation (launched in August 1903), as well as the intelligentsia unions of 1905:

establish a broad front against the Old Regime, from the zemstvo liberals to the socialist parties.[35]

The "bureau" of the union contained both Marxists and Populists. The former included several teachers from the city of Moscow. The PSR was represented by a group of zemstvo employees and former teachers associated with the party's Moscow Regional Bureau, most notably V. V. Kir'iakov, an important figure in the teachers' professional movement.[36] The moving spirit behind the union, as all participants concurred, was Sergei Ivanovich Akramovskii, an SR with considerable experience among Russia's rural teachers. Akramovskii arrived in Moscow as a delegate of the Saratov Teachers' Society with a long record of teaching, political activity, and arrests behind him. A priest's son, he graduated from the Kazan Theological Seminary in 1891 but chose teaching rather than a clerical career as more consistent with popular needs. During the early 1890s he taught in Petrovsk district, Saratov, where together with Malinovskii he helped organize a group which included one-third of the district's teachers and had some success conducting revolutionary propaganda among the peasantry. Akramovskii was arrested for distributing pamphlets such as "Tsar Hunger" and upon release was banned from teaching in Saratov. Subsequently he was active in populist circles and teacher organizing in various places. He was last employed by the Kursk zemstvo as a touring instructor in experimental adult peasant courses but again faced arrest for injecting politics into the curriculum. During the year prior to the Moscow Congress he appeared with other SR activists and *gastrolery* at teachers' courses in various provinces and laid the groundwork for a firmer organization (no doubt, the movement described above by *Revoliutsionnaia Rossiia).*[37]

Before his arrest and exile in October 1903, Akramovskii acted as the primary agent of the nonparty Union of Teachers, the major task of which, according to an SD member, was the mobilization of "teachers as an activist stratum close to peasants and workers, ready to conduct propaganda among the masses."[38] He visited teachers' assemblies, both legal and clandestine, distributing literature "of all political tendencies" throughout European Russia. According to the Moscow city teacher and Social Democrat A. F. Nasimovich, other members confined their activities to the center. A cache of illegal literature, "a huge laundry basket stuffed with SR and SD pamphlets," which also included works by Herzen, Lavrov, and Kropotkin, was kept at Nasimovich's apartment; numbers of *Iskra* were obtained through a local party source. All of this material was earmarked for distribution to teachers' circles throughout the country, largely by Akramovskii.[39] At some point in 1903 the union acquired a printing press, which was set up at the residence of P. M. Danilin, an SR. But in October-November 1903, and again in February 1904, arrests swept away many of the union's activists. Nasimovich and others managed to distribute an appeal among the 600 primary schoolteachers who attended the Third

Congress of Activists in Technical and Professional Education held in St. Petersburg over the holidays in 1903–4; this meeting assumed an explicitly political character and was closed by the authorities.[40] Nasimovich and others eluded the police dragnet and were able to save the union's store of literature by hiding it in the home of a priest. From there they continued its distribution, though at diminished levels.[41]

What then of the PSR-affiliated teachers' union? The testimony is conflicting. The Moscow Okhrana, for one, identified the nonparty union organized at the time of the Moscow Congress as none other than the "Union of Socialist Revolutionary Teachers," and with the arrests of late 1903 believed that it had dealt the party union a lethal blow. Two decades later, when two SD members of the union, Nasimovich and S. N. Dmitriev, examined the police files, they expressed their bewilderment, insisting that they had never belonged to the PSR and that the union in which both were active in 1903–4 was nonparty, which of course was true.[42] The confusion of the Tsarist police was matched by that of the PSR's Central Committee in Paris. In August 1903 *Revoliutsionnaia Rossiia* suggested that the nonparty Union of Teachers had adhered to the PSR, and the paper carried an appeal, "To All Russian Teachers," from the committee of the new SR Teachers' Union. Then in January 1904 readers were informed that in fact a party union had taken shape when some members of the nonparty union, already "gravitating toward the PSR," became disenchanted with the flabby and "indefinite" character of the organization, left it, and formed a party union more in line with their sympathies. Teachers, the editors argued, could scarcely be satisfied with Social Democratic literature, which, on the agrarian question, offered only the prospect of class differentiation and proletarianization for the vast majority of peasants. Not surprisingly, they claimed, SR literature held sway among both peasants and teachers.[43] In the six months since its foundation in May 1903 the PSR Teachers' Union did its best to meet this demand, establishing ties with teachers in ten, mainly central, provinces where initial contacts had been made at teachers' courses in June and July. The union supplied recruits with small libraries "intended to help teachers sort out their world view while fostering a critical attitude toward reality and comprehension of socialist ideas." The union had allocated twenty-five to thirty of these *bibliotechki* per district to be used free of charge. Rural teachers, who rarely had access to even the legal press, must have responded enthusiastically. During 1904 the union issued proclamations on the anniversary of the Emancipation of the serfs and against the war with Japan.[44]

Information on the party union derives from the PSR's émigré organ, which, citing "conspirative conditions," said nothing about the leadership or composition of the union. Writing twenty years later, Malinovskii offered an interesting hypothesis: the peripatetic Akramovskii played a key role in the PSR union as well as in the nonparty union. In fact, Malinovskii suggested that "the Moscow bureau of 1903 served on the one hand nonparty organizations and was itself nonparty, but in the person of its most active member [Akramovskii], who directly maintained all communications of the bureau with teachers throughout Russia—both nonparty revolutionary and party [teachers]—it was simultaneously the central bureau of the PSR union of teachers." Further, at a meeting of SR teachers in Kursk in May 1903, Breshkovskaia, who was about to go abroad, delegated Akramovskii as her successor for party work among teachers and supplied him with the addresses of SR teachers throughout the country.[45] Perhaps this was the founding meeting of the PSR Union. But perhaps also Akramovskii was less than forthright with party leaders about his activities. If the two unions were not one and the same, they had much in common.

Akramovskii died in 1922 and was unable to comment on Malinovskii's conclusion. In any case, the hypothesis does not seem that farfetched. Akramovskii was indeed an SR and remained a party member during the Revolution of 1905.[46] But he possessed a more flexible sense of reality than could be expected of the party leadership in emigration, which was locked in a polemical battle with its Marxist rivals over the future of the countryside. As an organizer with ten years of experience among teachers, he was less averse to forging alliances outside the party. The task at hand was making teachers conscious of their mission to enlighten the peasantry and of the need to struggle for their own liberation, which meant political struggle against the autocracy. All progressive forces should be utilized to this end, including zemstvo liberals.

Surely Akramovskii and others were sensitive to the fact that teachers did not attach the same significance to ideology and party labels as did the PSR Central Committee. To the rural teacher in his or her state of isolation and cultural deprivation, wranglings among socialist theorists must have seemed esoteric indeed: "My comrades and I did not see, did not even assume, any difference between the SRs and SDs. And between the Constitutional Democrats and the socialists we could only discern one difference: the constitutional democrats and their *Osvobozhdenie* wanted a 'constitution' and the SRs and SDs with their *Revoliutsionnaia Rossiia* and *Iskra* strove for a constituent assembly and a republic."[47] Almost *any* political literature was devoured by the book-starved teacher. Moreover, to the rural teacher, who often faced peasant indifference, clerical hostility, and official suspicion, a broad progressive coalition seemed to offer the best chance of support.

Teachers tended to view their world in bipolar terms, with "progressive" forces arrayed against the "dark" forces of ignorance and reaction. Pleve's world was also devoid of subtle shadings. But it would be erroneous to conclude, as he did, that a majority of teachers were revolutionaries. For the rural teacher, political activity continued to be a dangerous step; fear of dismissal loomed large. Even the concerted effort to recruit teachers launched by the PSR and others before 1905 could only begin to crack the crust of isolation, cultural retardation, and fear that characterized these "zemstvo rabbits."

Nevertheless, agitation among teachers was clearly on the upswing, hitting a peak in the summer of 1903 in the activities of mutual aid societies, at a major Northern Regional Educational Exhibition in Iaroslavl, and at summer courses, particularly those held in Kursk.[48] Such activity merely confirmed Pleve in his doubts about the political reliability of teachers and resulted in a wave of dismissals and arrests in late 1903 and 1904, as well as a hardening of official policy on summer courses.[49] After several years of relative toleration and rising expectations among teachers, this shift back toward repression served only to radicalize teachers. Official policy, as usual, tended to breathe life into the specter of revolution that haunted the regime.

Increasing numbers of teachers were thus drawn into the ambit of political opposition in the decade before 1905. These professionals favored the revolutionary parties, as the liberals regretfully noted.[50] This is scarcely surprising. Official ambivalence toward school and teacher had been amply demonstrated. The zemstvos were either unable or unwilling to make the kind of commitment expected by many teachers, either to improve material conditions or to grant teachers wider autonomy and a voice in zemstvo decisionmaking. Thus, many teachers viewed radical political and social change as a precondition for cultural and professional progress.

Furthermore, the major beneficiary of official repression and neglect, and of zemstvo indifference and impotence, was the PSR. Among politically active teachers the PSR held a dominant position, a fact admitted by SDs. It is well-known that teachers played an important role in SR organizations in the countryside such as the "peasant brotherhoods."[51] The reasons for SR strength are not difficult to divine. The PSR simply devoted more resources to work among teachers. In fact, Sletov, writing in July 1903, asserted that SDs who spoke at teachers' courses that summer had argued against wasting effort on the fruitless task of preaching socialism to an unresponsive peasantry.[52] That teachers were impressed with the relative merits of the SR program is doubtful, as Akramovskii had realized. For most teachers party programs remained of secondary importance and were needlessly divisive.[53]

This is not to say that SR propaganda had no attraction. Party appeals offered a scenario in which the rural teacher would play a pivotal role in the liberation of the masses, as an "intermediary between the avant-garde of the socialist movement [the urban intelligentsia and industrial proletariat] and the laboring peasantry."[54] By underscoring the importance of revolutionary work in the countryside and by placing them near the center of that activity, the PSR provided teachers much-needed empathy in their present privations and the assurance that ultimately they would receive recompense for their commitment to the enlightenment of the peasantry. One teacher, commenting that SR sympathies were common among rural teachers during this period, recalled, "I was extremely enthusiastic about the SR slogan 'through struggle will you find justice'!"[55]

In addition, SR ideology placed the teacher and other members of the "laboring intelligentsia" within the ranks of the narod, an unequivocal assertion that the interests of peasant and teacher were the same. Given that teacher-peasant relations were often strained, the assurance that within a reformed rural community the teacher's status would be greatly enhanced had to be attractive. In contrast, many SDs considered teachers to be "petty-bourgeois," unwilling to cast their lot with the proletariat, as Pokrovskii, who had lectured at summer courses, later recalled.

> Revolutionary teachers flocked after the SRs. The Social Democrats were definitely unpopular among teachers, for whom the emphasis on class evoked indignation. The average teacher was as poverty-stricken and hungry as the peasant, and so naively imagined that being impoverished he was also a proletarian. When accused of harboring petty-bourgeois tendencies, he would fly into a rage. "All I own is this *pidzhak,*" he cried, flapping the sleeves of his coat, "but you insist that beneath it hides the soul of a bourgeois."[56]

If the term "intellectual proletarian" had any social validity in prerevolutionary Russia, it certainly applied to the rural teacher. Given their low salaries, social distance from local elites, extreme subordination within the administration of schools, and disenfranchisement from local institutions (zemstvos and rural communities), it was natural that teachers would perceive themselves in this way.

The clash between this reality and a professional ideal that many had come to accept was a source of radicalism. The SRs offered teachers an alluring vision of social leveling and democratization of institutions. With the passage of the old order the bureaucratic walls that served to isolate the teacher, from both educated society and the peasantry, would crumble. Control over schools would devolve upon the local community and teachers themselves.

Yet this vision did not signal a rupture in the alliance between activist teachers and zemstvos. Since the mid-1890s, at least, the fate of the Russian teachers' movement had been closely linked with the fortunes of local self-government, and more often than not teachers perceived the relationship as an alliance against common foes, peasant ignorance, and official obscurantism. The durability of this relationship was much in evidence at the Moscow Congress. Indeed, this liberal-radical alliance underpinned the process of political mobilization in the provinces described above. Teachers' mobilization would have been much less likely if not for cooperation between revolutionaries and zemstvo liberals, and it was precisely a broad coalition of opposition forces that attracted teachers.

Nevertheless, teachers in Moscow had raised issues which called into question the very social and political nature of zemstvo institutions. The issue of teachers' influence on zemstvo decisionmaking, through local school sovety or commissions, provides a touchstone for measuring the depth of zemstvo liberalism and a test of the flexibility of these undemocratic institutions in accommodating the inevitable demands put forth by professionally conscious teachers.

A Tenuous Alliance: Zemstvos, Teachers, and the School Commission Experiment

By the eve of the 1905 revolution a certain consensus as to the imperatives of peasant schooling had taken shape within the zemstvo milieu, beginning with the provincial zemstvos and percolating down to the lethargic districts. When the Tver district zemstvo in 1902–3 considered turning its schools over to the Holy Synod, educated society raised a hue and cry and zemstvo opinion condemned the decision. Times had changed since the 1880s, when scarcely an eyebrow would have been raised over such a move. Despite the law of 1900 limiting zemstvo tax increases, the next four years saw intensive efforts in education.[57]

These included increased zemstvo concern for teachers' cultural needs, measured in support for teachers' societies and summer courses. Some zemstvos, generally the more liberal assemblies, raised the issue of legal status during the annual sessions of 1903–4. Here political opposition buttressed practical concern for teacher turnover. Zemstvo men complained of inspectoral capriciousness and meddling in zemstvo hiring of teachers. Some pointed to the disruptive effects of recent purges of teaching personnel in various locales. The Balashov (Saratov) assembly reviewed a series of "course" denunciations of irreligious and seditious behavior lodged, apparently anonymously, against local teachers. On the basis of these charges more than twenty teachers had been forced in autumn 1903 to leave their posts in Balashov district. Indeed, evidence suggested that arbitrary actions by school officials contributed to accelerating rates of turnover and dismissal on the eve of 1905.[58]

Nevertheless, zemstvos recognized that economic factors, above all else, were responsible for alarming levels of turnover and, indeed, the fact that some schools stood empty for lack of candidates. By 1903–4 zemstvos were increasingly responsive to the pleas of mutual-aid societies that salaries be increased, with supplements at five-year intervals.[59] Still, salary scales continued to vary tremendously between districts. In 1904, for example, the Suzdal zemstvo rejected a petition from the Vladimir Teachers' Society for increases, and local teachers continued to receive the low monthly wage of 20 rubles, which increased to 25 rubles after ten years of service! This compared unfavorably with other districts in Vladimir, accounting for the loss in the past five years of more than sixty teachers (there was a total of seventy zemstvo teachers in Suzdal in 1905).[60] As in the 1890s, salaries in the South were high, often reaching 500 rubles. Zemstvos in the central provinces complained that they could not compete with the wealthier zemstvos of Kherson, Tauride, and Kuban and had to sit idly witnessing the "flight southward of our best young teachers."[61]

Progress was slow and uneven. Studies of teachers' budgets undertaken by mutual aid societies revealed that many teachers, especially those with families, still found it impossible to make ends meet.[62] Replying to a questionnaire from the Simbirsk Society in 1904, one teacher remarked that a majority of teachers received "fifty to seventy kopecks a day, not more than is earned by an unskilled common laborer on a winter day in central Russia." In the Serdobsk (Saratov) zemstvo it was urged that "the earnings of teachers at least be equalized with those of metal workers."[63] On the eve of 1905 the rural teacher remained very much the intellectual proletarian described by Pokrovskii. The results were a continued decline in qualifications, high rates of turnover, and feminization of the profession.

Zemstvos also grappled with another issue of significance for teacher mobilization: their participation in forming educational policy. The issue of zemstvo school sovety or commissions with teacher representation had been forcefully raised at the Moscow Congress, suggesting the maturity of a movement eager to probe the boundaries of professional autonomy. Not only did this raise security concerns for the government on the eve of 1905, but it cut to the heart of zemstvo government. By counterposing ideals of expertise and democratization to traditional principles of social privilege, the school commission experiment revealed the limits of zemstvo liberalism and marked the first significant occasion the teacher-zemstvo alliance foundered before 1905, presaging the wreck of 1905. It helped, however, to crystallize teachers' identity as a profession.

By the turn of the century there were compelling reasons for involving teachers more closely in shaping zemstvo policy. Zemstvo programs were expanding and growing in complexity, while the institutional framework of school management had changed little since the 1874 School Statute. The staff of ministry inspectors had remained nearly static since 1876, rendering supervision perfunctory, and local school boards remained remote.[64] As for zemstvos, the days were gone when one member of the executive board *(uprava),* aided by a secretary, could effectively oversee district schools. Some zemstvos had resorted to hiring third element education "managers" who visited schools, prepared reports for the zemstvo assembly, and made recommendations to the executive board.[65] But this institution was not widespread before 1905 and was, in any case, a stopgap measure. Some form of regular discussion, involving zemstvo deputies and teachers, as specialists who best understood the operation of the school and peasant cultural demands, seemed a reasonable solution.

There was, moreover, strong precedent for such collegial deliberation in zemstvo medicine and other fields. Local congresses of physicians had played an important role in zemstvo policymaking as of the early 1870s.

During the same decade district zemstvos began to establish collegial organs to implement the recommendations of doctors' congresses and provide expert advice to zemstvo assemblies. Composed of zemstvo men and physicians, these medical councils *(vrachebno-sanitarnye sovety* or *komissii)* existed in 61 districts by the end of the decade. All was not harmonious between employees and zemstvo deputies. In some cases the latter, affronted by the "pretensions" of the physicians, dissolved the councils; in others the doctors handed in collective resignations when zemstvo assemblies failed to implement medical reforms deemed vital by the employees. Yet, despite setbacks, collegial medical organization gradually received acceptance in the zemstvo milieu. By 1890 medical councils had been set up in 165 (46 percent) district zemstvos and by 1898 in 231 (65 percent). On the eve of World War I such organs were active in nearly all zemstvos.[66] From this institutional base doctors were able to influence the evolution of zemstvo medicine into the world's first free health care system.[67] The medical councils also played an important role in professional development. Councils had obtained rights that had previously belonged exclusively to executive boards: nomination of candidates to doctors' and feldshers' posts, drawing up budgets, and direct appeal to the zemstvo assembly.[68] Medical councils convened several times a year and the physician S. I. Igumnov remarked that this greatly facilitated the development of a corporate consciousness and exerted a healthy influence on the collective "psyche" of zemstvo doctors, who, like teachers, spent much of the year in isolation. Professional morale had risen as a result.[69]

Teachers, with an eye to the trail blazed by physicians, began to argue for a similar direction in education, a field in which they increasingly felt that *they* were the experts. District teachers' congresses and mutual aid societies raised the issue after 1900, and zemstvo school councils with elected teacher representation received strong endorsement at the Moscow Congress of 1902–3.[70] Realization of such a project depended on a favorable response from the zemstvos and a measure of toleration on the part of the government.

Some zemstvos had established commissions to coordinate education programs during the 1890s, but expansion of these to include teachers came relatively late. One of the first, certainly the best publicized, came in 1900–1 when the Saratov district zemstvo voted to invite twenty teachers to discuss "internal school affairs" with nine zemstvo deputies and the local inspector, N. N. Lozanov. The expanded school commission first met in February 1901 and, despite its obvious limitations (teachers lacked voting rights), was hailed in the St. Petersburg press as a "step forward."[71] Zemstvo teachers provided valuable, first-hand information on a variety of subjects: peasant receptivity to zemstvo projects, particularly recent innovations in adult education; the vexing problem of peasant labor demands on their children and the deleterious effect it had on attendance; curricula; and other issues. Teachers drew from personal experience, for example, the techniques used to spark peasant interest in Sunday public readings, and in many cases the opinions of teachers were accepted by the zemstvo men. The Saratov teachers openly discussed their strained relations with village priests and others and in so doing were able to raise certain aspects of the problem of the teacher's difficult legal status.[72] The commission's deliberations were substantive and teachers clearly contributed to their success.

Formation of school commissions or sovety with teachers' participation or expansion of existing organs to include teachers occurred in Tver, Moscow, Novgorod, Kursk, and other provinces during this period,[73] but it was the Moscow Congress, with its strong endorsement of collegial management, that lent real impetus to this movement. This was evident in Moscow province, where mutual aid societies in Mozhaisk, Serpukhov, Podolsk, and Dmitrov districts raised the issue during winter 1902–3. Pressure from teachers for a wider role in zemstvo decisionmaking was especially intense in Dmitrov, where, after hearing reports from their delegates to the Moscow Congress, teachers petitioned the zemstvo to form a school *sovet* to which they would elect their own representatives.[74] Collegial management was endorsed, in principle, by a September 1903 meeting of district zemstvo board chairmen convened by D. N. Shipov, the provincial zemstvo leader.[75] In only a handful of zemstvo assemblies, however, did the idea meet with sympathy; in most cases it drew strong opposition from school officials and the reactionary press. Resolutions to establish consultative organs with teacher representation passed in only three district assemblies—Moscow, Dmitrov and Volokalamsk—though in each the principle of election by peers was shelved in favor of nomination by the zemstvo.[76]

Efforts to involve teachers more closely in the management of zemstvo education were not limited to Moscow. Under the twin pressures of calls for efficient organization and growing demands by teachers, a number of zemstvos, generally the more liberal assemblies, moved to accord teachers the status of partners—junior partners to be sure—in their efforts to transform a backward peasant society through enlightenment. In Smolensk, for example, the local mutual aid society raised the issue of school sovety in early 1904. Teachers responded with enthusiasm to a project submitted by the society's chairman, B. T. Sadovskii (also chairman of the zemstvo board) and the nationally renowned zemstvo doctor D. N. Zhbankov. But only three district zemstvos accepted the society's petition to establish school councils that utilized teachers' expertise.[77] In Tula only the Bogorodits zemstvo accepted a proposal for a sovet offered by M. D. Ershov, a zemstvo liberal who had attended the Moscow Congress. The Bogorodits zemstvo was the most progressive in the province, and its decision was overturned by provincial authorities.[78] Similar results came in neighboring Tambov province, where only Morshansk and Borisoglebsk endorsed school councils. Among district zemstvos in Vladimir, only the liberal stronghold of Kovrov decided in 1904 to organize a collegial council with teacher representation.[79]

The majority of zemstvo men were less enthusiastic about third element demands for a larger share in making education policy, and on this issue they found common ground with government officials. Most of the resolutions to establish school councils were promptly protested by provincial officials, who took advantage of ambiguity in the 1890 Zemstvo Statute concerning the rights of zemstvos to enlist outside expert advice. From a welter of arcane interpretations and appeals on this question to the Senate emerges the simple fact that Ministry of Interior and provincial officials viewed the school council experiment as a crucial confrontation with liberal zemstvo activists on the battlefield of public education and as an opportunity to contain the process of teachers' mobilization. For them the school sovety raised three issues that had less to do with education than with sharpening political conflicts in provincial Russia.[80]

Control over schools was a prime concern. In protesting these enterprises local officials, as well as MVD auditors of zemstvos in Kursk, Moscow, and Viatka, insisted that zemstvos were exceeding their legal competence and that the sovety threatened to give zemstvo activists an overweening influence over teachers. Second, Pleve and his lieutenants seized upon the school councils and the wider specter of a usurping third element "bureaucracy" in an attempt to pry the basically loyalist and conservative zemstvo majority from its tentative alliance with liberal zemstvo leaders. Official warnings that collegial organs in education might well eclipse the "enfranchised" zemstvo men, as had already happened in zemstvo medicine, found some resonance among rank-and-file gentry.[81] Finally, the zemstvo school councils raised very real security concerns for government officials. Under the tolerant eye of liberal zemstvo men, radical teachers might exploit these collegial organs to rally rural teachers around a revolutionary program. Councils formed to advise zemstvos on matters of school texts and hygiene might be transformed into radical committees waging propaganda among the peasantry. In the wake of the 1902 agrarian revolts and with Pleve's succession as minister of the interior, the security apparatus became convinced that zemstvo institutions harbored radical employees and that the success of the revolutionary movement in the provinces was predicated on support from the legal opposition in the zemstvos.[82] In this light the seemingly innocuous school sovety might embody a strategic link between urban radicals and the countryside.

Such concerns played a role in the fate of the zemstvo school council in Elets district, Orel province. Elets had been the most active zemstvo in the province in education. Efforts were spearheaded by a group of progressive deputies led by P. Ia. Bakhteiarov, board chairman from 1897 to 1906, and A. A. Stakhovich, gentry marshal and chairman of the district school board since 1897 and, by all accounts, the moving spirit in the zemstvo's drive to educate the peasantry. Stakhovich, a moderate liberal in the Shipov mold, had attended the Moscow Congress as an "expert" and brought forty teachers from Elets at zemstvo or personal expense. V. A. Vargunin, a wealthy landowner and doctor who founded a number of schools at his own expense, also played a key role in local education. According to the police, Vargunin organized meetings of teachers at his estate, and the district police chief was convinced that all "criminal proclamations" that turned up in haycocks in Elets emanated from the doctor's estate.[83]

On the initiative of these people the Elets zemstvo in September 1903 resolved to establish a school council composed of seven zemstvo men and seven teachers elected by their peers. Local officials moved to quash the project, alleging that a number of teachers elected to participate in the council were politically suspect. One had recently been dismissed, another placed under surveillance, and Tat'iana Solopova was arrested on December 1, 1903. Solopova had taught at the same school since 1890, and the local inspector reported that she was a dedicated professional and active in the local community. She had only hung Leo Tolstoi's portrait on the school wall.[84] But local police smelled sedition of a more alarming brand. After Solopova's arrest revolutionary proclamations aimed at teachers spread through the district, signed by the "Committee of Russian SR Teachers," the "Orel Teachers' Committee," and the PSR. In light of this agitation, the inspector issued a warning to all teachers not to attend the first meeting of the sovet scheduled for February 1904 or risk dismissal. The zemstvo board cancelled the meeting.[85]

It was in Novotorzhok, Tver, that both official security concerns and conservative gentry fears of third element ascendancy were put to the test. Since the 1860s the Novotorzhok zemstvo had been the most liberal in Tver province, in fact, in all of Russia. Novotorzhok was home to liberals like the Bakunins (younger brothers of the famed anarchist), Petrunkevichs, and Miliukovs. Tver province provided more activists for the liberal movement of the 1890s and early 1900s than any other province, and many of these won their spurs in Novotorzhok. The district zemstvo was especially active in education, the "pride" of the Novotorzhok zemstvo men, according to Boris Sturmer, a landowner and former zemstvo deputy from nearby Kashin district who conducted the MVD's audit of Tver province. In 1897 there were 58 schools with 67 teachers. By 1903–4 the district could boast 105 schools with 142 teachers.[86]

Since the 1870s Novotorzhok had also been a haven for third element personnel, including radical teachers, dismissed elsewhere for political activities. Some loose form of teacher organization had existed in Novotorzhok and neighboring districts from the mid-1890s. In 1900 a new zemstvo board led by N. A. Balavenskii and younger zemstvo activists authorized formation of a school commission which accorded teachers a larger role in zemstvo policymaking.[87]

In the government's view, two factors had a decisive effect on the subsequent radicalization of teachers in Novotorzhok and transformation of the zemstvo school commission into a "revolutionary committee." One was zemstvo recruitment policy. Despite inspectoral vigilance, liberal zemstvo leaders managed to hire radical teachers, particularly from Slavianoserbsk district, Ekaterinoslav province. Under a liberal leadership the Slavianoserbsk zemstvo had made remarkable strides in building schools and initiating adult education programs. Starting salaries had been set at 300 rubles with supplements. A school commission was formed with wide competence, including nomination of candidates. The fruits of this system were quickly apparent. In 1901 Slavianoserbsk boasted a cadre of teachers with relatively high qualifications: 6 percent had higher educations (quite unusual), 50 percent complete secondary schooling, 25 percent came from normal schools, and only a small minority from diocesan schools. Many of these teachers were revolutionaries, and massive dismissals in 1902 swept many of them away. Some, taking advantage of links between revolutionary organizations in Tver and Ekaterinoslav, found employment with the Novotorzhok zemstvo. It was these teachers from the South, according to MVD auditors, armed with their experience in Slavianoserbsk, who had a considerable impact on events in Novotorzhok.[88]

The Moscow Congress, which had been attended by a large delegation of teachers from Novotorzhok, had an even greater impact. "Teachers became unrecognizable," reported the provincial school director, "and relations with the school administration became sharply strained." Teachers ceased conducting routine business with their superiors and "comported themselves with extreme defiance." The Novotorzhok school commission was expanded to include twenty-eight teachers. Meeting under the chairmanship of Balavenskii, who MVD auditors described as the "tool" of radical teachers, the commission stepped up its activities. Under the pretext of meeting to discuss repairs to school buildings, this "committee of twenty-eight, in fact, manages all education business in the district."[89]

The reconstituted commission won the right to recommend candidates to the executive board. According to the inspector, N. V. Lileev, the commission did its utmost to recruit candidates who shared the radical views of its members, offering positions in Novotorzhok to victims of repression elsewhere (for example, to Akramovskii, the former teacher from Kursk and major activist of the illegal Union of Teachers). Conversely, the commission tried to squeeze out conservative teachers, for example, one who preferred to use religious texts in adult readings and another who taught at a school close to a factory but failed to use this opportunity to conduct propaganda among the workers. When these teachers appealed to the inspector for protection they were condemned by a teachers' "court of honor" *(sud chesti)* and then boycotted by their fellows.

The commission's primary task, as officials saw it, was to organize propaganda among the masses. Its members, who were elected by their peers at a 1 to 5 ratio, compiled lists of works to stock school libraries. These went well beyond ministry catalogs restricting the content of these libraries. Lileev found copies of Tolstoi's *Resurrection* and his "Appeal to the People," as well as works by Maksim Gorkii and Pushkin's "The Captain's Daughter," which included illustrations of gentry being hung by "mutinous rabble," which the inspector saw as inflaming landowner-peasant relations. The commission also sought to influence the content of "popular readings" *(narodyne chteniia)* held for the adult population by "tendentious selection of readings calculated to elicit among peasants hostility toward the privileged and convince them of the need to oppose all directives of the government and shake religious convictions." Readings dealt with the Razin and Pugachev rebellions, the Finnish nationalist struggle, the agrarian question, and recent disturbances in Kharkov and Poltava. Local priests reported that religiosity among peasants was declining and ascribed this, in large part, to teachers' agitation. Year-end examinations found pupils woefully deficient in catechism *(zakon bozhii),* and in the course of visits to schools the MVD auditors found the following written in pupils' notebooks: "In times of plenty the pastor makes brilliant speeches, but in times of need he hastens to strip the last shirt off the peasant's back"; "the peasant went off to sell tar in order to give a tenth of the proceeds to the priest, but at home he has left a wife and children without bread." In addition, local officials alleged that the school commission helped circulate revolutionary leaflets in the district, and in the town of Torzhok police turned up a cache of materials that included an appeal from the Union of Teachers.[90]

Police moved to crush the commission. Arrests of prominent members followed completion of the MVD audit in November 1903. Then in early 1904 the government took drastic action. It overturned recent elections that had returned Balavenskii and other zemstvo leaders and, in their stead, installed a government-appointed executive board (similar action was taken against the Tver provincial zemstvo). Leading liberals, I. I. Petrunkevich, A. I. Bakunin, and M. I. Litvinov, were banished from Tver. In response to these actions third element personnel resigned in protest; in Novotorzhok these included all eleven doctors, fifteen feldshers, two technicians, two agronomists and forty-seven teachers (not counting another ten teachers dismissed shortly after). On March 12, 1904, the Department of Police issued a circular to all governors banning the Novotorzhok teachers from any post in the empire. Lileev was given a free hand in finding their replacements.[91]

It is difficult to determine the extent of zemstvo experimentation with school councils and commissions. The high point seems to have been 1905 when, according to Ministry of Education information, thirty-seven district zemstvos adopted resolutions to set up councils with teacher representation or widen the composition and competence of existing bodies. Many of these decisions came in response to teachers' petitions. Some were protested by provincial authorities, others were overturned by zemstvo assemblies the following year, and some were put into effect. Zemstvo resolutions on this question tapered off considerably in 1906. According to a survey conducted that year by the Vologda zemstvo, of fifty-nine zemstvos providing information, school councils existed in twenty-eight. But teachers participated in only eleven of these (in two of these not on a regular basis). In only three cases (Elets, Saratov, and Voronezh) did teachers elect their own representatives, and only in Elets did they have voting rights.[92]

Overall, the school council experiment must be judged a failure. Nevertheless, it can tell us much about the rise of the Russian teachers' movement and, more broadly, about politics in provincial Russia on the eve of 1905. Despite teachers' interest, they were unable to solidify a position comparable to that achieved by zemstvo physicians. Why this was so is not difficult to explain. Given its view of teachers as a security risk, the government was hostile to the enterprise. At the same time the overwhelming majority of district zemstvos proved unwilling to grant teachers a role in policymaking, no matter how modest. Because of their more advanced educations and esoteric skills, urbanity, greater social proximity to the zemstvo gentry (one can cite many cases of zemstvo men simultaneously serving as doctors), and also because medicine was still a male-dominated profession, zemstvo physicians managed to earn grudging recognition as "experts" and a corresponding influence in zemstvo affairs, which teachers were never able to approach.

But timing was also a factor. Teachers' demands for greater input through school sovety came at a time when many zemstvo men were questioning the role played by employees in statistics and medicine, seeing collegial management in these areas as a threat to the prerogatives of the "enfranchised" second element.[93] No doubt some conservatives, fearful that they were losing control of zemstvo affairs (above all, zemstvo budgets) to third element professionals, also shared the government's growing concern about employee involvement in rural propaganda. Heading off such alarming trends in the field of public education seemed only prudent.

Indeed, there was some substance behind conservative concerns, since the demands for school sovety reflected the maturation and politicization of the teachers' movement after the turn of the century. Claims to autonomy were, doubtless, advanced primarily by the activist minority, which recognized the value of school councils in mobilizing less developed teachers. Given the rapid popularization of this issue after 1902, these hopes appeared justified. Moreover, the Novotorzhok experiment indicated that collegial organs could be used to organize rural teachers against the existing social and political order. Officials conceded that the school councils in Novotorzhok and Slavianoserbsk were exceptional but cautioned that they were the advance signals of trends already evident elsewhere.[94]

Conservatives in government and zemstvos could take comfort from the fact that these hotbeds of teacher radicalism were purged but seemed oblivious to the deeper implications of the stymied school sovety and to the broader pattern of politicization which this experiment reflected. For increasing numbers of teachers, official intransigence and the zemstvos' apparent lack of receptivity on this issue caused profound dissatisfaction, expressed in growing antipathy to the bureaucracy (above all the inspectorate) and also disillusionment with the existing undemocratic zemstvos, which by and large failed to accommodate the modest demands of teachers for a larger voice in the making of education policy. The more perceptive teachers sensed the vital connection between autocracy and gentry domination of the countryside and concluded that only a broad political struggle could secure a measure of professional autonomy.

The latter feeling was not yet sharply defined. Still, within a year of the Moscow Congress contemporaries noted a perceptible change in the alliance between activist teachers and zemstvos forged in the past decade and just affirmed in Moscow. The Third Congress on Technical and Professional Education met in St. Petersburg over the Christmas recess of 1903–4 and was attended by hundreds of teachers and many people who had taken part in the Moscow Congress. The zemstvos were again hailed as a progressive force in education, in sharp contrast with the government, but "the tone was more restrained . . . and in private conversations and gatherings during the congress began to sound a sharp dissatisfaction with the existing zemstvo."[95] Petr Dolgorukov expressed the anxiety of zemstvo liberals over the apparent fragility of the zemstvo-teacher alliance at a session of the *Beseda* group shortly after the Technical Education Congress:

> At the time of the congress in St. Petersburg Social Democratic circles organized meetings to which they attracted teachers attending the congress. This is a great pity since we would have preferred to see them in the ranks of the zemstvo men. Regrettably, the zemstvos do not provide a sufficient rallying point. It is necessary to exert an influence on the lively elements of society, otherwise you risk remaining at the tail end of events.[96]

For liberals in the zemstvos, who saw in teachers a vital link with the rural masses, these were danger signs. Activist teachers stood considerably to the left of their patrons in the zemstvos. The growth of revolutionary teachers' unions and the influence of revolutionary parties, particularly the PSR, among teachers attested to this fact. For these teachers the failure of the school commission experiment called into question the whole scenario of the liberals for Russia's transformation, a new, democratic social and political order not based on estates, in which the importance of property and privilege would be diminished and criteria of service and expertise enhanced. Could the zemstvos, which seemed incapable of putting these principles into effect in a limited sphere like education management, reasonably be expected to lead a national movement for the country's wider democratic transformation? Before answers to this question could be formulated and the deeper contradictions in teachers' status resolved, teachers were suddenly thrust into the vortex of the 1905 revolution, which confronted them with stark new perils and possibilities.

6. The Teachers' Movement and Revolutionary Politics in 1905

January 9, 1905, when government troops fired into columns of peaceful Petersburg workers attempting to deliver a petition to Nicholas II, conventionally marks the beginning of the Russian Revolution of 1905. Followed by a wave of strikes throughout the empire, "Bloody Sunday" signaled the start of mass political action against the autocracy (at least in urban Russia) and the complete bankruptcy of the Old Regime in the eyes of much of educated, articulate society. With the government's ruthless repudiation of the workers' initiative, society and autocracy were set on a collision course.

The crisis of the Old Regime was, of course, already well advanced before the Petersburg workers and their families left their dreary industrial suburbs that fateful morning. The Liberation Movement had stalled somewhat in early 1904 with the onset of the war with Japan and moratorium placed on the kind of legal professional gatherings which in recent years had provided a forum for incipient political organization. By late summer, however, public opposition to the bureaucracy was on the upswing again, more general and more politically explicit than ever before.

The government's predicament was highlighted by a series of embarrassing military defeats in the Far East, which, like the famine and cholera of 1891–92, underscored Russia's backwardness in every area, compared not only with the West but even with Japan. Not the least of these was culture, and especially rural education. Internal crisis aside, the unsuccessful confrontation with Japan would probably have been enough to cause great concern over public education. Critics of autocracy dusted off the old aphorism that it was the Prussian teacher who proved victorious at Sedan and suggested that Japan's military prowess stemmed from the rapid strides achieved in mass education during the Meiji era.[1] In education, as in other areas of national life, it had become increasingly clear that real progress was possible only after basic political transformation. From autumn 1904, this was precisely what educated Russian society demanded.

The resurgent Liberation Movement, furthermore, benefited from a shift in government policy. The assassination on July 15, 1904, of the Minister of Interior Pleve, who was blown up in broad daylight in the streets of St. Petersburg by a former university student and operative of the PSR's terrorist organization, signaled a crisis of confidence for the government and ushered in a period of uncertainty as how best to deal with the mounting wave of opposition. A solid month elapsed before Nicholas II appointed a new minister, Prince Sviatopolk-Mirskii, who proclaimed the government's "trust" in educated society and embarked on a series of measures designed to placate the moderate opposition: an amnesty which returned from exile, among others, leading activists in the teachers' movement; relaxation of the censorship; end of the campaign against the zemstvos and rehabilitation of leading zemstvo activists; abolition of corporal punishment.[2]

Rather than putting a break on the locomotive of opposition, this "government springtime" bolstered the clamor for constitutional reform. With Pleve absent from the scene and the administration apparently amenable to reform, the public was all the more prepared to test the limits of the new political situation and engage in overt political activity. Opposition now swept up many who had previously left this arena to professional revolutionaries. Wide sections of the so-called democratic intelligentsia were affected, as were professional people who had not yet committed to one of the existing political parties and moderate elements in the zemstvos.

This political ferment was loosely orchestrated by the Union of Liberation, which represented a broad spectrum of opinion, from the radical professional intelligentsia to the leftwing of the zemstvos, the so-called zemstvo-constitutionalists. A diversity of political and social views reigned, but there was general consensus on the need for a constitutional regime and extensive civil liberties, and by late 1904 a majority of the union leadership probably shared with the revolutionary parties a commitment to the convocation of a constituent assembly elected on the basis of a democratic "four-tail" suffrage (universal, equal, secret, and direct).[3] In October 1904 the Union of Liberation adopted a plan to organize the articulate elements of Russian society around these demands and apply increased pressure upon the wavering autocracy. Targeted directly was the zemstvo milieu, first through the national Congress of Zemstvo Representatives (which met in early November and adopted a resolution in favor of a constitution but opposed to democratic suffrage) and then through the winter sessions of provincial zemstvos which echoed demands for political reforms. As for the intelligentsia, the union initiated a series of political "banquets" around the country and also utilized meetings of cultural, scholarly, and professional societies. The aims of the *osvobozhdentsy* were twofold: to garner support among the intelligentsia for radical political resolutions and to lay the groundwork for their organization into political-professional unions, to be joined eventually into a *Soiuz soiuzov* which would lay the basis for the organization of a liberal political party.[4]

The union's tactics met with considerable success. Even the inherently loyal and moderate zemstvos passed constitutionalist resolutions, while many of the intelligentsia gatherings went further, calling for a constituent assembly as well as social reforms. Furthermore, a number of intelligentsia *soiuzy* were formed in the course of the banquet campaign in late 1904 (engineers, physicians, academics).[5] Thus, even before the decisive events of January 9, the autocracy was confronted with an increasingly vocal and organized opposition in educated society. And after Bloody Sunday the government was also besieged by a powerful workers' movement, which supported to some degree the political demands of society while pursuing more radical social and economic changes.

The movement for political reform was for the most part limited to urban Russia. The attitude of the largely inarticulate, "dark" peasant masses to the ensuing struggle between government and society was not easy to divine at the end of 1904 or early 1905, but as the revolutionary crisis unfolded educated society was compelled to consider the political physiognomy of the peasantry and the role it would play in the revolution. It was during moments of national crisis and imminent change that the problem of "two Russias" seemed most critical and the potential of the rural intelligentsia as a link between society and the narod loomed large.

By virtue of their strategic position and numbers, teachers again occupied an important place, but the question of the peasantry's role in the revolution and thus of the teacher's involvement in politics provoked a variety of responses. For the SRs, peasant aspirations were inherently progressive. It remained only to articulate these aspirations and organize the narod for active struggle. Teachers were summoned to assist in this undertaking, to broaden SR influence in the countryside and act as "enlighteners" in the broadest cultural and political sense. The Social Democrats, while initially devoting less attention to the countryside, nevertheless recognized the need to extend party activity into the rural milieu and hence understood the importance of rural teachers.

Before 1905 the nonrevolutionary intelligentsia and liberal zemstvo oppositionists viewed the peasantry as a largely passive or negative factor in the political struggle. They saw the "enlightenment" of the narod in more limited, gradualist terms while subscribing to a more modest role for the teacher. As an agent of cultural change, it was the teacher's task to gradually prepare the rural masses for eventual participation in national life by uplifting and integrating the peasantry with the wider society. In this process the schoolteacher donned the mantle of "enlightener" *(prosvetitel')* rather than that of "liberator" *(osvoboditel')* or, as the SRs would have put it, "fighter" *(borets)* for the popular will and welfare. Implicit in the liberal scenario was the hope that the political struggle between society and the Old Regime could be largely contained within the elites, the upper echelons of the professional intelligentsia and especially zemstvo men, who believed that by virtue of culture and long experience in local self-government they were most fit to assume a leading role in national affairs, as well as oversee the subsequent political education of the peasantry.

With the outbreak of revolution, liberal assumptions began to dissolve. In a period of flux and increasing activism by the masses even the more moderate opponents of the autocracy recognized that the peasantry and its aspirations had to be reckoned with. But what the orientation of the narod would be was not at all clear; in a political sense the peasantry remained for educated society a sphinx. Would the peasantry rally to the defense of the autocracy and conservative principles in something like a modern Russian version of the Vendée? Evidence of such a possibility, as we will see, was not lacking. Many educated Russians, moreover, soon confronted the possibility that the narod might seek its own solution to its grievances, a solution that might go well beyond anything envisioned by liberal society. Fears of a modern Pugachev movement increased, as from February through March 1905 various provinces were affected by a mounting agrarian movement reminiscent of the disorders of 1902 in Kharkov and Poltava. In response, liberals in the zemstvos and other adherents of the Liberation Movement before October 1905 attempted to "go to the people," hoping to channel the peasant movement into "legal" (moderate) and "conscious" (organized) forms. The most important manifestation of this orientation, as we will see, was the movement to organize peasant unions.

Teachers' participation in the Liberation Movement suddenly acquired real urgency in the eyes of educated society. To the degree that the posture of peasant Russia became a factor that no serious political force could afford to ignore, opposition elements perceived the potential significance of rural intellectuals like teachers who might provide an invaluable link with a milieu from which society felt dangerously divorced. Speaking for the liberal zemstvo opposition, Petr Dolgorukov underscored the potential of the third element as a political wedge into the countryside.

> We must now forge a link between ourselves and the population, and prepare the latter for more conscious and active participation in the current liberation movement. In view of our own small numbers, we have to find mediators *(posredniki),* translators *(perevodchiki),* in order to communicate with the population. This role can be assumed by zemstvo employees—doctors, teachers, technicians, etc.—who stand close to the masses.[6]

As activists in the Liberation Movement contemplated the prospects of constitutional transformation and participation in a national electoral campaign, the same question of links with the peasantry presented itself. As early as March 1905 (after publication of the Bulygin Rescript promising a consultative assembly), the lawyer and liberationist V. A. Miakotin remarked that even zemstvo activists possessed few solid ties with the rural milieu. He asked, "What forces now exist in the countryside that would be able to carry on electoral agitation?" and answered, "the rural intelligentsia," among which he counted teachers, feldshers, midwives, and peasants who were products of the zemstvo school. Once again, as in the wake of the cholera riots of 1892, the liberal press called upon teachers to shake themselves from their "wintry sleep" and plunge into the thick of national life. But now, in the deepening crisis of early 1905, the stakes were higher. Fostering broad "political enlightenment" and actively intervening in popular affairs replaced nurturing gradual cultural change as teachers' public duty.[7]

At first there was little response. Critics from educated society reproached teachers for their "inertness *(nepodvizhnost')* and excessively 'correct' attitude toward current events," at a time when all Russian society was stirring. V. N. Ladyzhenskii, a zemstvo man and member of the Penza Teachers' Society, explained as follows the apparent "silence" of teachers at a time when "one great idea of general reform had seized hold of all thinking society":

> The teacher has not kept silent because he is overwhelmed by poverty. On the contrary, one would think that this would compel him to raise his voice to express his urgent needs and lawful demands. He has remained silent due to his pitiful juridical position. The governor's office can at any moment deprive him of his last crust of bread; he can be dismissed by the school board at the slightest pretext or rumor. This is why the teacher has been "silent" and has remained silent to this time, when his voice is so needed.[8]

A "rural teacher" from Ekaterinoslav province put the dilemma this way: "Really, it is difficult for me to imagine a schoolteacher who is not silent: at the very moment he becomes a *person* with independent convictions he will cease to be a teacher."[9]

The obstacles in the way of organizing teachers for direct participation in the Liberation Movement were, indeed, formidable. Many teachers remained deaf to the appeals of society, oblivious to the imperatives of political involvement that seemed inherent in the very position of the rural teacher: the realization that political struggle could serve to close the gap between the reality of the teacher's existence—isolation, cultural deprivation, and *bespravie*—and the ideal of the *narodyni uchitel'* as an effective and influential agent of enlightenment in the countryside. But many others, in unprecedented numbers, were ready to plunge headlong into the revolution, taking advantage of a period of administrative disarray, spurred on by the demands of both society and the narod, and with the firm belief that only an end to the Old Regime could assure realization of their own potential as professionals and ensure the success of popular enlightenment:

> Let no one be confused or deceived by our silence! I say "our" since I firmly believe that there are many of "us," only we do not know each other. The

> teacher, in any case, is from the narod and for the narod, and not against it. We are silent because we have not yet become accustomed to speaking, because we are so disunited and each speaks in isolation. Do not think that the teacher will just sit with folded hands.[10]

Indeed, the generalized mood of expectancy and defiance that gripped educated society after Pleve's assassination began to percolate into the rural backwaters where teachers were beginning the new school year. N. A. Malinovskii discerned a "miraculous transmutation *(volshebnoe prevrashchenie)* among even those teachers who previously did not want to hear about revolution or about anything other than their base, self-interested existence."[11] A young teacher from Balakhnia district, Nizhegorod province, Ivan Samokhvalov recounted how the general sense of exhilaration experienced by society affected local teachers who began to meet frequently in the autumn of 1904. They engaged in "heated discussions" over political issues, pledging themselves to "struggle against the oppressive autocracy and for the popular good." As a first step Samokhvalov and associates resolved to purge from both classroom instruction and official correspondence the Russian language "hard sign" and other calligraphic vestiges enforced by the Ministry of Education, as well as to introduce more natural science into their curricula.[12] Petty acts of defiance to be sure, these were, nonetheless, symptomatic of a larger mood sweeping Russian society.

Some rural teachers took part in political banquets in Saratov, Orel, and elsewhere in autumn 1904.[13] But for the most part the banquet campaign was a city phenomenon, encompassing the urban intelligentsia and workers. Politically, urban Russia ran far ahead of the countryside, organizing around existing learned and professional associations and finding a voice in a new, radical press eager to test the limits of a relaxed censorship. Rural teachers, bound to the countryside, remained inarticulate and poorly organized. The problem was one of mobilizing teachers to take an active part in the Liberation Movement and finding an appropriate organizational framework.

For much of the nonrevolutionary professional intelligentsia, legal corporate association provided the initial organizational framework for political articulation, education, and mobilization during the initial months of revolutionary upsurge in 1904–05. The next step was usually participation in nonparty formations, the so-called political-professional unions, followed by adherence to political parties with definite programs. This was the political terrain traversed by large sections of Russian society during the 1905 revolution.

Teachers took their first steps along this road; they utilized the mutual aid societies which managed to survive Pleve's attack on teachers' association and were, indeed, energized by the Moscow Congress of 1902–3. A number of local teachers' societies overstepped the bounds of narrow material assistance, some passing more or less explicit political resolutions as early as the end of 1904 and early 1905. In late October (or early November) 1904 the Saratov Teachers' Society, called for "renovation of the existing political structure *(stroi)*."[14] The Saratov Society was dominated by radical third element personnel; the involvement of rank-and-file teachers in this affair, however, is unclear. On November 28, 1904, some two hundred thirty to two hundred fifty members of the St. Petersburg Teachers' Society endorsed a resolution calling for political reform. Official education policy was subjected to a withering attack, and the assembled members—city teachers and a group of "educational activists"—concluded that the "task of popular enlightenment" could only be advanced after Russians secured civil liberties and a democratic constitutional regime. "Here, for the first time in an open teachers' assembly," recalled the city teacher and Social Democrat L. R. Menzhinskaia, "was pronounced the word 'constitution.' "[15] The Nizhegorod Teachers' Society, one of the oldest in the country, urged societies throughout the empire to raise the issue of teachers' depressed legal status in the context of political reform.[16]

The Nizhegorod appeal sparked substantial response. Within the Nizhegorod Society itself a special report on the issue of legal status was read before a packed assembly on December 29, 1904, reportedly attended by 500 persons. Demands for full civil freedoms and even the convocation of a constituent assembly were raised. The Tauride Society raised the issue of legal status, civil freedoms, constitutional reform, and immediate cessation of the war, while the Tula Society called for freedom of association and assembly "without preliminary sanction" *(iavochnym poriadkom)* and equalization of all Russian citizens in civil and political rights.[17] The Simbirsk Teachers' Society on January 6, 1905, called for substantial increase in zemstvo representation on local school boards; teacher representation on these boards as well as in zemstvo assemblies; removal of the inspectorate's police power over teachers; transfer of primary education to the zemstvos. The Simbirsk Society agreed with its Nizhegorod counterpart that any improvement in the teacher's juridical position was contingent upon a "general improvement of the conditions of Russian existence," a euphemism for political reform. An assembly of the Iaroslavl Teachers' Society was even more oppositional in tone. The government's record in the field of education was assailed in a fiery speech by O. N. Florovskaia, wife of a local doctor and, as police reports were quick to point out, sister of the famed revolutionary populist Vera Figner. Noting that the state found it possible to spend fifteen million rubles on rural police *(strazhniki)* while allocating only miserable sums for teachers' salaries, she argued that the teacher's lot would change for the better only after a constitutional regime was installed. The provincial school director Nasilov blamed this agitation squarely on the nonteacher "associate members," the radical third element people who had assumed leadership of the society in December 1903.[18]

Just how many teachers took part in these meetings in late December

1904 and early January 1905 is difficult to determine. In the Petersburg Society urban residence insured substantial teacher participation, while sessions in the provinces, given their heterogeneous composition, were more typical of other manifestations of the banquet campaign.[19] Police reported that a meeting of the Kaluga Society on January 3 attracted an unprecedented 300 persons, but only 40 to 50 of these were teachers. The remainder were "outsiders" *(postoronnaia publika):* zemstvo employees, student youth, "worker intelligentsia" *(rabochie-intelligenty),* urban lower classes *(prostoi narod),* and local revolutionaries. Revolutionary speeches and proclamations "To Teachers" were in evidence, and the assembly passed a resolution demanding a constituent assembly. The winter assembly of the Voronezh Teachers' Society, which according to police reports was attended by at least one hundred members, mostly rural teachers from Voronezh and Korotoiak districts, took on an "especially stormy character." Radical members, led by Andrei Kravchenko, a rural teacher and SR, dominated the proceedings. The society's executive board, which included two school officials, was repudiated for not having done enough to satisfy teachers' cultural and other needs. A new board, dominated by liberal zemstvo activists, third element, and radical teachers promised to raise political issues at the next meeting.[20] A similar radicalization and change of leadership occurred at the same time within the Irkutsk Society in Siberia, while in the Samara Society such a turnabout was narrowly averted by its conservative leadership.[21]

School officials took comfort in the fact that the rank and file seemed untouched by these events. Up to this point these officials had been largely successful in controlling the mutual aid societies, ensuring that they remained unresponsive to teachers' needs. The deepening revolutionary crisis, however, undercut their position. Activists in the societies were now ready to shed their role as beneficent associations, challenge the patriarchal regime which policed the profession, and popularize the view that improvement of teachers' status and promotion of public education were possible only with the demise of the autocracy. Aid in coordinating these efforts soon came from the two capitals, Moscow and St. Petersburg.

A Teachers' Union: Professional or Political?

The idea of organizing a national teachers' union in Russia was, of course, not a new one. Russian activists had long admired the accomplishments of their colleagues abroad, particularly in Germany, where 100,000 teachers were organized in a federation of professional unions, and the Moscow Congress had adopted a model statute for a "union" of mutual aid societies which failed to gain official support.[22] With the outbreak of revolution in 1905 the idea of forming an All-Russian Teachers' Union, *Vserossiiskii soiuz uchitelei i deiatelei po narodnomu obrazovaniiu* (VSU), without official sanction, arose among city teachers and others active in education in both Moscow and St Petersburg. Many of these people had been close to the Union of Liberation and represented a wide spectrum of political opinion ranging from liberal (future Kadets) to radical (future members of the Popular Socialist party or Trudoviki) to adherents of the PSR and even the Social Democratic party. Like other "political professional unions" which succeeded the Union of Liberation, the Teachers' Union aimed to unite the politically diverse but unaffiliated elements among teachers, who, in the words of N. I. Popova, a Moscow teacher, member of the Union of Liberation, and future SR, "could play an immense political role by virtue of their closeness to the masses."[23]

In St. Petersburg these efforts centered around the local mutual aid society's Ushinskii Commission, which had been charged with preparation for a second congress of teachers' societies (scheduled for December 1905), and in a "club" representing city teachers of "all progressive political currents." The Petersburg teachers, most of whom were relatively well educated women (a significant number were graduates of the Bestuzhev Women's Higher Education Courses), were, by Russian standards, well organized.[24] It was among these teachers, meeting with other education activists and instructors in secondary schools, that the idea of a teachers' union, similar to the unions of engineers and of others already formed, was discussed from January 1905. These deliberations resulted in the compilation of a rudimentary program or "Memorandum on the Needs of Public Education" *(zapiska o nuzhdakh narodnago prosveschcheniia)* adopted by an assembly of teachers and education activists held in the building of the Imperial Free Economic Society on March 12, 1905, and signed by 256 persons.[25]

The Petersburg activists located the roots of Russia's educational backwardness, compared even with some "Asiatic states," in the "existing governmental and social system, and we [the activists] are convinced that the regime consciously hinders the enlightenment of the narod in order to maintain itself in power." Specific charges were leveled at policies that tended to keep teachers in a state of disassociation and cultural deprivation. Although there was some dissent on the question of secularization of the school, a majority agreed that the following reforms should constitute the foundation for a "free and democratic school": (1) introduction of the "ladder system," which would make secondary and higher institutions more accessible to graduates of lower schools, many of which had been designed as dead ends for children of the lower classes; (2) introduction of universal and free schooling; (3) a secular, general education curriculum with instruction in the native language of the population; (4) control over schools by local institutions such as zemstvos, with teachers' representation. The "Memorandum" ended with the usual call for immediate political reforms, including convocation of a constituent assembly elected by four-tail suffrage, and also indicated that educational reform would have to be accompanied by measures to promote the "economic welfare of the laboring classes."[26]

The Petersburg teachers constituted themselves a union, elected an executive bureau, and began a national membership drive, mailing copies of the memorandum to provincial teachers' societies and to zemstvo and municipal institutions.[27] The new bureau urged zemstvos to aid in distributing copies of the program among teachers while providing the latter with means for assembly. Local teachers' societies were urged to convene gatherings of their members to discuss the document and to begin organizing local sections of the union.[28] By early April adherents of the Petersburg statement exceeded a thousand persons, and anxious provincial authorities bombarded the Ministry of Interior with reports of organizing activities in their bailiwicks, some pledging to do everything possible to prevent dissemination of the "criminal appeal" among teachers.[29]

Meanwhile, in Moscow efforts to launch a national union proceeded no less intensively. Here too a group of teachers and experts close to the Union of Liberation provided the initial organizational thrust. Aside from Popova and her husband, M. N. Popov (a university instructor), these included V. P. Vakhterov and his wife, N. V. Chekhov, who had moved to Moscow after the administrative assault on the Tver zemstvo, and I. N. Sakharov, the lawyer who had chaired the Legal Commission at the Moscow Congress. Most were moderate populists in orientation; Sakharov was a future Kadet. An influential group of Social Democrats, subsequently organized into a "lecture group" attached to the party's Moscow Committee, was also involved.[30]

The Pedagogical Society attached to Moscow University assumed the role of midwife for the union. Founded in 1898 by liberal university professors, the Moscow Pedagogical Society in subsequent years had attracted teachers in primary and secondary schools (in 1904 there were 889 members from these categories, comprising 86 percent of the membership). Democratization had drawn increased attention to the problems of the primary school and teachers and set the stage for the society's radicalization in late 1904, when a majority of members sought to utilize the society as a political forum. Conservative professors resigned in protest, and a radical new leadership was elected in their place, drawn largely from young university and secondary instructors from the society's Historical Section. These included some of Russia's most promising young historians, many of whom were strongly influenced by Marxism and were already gravitating toward the Social Democrats. N. A. Rozhkov, installed as chairman of the society, had been close to the Union of Liberation, but according to an associate he was already moving toward the Bolsheviks. Because of his previous activity as a lecturer at summer courses around the country, Rozhkov enjoyed wide popularity among teachers, and not only in Moscow. M. N. Pokrovskii, who occupied a similar political position, was elected associate chairman.[31]

Under its new leadership the society on January 22 joined its voice to the resolutions adopted by the Kaluga, Petersburg, and other teachers' societies. It strongly censured the administration's overall approach to education and to teachers in particular and underscored the vital link between educational and political reforms. Shortly thereafter, in response to a plan worked out by I. Ia. Gerd, the idea of a teachers' union that would encompass all pedagogues, from the rural schoolteacher to the university professor, was raised for discussion. Gerd's project, which was printed in *Russkiia vedomosti,* outlined a series of measures to improve the "intellectual, moral, and material position" of teachers and argued that only an All-Russian Union of Educators could realize these reforms.[32] Response from teachers was favorable. The Pedagogical Society received, among others, a letter from twenty-three teachers in the rural settlement of Dubovka (Tsaritsyn district) in Saratov province who urged that the society pay special attention to the depressed legal status of elementary schoolteachers and include the demand that teachers be granted a voice in school management at the local level. The Dubovka teachers pointed out that unification of teachers was imperative, not only from a professional standpoint but from a political one as well, arguing that teachers, "as the most important intellectual force in the countryside, should be accepted as expressing both their own needs and those of the narod in current discussions of state reforms."[33] This was the first response from rural teachers to the organizing efforts underway in the capitals, and it was indicative of the wide, extraprofessional tasks that many teachers foresaw for their nascent organization.

On February 26, after hearing a report by N. S. Felitis, "The History of the German Teachers' Union," the Moscow Pedagogical Society accepted in principle the idea of forming a union, and concrete organizational efforts began in earnest.[34] Having established liaison with the Bureau in Petersburg, by mid-March, plans were underway to convene a national congress of teachers in Moscow in early April. In the words of N. I. Popova, this would be the first time they "could freely express, without restraint, their most pressing needs and dreams, and feel themselves not abandoned in some backwater *(medvezhii ugol),* isolated and forgotten by the whole world, but members of one comradely teachers' family, instilled with the same feelings and strivings."[35]

The congress convened April 11–13, 1905, in the luxurious residence of Varvara A. Morozova, merchant's wife and owner of the liberal Moscow daily *Russkiia vedomosti,* who opened her home for a variety of political gatherings during this period. The mood was one of euphoria, the same sense of exhilaration felt by other groups that met "without official sanction" *(iavochym poriadkom)* during early 1905. But the April meeting also revealed the first rift within the teachers' movement, over its political program. One hundred fifty-two delegates from thirty provinces attended; not surprisingly, the two capitals were heavily represented (by fifty-eight individuals). The Moscow Pedagogical Society made a special effort to attract rural teachers, utilizing contacts made at the Moscow Congress of mutual aid societies and the Third Technical Education Congress.[36] In some cases delegates were formally elected from existing teachers' societies or other groups. This appears to have been the case, for example, in Rostov-on-Don. The Iaroslavl Society's executive board chose two teachers: V. K. Burtsev, from a railway school, and G. A. Sokolov, a rural teacher. Burtsev recalls that both had to be supplied with new shoes for the trip since each had ruined theirs, one crossing the ice on the Volga, the other walking seventeen versts along mud-clogged roads to their rendezvous in the provincial capital. There they were provided with addresses in Moscow for overnight lodging without police registration. They left during the Orthodox Holy Week and so avoided arousing the suspicion of school authorities.[37] Much less is known concerning the identities of other provincial delegates. Many carried no official accreditation from local teachers' organizations, and those who arrived at Morozova's decided to constitute themselves a "preparatory conference" for the formation of the union, rather than a "constituent congress," and to adopt a provisional statute.

Discussion centered on the union's "professional" tasks as well as "political" aims. There was little disagreement regarding educational reforms, and in the main the participants simply reiterated the points contained in the Petersburg memorandum. Despite some protests occasioned by excessive populist qualms about ramming anything down the throat of the narod, compulsory schooling was accepted. In spite of the arguments of opponents of secularization, the demand that catechism be dropped as a mandatory subject was reaffirmed. In short, the union would wage a "struggle for a radical reorganization of public education in Russia on the basis of freedom, democratization, and decentralization."[38] Whether the Teachers' Union should adopt "political" tasks, and what these should be, occasioned more debate. This dispute reflected the different attitudes of the major political parties toward teachers and other members of the democratic intelligentsia in general, and toward the intelligenty unions in particular. Since the issue would hound the Teachers' Union throughout its existence, it is worth briefly examining these attitudes.

The liberals hoped to unite the majority of the Russian intelligentsia, from academicians and jurists to rural teachers and feldshers, into a broad party espousing constitutional reform based on universal and equal suffrage and a peaceful transition to a new order. This was the strategy that Petr Struve had outlined in October 1904, and it motivated the formation of unions of intelligenty, which would unite members of a given profession not so much on the basis of specific professional interests as on acceptance of the liberals' political agenda. In teachers and others, the liberals could, ideally, find a medium for the popularization of their program among the masses.[39] The "liberationist" strategy found support among the education activists who directed the Teachers' Union: G. A. Fal'bork was a liberal deputy of the Petersburg city duma and a future Kadet (V. P. Vakhterov ran on the Kadet party list in elections to the Second Duma); Charnoluskii, P. A. Miakotin, and other union leaders subsequently were charter members of the moderate Popular Socialist party. The team of Moscow education writers, Tulupov and Shestakov, were in the same mold. In political terms N. V. Chekhov, Vakhterov, and other union leaders belonged to that amorphous political world that would later be termed "left of the Kadets"; they were not revolutionaries, but their brand of liberalism was imbued with a strong democratism and populist ethos. They supported the "liberationist" notion that the new union should pursue political aims, couched in the hazy formulation "struggle for the political liberation of Russia and for wide socioeconomic reforms." The intent of this plank was twofold. First, union organizers insisted that the organization be political (and illegal, since they rejected the idea of petitioning the government for its registration) in order to separate progressive teachers from the reactionary element and to elicit some form of commitment from rank-and-file teachers. Second, the formula was left general enough to attract all progressive pedagogues, the large number who were not associated with any political party, as well as firm adherents of the major socialist parties.

The Socialist Revolutionaries candidly admitted that the intelligentsia unions had originated within the Union of Liberation, and they had few illusions about the liberals' plan to coopt them. Nevertheless, SRs remained convinced that the democratic intelligentsia constituted a distinct social formation, intrinsically opposed to bourgeois society, which could not be constricted within the narrow limits of the liberation program. Had not the Pirogov congress of doctors in March 1905 already endorsed the idea of "transfer of land to the narod?" And had not the agronomists called for confiscation of private landholdings to benefit the peasantry? Supremely confident of their ability to move the "politically undifferentiated mass" of the intelligentsia leftward, to vanquish the liberals on a battlefield chosen by the latter, the SRs threw themselves headlong into the movement to organize the "political-professional unions." Such organizations could be of inestimable value to a relatively small, conspirative party like the PSR, in terms of recruitment, "ideological influence," and the like.[40] And what milieu could promise greater dividends than teachers, a group on which the PSR had been expending considerable resources to woo in recent years?

At the April meeting in Moscow the SRs therefore agreed to take part in the projected All-Russian Union of Teachers, accepting the above political formula. Socialist Revolutionary representatives confidently predicted that the mass of teachers would eventually be won over to their program, since their socialist rivals, the SDs, had nothing to offer the peasantry but post-Emancipation "cutoffs" *(otrezki)* and thus could not attract teachers committed to political work in the countryside. Finally, twelve SRs issued a statement to the effect that they were not fully satisfied with the union's statute as it then stood but expressed the hope that as the union struck root in the provinces "our comrades in the locales . . . will demand significant changes and amendments."[41] In a distinct minority at the meeting, the SRs remained optimistic concerning their prospects and called for unity among teachers, tactfully noting that they had not come to sow discord along party lines.

Not so the Social Democrats, who also took an active part in political organization among the intelligentsia in early 1905. S. I. Mitskevich, a Bolshevik physician involved in this campaign, active in the Union of Medical Personnel in particular, has left a vivid account of this period. Social Democrats played a prominent role in the organization of the Teachers' Union in Petersburg (according to Menzhinskaia, the delegation attending the April conference from that city included a strong SD contingent) and particularly in Moscow through the Bolshevik-dominated "lecture group," which included Rozhkov and Pokrovskii, the former city teacher I. I. Skvortsov-Stepanov, Kirik Levin, as well as the city teachers Nasimovich, Filatov, Dmitriev, and others who before 1905 had been involved in the nonparty revolutionary Union of Teachers and who in early 1905 were active in the organization of a professional "corporation" of Moscow city teachers.[42] All of these people participated in the April conference in Moscow. Rozhkov, who was elected chairman of the gathering, later remarked that, although a minority, "we Bolsheviks had a solid group at the congress."[43] In fact, as subsequent voting would demonstrate, the SDs were twice as strong at the conference as the Socialist Revolutionaries. Yet the tactic they pursued there was quite different.

Mitskevich notes that as early as March 1905 there was considerable debate within the Moscow "lecture group" concerning participation in the intelligentsia unions. The local party leadership tended to disapprove of it, as did the Bolshevik leadership in emigration. Later on, Social Democrats who had taken part in this movement and who had "overestimated" its significance were taken to task by V. D. Bonch-Bruevich, clearly expressing Lenin's opinion in the Bolshevik organ *Proletarii:*

> Our comrades forgot precisely that all these congresses were important to the liberationists, not only as a platform for propagating their moderate and calculated program, but also to deflect the wavering forces of the intermediary-class *(mezhduklassovaia)* intelligentsia away from social-democratic propaganda. The liberationists well know that it is namely with the SDs that they will soon have to do battle to the death, and the [degree] of success enjoyed by these constitutionalists can only spell failure for the party of the proletariat.[44]

It is well known that Lenin had a distinct aversion toward the Union of Liberation (John Keep has termed it as "psychosis") and to its offspring, the intelligentsia unions. Although a formal resolution condemning the Social

Democrats' participation in the unions was not adopted until late April, at the Third Party Congress (Bolshevik) in London, the position of the party leadership was conveyed sometime earlier to party members in Russia.[45] Only in this way, it seems can one explain the confrontational tactics pursued by the SDs in Moscow, despite the misgivings of some local party activists.

The Social Democrats at the conference (and a majority of these appear to have been Bolsheviks) immediately objected to the amorphousness of the proposed political plank. The first salvo was fired by the Minsk teacher and Jewish Bundist M. Ia. Frumkina, who argued that such an "indefinite" statement would reduce the Teachers' Union to an appendage of the liberals. She also urged stricter demarcation between adherents of the socialist parties, particularly on the agrarian question, and boldly contended that Social Democratic teachers "cannot enter a union that does not place on its banner the SDs' program-minimum [including demand for a democratic republic, the eight-hour day for workers, and so on], because in doing so they would betray their program and to a significant degree would becloud the class consciousness of the proletariat." As "proletarians" themselves only one option was open to teachers: place their union under the standard of the Social Democrats and, together with the Russian proletariat, carry on the revolutionary struggle for the attainment of socialism.[46]

After this and other SD statements the mood at the conference, recalled Pokrovskii, "quickly turned against us."[47] In response to the strident appeals of the SD delegates, others offered conciliatory calls for unity among all progressive teachers. It was the task of the schoolteacher, argued a certain S., to "awaken the popular masses to political life," a protean task that would necessitate the cooperation of all political forces that accepted the need for a democratic constitution and reforms "in the interests of the laboring masses." Kiriakov likewise argued for a united front against the autocracy and cited the Conference of Oppositional and Revolutionary Parties held in Paris in September 1904 (from which the SDs had abstained) as a model.

But these calls for unity had little visible effect on the SD representatives, who continued to insist that the political program proposed by the union organizers was that of the "bourgeois democratic party," to which teachers should not subscribe. Such accusations drew angry retorts directed against SD speakers who had the audacity to characterize such luminaries of the teachers' movement as N. F. Bunakov and Vakhterov as "bourgeois," and the censure of those "who out of fear for the purity of distant ideals sacrifice essential tasks and call for disunity."

Faced with this storm of indignation the SDs shifted gears, urging that the union adopt no political platform and remain a purely "professional" association. They were apparently supported by some delegates who pointed out that such a union would be able to encompass the "as yet politically untouched and timid *(robkie)* teachers," who might easily be repulsed by adoption of a "radical political banner." But this consideration was lightly dismissed by others who argued that a political program was essential if the union was to protect itself from "reactionary and undemocratic elements."[48]

In the final analysis the SDs' call for a purely professional union (even though they pointed out that this would in no way inhibit political activity by teachers as individuals) could not strike a sympathetic chord among teachers. After all, a major lesson of the teachers' movement in recent years had been the connection between teachers' professional status and the whole structure of the Old Regime, which, by contrivance and neglect, maintained them in a state of bondage. Politics and professional interests were inseparable. The iron logic of the Social Democrats, that if teachers entered the projected "political-professional union" they would only be serving the class interests of bourgeois society, appeared tortuous and incomprehensible to most teachers.

> The proposition could not even pop into the head of a conscious schoolteacher that the first paragraph of the union [statute], a free school, could possibly be achieved without alteration of the bureaucratic system; that he, proverbially without rights, subjected to the *nadzor* of ten Arguses, humiliated in the pedagogical principles dearest to him, could become a free teacher of a free school? And if he adopts the political credo linking him with the Teachers' Union, in the words of Mr. Rozhkov, he will become a tool, he will fall into the nets of the liberal-bourgeois party and will unconsciously pursue a class political line. What horrors! Receiving 200–300 rubles salary, living not better than a worker, and not even in a position to defend his own interests, the teacher will become a representative of class egoism and agrarian rapaciousness if, God forbid, he joins a professional-political union of teachers.[49]

For many teachers, as for other professionals, the political-professional unions seemed a logical step in their own maturation: "for those strata of teachers which had recently, some only after the past stormy winter, awoken to political work, the union was the first necessary step toward party work and at the same time provided the possibility to feel themselves free citizens." Unable to comprehend the Marxist notions of "class" and the "hegemony" of the proletariat in the Russian revolutionary movement, these teachers were clearly put off by what seemed an intractable position taken by the SDs, at a time when the primary consideration for those who had come to Moscow was unity among progressive teachers. This was the prevailing mood at the April conference. Teachers' impatience with dissentious party squabbling was relayed during the second day of the gathering in a statement by a group of Vologda teachers which concluded: "Let's drop these party quarrels *(podal'she ot partiinykh sporov):* fewer words, more action."[50]

The Social Democrats' position was consequently rejected by a majority

(96 to 23). The Teachers' Union would pursue "political" as well as "professional" tasks; a constituent assembly elected on a four-tail, full civil freedoms; and [though unspecified] socioeconomic reforms. The SDs issued a statement that under these conditions they could not enter the union. Yet, since the Moscow gathering was designated as "preparatory" and a fully "constituent" congress of delegates from local teachers' groups was planned for early June in St. Petersburg, this decision remained provisional. During the following weeks Social Democrats in Moscow, St. Petersburg, and elsewhere continued to play a role in union organizing activities, doing all they could to send supporters of their position to the June Congress.[51]

Yet the Social Democrats' boycott of the Teachers' Union (the Mensheviks' *Iskra* also recommended against participation in the *soiuzy*)[54] was never solid. V. K. Burtsev, for example, who had been close to SD circles in Iaroslavl since 1904 and who represented the Iaroslavl Teachers' Society at the April conference, remained in the union throughout its life and insisted that its political platform was well suited to the organization of teachers "who had just entered political struggle and were fearful of any party differences and dampening *(raskolachivanie)* of their revolutionary enthusiasm."[52] Mitskevich and others continued to question the monolithic view adopted toward the democratic intelligentsia: "our task was to sever the more radical strata of the *raznochintsy* intelligenty away from union with the moderate liberals." A Menshevik, P. Lavrov, argued along similar lines.[53]

So did Mikhail Pokrovskii, who in early summer 1905 questioned party policy toward groups like teachers and insisted that, in pursuing their boycott tactic, the SDs had surrendered this high ground to the liberals and, particularly, to the SRs. Pokrovskii's contention that Russian Marxists had overestimated the "liberationist" bogey drew a sarcastic blast from the editorial pen of Lenin, but twenty years later the dean of Soviet historians again questioned the premises underlying Bolshevik attitudes toward teachers during 1905, this time in an apparently unpublished manuscript which deserves to be quoted at length:

> At the time this was the basic directive regarding the professional-political unions: demand that a union accept our program and in case of refusal shake the dust from our feet, leaving the union prey to the SRs and liberationists, who were already in a state of decomposition at this time. This tactic was motivated by the concern that otherwise the workers, seeing us together with the "bourgeoisie," would not understand where the class boundary lay and would themselves begin to listen to the speeches of bourgeois agitators, with whom we Bolsheviks stewed together in the same juice in the "professional-political unions." Very likely, in regard to such unions as professors, lawyers, and engineers, such a tactic was completely correct. But to this day it is not clear to me how nobody understood that toward rural teachers who constituted a direct channel to the village and the peasant, the approach had to be different. Or that any conscious or even semiconscious worker would have

> taken the shabby rural enlightener for a "bourgeois." Only some of our green agitators were capable of this, at meetings telling the teacher that possibly tomorrow they "would have to shoot at them" (literally). The teachers did not comprehend all this and became terribly agitated. For the Bolsheviks to acquire any influence among teachers it was necessary to have contact with them over a long period and gradually wean them . . . but at the congresses of the union, against the backdrop of our statements, for the most part in the vein just described, the influence of the SRs was almighty and the last of the Mohicans of the "liberationists" retreated before them. The SRs stressed that they did not recognize any class partitions, that they summoned the "whole narod" to struggle against the autocracy and that they did not pose any programmatic ultimatums. The petty-bourgeois teachers followed them in a herd.[54]

Based on his experience at summer courses, Pokrovskii, in contrast to party activists in Moscow or Petersburg, had a keen understanding of the rural teacher's world view. The teacher's world was starkly manichean. On the one side stood reactionary, "dark" Russia, a configuration of bureaucracy, popular ignorance, and clerical hostility that hampered teachers' modest efforts at enlightenment. On the other side was progressive Russia, the intelligentsia and educated society, with which teachers strongly identified. The division of this society along party or class lines was something teachers found difficult to comprehend or accept. Those who preached a united front of all progressive forces against the Old Regime found teachers a receptive audience. For the majority of teachers the choice was not between joining a union with a "political" platform or one that would ostensibly limit itself to more narrow "professional" tasks. In either case the union would have been illegal, a point little remarked on during the platform debates but a fact that would have tended to alienate the more conservative and timid elements. The real choice facing teachers was whether to remain within the modest limits of teacher association permitted by the authorities, the mutual aid societies, or to adhere to an illegal teachers' union. This question, and that of whether the union would pursue political aims, was decided within provincial teachers' societies during the spring and early summer of 1905.

"Spring Thunder" in the Teachers' Societies

To this point teachers themselves had been largely quiescent. School officials could take comfort that the winter banquet campaign had registered only a faint tremor among the mass of Russia's rural teachers. Such complacency proved unfounded. Between late April and June 1905 a "spring thunder" shook the mutual aid societies and the teacher out of a long, wintry sleep.[55] For the first time teachers felt free to fully articulate their grievances and aspirations, and they explicitly linked their own fate to the general struggle for political liberation. They did so in unprecedented numbers; the spring 1905 assemblies marked a high point in attendance and participation. Most significant was a new assertiveness displayed by the rank and file. As a member of the Irkutsk Society recalled, the "gallery" finally came out in force and spoke its word, a reference to rural teachers who had previously, if they attended the society's sessions, sat in silence.[56]

By spring 1905 even teachers in provincial backwaters sensed what had been perceived months earlier in urban society: the balance of forces between supporters of the old order and its opponents had shifted. Russia was engulfed in revolution, the bureaucracy was in disarray, and government concessions only emboldened and deepened the opposition. Publication of the Decree of February 18 to the Ruling Senate marked an important stage in this process. Issued in conjunction with the Bulygin Rescript, which promised a consultative national assembly, the decree granted the right of petition on questions of "state welfare" to individuals and institutions. The Council of Ministers would consider these addresses from the population. This was a significant event. Indeed, in terms of extending political discourse and heightening agitation, the February 18 acts played a role in the 1905 revolution similar to Louis XVI's consent to national elections and convocation of the Estates-General in France in 1788–89. The moderate liberal V. A. Maklakov later remarked that the decree sealed the fate of autocracy in Russia. Placing as it did a stamp of legality on political activity, he argued, it greatly facilitated agitation among wide sectors of the intelligentsia and lent impetus to the campaign to form political-professional unions.[57] The decree did provide a pretext for political discussion which was eagerly seized by all manner of organizations—zemstvos, agricultural, learned, and professional societies—sparking a nation-wide petition campaign which reached down even to the village level.

Teachers' involvement in this campaign was at first largely limited to individuals lending a hand in the formulation of peasant addresses. Most rural teachers could not visit provincial towns until the Easter holidays in late April or the end of the school year. Therefore, only a few mutual aid societies responded with alacrity. In late February the Vologda Society informed the government that improvement in teachers' status was possible only with the establishment of a "legal order" and constitutional reform.[58] An assembly of the Voronezh Teachers' Society on February 25, attended by 150 members, went further, assuming, "a genuinely revolutionary and criminal character." Discussion centered on two reports linking "teachers' status with government disorder in general and the dire economic status of the peasantry in particular." As in January the proceedings were dominated by liberal zemstvo men, third element radicals, local party activists (including Iu. P. Makhnovets, a former teacher and sister of the renowned Social Democrat Akimov-Makhnovets), former teachers like Gonorskii, who had recently been dismissed for "political unreliability, the teacher Kravchenko, and the priest S. I. Serebrianskii, a future Peasant

Union activist from Valuiki district. School officials were forced to admit that rank-and-file teachers also took part in the discussions and supported resolutions favoring a constituent assembly, civil freedoms, teacher participation in a future "small zemstvo unit," and a complete overhaul of the educational administration, including increased teacher influence in school management. Finally, the Voronezh teachers readily accepted the obligation to bring the Liberation Movement to the narod: "in light of the acts of February 18, we teachers demand the right to explain to the population the significance of national elections so that it can react to them in a conscious manner."[59] At this critical juncture, they argued, peasant political education was the teacher's moral duty.

The Voronezh meeting presaged a wider movement, one which began to encompass most of the teachers' societies during the spring. The key issues were adumbrated: the connection between teachers' status and political reform; the potential role of teachers as political activists attempting to hitch the lumbering peasant cart to the speedy locomotive that was urban Russia in revolution. The governor of Voronezh charged that the local teachers' society intended to "unite teachers into an antigovernment group aimed at disseminating among the peasantry ideas about changes in the existing state and social structures," and local police asserted that in Voronezh, Valuiki, and Zemliansk districts teachers and lower level medical personnel were already organizing for this purpose.[60] Other teacher's societies followed the lead of Voronezh, resolving to utilize the Decree of February 18 to mobilize teachers.[61]

Official response to this incipient movement was confused. The Voronezh governor recommended closure of the society, while other officials complained that the February Decree had tied their hands and had lent an air of semilegality to overtly oppositional, even revolutionary, activities. They received some comfort from a Ministry of Interior circular issued to provincial governors on April 12, 1905, which warned that any attempt to exploit the decree in order to "threaten the state order or the public peace" would not be tolerated. Furthermore, the circular laid down guidelines for meetings of zemstvos, professional associations, and rural communes: "outsiders" would not be permitted to participate in political discussions; all societies operating under special statutes (for example, teachers' societies) would have to conduct discussions behind closed doors; the resolutions adopted and forwarded to the Council of Ministers were not to be published in the press.[62]

The MVD circular offered local authorities some leverage, but it did not erase the central fact that the government had made a major concession to public opinion. Russian society tended to interpret the decree in the widest sense, as a full-scale government retreat. Teachers were no exception. And so, when after the Moscow Conference Teachers' Union organizers appealed to provincial teachers' societies to discuss the union's tentative program and form local affiliates, they unleashed a storm of protest against school officials, sparked unprecedented discussion by teachers of educational and general reforms, and launched a political campaign that would ultimately mobilize many of Russia's "zemstvo rabbits."[63]

Among the first to respond was the Nizhegorod Society. It summoned an "extraordinary" assembly on April 19, which was well attended by rural teachers who were provided lodging at the society's student dormitory, vacated for the holidays. Nizhegorod had failed to send representatives to the April conference, but the packed assembly enthusiastically endorsed the union organizing efforts underway in the old capital. The society rejected the notion of a consultative national assembly outlined in the Bulygin Rescript and refused to cooperate with the city government, which was considering the state's proposals. As a certain Kolosov put it, "there can be nothing in common between the tasks of the Teachers' Union and the current activity of the municipal duma," which he characterized as a "tavern proprietors' organization" *(traktirno-domovladel'cheskaia organizatsiia).* Concerning the more liberal zemstvo, the teachers were cautiously optimistic. Speakers argued vehemently that teachers should be accorded a voice in the future management of education, equivalent to that of the elected second element in zemstvos and municipal government. Elections of society officers returned a board with a decisively radical complexion, dominated by teachers and third element people.[64]

On the following day a "private conference of city and rural teachers," attended by 200 persons, discussed the recent wave of conservative, patriotic agitation directed against rural intelligenty and how best to combat the "dark forces" of the countryside in what was viewed as a crucial contest for the hearts and minds of the peasantry. Teachers favored an activist, confrontational approach to rightist propaganda and were clearly dissatisfied with the position taken by local zemstvos, which did little more than inform the minister of interior of the impossibility of continuing normal operations as long as this campaign continued unchecked. The Teachers' Society allocated funds for the purchase of inexpensive political literature published by "Donskaia Rech'" and "Molot," and a special commission sent free of charge to rural teachers "progressive" brochures with the official stamp of the liberal school inspector N. N. Iordanskii affixed in order to escape detection. Only in this way, teachers reasoned, could they both inform themselves and enlighten the rural masses concerning the "issues of the day."[65]

Nizhegorod could boast of a fairly well-developed network of district filial teachers' societies, and it was here that the organizational efforts begun in the provincial capital now were continued. This activity was particularly successful in Balakhnia, a lively district that included the industrial suburb of Sormovo. Here the local teachers' society met on May 1 and May 15. Much discussion was devoted to recent disciplinary action taken by the inspector, a certain Kroliunitskii, against several teachers. A teachers' organization, bound by "collective responsibility" *(krugovaia po-*

ruka) and pledged to boycott the posts of teachers unjustly dismissed, was deemed the most effective way to counter arbitrary "police actions" by school authorities. The Balakhnia teachers decided to set up a special fund to aid teachers repressed for political or progressive pedagogical activity; previously they had consented to the zemstvo deducting 1 percent of their salaries to aid Red Cross relief work in the Far East, but now they requested return of these funds to support this fund for teachers. The Petersburg *zapiska* was accepted, and eighty-seven, presumably all members of the local society, adhered to the Teachers' Union, electing three delegates to the upcoming constituent congress.[66]

The union movement soon swept up teachers' associations throughout the province, although some, like Arzamas district, did not form union groups until fall 1905. Even the teachers of Semenov district, described by the correspondent of *Nizhegorodskii listok* as "gray . . . isolated from cultural life . . . incapable of comprehending even the most commonplace terms, such as 'bureaucracy' . . . since the majority don't read newspapers," even these "zemstvo rabbits" stirred. Meeting in late May they decided to form a filial section of the provincial society (an association had not existed in the district), and many, "in order to keep abreast of contemporary life," resolved to subscribe to the radical Petersburg daily *Syn otechestva*. Although the local zemstvo refused to distribute the union materials sent from the bureau, the Semenov teachers found out about the union from colleagues in neighboring Makarev district, where the more liberal zemstvo had divulged the contents of parcels received from Petersburg. Accordingly, of the fifty to sixty teachers who gathered in Semenov, forty-five joined the union, recognizing that its program should include political tasks shared by all progressive parties, above all "democratization of the existing public order on the basis of the four-tail franchise." In general, the response of teachers in Nizhegorod province to the union was positive; by the end of the year there were some five hundred members province wide.[67]

In other provinces a number of mutual aid societies met on April 22, and in each instance discussion revolved around political issues, to the discomfort of local authorities. Sixty members took part in an assembly of the Borisoglebsk (Tambov) Society, augmented by a throng of some two hundred fifty students and other "outsiders," many of whom, according to the local inspector, registered as members just before the start of the session and helped radicalize the proceedings. Predictably, the burning question of legal status held a central place. Several teachers who had suffered disciplinary action for "political unreliability" recounted their personal histories, and others described a recent wave of "nightly attacks" against teachers and ascribed this movement to agitation by police and clergy "who proclaim from the pulpit the fable that [striking] workers have been bought with 18 million rubles [presumably by British or Japanese agents] and openly slander intelligenty as traitors and rural teachers as purveyors of pernicious ideas." A telegram was read aloud from the governor, who warned against any discussion of the *zapiska* of March 12, which in turn evoked loud protests that such a ban was illegal in light of the Decree of February 18. The zapiska and the Moscow resolutions were then accepted by the assembly, which adhered (according to one account, unanimously) to the union. Elsewhere in Tambov province efforts to organize local union groups were pursued outside the mutual aid societies.[68]

One of the more dramatic assemblies of April 22 was that of the Ekaterinoslav Teachers' Society. Founded in 1898, this association had been well endowed with grants from local self-government and private benefactors and in a few years managed to amass a small fortune of 15,000 rubles. Yet the society had been lifeless. Attempts by activist members to broaden its services had been repeatedly thwarted by a conservative leadership which preferred to act as trustee over the society's treasury, jealously issuing loans to members, unresponsive to the wider and varied needs of teachers. The society's executive board was dominated by bureaucrats and reactionaries: the provincial school director K. T. Kalabanovskii, Inspector M. V. Osterman (subsequently a member of the right-wing Union of Russian People who teachers nicknamed the "Vulture"), two secondary school directors, and three teachers described by one society member as *chekhovskie futliary* (persons with their heads in the sand). Under their stewardship the society had suffered a precipitous drop in membership since 1902, and its record paled in comparison with even the modest achievements of teachers' societies in other provinces.[69]

Discontent with this record boiled over in early 1905. Impressed by the militant statements issued by the Kaluga, Nizhegorod, and other societies earlier in the year, Ekaterinoslav teachers began to clamor for a new deal and speedy convocation of the membership in order to turn the society around. A meeting was scheduled for February 25 but was then cancelled by director Kalabanovskii, who feared that given the "alarming mood" of local society an assembly of teachers in Ekaterinoslav might easily turn into a political demonstration. The board's decision, as well as its past record, was then subjected to a barrage of criticism in the press by disaffected members.[70] Under this pressure, and apparently shaken by government concessions on rights of speech and assembly (the original cancellation had come prior to publication of the February 18 Decree), the board caved in. When 138 members of the society met on April 22, most were in an angry mood.

The teachers S. F. Samoilenko and Mariia Zheits asked why the society had not responded to the important questions raised at the Moscow Congress of 1902–03 and the Third Technical Education Congress a year later. N. M. Liamtsev excoriated the board for ignoring the cultural needs of the membership, concluding that the board "had not fulfilled that morally unifying role which teachers, who are spiritually disunited and toil in isolation, have a right to expect of it." Kalabanovskii and his confederates were compelled to defend past policies. In response to Liamtsev's reproach that the board had not even attempted to secure free medical aid for teachers (a standard function of the mutual aid societies) Kalabanovskii discounted such assistance, arguing that physicians would not pay sufficient attention to patients without fees. This drew an angry retort from doctor A. L. Karavaev (subsequently an SR deputy in the Second Duma), who accused the director of obfuscation and slander of the medical profession. Finally, G. N. Maltapar, a teacher in a railway school from Novomoskovsk district summed up the prevailing mood, arguing that the times dictated a more activist stance on the society's part.

> Now at a time when public conditions have eased somewhat, the Teachers' Society must assume the grand task of spiritual unification of teachers; this is the sole path to an intelligent personal existence and productive public work. Libraries, congresses, courses, here are just a few of the tasks which our Society can pursue in the immediate future.

Other members called for a drastic revision of the budget submitted by the board in order to cover new projects, including subscriptions to progressive newspapers for teachers and a central teachers' library.[71]

Not surprisingly, wider political questions meshed with professional interests. "Rural teachers stand so close to the very source of popular life and . . . fully comprehend the cultural-legal serfdom in which the Russian peasantry is still mired." Thus, the assembly considered it a "moral and civic obligation to lend its voice to the chorus of all thinking and feeling Russia and, in accord with the February Decree, to speak out on questions of state structure and popular well-being." Despite Kalabanovskii's threat that it would lead to the society's closure, the Petersburg zapiska was read and accepted by a large majority. Legal arguments against this resolution were pushed aside by A. M. Aleksandrov, a radical lawyer well known for his involvement in political trials. Teachers, he argued, had the right to fully discuss political issues. This right was firmly anchored upon the acts of February 18. As for the MVD circular to the governors, since it had not been issued through the Senate it lacked the force of law and therefore could not be used to amend the rights granted by the decree. Besides, he added, the voice of elements like teachers was needed to balance that of moderates like D. N. Shipov who were already beginning to organize politically. Most importantly, the narod had to be organized and its voice heard. That teachers had an obligation to aid in this process of political enlightenment was accepted as axiomatic by those at the April 22 assembly: "Each of us," later remarked a teacher from Novomoskovsk district, "felt in himself a revolutionary spark and hastened to carry it into every remote corner of the province."[72]

The assembly resulted in an unprecedented flurry of activity by the Ekaterinoslav Society under the energetic leadership of a new board (not a single member of the old board was reelected). Kalabanovskii, with prompting from the curator of the Odessa school district, launched a counteroffensive and refused to hand over the society's funds. Disciplinary action was taken against three of the more outspoken teachers and new board members: A. A. Poliakov, Maltapar and Prokhor Diinega, members of the PSR. Closure of the society was narrowly averted, but this mattered little since activist teachers had already organized a section of the Teachers' Union for which the society served mainly as a legal front.[73] This process was replicated in most other provinces where the mutual aid societies played the role of midwife to the illegal unions. The Ekaterinoslav union was among the best organized and most radical in the country (in addition to being among the most savagely repressed). In large measure this was because of the intensity of the revolution in this province as well as the influence exerted on the teachers' movement by railway teachers who worked on the Ekaterininskaia Railway, militants who were more closely tied with political developments than the majority of rural teachers.[74] But the history of teacher association in Ekaterinoslav was also a factor. Antipathy toward local authorities, who in the recent past had retarded the growth of corporate activity among teachers, was manifest at nearly all meetings of teachers' societies in 1905. Nowhere was it more pronounced than in Ekaterinoslav.

A similar backlash occurred in the Samara Society. Here the villain was the society's chairman, school inspector I. S. Kliuzhev (later an Octobrist deputy and education expert in the second, third, and fourth Dumas). As in Ekaterinoslav, discontent with the leadership (in this case, that of Kliuzhev) had been brewing for some time: it came to a head during the first months of 1905 and ended in full-scale revolt. Aside from phlegmatic leadership, Kliuzhev was accused of conspiring with the governor to suppress the reports of delegates returning from the Moscow Congress in 1903. As the zemstvo man D. D. Protopopov put it, the teachers of Samara province had suffered long enough at Kliuzhev's "velvety paws" *(barkhatnye lapki).*[75] For them the revolution offered the opportunity to exact vengeance (not an insignificant motive in the teachers' movement of 1905) and, more importantly, to make teachers' association more responsive to the needs of the membership.

To this end pressure was applied from all directions. In the city of Samara radical members of the society clamored for convocation of a general assembly to deal with questions like legal status. By January 1905 it was a foregone conclusion that any discussion of this sensitive issue would carry explicitly political overtones, and chairman Kliuzhev strove mightily to head off such a meeting. Teachers in the districts called for reorganization of the society on the basis of the principles of the Moscow Congress.[76] The result of this agitation was a meeting of the society on April 22, attended by 145 members, which Kliuzhev and other officials refused on very questionable grounds to recognize as legal. Those in attendance called for an end to Kliuzhev's "dictatorship" and voted to exclude him from the society altogether. A new board was elected, composed of local radicals and headed by the liberal member of the Nikolaev zemstvo board, Protopopov. Resolutions put forward by the new leadership were accepted and then forwarded, in accordance with the February Decree, to the Council of Ministers. Samara teachers endorsed the Petersburg zapiska of March 12 and voted to form a local section of the Teachers' Union.[77]

Supported by the governor, Kliuzhev and his supporters mustered their forces for a counterattack and called an assembly of the society for May 26. But the new board, in the words of police chief Trepov, "had behind it numerical strength and the authority of liberal activists who everywhere introduce political questions and entice the credulous on to the path of agitation against the government." By a vote of 100 to 40 this assembly affirmed the decisions of April 22.[78] Three days later the board convened another meeting; this time it was attended by some 300 teachers, then on summer recess, by "outsiders and even *Jews*" (emphasis in original). According to police reports, the participants dealt exclusively with political questions. Revolutionary proclamations were distributed, as was the brochure "Universal Electoral Rights in the West" by V. V. Vodovozov. Speakers expounded on the programs of the SR and SD parties (for example, on the agrarian question), and the zemstvo employee A. K. Klafton urged teachers to return to their villages and convince peasants to compile communal addresses calling for an end to the war. Teachers chose delegates to the upcoming union congress and members of the local union bureau, most of whom were leftists. Local authorities raised a hue and cry for permission to close the society, which was finally suspended for six months as of August. By then, however, a teachers' union had already taken shape in Samara; by late June some one hundred fifty teachers had joined (of these only five taught in secondary schools). As in other parts of the country it was predominantly primary schoolteachers, rather than their more privileged colleagues in secondary schools, who responded to the union's appeal.[79]

By various means news of the union filtered down to teachers in the rural backwaters of Samara province. In Novouzensk district, assistance came from a rather unexpected quarter. Here in mid-May was held one of the rare official teachers' congresses. A congress had not been held in Novouzensk for over thirty years, so it was organized on the basis of the "temporary rules" of 1899. What made this meeting unique, apart from its timing (during the revolutionary year 1905), was that it took place under the supervision of a school inspector sympathetic to the aims of the Teachers' Union, V. G. Arkhangel'skii, an SR who later served as a deputy in the Second Duma.[80] The atmosphere was thus conducive to open discussion, particularly outside of the congress's official sessions where "in unconstrained, simple circumstances [sitting] before a cup of tea or mug of beer, teachers freely discussed those issues that most concerned them." After a week of such discussion the Nouvouzensk teachers adopted a resolution calling for basic educational and professional reforms, which, they reasoned, could only be secured by fundamental political changes, including establishment of a constituent assembly. Meanwhile, they urged that the zemstvo be more responsive to teachers' cultural needs (in providing reading materials, and so on) and that they be accorded a voice in zemstvo decisionmaking, both through a school commission and in the zemstvo assembly.[81] Finally, a majority accepted the program of the Teachers' Union.

As in Samara the Easter holidays witnessed a sharp turn toward radicalism in the Vladimir Teachers' Society. In a meeting on April 23, described by Governor Leont'ev as an "anarchist mob" *(sborishche anarkhistov),* the Vladimir teachers echoed the now familiar medley of professional and political demands. Fierce attacks were mounted against local school officials, in particular a certain inspector Kazanskii, who was denounced for the recent dismissal of a female rural teacher from Sudogoda district for "political unreliability." The beleaguered Kazanskii tried to defend his twelve-year record as inspector, admitting, however, that the filing of political reports on teaching personnel had been a routine feature of that career. He was shouted out of the hall. A correspondent for *Severyni krai,* writing under the pseudonym "Restless," described the scene as "electrifying": "all present felt that their old nanny, the bureaucracy, was really singing with its toothless mouth and halting tongue its own funeral dirge."[82]

Given this mood of hopeful defiance, adherence to the union, both the *zapiska* and the program drawn up at the Moscow conference in April, was a foregone conclusion. Within days the Vladimir Society's board distributed these materials to teachers throughout the province along with the suggestion that they organize at the volost level and select delegates to a second assembly scheduled for May 22.[83] Accordingly, a series of local teachers' conferences were held throughout the province during the first weeks of May. School officials bombarded their subordinates with warnings not to leave their schools and in some places were successful in aborting the volost conferences. But in numerous locales meetings were held, the union's program discussed, and delegates elected; in Murom district teachers came together with the blessing of their inspector! Undaunted, Governor Leont'ev invoked an emergency clause in the provincial statute to cancel the May 22 gathering and demanded that the Ministry of Education close the Teachers' Society altogether (this he finally achieved in August). City police did their best to detain and "register" all teachers arriving in Vladimir, but, given that the town was crowded owing to a local religious holiday, some seventy teacher delegates were able to slip into the city undetected.[84] As in other parts of the country a significant number of teachers embraced the notion of an illegal professional union with explicit political aims. By summer's end more than two hundred teachers had joined the union in Vladimir province (in 1903 there were 853 teachers in zemstvo schools there). The organization was especially strong in Pokrov district where, according to a Social Democratic observer, SR influence among teachers was widespread and where teachers were closely involved in political work among the peasantry.[85]

In April 1905 other teachers' societies, in Viatka, Tomsk and elsewhere, responded in similar fashion to the imperatives of Russia's Liberation Movement and, more specifically, to the appeals of union organizers in Moscow and Petersburg.[86] The movement really gained momentum, however, from mid-May, after most teachers were free from their direct duties. A series of mutual aid societies managed to convene their memberships during May and early June: Voronezh (twice), Kostroma, Kaluga, Irkutsk, Kazan, Iaroslavl, Yalta (section of the Tauride Society), Pskov, Penza, Kursk, Saratov, as well as the filial sections of various provincial societies.[87] In some cases local authorities were able to head off (Chernigov, Perm) or delay (Arkhangel) meetings of teachers' societies, but they could not forestall the inevitable explosion or shield teachers from the current "Time of Troubles." Politically active teachers and union organizers found ways to circumvent official proscriptions placed on legal professional associations.[88] For one reason or another some mutual aid societies (Smolensk, Tver, Novgorod) did not meet until late summer.[89] In countless other locales teachers during this period utilized less structured forums, such as private conferences or informal gatherings organized by sympathetic zemstvo activists, in order to discuss both professional and political issues.[90]

Teachers stirred from the Baltic to Black Seas, and from the western borderlands (including Russian Poland) to Baikal, attending the spring sessions in unprecedented numbers.[91] Self-serving reports by school officials averred that nonteacher radicals (including former teachers) steered the discussions toward political issues, while the rank and file sat passive and uncomprehending, but more candid police analyses, as well as some MNP reports, admitted that rural teachers assumed an increasingly active role in the assemblies. They contrasted teachers' passivity during the winter sessions with their posture in the spring meetings. In the case of the Iaroslavl Society, which met three times during the year (January 4, May 22, and August 4), local authorities pointed not only to a numerical increase in "active" members present at the sessions, "arriving from even the most distant corners of the most isolated district in the province," but also increased participation in the proceedings, a pattern confirmed for other societies.[92] Teachers were clearly concerned with more than the narrow material interests served by the mutual aid societies. A special government investigator sent to Saratov after the tumultuous May assembly of the local teachers' society concluded that only a small minority of teachers attended with "good intentions" and that these represented mainly older individuals with families for whom the society's normal functions (aid in children's education, and so on) were paramount.[93] By contrast, the majority evinced a radical mood and a keen interest in wider questions, both professional and political, which were seen to be closely related.

In all of the April-June meetings, without exception, teachers discussed a broad range of professional needs, in striking contrast to contemporary gatherings of upper-level professions, such as lawyers, engineers, agronomists, where deliberations were more or less restricted to political questions. Some demanded substantial increases in teachers' salaries while stipulating that the burden of such remuneration not be borne by the peasantry. Others indicated educational reforms ranging from the global (secularization, universality) to the minute (reform of Russian calligraphy). In nearly every instance teachers pointed to specific measures designed to ease cultural deprivation, and everywhere they addressed the question of legal status—the same nexus of issues that the government had doggedly worked to suppress during and after the Moscow Congress of 1902–3. In many cases teachers drew up detailed lists of reforms covering every aspect of school management and teachers' professional and personal lives, all designed to make the teacher, if not master in the school, at least an independent and authoritative entity within a reformed education system.[94] Equally widespread was a pronounced antipathy toward school officials, who in their position as "permanent members" of the mutual aid societies fell victim to a torrent of criticism from their aroused subordinates. In the midst of the spring maelstrom the curator of the Moscow school district on June 7, 1905, could only charge his hapless deputies, in the face of "personal insults and censure," to remain at their posts, "standing firmly on the basis of law."[95]

For teachers the satisfaction derived from seeing their superiors humbled was fleeting (expulsion of school officials and reactionaries from membership in the societies was a symbolic gesture). Teachers required firmer guarantees. Therefore, in nearly all teachers' assemblies of this period deliberation over professional and educational questions led inexorably to political demands: that the limited and provisional freedom of assembly bestowed by the Decree of February 18 be secured and broadened and that a constitutional order, often coupled with the demand for a constituent assembly elected by four-tail suffrage, be installed to secure both professional and other reforms. In some societies—Saratov and Voronezh, both heavily influenced by local PSR organizations, Iaroslavl, where the board was dominated by SDs and SRs, Kostroma, and others—nationalization of land, the eight-hour day, and other socioeconomic reforms were placed on the agenda.[96]

Most importantly, perhaps, the spring movement revealed a new sensitivity on the part of teachers to the political moment and to the role they might play in the revolution, above all the task of bringing the Liberation Movement to the narod:

> The liberationist-constitutional movement, which began in Russia from September 1904, has rapidly encompassed the country, penetrating everywhere, and at the present moment has achieved striking, concrete results. The government is powerless and stands alone in the midst of the hostile revolu-

> tionary camp which approaches like an ominous cloud . . . Agrarian rebellions point already to disaffection among the narod as well . . . regrettably, the latter still does not fully comprehend the present moment; within it still reigns a "dark force," this "black hundred" which impedes us, the intelligentsia, from merging with the narod, which tries to tear it away from us. Among the mass of unions—lawyer, doctors, professors, students, industrialists, workers, etc.—only a union of teachers is lacking. And you, sirs, must penetrate into the popular mass, enlighten and transform it and help the narod all the more quickly to emerge from the murk into the light.[97]

In Yalta on May 15 Vasili Vakhterov, from the Moscow Bureau of the Teachers' Union, pointing to the "unprecedented gulf between educated and uneducated classes" in Russia, put essentially the same tasks before an audience of teachers.[98]

These, of course, were the entreaties of educated Russians concerned about the attitude of the popular masses in the ensuing struggle between the Old Regime and the opposition. Faced with alarmingly mixed signals from the countryside (sporadic agrarian violence, anti-intelligentsia agitation, peasant petitions supporting the political demands of educated society), liberals urged teachers to organize for both professional and political purposes. Authorities admitted that such appeals did not fall on deaf ears. Reporting on the May 29–31 sessions of the Saratov Society, the local okhrana chief noted that at the close of the meeting teachers "quite openly remarked that after such discussions they would act dishonorably if they did not begin strenuous propaganda among the narod." In this frame of mind, he warned, some two hundred teachers dispersed to their villages.[99] While remarkable, these developments should not have come as a complete surprise to the government. During the past decade many teachers had internalized a professional ethos which placed a premium on "public" activism beyond the confines of the village school. The tumultuous events of early 1905 focused and magnified such imperatives but did not signal a break with the past.

As the same time teachers were conscious of the difficulties and dangers involved in political work in the countryside. Many teachers' assemblies addressed the thorny issue of "black hundred" agitation against the intelligentsia, particularly in Saratov province, the scene of an intense antiliberationist campaign waged by clerics and others among the masses. The Saratov Teachers' Society angrily resolved to exclude Archbishop Germogen, accused of inspiring much of this agitation, from "honorary membership" in the society.[100] More significantly, teachers in various locales vowed to combat reactionary propaganda by means of direct political "enlightenment" in the countryside and expressed the hope that zemstvos would come to the aid of rural intelligenty in securing popular political literature.

By spring 1905 some teachers had already suffered for political activity and a number of the assemblies of that period discussed methods of self-defense. In some cases teachers resolved to set up special funds to aid colleagues dismissed for "political unreliability" and discussed the idea of boycotting posts of dismissed teachers. (Both measures soon became crucial components in the tactical program of the Teachers' Union.) Given the meager material means available to teachers' associations, it was hoped that zemstvos and other institutions would support such tactics. Regarding local self-government teachers remained cautiously optimistic. Many assemblies demanded greater influence for teachers in the formulation of zemstvo policy through school commissions and the like, and in some instances teachers criticized the record of zemstvos in public education and openly assailed the undemocratic electoral basis of local institutions.[101] This same guarded posture was maintained by the delegates who met in early June at the Teachers' Union's Constituent Congress: hope that zemstvos and city governments would support the demands and activities of teachers, but stipulation that the union would struggle for the transfer of education wholly into the hands of local self-government based on a democratic franchise.

Finally, a majority of teachers' societies debated the question of adherence to the union and acceptance of the program hammered out in Petersburg and Moscow. In most cases the controversy over the union's platform, which had dominated the Moscow conference of early April, caused no undue furor, and delegates to the scheduled congress in the capital were chosen to represent local union groups (at a ratio of no less than 1 to 25). Most local activists found it difficult to grasp the arguments of Social Democrats that the union eschew political statements. The intrinsic connection between professional interests and political demands had run like a red thread through the discussions that spring. Teachers' buoyant optimism, on the one hand, and the specter of black hundred agitation and official backlash, on the other, seemed to dictate solidarity among all "progressive" forces. Returning from an illegal teachers' meeting in Viatka, a certain Z. Liutina expressed her impatience with the incessant wrangling between SR and SD speakers "when at present so much precious time is slipping away."[102] Members of the Voronezh Teachers' Society, who unanimously accepted the professional-political platform on May 12, argued that many teachers were as yet politically immature. For such persons a union with a more general political program than that offered by the existing parties could prove a valuable school, without alienating those teachers who already subscribed to a specific, but progressive, program.[103] For the majority of teacher activists these arguments were persuasive.

In some locales, however, teachers refused to accept the union platform. Some groups split over the issue, although motives are not always easy to untangle. In Riga and elsewhere in the Baltic, Social Democrats dominated the teachers' movement, and most groups decided against joining the All-Russian Union.[104] Local SDs succeeded in having the union's program rejected by majorities in the Kaluga and Pskov societies, where they argued that such a "terse and hazy *(tumannaia)* political credo may, in the final analysis, result in teachers' associations becoming the tools of a liberal-bourgeois party."[105] As already noted, Social Democrats had substantial influence among teachers in the two capitals. Indeed, a good deal of SD strength at the June congress appears to have derived from Petersburg and Moscow.[106] Elsewhere it is somewhat more difficult to ascribe dissent over the union's platform to direct sympathy with the SDs' position. In Tobolsk, for example, a rift over this issue was forced by moderate elements fearful of any attempt to involve teachers' associations in political activity.[107] Ultimately, the issue was resolved, if only temporarily, at the First (Constituent) Congress of the union held in Petersburg and Finland between June 7 and 10, 1905.

The First Congress of the All-Russian Teachers' Union and Official Response

By June 1905, revolution had progressed rapidly in town and countryside. Peasant disturbances increased markedly in April and May, as did the number of urban workers on strike. Demands that they aid in police actions against civil disorders placed an increasing strain on available troops in European Russia. The naval debacle at Tsushima (May 14) heightened opposition in moderate and radical society, and news leaked to the press a week later concerning the government's reform agenda, a consultative assembly elected by a narrow franchise and indirect elections, failed to dampen the revolutionary spirit among the intelligentsia. The Union of Unions held its first congress in early May and, in concert with the Union of Railwaymen, was already discussing the possibility of a general strike to bring down the autocracy.[108]

It was in this climate that the Teachers' Union, already represented in the Union of Unions, held its constituent congress. By June 7 some 170 delegates had gathered in the capital representing 81 union groups from 34 provinces with 4,668 members, as well as strong contingents from Petersburg (33 delegates, 865 members) and Moscow (2 delegates and 165 members). Roughly half of existing local groups sent representatives.[109] Police harassment forced the delegates to reconvene after one day in a hotel in Iustila, Finland, but this minor irritant did not dampen the buoyant mood carried over from the spring assemblies and enthusiastically related twenty years later by I. S. Samokhvalov, a delegate from Balakhnia district (Nizhegorod):

> No other meeting during my subsequent life had one-tenth the impact of this first teachers' congress. To struggle against darkness and evil, the war, injustice and poverty, all of it heaped high by the Tsarist autocracy, as well as

> the quality of our existence; to struggle together with our comrades under the banner of enlightenment for popular justice and welfare—these became the articles of my faith at this congress. At the time I was 21 years old.[110]

As expected, the vexing issue of the union's "professional-political platform" headed the agenda. Social Democrats had lobbied energetically for their point of view since April and reckoned that, along with nonparty supporters of a strictly professional platform, they represented nearly one thousand teachers and other education activists.[111] As in Moscow, the SDs demanded that teachers draw a sharp line between themselves and Russian liberalism and recognize the "hegemony" of the proletariat in the general onslaught against Tsarism. I. I. Skvortsov-Stepanov (Moscow) argued rather optimistically that "the era of party organization has now dawned; we have stepped onto the path of Western European [style] political struggle . . . now anyone involved in politics must belong to a party . . . not to monstrosities like the unions and the Union of Unions, which include the likes of [Prince] S. N. Trubetskoi, groveling before the throne." Rozhkov argued that the SDs, in adhering to a union which accepted political tasks, could easily find themselves in an untenable position: "a majority of the delegates may decide to send greetings to the zemstvo men and the impression will be given that it is speaking for the whole union." A Petersburg delegate, Menzhinskaia, put the issue more bluntly: "Do you teachers really imagine that your needs can be satisfied outside the class struggle of the proletariat? The union will lead you to support liberal-bourgeois elements. We know what is hidden behind the word 'political' . . . the *liberationist* program."[112]

Some delegates insisted as vehemently that the union adopt the program of the PSR ("the rural teacher must act as an SR, otherwise the peasants will not heed him," argued a Voronezh delegate). But the majority of speakers, SRs included, preached unity of all progressive elements around a political program minimum: a four-tail constituent assembly and civil freedoms. Sobol'ev, from Perm, dismissed the assertion that teachers might unwittingly become the tool of the bourgeoisie and warned that, as the SDs fostered sectarianism, a real danger, a dictatorship of the "black hundreds," loomed on the horizon. Others argued that some political program was essential to keep conservative elements out of the union. Emotion as well as political calculation dictated the inclusion of political tasks. As Zhebuneva (Ekaterinoslav) put it: "The word 'political' signifies our mood, not a program."[113]

So with head and heart a majority (109 to 40, with 9 abstentions) voted to retain the program's political component. Thirty-one Social Democrats, acting on party directives, then demonstratively walked out of the congress (9 votes had come from nonparty supporters of a professional union). Only later, in autumn 1905, did they attempt, without much success, to organize a rival "purely professional" teachers' union. The Marxists' withdrawal from the union was by no means complete since many SDs remained in local sections of the union.[114]

The remaining delegates voiced profound regret over the decision of the Social Democrats and then moved onto further business. The union's program was discussed point by point, with substantial debate over only the question of compulsory primary schooling and exclusion of catechism *(zakon bozhii)* as a compulsory subject (the SRs pressed for total eradication of religious training from the curriculum). A minor controversy erupted when representatives of the St. Petersburg Union of Secondary School Instructors and similar organizations demanded full autonomous status as a condition for their entry into the All-Russian Union. These organizations were, as yet, weakly developed: the secondary teachers admitted that their fellows were politically inert compared to Russia's *narodyne* teachers but argued that the special problems of the middle school demanded separate organization. A large majority of delegates rejected such an arrangement as a compromise of the principles of democratization of public education and of a unified ladder system assuring access to secondary and higher institutions for children of the lower classes.[115] With the withdrawal of the SDs and members of the secondary school unions, the remaining delegates accepted a final statute which obliged them to struggle for both "the political freedom of Russia and transfer of power into the hands of the people" and for a "radical reorganization of public education in Russia on the bases of freedom, democratization, and decentralization."

Toward realization of this program the union could offer its members few specific guidelines. Regarding school reform, the congress made several tactical suggestions: ignore all ministry catalogs regulating curricula, libraries, and the like; boycott all school officials who refused to support the union's program (and if possible involve the population in such protests); and, if any member suffered dismissal for such activities, he or she should be supported through "mutual insurance" funds and boycott of his or her post. Zemstvo support would be vital to the success of such tactics and the union's bureau promised to issue an appeal to all institutions of self-government before the start of the school year in September.[116] The prospects for such aid were unclear. Surely G. A. Fal'bork was overly sanguine when he told the delegates that the "participation of zemstvo activists in the Union of Unions commits them, in particular, to cooperation" with the Teachers' Union. Here was a prediction hardly based on a sober assessment of the social and political realities governing the gentry-dominated zemstvos.

Echoing the spring assemblies, the delegates in Finland pledged themselves and their constituents to intensive political work among the rural masses. Fal'bork, who was elected to the union's Central Bureau, insisted that the Teachers' Union could play a great role in the campaign for a constituent assembly: "It [the union] stands as the most powerful order of political missionaries with which, in terms of its [numerical] strength and proximity to the very wellsprings of peasant Russia, only a union of clergy could compare." He then advised teachers how to conduct rural propaganda. Begin with discussion of the war and peasant poverty, and "from these questions you will compel the peasants themselves to arrive at the fundamental political conclusion."[117]

An unidentified delegate from a union group in northern Russia offered additional advice drawn from personal experience (both his and Fal'bork's speech were subsequently distributed by the union's bureau to local groups as a guideline on tactics). Describing the success of his local group in waging a propaganda campaign among the rural population, the northerner urged all teachers to devote themselves to the protean task of advancing peasant political consciousness. As for the threat of administrative reprisals, damn the consequences: "we are not teachers, but citizens and propagandists . . . [we] all belong to the narod; we are young and if we can no longer teach children then we can chop wood." The most pressing goal, he pointed out, was an end to the autocracy and convening of a constituent assembly. Toward this end teachers should urge the peasantry to refuse payment of taxes to the government. The primacy of political over professional tasks constituted the overriding theme of the northerner's fiery speech, which ended with a stirring appeal:

> I repeat, in our work we have looked upon ourselves as people who are, in essence, the property of the narod, sacrificing ourselves totally for it. In terms of belongings, in terms of personality, we have nothing left that is our own. We have been socialized *(My sotsializirovany).*[118]

Before departing Finland the union delegates passed a number of political resolutions: condemnation of the Bulygin constitution; an end to the death penalty and immediate cessation of the war; emancipation of Jews. But the dominant message that was carried back to the provinces was that teachers should organize themselves to bring the Liberation Movement to the narod, a phenomenon that will be examined in the following chapter.

Efforts to mobilize teachers as "political missionaries" deeply concerned officials in the provinces and in St. Petersburg. On June 21, 1905, Minister of Education V. G. Glazov issued a circular to his subordinates urging them to bend every effort to prevent the organization of teachers' unions. In the wake of the spring movement local authorities deluged the MVD and MNP with requests that teachers' mutual aid societies be closed and that their statutes be amended to remove undesirable elements and insure greater official control. A number of societies were actually closed for periods of time ranging from six months to a year.[119] But by this time, in the opinion of teacher activists, the societies had already served their function. Despite a barrage of warnings against "illegal assemblies" from the ministry and local officials, the focus of activity had switched to the illegal union organizations, and where mutual aid societies survived they often served as legal front organizations for the union.[120]

The Ministry of Education deemed threats alone to be insufficient and simultaneously considered moderate reforms and concessions, in public education generally and over the issue of teachers' status in particular. As in other spheres (press censorship, industrial relations, the agrarian question), the Revolution of 1905 sparked a flurry of bureaucratic discussion of reform. For the most part these deliberations behind locked chancellery doors remained just that, since little of practical significance resulted. Still, they reveal the extent to which the government was willing to go to respond to teachers' grievances.

As early as March-April 1905, *Pravitel'stvennyi vestnik* reported that discussion was underway in the ministry regarding various reforms, including less restrictive rules on teachers' summer courses and local congresses, which had in recent years been driven near the point of extinction. In late May a special "conference" of provincial school directors for the Petersburg district examined teachers' status and how to improve it, both "materially and morally." The directors recommended that salaries be raised to a 360-ruble minimum but also noted that recently teacher complaints over material status had taken a back seat to other grievances, particularly their subordinate status in relation to rural officials. They urged inspectors to defend teachers against the arbitrary demands of local authorities. Some directors supported greater input from teachers regarding the conduct of year-end school examinations as well as some form of consultative representation on local school boards.[121]

The most ambitious attempt by the ministry to come to grips with the "teachers' question" was the formation of a "commission to improve teachers' status" under the chairmanship of Count A. A. Musin-Pushkin. The commission convened in late September 1905, and its final report was put before the minister of education on December 8. Members included liberal officials like V. A. Latyshev (acting curator of the Petersburg school district) but also conservatives, like the representative from the Ministry of Interior, the notorious reactionary V. M. Purishkevich, who viewed schoolteachers, almost by definition, as a seditious lot.[122] The unique feature of the Musin-Pushkin commission was that its deliberations were based largely on material collected from local conferences of teachers and school officials. These were organized in twenty-nine towns, mostly in the borderlands (Vilno and Orenburg districts, the Kuban and Caucasus), between May and October 1905. All were chaired by the head of the ministry's pension fund, V. D. Mut'ev, and his assistant S. O. Turzhanskii, both of whom served on the commission. Participation of teachers in these conferences appears to have been minimal, particularly in the case of those from rural schools. Some forty zemstvo teachers took part in the conference in Simferopol on August 31, but there were complaints that all teachers wishing to attend the sessions were not permitted and that most of those in attendance were appointed by local school officials.

That the ministry began to organize these conferences in May, after the beginning of the spring movement in the teachers' societies and the start of Union activities, was more than coincidental. While official presence at these gatherings undoubtedly tended to diminish candor, teachers expressed some very pressing needs. Predictably they complained of beggarly salaries and pensions, but they also told Mut'ev of constant interference by volost officials, clergy, land captains, and gentry marshals, both in running the school and in teachers' private lives. In cases of conflict with such persons, Mut'ev concluded, teachers were in an unenviable position. Even when school inspectors judged teachers' conduct to be correct, they often felt compelled to transfer them to another school in order to avoid further confrontation. Evidence suggests that teachers also complained about the interference of the inspectorate in matters not related specifically to teaching *(uchebnaia chast')* and pointed to the need for satisfaction of cultural and other professional needs (access to reading material, regular congresses).[123]

Little came of these officially sponsored discussions. True, the Musin-Pushkin commission did recommend increases in teachers salaries to 360 rubles, with a 60 ruble supplement for lodging and supplements designed to double the base pay rate after twenty-five years of service. But these prescriptions remained on paper; after 1908 the ministry, State Duma, and zemstvos were still trying to increase salaries to these levels. The Ministry of Education did request the Ministry of Interior in July to restrain its land captains from meddling in school affairs (Mut'ev's reports had devoted much attention to this problem) and also promised to make it easier for teachers belonging to the peasant estate to receive the rank of "honored citizenship" *(pochetnoe grazhdanstvo)* after twelve years of service.[124]

This was hardly an agenda capable of satisfying teachers' varied demands, let alone of undercutting the movement that had gained momentum through spring and early summer. The teachers' "silence" during the initial months of the revolution had been broken, shattered by the twin pressures of professional interests and political imperatives. Teachers embraced political activism as a way to resolve problems of professional status. During the past decade teachers' rising professional consciousness and attempts to deal with isolation and cultural deprivation had been repeatedly frustrated by official policies designed to sharply circumscribe autonomy and insulate teachers from ideas and social movements in Russian educated society. Teachers came to perceive these policies as inimical to their basic role as educators. But this was not all, since during the past decade of professional association teachers had also internalized an ethos which cast them in roles transcending the confines of the village school, as public activists and multipurpose cultural agents within peasant society. Official perspectives on peasant schooling and the rural teacher's role could hardly accommodate teachers' evolving professional consciousness.

The circumstances of 1905 finally allowed teachers to give full expression to their professional grievances and aspirations, and political opposition, latent during recent years, became overt and full-blown. What lent this movement a sharp edge was teachers' willingness to assume the role of political activists in the Russian countryside. Russian society and the urban intelligentsia exerted considerable pressure in this direction, and by summer 1905 even the zemstvos were urging teachers to intervene in rural politics. Ultimately, the success or failure of teachers' efforts would be decided in the countryside. We now shift our focus from the relatively solid ground of professional meetings to the more difficult terrain of rural Russia.

7. Teachers in the Countryside, February–October 1905

Within the rural community, as we have seen, the teacher was an "outsider," legally, socially, and culturally, a reality that was not only recognized by political groups seeking to recruit teachers as links to the peasantry, but concerned teachers themselves. Hence the teachers' movement heartily endorsed the "small zemstvo unit" in which rural intelligenty, women included, would be enfranchised, and the teacher's right to participate in the rural assembly *(skhod).* It also explains why delegates to the Moscow Congress rejected any proposal that seemed to preserve the gulf separating teachers from the masses.[1] Everyday teacher-peasant relations were marked by tension and ambiguity, the result of feminization, turnover, and peasant suspicion of the secular, rationalist values represented by the school and teacher.

But teachers' status in the village was not immutable. Peasant isolation was eroding under the impact of increased peasant contacts with the city, increasing literacy and simply more frequent contact with the third element. Surveys of rural opinion evidenced growing acceptance of the value of schooling and suggested that, if peasants were dissatisfied with the zemstvo school, this was often because the course of instruction was limited to three years and rates of recidivism were high.[2] Moreover, a survey conducted in early 1905 by the Saratov zemstvo asked 328 rural "correspondents" (peasants, teachers, rural officials) to comment on the population's attitude toward the intelligentsia. In only 34 cases were peasant attitudes toward teachers and medical personnel described as hostile; this compared favorably with the negative ratings attached to peasant relations with land captains (88), communal officials (118), local police (126), and clerics (77).[3]

It is difficult to generalize about teacher-peasant relations. Aloofness and suspicion on both sides continued to characterize their interactions in a good many cases, and it seems safe to say that on the eve of 1905 the majority of teachers remained largely uninvolved in rural affairs, leading a rather inconspicuous existence in the classroom. All of this changed with the onset of revolution. Teachers were thrust into the eye of a wider political storm. In some cases, under pressure from outside events and forces, the tensions that had characterized teachers' relations with peasants burst the boundaries of normal routine, generating a fierce backlash against these carriers of an alien culture. Yet many teachers achieved an unprecedented authority, the status of notables in the village. In many cases, pressure "from below" served as an impetus to activism by teachers, whose influence in local affairs soared as national events impinged upon the parochial world of rural Russia and they were called upon to function in unaccustomed roles as political propagandists, interpreters of happenings beyond the community and popular tribunes.

Anti-Intelligentsia Agitation in Early 1905 and the Problem of a Rural "Black Hundred" Movement

Peasant monarchism and conservative values had long been nurtured by supporters of the old order. Conflict between zemstvos and church, teachers and clerics, had heated up with recent zemstvo efforts in popular education which competed with church-run schools. Judging from teachers' memoirs, tension between clerics and teachers appears to have been endemic, not only because they were rival "authorities" competing for the hearts and minds of the peasantry, but also because of specific conflicts within the school.[4] Teachers often complained that priests were not fulfilling their obligation to teach religious classes *(zakon bozhii),* forcing teachers to shoulder these duties without pay since ministry catalogs reckoned this a compulsory subject in which pupils would be examined before graduation.[5] Teachers in Saratov, Tula, and elsewhere complained on the eve of 1905 that dismissals of teachers on political grounds could often be traced to denunciations by priests. Among the Legal Theses of the Moscow Congress was the demand that teachers not be dismissed on the basis of cleric-inspired calumny.[6] In late 1904, with the growth of opposition, Russian military reversals in the Far East, and unrest among the national minorities, patriotic clerical agitation among the Orthodox masses assumed the dimensions of a full-blown campaign.

The beginning of hostilities with Japan in early 1904 had been greeted with a wave of patriotic fervor in nearly all segments of Russian society. With the drawn-out stalemate in the Far East, this sentiment rapidly dissipated in urban society. Apparently, it had more staying power in the countryside, where monarchist agitation by clerics and rural officials commonly took the form of attacks on the intelligentsia and liberal gentry as alien strata interposing themselves between tsar and narod, acting as a fifth column at a time when the fatherland was locked in mortal combat with a foreign foe. "Internal sedition" was linked in this campaign with Russia's "external enemies," and the loyalist peasantry was called upon to resist both. A common theme was that the Russian intelligentsia was subsidized by Japan and England—18 million rubles was a frequently cited pricetag for this act of treason. In the villages, teachers and other zemstvo employees were branded from the pulpit as "Japanese agents," "enemies of the Fatherland," and "minions of the Antichrist."

Nowhere was this agitation more evident, and its apparent effect on the population more ominous, than in Saratov in late 1904-early 1905, when clerics, abetted by local authorities, orchestrated a campaign against the third element aimed at neutralizing their secular rivals and appealing to peasant monarchism in the face of mounting opposition in urban Russia. Priests in Kuznetsk and other districts inveighed against the sacrilegious behavior of teachers, and rural communes compiled decisions that the culprits be dismissed. Heeding warnings of their pastors that zemstvo schools had a depraving influence on the younger generation, undermining respect for their elders, and even leading to "revolt and mob law," peasants in scattered locales demanded their closure. Some teachers reported sharp drops in attendance, as parents pulled their morally endangered children out of school.[7]

The Saratov zemstvo's experimental "repeater courses" for adolescents and adults, in particular, fell under a cloud of popular suspicion. Designed to combat recidivism among primary school graduates and supplement the three-year program, the repeater courses had been initiated by the provincial zemstvo in three districts in 1902–3. Touring teachers, all men with considerable experience, offered these classes in two or three villages in a given district. So successful was the endeavor that the zemstvo funded courses in eight districts for 1904–5, where they were targeted by clerics and local officials who charged that they were used for political propaganda. Serious conflicts arose in at least five districts, and in early April 1905 the zemstvo felt compelled to suspend them throughout the province.[8]

Indeed, clerical agitation against rural intelligenty in Saratov assumed, according to the zemstvo, a "systematic" character and was led by the reactionary archbishop of Saratov, Germogen, whose pastoral letters to the faithful were an open invitation to attack teachers, medical personnel, and other "seditious persons." Reports suggested that such agitation was strongly supported by rural police. In some places there were threats of violence, and teachers, doctors, and medical assistants abandoned their posts. In the large village of Elan, Atkarsk (population 18,000) a drunken mob was incited to loot the zemstvo school and was reported to have boasted that "for the murder of the teacher they would receive only thanks from the authorities and would have to answer for it less than for killing a frog." Peasant suspicion in Elan had been cultivated by local clergy.[9]

Anti-intelligentsia agitation in Saratov became so widespread that the zemstvo threatened termination of all services and appealed to the Ministry of Interior, the Holy Synod, and governor Petr Stolypin to help restore order and rein in the police. Ominously the zemstvo predicted that if agitation was allowed to go on unchecked into an anticipated period of cholera, provincial authorities would have a calamity on their hands. In March the zemstvo itself issued an emergency circular to volost offices urging rural officials to combat the slander campaign conducted by "dark forces" against the intelligentsia.[10] As for Stolypin, he ordered his land captains and police to explain to the population that teachers and other third element personnel were "state servants" and agitation against them was a criminal act. Pledging that the "peaceful activity" of rural intelligenty would be protected by the authorities, he assured the zemstvo of Germogen's promise that all efforts of his clergy would be directed toward instilling "peace and love" among the masses. At the same time Stolypin warned that "both clergy and civil authorities are obliged to explain to the population the criminality of revolutionary brochures and appeals which in recent times have been distributed in great quantities in the villages." Pointedly he called on teachers to join this effort.[11]

What teachers labeled a rural "black hundred" movement was not confined to Saratov. Evidence of rightist agitation and peasant reaction against "unpatriotic" and "seditious" teachers surfaced in Nizhegorod province. In response to a survey conducted by the Nizhegorod Teachers' Society, one teacher remarked that, "given the present mood of peasants and vigilance of clergy and police, it is not altogether safe for teachers to gather."[12] Similar reports came from Novgorod, Kherson, Poltava, Tambov, Arkhangel, and other provinces.[13] In one village in Samara the local priest, upon reading the imperial acts of February 18 from the pulpit, exhorted his parishioners to repudiate teachers "who eat meat during religious fasts." The Samara zemstvo assembly resolved to counter the campaign against the third element through wide dissemination of the February Decree and Bulygin Rescript, which demonstrated that the tsar himself had placed political reform on the national agenda.[14] In Kharkov province the Sumy Agricultural Society appealed to the government to take firm action, noting that "in every church appeals are read summoning the population to rise up against 'internal enemies'."[15]

As in Saratov there was evidence of official inspiration. In Moscow province the bishop of Serpukhov, Nikon, circulated an inflammatory tract, "A Voice from the Hermitage of St. Sergei concerning the Unfortunate Events of Recent Times," attacking the political opposition and intelligentsia. Religious authorities in Perm disseminated a similar pamphlet, while in Novgorod in early 1905 a mysterious "People's Union" issued a proclamation to "peasants, townsmen, and working people" urging them to resist the constitutionalist machinations of lawyers, writers, teachers, students, and "titled zemstvo men" (Dolgorukovs, Trubetskoi), who, like the boyars of Muscovy had plunged Russia into a new "time of troubles" and wished to limit the tsar's autocratic powers. Similar themes were adumbrated in reactionary newspapers, which found their way into village reading rooms. In Penza province attacks on teachers and others were reprinted from the reactionary press in the official gazette *(vedomosti)* and sent to all volost offices. As the local school board pointed out, this imparted an official stamp of approval to rightist agitation.[16]

Aside from active encouragement by local officials, contradictory signals emanating from St. Petersburg seemed to condone anti-intelligentsia propaganda. The political concessions of February 18 were accompanied by another, very different, document, intended to isolate the Liberation Movement from the presumably loyal masses. The Manifesto of February 18, inspired by the aging archconservative Pobedonostsev, called on "all true Russians" to defend the fatherland from foreign foes and protect the "true autocracy" from internal enemies.[17] What effect this appeal had in stirring patriotic sentiment is not clear. In some locales officials attempted to conceal the decree and rescript in favor of the manifesto; in one instance a village priest read the decree "through his teeth," rendering it unintelligible to his peasant listeners. The manifesto was at best an inflammatory document and at worst a thinly veiled summons to civil war. The Saratov zemstvo warned that it could easily be interpreted among the narod as a license to bash rural intelligenty and urged wide dissemination of the Bulygin Rescript in order to "calm the population and dispel the agitation of both the revolutionary parties and no less revolutionary guardians of state order."[18]

Organized teachers were soon compelled to grapple with the problem of black hundred agitation in the countryside. Ascribing its success to popular ignorance, teachers concurred that the most powerful antidote was political enlightenment. Teacher activists were confident that the anti-intelligentsia manifestations in Saratov and elsewhere were ephemeral, that the barriers between peasant and intelligent were essentially artificial and would be swept away with the old order and with the expected democratization of education and integration of the peasantry into the newly emergent political life of the nation, a process they hoped to assist.

As they suspected, peasant suspicion and conservatism were not immutable but were eroding under the long-term pressures of industrialization, increasing urban-rural contacts, and literacy. In the short run specific events had a profound effect on peasant attitudes. This was certainly the case with the war and revolutionary events of 1904–5, which, in unprecedented fashion, impinged on the Russian village, confronting the peasantry with a bewildering array of new political concepts and ideologies. The success of any political activity by teachers among the rural masses was ultimately predicated upon an appreciable shift in popular concerns and interests from its traditional focus on the local community to wider, national events.

Teachers and Rural Politics in Spring and Summer 1905

Although it is questionable whether popular support for the war with Japan ever ran very deep, charges of the intelligentsia's disloyalty did strike a chord in the countryside.[19] Unfortunately for supporters of the regime, the credibility of such claims was eroding among the rural masses, the result of Russian military defeats and popular disaffection with the war and of the peasantry's exposure to more compelling explanations for Russia's military debacle and internal crisis. Somewhat paradoxically, it was news from Port Arthur and Liao-Yang that sparked peasants' interest in Russia's domestic politics and helped shape a rural audience receptive to liberal and radical propaganda. This shift in popular interest confronted rural intelligenty like teachers with new tasks and possibilities.

Symptomatic of this shift was an unprecedented peasant interest in the press owing primarily to the war: "According to local people such reading has increased ten-fold. It is not rare for a whole village to pool money for a subscription . . . the paper is passed house to house and eventually reduced to shreds."[20] Rural correspondents of the Moscow zemstvo noted a similar pattern in 1905: "Compared with last year newspapers are subscribed to on a massive scale so that there is not a village in the area where they don't receive some kind of paper." The Moscow zemstvo demonstrated that peasant interest, initially sparked by news from the front, was sustained through 1905 by a barrage of information on domestic affairs: the mounting wave of opposition in the cities, industrial strikes, and initial outbreaks of peasant activism against private landowners beginning in Kursk, Orel, and Chernigov provinces as early as February 1905.[21] Only after the government's dissolution of the First Duma in July 1906, and with it hopes for legislated agrarian reform, did peasants' interest slacken.[22]

Peasant readers became more discriminating as well. Various sources attest that under the impact of continued military defeats and the war's toll in peasant sons and requisitioned horses, peasants became disillusioned with conservative papers like *Russkiia chteniia*, *Svet*, and *Sel'skii vestnik*, which had enjoyed a kind of hegemony in the village during the initial stages of the conflict. Instead, peasants expressed preference for liberal dailies like Sytin's *Russkoe slovo*, which attained the largest circulation in Russia, or more radical fare.[23] While conservative papers continued to sound the old note of strident patriotism, the liberal or radical papers offered increasingly persuasive explanations for Russia's present predicament and for the growth of the opposition movement, as well as providing more comprehensive coverage of domestic news. In short, the village was flooded by an unprecedented deluge of information, much of it from the press, some, no doubt, in the form of rumor picked up in markets. Whatever the source, this information, particularly anything dealing with the agrarian question, cried out for explication and interpretation. Arcane political concepts and terminology, much of it borrowed from foreign sources, demanded explanation, and the printed word often required literate decoders. Not surprisingly, peasants turned to literate fellow villagers, rural clerics, and the rural intelligentsia for assistance. Although evidence is fragmentary, it is clear that teachers, in increasing numbers, attempted to meet these demands and that this process continued through 1905.[24]

In Kursk province, peasant interest in the war inspired teachers to organize evening and Sunday "courses" at which current events were discussed. In Odessa district zemstvo teachers reported widespread popular requests that they help decipher contemporary political events: "peasants come to teachers asking that they explain an incomprehensible section in newspapers, in the main *Syn otechestva*." A certain G. N. Vozkov related his experience: "In my village are many soldiers' wives who came to me with newspapers and implored, 'Read, for God's sake, how things are going at the front; perhaps my husband has already been killed and if so I want to know.' " So Vozkov read about the Russian losses at Mukden (February 25) and the naval disaster in the Tsushima Straits (May 14). The land captain tried to persuade villagers that all such news was a lie, "but then the peasants went to the neighboring village where the news was confirmed, and trust in the teacher was solidified."[25] A teacher from Ekaterinoslav province recalled how each evening villagers gathered at the school to discuss both the progress of the war and domestic events.[26] In Klin district (Moscow) a zemstvo teacher, A. S. Kondrat'eva, was dismissed from her post in spring 1905 for explaining Russian military defeats in the context of superior cultural opportunities enjoyed by the Japanese, while in Russia the bureaucracy consciously tried to keep the masses in a state of stupefying ignorance. Kondrat'eva's dismissal was protested by other teachers and third element personnel, who insisted that she had merely acted in a "manner that society deems to be the moral duty of any educated activist."[27] Similar cases of explication and official harassment were reported from other locales.

Teachers were on the horns of a dilemma. As they pointed out in the Nizhegorod zemstvo school commission, peasants "beg the literate person, the teacher in particular, to read from newspapers and books about current events and explain what is incomprehensible." But teachers had to be wary of "giving grounds for unpleasantness," including dismissal, in acceding to peasant demands. Yet they also risked incurring popular distrust by refusing to meet such requests. The zemstvo commission echoed the demands of teachers' assemblies that "satisfaction of the intellectual needs of the population be recognized as fully legal" and that teachers be allowed to use all materials passed by the general censor in efforts to advance the political enlightenment of the masses. Based on experiences related by provincial members, the Teachers' Union recommended that, in conducting propaganda among the peasantry, teachers begin with Russia's military defeats and then move on to broader criticism of the existing political and social order.[28]

The government itself provided an additional impetus for peasant involvement in politics during 1905 and unwittingly encouraged rural intelligenty to enter the fray. As was true with other corporate bodies, the Decree of February 18, 1905, granted rural communes the right to forward petitions to the Council of Ministers (and through this body to the tsar) concerning "improvements in the organization of the state and the people's situation." As we have seen, the decree was widely utilized by educated society, teachers included, to voice political and other demands. But, as the Soviet historian E. D. Chermenskii has pointed out, this concession was targeted, above all, at the peasantry, "to fortify monarchist illusions . . . and direct the peasant movement into the peaceful channel of a petition campaign." Faith in redress of popular grievances at the hands of the tsar was still strong among the peasantry, and the prospect of a direct line to Nicholas II had to be alluring. Accordingly, the peasantry responded with some sixty thousand communal decisions *(prigovory)* during the spring and summer of 1905.[29] Only a small percentage of these were ever published, and it would be a perilous task to attempt more than general comment on this petition campaign. In some locales peasants adopted patriotic addresses to the throne critical of the opposition. According to some reports, rural officials extorted communal decisions of this type or concealed the February 18 decree.[30]

In many instances, however, peasants avidly took advantage of the decree to voice their concerns, especially economic grievances. Increase in peasant landholdings at the expense of private estates, church and state lands figured prominently in most *prigovory,* although the exact terms of such reform (for example, the question of redemption) were often unspecified, and there was wide regional variation in economic demands. As a third element observer put it, "peasants looked upon their petitions not from the point of view of their public effect *(obshchestvennyi effect),* as did zemstvo men and the intelligentsia, but expected that the government actually deal with their declarations, all the more in that among the latter were recountings of old quarrels with landowners and other needs of a parochial nature."[31]

Yet peasant petitions of this period also addressed wider issues, echoing the demands of educated society for democratization of education (this was a near-universal peasant demand), civil freedoms, an end to the war, political amnesty, controls over police and officials, reform of local government, and convocation of a national legislative assembly elected by democratic franchise.[32] Such political demands emanating from the village were a source of consternation in official circles. At the same time that the authorities had to grapple with traditional forms of agrarian activism directed against nonpeasant property, here was evidence that there existed some degree of popular support for the political demands of educated society. By and large, local officials tended to discount this phenomenon, believing, until the elections to the First Duma, in the innate political conservatism of the peasantry. Denying that the political component in peasant addresses reflected genuine rural concerns, provincial authorities were quick to detect the work of outside hands in these endeavors and ascribed them to the machinations of "agitators" from the city or, more frequently, to third element intelligenty operating as rural cadres for liberal zemstvo elements or revolutionary parties. The governor of Novgorod insisted that communal addresses containing "the usual demands for state reform" were compiled by teachers and other persons "alien to the peasantry" and that peasants affixed their signatures to these documents without reading or discussing their contents, "under the guise of petitions for an increase in allotment land."[33]

There is a kernel of truth in such allegations. Just as they utilized the February decree to voice their own professional and political demands, teachers and other intelligenty interpreted the government act as providing some "legal basis" for agitation among the peasantry:

> Without the right of petition sanctioned by the Decree of February 18 and recognition of constitutionalist demands in the Bulygin Rescript, one could never have expected from the intelligentsia any significant constitutionalist propaganda. And without these acts, peasants would undoubtedly have reacted quite differently to statements made by the intelligentsia. The petition movement, which became fairly widespread, would have assumed "without this legal basis" a largely fortuitous character.

Zemstvo liberals drew the same conclusion and encouraged their employees to wage a constitutionalist campaign in the village during spring and summer 1905, and the Teachers' Union recommended that its members arm themselves with copies of the decree and rescript and initiate open political discussions with peasants.[34]

All of this caught the authorities off guard. While granting peasants the right of petition, the government moved simultaneously to ensure official control over the process, as well as to limit the influence of outsiders. Already on February 27, 1905, the MVD instructed land captains to tour the volosts in March in order to elicit popular opinion on the agrarian question and to "explain to peasants the true meaning of projected reforms [the Bulygin prescription for a consultative assembly] and advise them to come namely to the land captain for counsel and explanations." A subsequent circular from the ministry stated that persons not legally part of the rural commune could not take part in the compilation of petitions, thus disqualifying most teachers and third element personnel.[35]

Nevertheless, many rural intelligenty took an active part in the petition campaign, some suffering administrative reprisals. In the village of Ivanovka Vtoraia, Balashov district (Saratov) in March 1905 peasants adopted an address containing demands for political reform and nationalization of lands. In connection with this episode Governor Stolypin ordered the dismissal of the manager of the zemstvo's education department and all three teachers in the local zemstvo school, reputed to be one of the best in the province. All were members of the local Teachers' Union (VSU) organization, which had some success in boycotting their posts at the start of the 1905–6 school year. In Vesegon (Tver) in May a zemstvo

"The Village 'Intellectuals': School Teachers, Veterinaries, etc.—who almost invariably try to bring real light to the peasants." Source: William E. Walling, *Russia's Message: The People against the Czar* (New York, 1917), p. 190.

teacher, A. M. Gorshechnikov, who had taught in the same school for twenty-five years (no mean achievement) and was revered by the local population, was dismissed for political propaganda, which consisted of reading, at peasant request, from newspapers, explaining the significance of recent government decrees, and drawing up an outline of a communal *prigovor,* adapted from a peasant petition printed in *Birzhevye vedomosti.* Peasants commonly borrowed from other addresses printed in the press. In Tiraspol district (Kherson) a zemstvo teacher, Volkov (also a member of the local teachers' union), lost his job for his part in the formulation of a communal address from the village of Slavianoserbka. Volkov, allegedly, was guilty of nothing more than acquainting local peasants with notices in the press.[36]

In the village of Lokhnia, Sumy district (Kharkov) peasants requested the zemstvo teacher L. N. Skrynnikov to read them the Bulygin Rescript, which volost officials had attempted to conceal. Skrynnikov's assent to this request sent the local land captain into a paroxysm of rage at a session of the district school board, where he screamed that all teachers in Sumy district were agitators and "anarchists." Skrynnikov was subjected to a police search.[37] In Beloozersk (Novgorod) an agronomist, a doctor, and four teachers were arrested for helping peasants in three volosts draw up a petition. Similar cases were reported in Vladimir province and elsewhere.[38]

Under these circumstances rural intelligenty were placed in a quandary. On the one hand, local officials were highly suspicious of any political activity, no matter how modest. Many no doubt viewed the February decree not as a safety valve for peasant grievances, but as opening a Pandora's box of popular discontent, easily exploited by antigovernment elements to rally mass support and raise peasant hopes for a radical land solution. Accordingly, during the summer of 1905 a number of governors, pointing out that zemstvo employees frequently participated in the formulation of peasant addresses that "threatened private landownership and the Fundamental Laws of the Empire," warned zemstvos to curb such activities on the part of the third element.[39] Teachers and others argued that they were merely responding to peasant pressure that they "explain the essence of constitutionalism and the connection between local needs and those of a general-state character."[40] Just as vehemently did teachers insist that they did not hoodwink peasants into signing *prigovory* that contained political demands.

Novozybkov district (Chernigov) provides a case in point. In July 1905 a number of communal assemblies petitioned the tsar for transfer of land to the peasantry, an amnesty, and immediate convocation of a national assembly elected by four-tail suffrage under conditions of full civil and political liberties. Implicated and arrested in this affair were a zemstvo teacher of local peasant origin, I. Ia. Busev, a student of a technical institute (also a local lad), and two peasants. Each insisted that the petitions had been drawn up at the request of local communities. The peasants of Novyi Ropsk, according to Busev, "in reading newspapers noticed the petitions printed there and told me precisely which points they wished to include in their petition." Such requests began six weeks before the Novyi Ropsk *prigovor* was actually drawn up. Obviously self-preservation was a motive in the testimony of the accused, but the depositions of local peasants corroborated the fact that they themselves had felt the need to address the tsar with political and other demands. Moreover, during the course of several months prior to July 1905 the volost elder and rural police had tried to convince peasants to sign a loyalist statement. Their refusal, as Busev pointed out, attested to some degree of peasant political "consciousness." It is also worth pointing out that the arrests of Busev and his comrades were actively resisted by local peasants.

Allegations that Busev and his fellow "agitators" had somehow incited peasants to sign petitions that did not reflect rural opinion were groundless. Peasant political consciousness, he argued, was advancing: Busev and his confederates merely acted as "midwives for 'seditious ideas' with which the peasantry was already pregnant." A fairly accurate characterization of the activity of rural intelligenty in this period was provided by K. V. Sivkov, who analyzed a number of peasant petitions and concurred that the role of intelligenty was ancillary: they focused and articulated peasant opinion and engaged in broad political enlightenment. He drew a sharp distinction between the "arbitrary" power used by officials to extort patriotic addresses and the "moral authority" exercised by teachers and others. "No 'agitator,'" Sivkov pointed out, "can force a peasant to sign an address not corresponding to his own wishes and needs."[41] This seems self-evident and is strongly supported by what we know of teacher-peasant relations. If peasants had not been increasingly receptive to the political demands of urban society, no amount of propaganda by the rural intelligentsia would have had much effect. Quite the contrary, the kind of chauvinistic, anti-intelligentsia manifestations that occurred in Saratov and elsewhere would have dominated peasant-intelligent relations during the revolution. In fact, the evidence suggests that for many teachers involvement in rural politics came as a direct result of popular demand for information and alternative interpretations of current events to those offered by clergy, rural officials, or the land captain. This pressure "from below" was undoubtedly an important factor in drawing many rural teachers into the Liberation Movement and then into more significant efforts like peasant political organization.[42]

But were teachers prepared to assume the burden of political enlightenment? As we have seen, the evidence suggests that many did not possess sufficient understanding of the social and political issues confronting Russia.[43] Developing this understanding was thus a principal task assumed by Teachers' Union groups, first during the spring, but more intensively after the start of the new school year in September 1905. The Iaroslavl Teachers' Society established a special commission to provide rural members with political literature. The society's leadership (and that of the local VSU group) was composed mainly of SDs and SRs, but it stockpiled pamphlets of all progressive tendencies, with the exception of liberal literature on the agrarian question. The project was supported financially by sympathetic zemstvo liberals. The Iaroslavl teachers' union also circulated an "outline" for a village political meeting in which teachers were advised on how to conduct rural agitation. Compiled by V. K. Burtsev, the outline contained statistical data on gentry and peasant landholdings and information on political reforms. Teachers were also sent copies of the radical daily *Severnyi krai.* All of these efforts were intended to keep rural teachers abreast of current events and place them in a position of informed "moral authority" within the community. In Nizhegorod and in Klin district (Moscow) union groups organized a network of political libraries, and urban members were urged to send newspapers to their rural comrades.[44] In Viatka, teachers' organizations distributed collections of political literature. One of these was cataloged by school officials investigating a teacher in Nolinsk district, Ivan Sivkov, a union member suspected of waging revolutionary propaganda among peasants. For the most part, Sivkov's cache (thirty titles) consisted of brochures on the Duma and other reforms. These had been passed by the censor, and officials were able to uncover only one illegal item, A. V. Peshekhonov's populist tract *Khleb, svet i svoboda.*[45] Union efforts intensified in autumn 1905. The Moscow Regional Organization of the VSU distributed large amounts of literature among teachers in the central provinces and dispatched a team of political "lecturers" into the countryside. The Central Bureau in St. Petersburg made similar efforts. Literature was selected regardless of party provenance, but decided preference was given to works "supporting full democratization of the political system and on economic questions those of a socialist hue."[46]

Union efforts reinforced popular demands that teachers become involved in rural politics. These pressures were compelling, but many teachers remained timid "zemstvo rabbits," vulnerable in the face of a legion of "dark forces"—clergy, officials, conservative peasants, and gentry—bent on maintaining the traditional social and power structures of rural Russia. In this light, another impetus for teachers' involvement in politics came from their liberal zemstvo allies, to whom teachers had traditionally looked for support against the bureaucracy. The zemstvo opposition, particularly its left, constitutionalist wing, sought in the rural intelligentsia a "mediating" stratum between the masses and educated society. The problem of a link with the narod acquired urgency for the zemstvo opposition in the deepening crisis of 1905. Liberals were concerned with the problem of peasant monarchism, that the autocracy might effectively appeal to the loyal masses against the opposition. If a constitution was won, the attitude of the peasant majority would be crucial. More ominously, there was concern, shared by some on the left, that peasant activism, beginning already in February 1905, might be wholly destructive and indiscriminate: spontaneous *bunt* directed not only against gentry property and officialdom, but also against "culture" (schools, zemstvo clinics) and the intelligentsia, often lumped in the peasant mind together with traditional privileged and exploiting elements as "gentlefolk." Both concerns were underscored by the anti-intelligentsia agitation of early 1905. Who could better provide a link with the peasantry than the liberals' junior partners in the effort to bring cultural enlightenment to the narod, now that the times called for popular political education? Teachers shared the liberals' concerns, and many continued to look to the zemstvo activists as powerful allies.

Teacher and Zemstvo before October: Cooperation and Conflict

The zemstvo opposition of 1904–5, as Roberta Manning and others have demonstrated, was a movement of inherent contradictions. The roots of gentry opposition to the Russian government were varied and complex: profound social and psychological alienation from an irresponsible ruling bureaucracy; opposition to bureaucratic meddling in the affairs of local government, a preserve of local power and prestige to which important sectors of the landed gentry had come to attach some importance; the agrarian crisis, which the gentry blamed on the regime's policies of industrialization and viewed as a threat not only to their own economic well-being, but to their security as well since it contributed to peasant discontent.[47] The gentry's disenchantment with the regime was only exacerbated by recent military setbacks and the onset of revolution in town and country. Under these circumstances rank-and-file zemstvo men, at heart conservative or reactionary, came to accept the arguments of zemstvo liberals that the only way out of the country's impasse was a constitution. By early 1905 a majority of provincial zemstvos had adopted resolutions calling for a national legislative body elected by broad franchise. In line with much of public opinion, zemstvo men were dissatisfied with the Bulygin prescriptions for a consultative assembly, government temporizing on promised reforms, and their own exclusion from bureaucratic deliberations over the latter. Hence, the zemstvos drifted leftward, and the liberal zemstvo leadership, which had dominated zemstvo affairs since the mid-1890s, was at the height of its influence.

Zemstvo opposition peaked in early summer 1905 in the wake of the Tsushima naval disaster and the failure of the June 6th deputation to Nicholas II, at which time zemstvo spokesmen made one final effort to impress upon the tsar the necessity for a speedy convocation of elected representatives. These developments, coupled with the continuing wave of peasant disorders through early summer, the urban workers' movement, and radicalization of the intelligentsia represented in the Union of Unions, compelled leading zemstvo men to search for fresh tactics.[48] In a radical and uneasy departure, they decided to abandon for the moment the path of petitioning the government in order to press the cause of political reform directly before the narod.

This new course was charted at two meetings of zemstvo activists held in Moscow in early July: a general Congress of Zemstvo and Municipal Deputies and a Conference of "Zemstvo-Constitutionalists," representing left-wing zemstvo opinion. Mass politics had been alien to most zemstvo men. Traditionally, even liberal zemtsy had regarded the peasantry as the passive object of zemstvo concern, seeing themselves as the natural leaders and conscience of the nation, the "nonclass" spokesmen for all social groups, by virtue of education, experience in local government, and principled stand against the bureaucracy. But with the advent of mass politics, imminent elections to some kind of national assembly, and strong competition for the narod from parties to the left, the zemstvo opposition had to reconsider its relationship to the peasantry. Moreover, the zemstvo gentry, including its left flank, which supported some form of compulsory expropriation, with compensation, to benefit the peasantry, hoped to avert rural rebellion and steer the peasant movement into peaceful channels while at the same time garnering popular support to pressure the government into further concessions. All of these considerations seemed to dictate a more aggressive approach, a "going to the people." Accordingly, the Zemstvo Congress adopted by a crushing majority an "Appeal to the People," which outlined the liberals' program of moderate reform, and urged local zemstvo activists to organize mass meetings to explain to the peasantry the inadequacies of the Bulygin project, conduct liberal propaganda, and lay the groundwork for an electoral campaign.[49] At the Conference of Zemstvo-Constitutionalists, Petr Dolgorukov and others argued that liberal zemstvo men must unite with "broad popular *(obshchenarodnye)* forces." The zemstvos' alienation from the masses was already being exploited by the revolutionaries, they warned, and it was now necessary to "intervene in the very thick of life in order to influence the course of the popular movement which is proceeding in a whirl." Sensing their lack of ties to this movement and numerical weakness, liberals argued that zemstvo men should work closely with "wide strata of the intelligentsia" united in the Union of Unions, in particular the third element. Dolgorukov pointed out that in his native Sudzha district (Kursk) there were only four zemstvo-constitutionalists, but sixty zemstvo employees enrolled in various political-professional unions, and he warned that zemstvo men, "acting by ourselves, would prove completely powerless as soon as we began practical work in the locales."[50]

With this in mind a number of zemstvos made overtures to teachers and other rural intelligenty, and this encouragement often played a significant role in teachers' political mobilization during summer 1905. Aside from attempts to disseminate political literature directly among the peasant population,[51] various zemstvos directed their efforts at the political enlightenment of rural teachers and, via them, the narod. The Iaroslavl zemstvo worked directly with teachers' organizations to supply teachers with political literature. At the Samara zemstvo assembly in late June the liberal deputy N. A. Shishkov urged direct propaganda among the masses, and the zemstvo allocated 5,000 rubles for dissemination of popular brochures and another 6,440 to provide rural teachers with newspapers. Acting on a resolution of the zemstvo assembly of May 31, the Vologda zemstvo agreed to send each teacher free of charge the radical daily *Syn otechestva,* urging them to share its contents with peasants.[52] Other zemstvos initiated similar measures, and during the sessions of September and early October 1905 a large number of district zemstvos began or increased subsidies for teachers' subscriptions.[53]

Some zemstvo men went beyond these tentative efforts during summer 1905 and actively encouraged teachers to unite, both in pursuit of their own professional needs and to carry the Liberation Movement to the masses, by, among other things, promoting peasant political organization. This reflected a growing tendency on the part of the more radical zemstvo men to search for an ally to the left capable of organizing the peasantry to exert maximum pressure on the Old Regime while at the same time ensuring that peasant demands were expressed through orderly, "legal" channels (the parliamentary machinery of a new political order) and averting the violence and social conflict associated with traditional forms of peasant activism.

In Balashov district (Saratov), for example, the chairman of the zemstvo board, K. B. Veselovskii, brother of the zemstvo historian, organized, under the guise of a "conference of popular librarians," a political meeting attended by seventy teachers, who decided to join the VSU. Veselovskii, supported by the teacher unionists Vedeniapin, Vinokurov, and Dokunin (delegate to the Moscow Congress of 1902), urged teachers to carry political propaganda to the peasantry, promising that the zemstvo would rally to their defense in case of retaliation from the school authorities.[54] Likewise, in Tiraspol district (Kherson) police ascribed a major role in the radicalization of teachers during summer 1905 to a group of third element employees led by Boris Nikitin, a member of the zemstvo board. According to the Okhrana, Nikitin personally waged propaganda among the peasantry (distributing the February acts, being involved in the petition campaign) and sought to enlist teachers in this work. In late May 1905 he helped organize a local chapter of the VSU which sent delegates to the June congress in Finland, and on July 24 Nikitin and his confederates arranged a clandestine meeting of teachers across the river in Bessarabia province at which they laid out a general plan of agitation among the peasants of Tiraspol district. Authorities pointed out that the local peasantry was relatively well off and blamed the increase in peasant discontent on the agitation of teachers and other third element employees conducted in the spirit of the Peasant Union.[55]

Zemstvo activists in Viatka made similar efforts to enlist teachers. On July 17, 1905, an assembly of teachers in Malmyzh district heard V. Batuev convey his impressions of the recent Zemstvo Congress. Batuev criticized the Bulygin project for a State Duma and exhorted teachers to "actively oppose the government and to that end exert their influence on peasants and workers." In neighboring Urzhum a series of teachers' meetings were arranged by the chairman of the zemstvo board Depreis, a zemstvo deputy Matveev, and employees. As Batuev had done, Depreis on July 14 told teachers about the resolutions passed by the Zemstvo Congress. Two weeks later a larger gathering was held. Here teachers decided to form a local section of the Teachers' Union and resolved to return to their villages at the start of the new school year and actively publicize the idea of a constitution or "popular rule," among the peasantry. Final plans for this campaign, including distribution of literature to teachers through the zemstvo post and by special third element couriers, were laid at an assembly on August 28, just before teachers returned to their schools. According to police, revolutionary proclamations were handed out and an inflammatory speech delivered by a zemstvo teacher and SR, Pavel Vtorov, who shouted: "Long live liberty; let us have the same freedom with which was crowned our simpleton Kolia"—in other words, down with the autocracy.[56]

As had been true in the early 1900s, official reports for mid-1905 stress either the active encouragement of or acquiescence in the radical activities of zemstvo employees by zemstvo activists.[57] In Voronezh, where teachers had formed a section of the VSU in May, liberal zemtsy, aided by their third element allies, continued to promote teachers' political mobilization through the summer. A "congress" of teachers from several districts was held for this purpose at the zemstvo board in Valuiki on July 3, 1905, and on August 14–15 a larger gathering of Teachers' Union members met in Voronezh under the chairmanship of V. A. Kil'chevskii, a former member of the provincial zemstvo board. Here the aim was clearly to prepare a campaign of propaganda and peasant political organization for the upcoming autumn. When police broke up the assembly, large quantities of SR and Peasant Union literature were uncovered. Six persons, including Kil'chevskii and the Teachers' Union leader A. V. Kravchenko, were arrested. The provincial Okhrana remarked that there had already been isolated cases of revolutionary agitation by teachers in villages during the summer and expected this to intensify after the start of the school year.[58] A similar pattern emerges in Kursk province, the center of reactionary gentry politics after 1905. Here individual zemstvo liberals encouraged rural intelligenty to carry the Liberation Movement to the peasantry. This was true of Dolgorukov in Sudzha, as well as in Lgov district, where the chairman of the zemstvo board, N. V. Shirkov, personally spoke at village meetings in favor of the Peasant Union. At meetings in July, Shirkov instructed teachers how to conduct antigovernment propaganda among the narod. In September conservative critics in the Lgov zemstvo charged that Shirkov was organizing the third element and peasantry to seize gentry estates.[59] On June 29, 1905, in neighboring Shchigry district an assembly attended by some thirty teachers was convened by the liberal chairman of the zemstvo's education commission, I. A. Mikhailov. Teachers openly condemned the war with Japan and labeled the existing regime "parasitic"; they decided to organize a section of the Teachers' Union, headed by Mikhailov, and vowed to support the formation of peasant unions in the district. This gathering drew an angry response from a majority of Shchigry zemstvo deputies led by the ultrareactionary N. E. Markov and the local marshal of nobility, A. A. Shchekin. The unlucky Mikhailov was forced from office at an emergency session of the zemstvo in early August, where zemstvo men also condemned the VSU program, particularly its plank calling for removal of religion as a compulsory subject in the school curriculum. The "godless" teachers were given a stiff warning not to attempt to shake the peasants' religious faith.[60]

Thus, liberal zemstvo men, who had supported the teachers' movement before 1905, played a significant role in drawing their teacher-clients into the Liberation Movement. Indeed, at the local level liberal politics correlated to a great degree with Teachers' Union activity. The strongest union groups in Kursk were in Sudzha, Lgov, and Shchigry districts. Likewise in Balashov and Saratov districts (Saratov), where there had been a tradition of zemstvo liberalism and alliance with the third element, the union struck deep roots.[61] Moreover, during summer 1905 individual zemtsy and their third element allies were groping toward a more concerted campaign of peasant mobilization, embodied in the Peasant Union, an organization with close ties to the teachers' movement. Not surprisingly, one can see strong correlation between teacher and third element involvement in the Peasant Union movement and liberal zemstvo activism at the district level.[62]

Unfortunately, the liberals did not constitute anything like a majority within the zemstvos. The bulk of the zemstvo gentry was at heart conservative, temporarily swayed into political opposition under the circumstances of early 1905. As the revolutionary movement deepened, particularly in the countryside after October, zemstvos veered sharply to the right, and former leaders like Dolgorukov and Shirkov, many of whom joined the Kadet party, were repudiated by the rank and file. In other cases (for example, Depreis and the Urzhum zemstvo), zemstvos which had previously encouraged teachers to engage in politics did an about-face in autumn 1905, threatening with dismissal any teachers who engaged in political discussions with peasants. The sharp reaction in August within the Shchigry zemstvo against teachers and their liberal supporters was a harbinger of things to come.

Zemstvo response to an appeal for support from the Teachers' Union in early September, issued in advance of the regular zemstvo sessions, told a similar tale. Although it was obvious that most zemstvo deputies did not accept elements of the union program (four-tail franchise and a constituent assembly), teachers hoped that zemstvos would rally behind them in conflicts with officialdom. The VSU proclaimed its political goals and notified zemstvos that its members would refuse to comply with the "purely formalistic demands of school officials," would disregard all ministry restrictions on school curricula and rural libraries, and "in the selection of books and periodicals would pay attention only to the quality of the publications and the requirements of the narod." Zemstvos were asked to defend teachers in the event of official persecution by continuing to issue salaries to those dismissed. The union also urged zemstvos to accord teachers a greater voice in the formulation of education policy and in matters of appointments, transfers, and dismissals through formation of school commissions. In conclusion, the union declared the government totally bankrupt, incapable of satisfying the needs of the narod or restoring calm:

> The time has come for the zemstvo and municipal institutions to demonstrate before the country that they actually merit the trust and sympathy which they have enjoyed in such measure from progressive society. The Russian teacher will await with deep interest to learn whether he can count on zemstvo and city activists as friends and allies in the struggle for liberation and enlightenment of the motherland.

Taking into account the "political backwardness of our public institutions," the appeal to zemstvos was composed with great care. Nothing was said about democratization of local government itself.[63] Nevertheless, most zemstvo assemblies refused to discuss the document, to the profound disappointment of teachers attending the zemstvo sessions: "As if there had been no revolution, as if all remained of old."[64] Predictably, positive response to the appeal came from the more liberal (fewer than ten) district zemstvos.[65] In Vladimir province, for example, only the Kovrov zemstvo registered its support; here the assembly was swayed by the arguments of liberals such as N. P. Muratov, N. M. Iordanskii, and G. A. Smirnov, all of whom had been prominent in the zemstvo opposition and had established close ties with the radical third element. As in 1904 the Kovrov zemtsy voted to invite teachers' representatives to participate in zemstvo sessions and to form a school commission with teacher representation.[66] In the remaining districts of Vladimir, zemstvos either reacted negatively or were silent on the union communiqué. This was the case in other provinces as well.[67]

As with other contemporary observers, teachers had misread the realities of zemstvo politics, viewing their liberal patrons who spearheaded the legal opposition before autumn 1905 as representative of zemstvo sentiment at the grass roots. As late as August 1905 the chairman of the Smolensk Teachers' Society could confidently predict widespread zemstvo support of activist teachers: "In the course of this past year Russia has experienced more than it has in the course of previous decades . . . the views of many public activists have radically shifted in recent times and now we will scarcely find in Smolensk province a zemstvo which would look upon teachers as chimney sweeps *(trubochisty)* as happened in the past."[68] In fact, the rank-and-file zemstvo gentry more readily subscribed to Pleve's view of the third element as usurping zemtsy prerogatives in zemstvo management and threatening the rural social order. This group was already moving to the right. Disturbed by the specter of revolution and placated by government concessions, such as the August 6 decree announcing elections to a consultative Duma elected by limited franchise as well as the end of the war, moderate and conservative zemstvo men began to desert their former liberal leaders and rally behind the forces of law and order.[69] This incipient zemstvo reaction became full blown after nationwide strikes in October, further official concessions in the October Manifesto, and the agrarian movement of autumn.

As the zemstvos moved to the right during the latter months of 1905, teachers moved leftward. This was reflected in heightened opposition to the Old Regime, including the *tsenzovye* zemstvos; identification with popular demands for radical social and economic reforms; and increased involvement in peasant political mobilization, most forcefully around the program of the All-Russian Peasant Union. Something should be said here concerning this organization, for as teachers became disillusioned over the prospects for moral and material support from the zemstvos during autumn 1905, they came to rely more heavily on mass organizations in the countryside, above all the peasant unions. Indeed, the fate of the teachers' movement was linked to that of mass organizations in the village.

The Peasant Unions and the Teachers' Movement

The idea of a peasant union—a corollary to the intelligentsia *soiuzy* capable of drawing the rural masses into the Liberation Movement against the autocracy—had been implicit in the program of the Union of Liberation and its offspring, the Union of Unions. Initial efforts in this direction came in late spring 1905 after the government acts of February 18, which, as we have seen, engendered peasant discussion of political and other issues (the *prigovor* campaign) while at the same time facilitating propaganda in the countryside by teachers and others. Peasant political organization followed naturally from this process of articulation of peasant needs.

The immediate impetus for the formation of peasant unions came in Moscow province in response to a conservative campaign engineered by the governor and gentry marshal Samarin to elicit patriotic addresses from the peasantry. This plan proved a fiasco. Peasant delegates who gathered in Moscow on May 5 were unwilling to adhere to loyalist resolutions; instead they adopted demands for a constitution and other reforms proposed by liberal and radical intellectuals grouped around the Moscow Agricultural Society and third element people connected with local zemstvo institutions. To achieve their aims the Moscow delegates endorsed the formation of an All-Russian Peasant Union "for self-defense from the exactions and violence [perpetrated] by any authority not elected by the population itself."[70]

During the early summer months Peasant Union groups began to coalesce in the provinces, largely in the district and provincial centers (organizations at the volost and village level were, in general, formed during the autumn, the result of increased agitation after the October Manifesto). In most cases initiative belonged to intelligenty, primarily third element people of varied political persuasions, and to the more "conscious," literate (and often younger) peasants.[71]

A number of zemstvos during the summer actively sought to involve peasant representatives in discussion of the agrarian and other questions, which facilitated peasant organization in some places. Commonly this took the form of expanding the composition of "economic" or "agricultural" sovety attached to zemstvo executive boards to include peasant communal delegates for open discussion of political and socioeconomic issues with zemstvo activists. In many cases the doors were thrown open to the public and sessions were attended by third element employees including rural teachers, many of whom spent summer vacation in district towns. Expansion of zemstvo sovety in this fashion took place in a series of provinces: Saratov, Moscow, Vladimir, Riazan, Tver, Tauride, Iaroslavl, Kazan, Kherson.[72] In Kovrov district the local zemstvo set up sessions of the "economic council" in the larger villages; at these meetings zemtsy, intelligenty, and peasants discussed a variety of issues: political reform, peasant legal status, education, and, of course, the land question.[73] In the Ukraine liberal zemstvo men utilized local agricultural societies in much the same way—opening the doors to peasants and others and expanding deliberations well beyond the routine business of farm machinery and the like.[74]

This phenomenon was unprecedented in the history of the zemstvos and represented a high watermark in the zemstvos' movement "to the people." Just three years earlier zemstvo men had been hesitant to involve peasants in the deliberations of Witte's Local Committees on the Needs of Agriculture. But the situation in 1905 was markedly different with the onset of a spontaneous and threatening agrarian movement, imminent political change, and the prospect of mass politics. In the face of these conditions many zemstvo men recognized the need to open a dialogue with the peasantry, both to elicit peasant opinion on reform and to attempt to steer the peasant movement into moderate, peaceful channels. Hence, many zemstvos were willing to open their doors in summer 1905.

As it turned out the expanded sessions of zemstvo "economic councils" and similar meetings proved to be excellent forums for the articulation of peasant *and* third element demands, many of which went beyond the agenda of the liberals, to say nothing of mainstream zemstvo gentry opinion; they also aided the political mobilization of the peasantry. Recounting a meeting of the Petrovsk (Saratov) zemstvo's "economic council" in June is illustrative. Attended by nearly two hundred representatives of rural communes as well as third element intelligenty (including teachers), this gathering adopted a radical resolution including demands for democratization of local self-government, a constituent assembly, and abolition of private landholdings. The participants formed a peasant union.

The liberal Saratov provincial zemstvo immediately endorsed the actions of the Petrovsk council and the notion of peasant unions as a means of "weakening the mounting class antagonism that threatens to turn into civil war." As noted above, zemstvo men in other locales supported the Peasant Union movement and encouraged their third element clients, including rural teachers, to propagate the union's program in the villages. It appears that such encouragement was a factor in the increasing political activism displayed by rural intelligenty. But the Petrovsk meeting had other consequences, ominous for the future of peasant political organizations and for the efforts of intelligenty to promote them. A special session of the Petrovsk zemstvo assembly was called, and the gentry landowners repudiated the actions of their own elected *uprava*, the members of which then resigned. A new, conservative board was then elected, signaling a fundamental turnabout in zemstvo policy in the district. In protest a mass resignation of zemstvo employees followed (at least one teacher was dismissed for taking part in the council session).[75] The zemstvo reaction in

Petrovsk, like the response of the Shchigry zemtsy to secularization of schooling and "godless" teachers, as well as the cool response of zemstvos to the Teachers' Union's September appeal, was a sign of things to come.

As for the Peasant Union, the organizing efforts of early summer resulted in a congress in Moscow (July 31–August 1) attended by more than one hundred peasant delegates from twenty-eight provinces, as well as some twenty-five intelligenty.[76] Certainly this gathering cannot be considered strictly representative of rural opinion; as one Union leader remarked, the peasant delegates tended to be drawn from the more literate, politically conscious elements, the so-called "peasant intelligentsia."[77] Neither can the Peasant Union be dismissed as not reflecting "genuine peasant" interests, as was charged by the conservative press, which labeled the congress a gathering of lawyers, journalists, and other intellectuals.

Such assertions were disproved by the union's subsequent success in striking roots in the countryside. For the Peasant Union offered a program calculated to appeal to wide strata of the peasantry. At the head of the agenda was the land question, and on this issue all delegates at the Moscow congress agreed that private landholdings should be abolished and that state, church, and gentry holdings should be transferred to the peasantry. Concerning compensation for private holdings, the delegates settled on a compromise formula: "Land must be confiscated from private owners partly with compensation, partly without." This resolution reflected no concern for gentry estates, only holdings purchased by peasants.

Final disposition of the land question, the delegates reasoned, would be left to a constituent assembly elected by four-tail franchise. As for the future political order, a constitutional monarchy was favored. A suggestion by an SD representative that the congress demand a democratic republic was rejected in deference to the peasantry's traditional reverence for the person of the tsar. Demands for civil freedoms, as well as free, compulsory education were included in the union's program.

On the question of tactics, the congress adopted a moderate line. There was no mention of land seizures or other forms of direct revolutionary action against *pomeshchiki* or government officials. Instead, the congress advocated boycotts of rural officials and land captains and political agitation. This was essentially a continuation of the petition campaign that had begun during the spring, linked with efforts to organize local peasant unions in order to bring maximum pressure to bear on the government.

When the Peasant Union convened its second congress in Moscow in early November the delegates displayed a somewhat more militant mood. By this time agrarian riots had become widespread, especially in the Black Earth and Volga regions, and the government applied military force to restore order. Some delegates, particularly those from Saratov, where the agrarian movement was strong and violent and where the peasant unions were dominated by the SRs, called for revolutionary land seizures and armed insurrection, not waiting for the problematical convention of a constituent assembly. But the majority still hoped for a nonviolent solution to peasant land hunger. While holding out the threat of insurrection as a last resort, they called for a stepped-up campaign of political organization and agricultural strikes, refusal to pay taxes or give recruits as means to counter government repression.[78]

In broad terms this was the program and tactical line that activist teachers would support during the latter months of 1905. These peaceful, nonrevolutionary methods of struggle against the Old Regime were fully consistent with those outlined at the June congress of the Teachers' Union and with the efforts at political enlightenment that teachers had been pursuing in the countryside since spring. Like the Teachers' Union the Peasant Union was essentially a nonconspiratorial, nonrevolutionary organization premised upon the conditions of "semilegality" pertaining in 1905 (this was particularly true after the government's apparent concession of civil freedoms in the October Manifesto). As was the case with the Teacher's Union this was both a source of strength (in terms of agitation and recruitment) and a fatal weakness, since such fairly open organizations required a measure of tolerance from the authorities or a situation of administrative disarray. As such, both unions were vulnerable to a concerted campaign of repression, particularly local Teachers' Union groups bereft of zemstvo support.

The moderate tactics of the Peasant Union were suited to the teachers' movement for another reason. Teachers distrusted spontaneous peasant activism. Peasant violence, spurred on by hunger, poverty, and ignorance *(temnota),* might turn from the landlord's estate to the school or zemstvo hospital. As a cultural activist, the teacher was suspicious of an elemental peasant movement that might sweep all "culture" away with the old order. There were still strong cultural, social, and ideological barriers between the narod and the rural intelligentsia, and there was no sure way of predicting in which direction popular fury might turn. The wave of anti-intelligentsia agitation of early 1905 served as a sobering reminder.

Aside from tactical considerations, the Peasant Union program was well suited to teachers. By and large it included the major political demands of the democratic intelligentsia, including democratization of education. The Peasant Union's sharp animus against officialdom was shared by teachers who labored under many of the same legal disabilities as peasants. Most significant, the union offered the peasantry a solution to the land question sufficiently radical to appeal to broad strata of the peasantry (in some locales peasant unions adopted a more radical stance, rejecting any compensation for private holdings). According to an estimate in *Syn otechestva* in early September, local organizations of the Peasant Union already existed in forty-two provinces, boasting some 100,000 members.[79] Still in its embryonic stage, the Peasant Union held out to the teachers' movement the promise of mass popular support in the face of growing zemstvo reaction and government repression.

Therefore, it is not surprising that politically active teachers threw themselves into agitational and organizational activity on behalf of the Peasant Union or that the bureau of the Teachers' Union, in September 1905, alerted its members to the significance of this organization.[80] In some locales (for example, Iaroslavl) teachers' unions were directly responsible for initiating peasant unions.[81] Support for the Peasant Union, it should be noted, came from nonparty teachers as well as adherents of the revolutionary parties, and amid the sharpening social and political conflicts of late 1905 the Peasant Union became the sheet anchor of the teachers' movement.

When teachers returned to their schools at the start of the 1905–6 school year in September, many were already committed to the tasks of popular political enlightenment and decided to place regular classroom work on a lower order or priority. More would arrive at this decision in the ensuing months. How many did so is another question. Affiliation with the Teachers' Union provides only an approximate indication of activism in 1905. In early June the VSU encompassed some 5,000 teachers and by the start of the school year in September had 7,000 members organized in 400 locals. Nonteachers, by necessity, played a leading role in the union, but the overwhelming majority of adherents were teachers in rural schools.[82] This represented only a fraction of those teaching in Russia's schools, and membership in 1905–6 never exceeded 13,000 to 14,000. Nor did these constitute a particularly well-organized army of political activists. Links between the bureau in St. Petersburg and provincial groups were, at best, tenuous, and the situation was only slightly better in the central provinces after the formation in late summer of a Moscow Regional Bureau. As for the rank and file, they were consistently negligent when it came to paying union dues, which jeopardized the union's ability to render basic services, such as aid to members repressed for political activity.[83] In general, the Teachers' Union shared the amorphousness that was endemic to the political-professional unions of 1905, with the exception of the Unions of Railwaymen and Post-Telegraph Employees, which benefited from control of the communications networks.

Still, the Teachers' Union represented a significant force of activists committed to the aims of professional organization and bringing the Liberation Movement to the masses. Adherence to the union was a decision not taken lightly. As a teacher from Pskov wrote to the Central Bureau, "the majority of rural teachers, as usual, trembles before the well-known directive of the minister of July 21 not to participate in any unions or assemblies whatsoever."[84] The union tended to represent the cream of politically conscious and militant teachers, with the partial exception of those who refused to join because they agreed with the Social Democrats' assessment of its political platform or those who formed national organizations in the borderlands. But teacher involvement in the Liberation Movement was not limited to adherents of the VSU. The scope of repression against teachers after autumn 1905 belies such an assumption. For every teacher who consciously embraced the union's program, including political propaganda among the rural masses, there were probably one or two others sympathetic to reform or revolution, who by force of circumstances actively abetted the growth of popular opposition.

The mood among teachers in September 1905 was unprecedented. A thirty-two-year old teacher in Volchansk district (Kharkov), Fedor G. Nikol'skii, remembered how he and his colleagues gathered in town as they did each year to receive the necessary school supplies from the zemstvo. "There was discussion of political themes and all discussion led to one conclusion: We can no longer live like this (*tak zhit' nel'zia*)." The Volchansk teachers, noted Nikol'skii, remained in town longer than usual to discuss a plan of agitation among the peasantry. Accepting that the peasants' faith in the tsar was too strong to be attacked, they decided to explain to the narod that only political reform could assure a solution to the problems of peasant poverty and ignorance. They vowed to concentrate their agitation against the landowners and bureaucracy and to work for the political organization of the peasantry. On the road back to their villages, Nikol'skii and the teacher of a neighboring school, I. F. Stepanenko, decided not to begin work in the classroom but "to give themselves wholly to the work outlined at the [teachers'] assembly."[85] They felt that momentous change was imminent, and they were right, though the catalyst was provided not by the countryside but by the revolutionary movement in the cities.

8. October and Its Aftermath

Rural Teachers and Peasant Revolution

Relative quiet reigned in the Russian countryside during September and early October 1905. The agrarian movement, which brought arson, illegal timber cuttings and pasturing, destruction of landowner's property, had affected various parts of the country since spring but reached a low ebb as peasants brought in the harvest.[1] In many regions the harvest would be poor, contributing to a steep rise in peasant activism against gentry estates from mid-October.[2] Political activity among the peasantry also increased dramatically during the same period, under the impact of the revolutionary movement in the cities.

In the towns, and along the rails that connected them, there was considerable ferment in late summer and early autumn. The urban proletariat, from factory operatives to printers, remained restive. Political demands added a sharp edge to workers' economic grievances, and this period saw a rash of strikes, most notably a walk-out by typesetters which shut down newspapers in Moscow for two weeks in late September. The student movement was again on the rise, the result of an ill-considered decision to reopen the universities at the end of August and grant them autonomy.

For much of educated society the regime's concession of a consultative national assembly elected on a limited franchise—weighted in favor of the possessing classes and the presumably loyal peasantry, and disenfranchising much of the intelligentsia and working class—was unacceptable. Conservative elements decided to participate in elections to this emasculated Duma. For them the revolution had ground to a merciful halt. Liberal opinion, including the zemstvo left and moderate elements in the intelligenty unions, adopted a compromise position: they would contest the elections but only with the aim of transforming the Duma into a legislative organ based on a democratic franchise. For much of the intelligentsia, however, including a majority in the Union of Unions, the Bulygin Duma was unacceptable.[3] For them the revolution had not run its course, and there was talk of a general political strike to force further concessions from the regime. Teachers shared this view. The Central Bureau of the VSU condemned the August 6 law, noting that it would disenfranchise most teachers and "insulate elections in the peasant curia from intelligentsia influence, leaving officials an open field for intimidation." Some bureau members argued for participation but with the goal of struggling for a constituent assembly elected on a four-tail franchise.[4] Most teachers in the provinces, however, insisted on an unconditional boycott. The union's Samara section, for example, on August 17 denounced the Duma law as "an attempt to deceive society and quash the mounting revolutionary movement."[5]

This ruse, as the Samara teachers predicted, was in vain, for during the second week of October urban Russia went on strike: the factory proletariat, intelligentsia, and, most importantly, the railwaymen, who by October 14–15 had halted traffic on most of the country's rail network.[6] Teachers in city schools joined the movement. In St. Petersburg a strike was organized by the VSU, the Secondary Teachers' Union, and a Social Democratic Union of City Teachers formed in September by teachers who had walked out of the June congress over the platform issue. The decision to strike was adopted at an assembly of some 1,000 teachers (including 500 from primary schools) held at the university on October 14, and all 350 city schools closed.[7] In Moscow the "corporation" of city teachers joined other city employees in the general strike. Teachers' strikes affected other cities as well.[8]

Under this pressure, and on the advice of many of his closest advisors, Nicholas II put his signature to the Manifesto of October 17, promising to extend both the powers and franchise of the Duma as well as grant his subjects freedom of speech, assembly, and union. These promises would be only partially realized during the ensuing months in a spate of "temporary rules," decrees, and the Fundamental Laws of April 1906. For the moment the government was chiefly concerned with fracturing the opposition and pacifying recalcitrant elements. By and large urban society viewed the promised freedoms as immediately operative, and the more radical elements were bent on utilizing them, as well as the confusion of local authorities, to press further demands on the regime or organize openly for another round. Instead of calming the population, the October Manifesto had the effect of stimulating further political activity, particularly in the cities, where the "days of freedom" saw an orgy of agitation and grass roots social organization, as well as a breakdown of government censorship. In army garrisons, soldiers interpreted the manifesto as a signal that the old rules no longer applied, and discipline fractured, generating mutinous outbreaks through October-December. With the cities engulfed in revolution, peasants sensed that the regime's punitive capabilities had run out and viewed the October Manifesto as legitimating their just grievances against landlords and officials. The result was not only a massive agrarian movement against gentry property in November-December, but also intensive peasant political activity and organizing efforts.[9]

For teachers, the October Manifesto tended to reinforce the primacy of political over professional tasks and by no means signaled the end of revolution. Quite the contrary, for only a national assembly elected on a democratic franchise, reasoned teachers, could guarantee the kind of basic reforms in state and society outlined in the program of the Teachers' Union. Besides, the Duma electoral system, based on curia and disproportionate representation for the possessing classes, looked supiciously like that of the zemstvos, with which teachers were becoming disenchanted.

Promulgation of the manifesto had a dramatic effect, as well, on political activity in the village. A zemstvo employee in Poltava contrasted the initial tentative forays of the intelligentsia into village politics after February 18 with the massive activity after October 17,

> when the rural intelligentsia breathed more freely and believed, as did all moderate elements of Russian society, that a Rubicon had been crossed and there was no returning to the past. At that time the intelligentsia lived through a period of political romanticism, instinctively believing that all the principles of the October Manifesto would be realized in the very near future . . . naive, but this was a wonderful time![10]

The union's efforts to organize teachers intensified after October 17. The Central Bureau appealed to all teachers to utilize the new freedoms and adhere to the VSU. The Iaroslavl union assured teachers that political agitation among the rural masses was now legal and offered assistance, including "lecturers," in setting up peasant meetings.[11] Even local school officials wondered about the manifesto's significance. In Perm, the director of schools asked his superiors whether the ministry's June 21 ban on the union was still in effect, noting that many teachers "consider this issue already resolved and without vacillation or query are now joining the union."[12] In fact, the ranks of the Teachers' Union swelled during the ensuing weeks.[13]

In some cases, local notables encouraged teachers to take advantage of the new freedoms. In Lokhvitsa district (Poltava), for example, the gentry marshal and ex-officio school board chairman A. F. Rusinov urged that teachers conduct mass meetings in their schools to discuss the manifesto. When the Lokhvitsa teachers, who had organized a section of the Teachers' Union, heeded this advice and also began to agitate for the formation of peasant unions, the same Rusinov hurriedly ordered them to cease all political discourse with the peasants. Clearly he had hoped, through the medium of the teachers, to convince peasants to peacefully await the Duma and thus avoid the kind of agrarian movement then sweeping over gentry estates in other parts of the country. When teachers *and* peasants interpreted the government's concessions as sanctioning open political activity, including organization of the peasantry around a program of land nationalization, Rusinov, who owned 205 *desiatiny,* and the rest of the school board countermanded their original circular.[14]

Such encouragement from school boards, or even zemstvos, was rare, and the manifesto helped solidify the provincial gentry's retreat from liberalism. Nevertheless, autumn 1905 saw the most intensive political activity on the part of teachers during the revolutionary era, in the main because the burgeoning peasant political movement pressured teachers to become involved and because growing social polarizations in the countryside compelled them to take sides. A member of a union group in Petersburg province, which had organized as early as March, described the situation.

> After October 18 one noticed a special upsurge; our group arranged meetings to explain the freedoms of October 17, organized workers and peasants, explained the tasks of the Peasant Union and proper attitude toward the Duma. The population was extremely pleased with these gatherings; deputations would come to fetch teachers from 20–30 versts away, the peasants listened avidly, and the teacher became a genuine friend of the narod.[15]

But if teachers now plunged into the uncharted and turbulent sea of post-October politics, they did so at great peril, without compass and buffeted by fierce crosswinds. Not only did the autocracy's concessions arouse diehard monarchist elements, but also teachers could no longer rely on former patrons and benefactors in the zemstvos. Instead, they and other rural intelligentsia, sought an ally and sheet anchor in an organized, "conscious" peasant movement pursuing a democratization of state and society in keeping with their own vision. Peasant activism in late 1905, however, was varied and complex. As earlier in the year, some "dark" elements of the population actively opposed the political activities of progressive teachers, and in some forms the peasant movement ran counter to the tactics supported by teachers. Teachers were wary of spontaneous peasant violence directed against landowners, which, like an elemental flood, might sweep them away as well.[16] Rural teachers found themselves in a difficult and vulnerable position, caught between the Scylla of a peasant jacquerie and the Charybdis of a vengeful reaction. Both the promise and peril of the postmanifesto situation were already evident when teachers came together for the first time since the June congress.

Charting a Course: The Moscow Regional Teachers' Congresses

At the very moment the October general strike ended in partial victory, a regional congress of Teachers' Union delegates met in Moscow on October 21, 1905.[17] The mood of the gathering, understandably, was one of optimism, well conveyed in the opening speech of the educator Vasili Vakhterov, who spoke of the immense role teachers had played and were destined to play in the Liberation Movement. The late Viacheslav Pleve, who Vakhterov characterized as the "most bitter enemy of the teacher," had himself recognized the potential of teachers to awaken the consciousness of the popular masses and had once remarked that, although the regime had nothing to fear from the zemstvo opposition, the rural teacher posed a real threat. Now, argued Vakhterov, it was the task of teachers to imprint the principles of constitutionalism, "the alphabet of freedom and equality," on the minds of the population.[18]

Most of the provincial delegates readily accepted this challenge. A delegate from Nikolsk district (Vologda), for instance, noted that teachers there were conducting liberationist agitation and waging a campaign against the clergy focusing on the high fees priests charged peasants for the performance of religious rites. In Shuia district (Vladimir) teachers actively agitated among workers and peasants and used schools for public meetings. Indeed, after publication of the manifesto local factory owners had requested that teachers "explain these freedoms" to the population. Other delegates stressed teachers' vital role, noting that peasants were often confused by current events and did not comprehend the significance of the October Manifesto or were disappointed over the absence of any reference to the land question. The delegates declared the manifesto to be inadequate and vowed to continue the struggle for a constituent assembly.[19]

Reflecting past divisions, a few voices (from Mozhaisk, Vologda) spoke out against the political radicalism of the Teachers' Union and called for its reorganization along purely professional lines, supporting democratization of education and improvement in teachers' material and legal status. But the majority agreed that the time had not yet arrived when teachers could pursue only narrowly professional aims. Rather they concurred with V. G. Tan (Bogoraz), the populist writer and ethnographer representing the Peasant Union Bureau, on the need to deliver a final blow to the Tsarist regime. Tan commented on the recent show of strength by the political-professional *soiuzy* during the general strike but pointed out that victory would be assured only after this movement encompassed the peasant millions. Recounting the short history of the Peasant Union, he called upon teachers to help advance this movement among the rural masses.[20] The delegates unanimously expressed sympathy with the Peasant Union and resolved to convene a second congress in Moscow two weeks later, timed to coincide with the Second Congress of the Peasant Union opening on November 6, when teachers hoped to join forces with a mass peasant movement and coordinate tactics for the impending struggle.

When the Second Moscow Regional Teachers' Congress met on that date (with 130 delegates from twelve provinces) the question of organized peasant support for the teachers' movement had become more pressing than ever.[21] The aura of optimism that had characterized the October congress was already clouded. Administrative repression in the countryside seemed imminent, as government troops acting under conditions of martial law began restoring order in locales touched by agrarian disorders. In various places local authorities kept a vigilant eye on the rural intelligentsia, suspicious of any political activity—even explaining the October

Manifesto to the peasantry (cases of outright concealment of this document by local officials appear to have been widespread).[22]

Meanwhile the prospect of zemstvo support for teachers' political activity faded rapidly. This point was underscored in Moscow by a teacher from Pokrov district (Vladimir) who advised his confederates not to expect much support from local self-government. Zemstvo response to the union's September appeal in his native province was symptomatic of the growing reaction within these institutions: the Viaznikov and Gorokhovets zemstvos had refused to consider the appeal; the Melenkov zemstvo had threatened to dismiss within twenty-four hours any teacher who dared join the union, and so on. Only the liberal Kovrov zemstvo had responded favorably. Accordingly, the unidentified delegate recommended that teachers rely solely on the peasantry, advice echoed by another delegate: "We don't need any defense from the zemstvo; the narod, the peasantry—here is our defense."[23]

This was the dominant theme at the Moscow Regional Congress of November 6–8: the gathering had been convened specifically to cement formal ties with the Peasant Union as well as assess the strength of this organization at the grass-roots level (the highpoint of the teachers' meeting was a joint session with the peasant delegates scheduled for the evening of November 8).[24] The viability of the Peasant Union was of paramount importance to rural intelligenty. Vakhterov, for one, pointed to the historical significance of the peasant congress, which would demonstrate that "conscious peasants are not hostile to the best strivings of the intelligentsia, that they are not against cultural interests, that they, more painfully than we, feel the whole horror of *muzhik* ignorance and backwardness."[25]

But here was the dilemma: peasant ignorance was still a reality. The sociocultural gulf between the narod and the intelligentsia still existed and proved a stumbling block to the intelligentsia's attempts at popular political enlightenment. This was reflected in scattered instances of popular, "antiliberationist" reaction against the rural intelligentsia during the post-October 17 period, a disturbing echo of the black hundred manifestations and pogroms which swept numerous cities and towns within a week of the manifesto's publication. Here was the dark side of the peasant movement of 1905. Politically active teachers had to ask themselves how virulent this reaction was and how best to deal with it. Conversely, they had to gauge the strength of the "conscious" peasant movement and decide how this current could be promoted. The problem of a rural black hundred, at a time of government repression and the righting of zemstvo institutions, was the most troublesome issue addressed by the teachers who met in Moscow.

The dimensions of peasant reaction against the intelligentsia during autumn 1905 are not easy to assess. Delegates to the November congress in Moscow concurred that local officials, clergy, gentry marshals, and zemstvo representatives on school boards were attempting to exploit peasant backwardness and suspicion. Some reported outright hostility on the part of the peasantry toward "women teacher-nihilists" (*uchitel'nitsy-nigilistki*) and the zemstvo school.[26] Such reports are confirmed by the press. The Nolinsk (Viatka) section of the Teachers' Union reported widespread clerical agitation against teacher "rebels" (*smutiany*), and from Vesegon (Tver) came news that local police, at the instigation of the new governor Sleptsov, had begun a full-scale campaign of calumny against teachers. It was rumored that impending political reforms were nothing more than an attempt by the "gentlemen" (*gospoda*) to reinstate serfdom, and it was reported that teacher-peasant relations had worsened significantly. Teachers had turned to the zemstvo board for defense, warning that they would be forced to leave their posts if conditions did not improve. *Severnyi krai* reported in early November that in Iurevets district (Kostroma), "in view of the alarming mood of the masses, already involved in pogroms and physical violence, has come an epoch of emigration of teaching personnel." Equally ominous news came from Gorodnia (Chernigov) and Tiraspol (Kherson).[27] Similar reports issued from the Volga region. In Samara province teachers and other zemstvo employees had held political meetings with peasants (mostly Molokane sectarians) in the settlement of Orlov-Gai after publication of the manifesto. The Orthodox majority reacted strenuously to these activities, drawing up a communal petition that the intelligenty be dismissed and also threatening physical attacks on the teachers and veterinarian. In the village of Obsharovka (Samara district) a peaceful "demonstration" organized by local intelligenty to celebrate the act of October 17 was set upon by an angry crowd of allegedly drunken peasants. The teachers and a zemstvo physician barely escaped with their lives. Their posts were boycotted by the local section of the Teachers' Union, and the district zemstvo grudgingly agreed to support its employees in this affair.[28]

Peasant political reaction was also prevalent in Moscow province. This was the case in Volokalamsk district, where S. T. Semenov (the peasant writer, Tolstoyan and Peasant Union activist) wrote that peasant hostility toward the intelligentsia ran high after October and that peasants feared that "strikers" from Moscow would soon pillage their villages and that the manifesto was a ruse by the gentry.[29] In Bronnitsy district a local teacher attempted to gather peasants in the school to explain the October "freedoms." "I had no idea," he later recalled, "that the dark narod, under provocation, had gathered to subject me to a 'strike' (*ustroit' mne 'zabastovku'*), that is, to beat me and, possibly, kill me." Rumor spread through the district that peasants would be convened in the schools and hoodwinked into signing political statements: under the phrase "abolition of the existing state structure" was allegedly concealed one that read "return the narod to the old serf order." The upshot of this agitation was a full-scale attack on the zemstvo school in the village of Malyshevo on the evening of November 12 when the building was being used for a meeting of the Bronnitsy zemstvo employees' mutual aid society. The forty teachers and medical personnel who had assembled to discuss a plan of political agitation among the population narrowly escaped to a nearby railway station. The school was destroyed.[30] Here, at one disturbing level, was the culmination of decades of peasant-intelligentsia relations and the efforts of teachers and others to narrow the social and cultural gulf separating the two. These and other reports prompted the Central Bureau of the union to issue a special appeal to the peasantry, "Who Has Sown Disorder in Russia?" (*Kto poseial smutu na Rusi*), insisting that in reality it was the enemies of the peasantry who stood to gain by instigating such attacks on the intelligentsia; it also requested the Soviet of Workers' Deputies to exert a salutary influence on the village through its proletarian members' contacts there.[31]

As for the teacher-delegates in Moscow there was little agreement as to the significance of the black hundred phenomenon in the countryside. A good number of delegates claimed that such manifestations were either absent in their locales or that reactionary agitation was easily rebuffed by local teachers' organizations. I. S. Samokhvalov from Balakhnia district (Nizhegorod) positively denied the possibility of black hundred currents among the peasantry. Samokhvalov had come to Moscow directly from the town of Balakhnia, where he had attended a meeting of teachers on October 22. This assembly was attacked by a crowd of *meshchane*, petty-traders, artisans, and drivers (*izvozchiki*); one fatality resulted, and Samokhvalov himself rose to speak at the Moscow congress with his face bruised and eyes blackened. Producing on the audience, according to E. O. Vakhterova, "a terrible impression when he removed his dark glasses," this teacher of peasant origin insisted that the real narod, the "laboring peasantry" could not be implicated in the black hundred movement, which was the work of social riffraff and dregs bought by the authorities: "This is the last pitiful maneuver of the present regime, possible only in town. In the village, among the peasantry, I am always in complete safety."[32]

Samokhvalov spoke with passion, but much of the evidence did not support his contention. Most delegates tended to agree with I. N. Sakharov, who, while admitting that opposition to the Liberation Movement existed among the rural masses, drew a sharp distinction between the phenomenon in its urban and rural guises. In the city the black hundreds were clearly recruited from declassé elements by the police and other diehard supporters of the Old Regime. Distrust of the Liberation Movement among the "unconscious" part of the peasantry, contended Sakharov, was a more complicated matter:

> Here we are dealing with one of the most awesome and unresolved legacies of our past, the spiritual abyss between the peasantry and intelligentsia. We bear no guilt in this, but we must carefully wrestle with the problem—artificially contrived ignorance on the part of the narod and its alienation from the best forces of the country.

Sakharov then went on to assure his listeners that the interests of the narod and the intelligentsia were the same. Both required civil freedoms. "We must acquaint the population with our ideals and must struggle for its interests; surety that this will be crowned with success is provided by the Peasant Union which will go hand in hand with us."[33]

Accepting that even the most credulous and "dark" peasant could be weaned from black hundred sympathies, the congress adopted a resolution reiterating that the political education of the masses was the teacher's main task. The delegates also empowered the Moscow Bureau of the Union to request the printers' union not to set type for reactionary newspapers like *Den'*, *Moskovskiia vedomosti*, and *Kievlianin*. This decision drew fire from the moderate "thick journal" *Vestnik Evropy*, which charged censorship from the left, warning teachers to take heed of the significance of free speech.[34] But such platitudes were irrelevant to teachers who blamed the reactionary press for helping foment anti-intelligentsia agitation since the beginning of 1905.

The threat of government reprisals, zemstvo reaction, and black hundred manifestations also reinforced the nonparty, "progressive" character of the Teachers' Union. At both Moscow Regional Congresses delegates concurred that the political coloration of literature and oral propaganda was up to the discretion of local groups and individual teachers. G. A. Sokolov remarked that in Vladimir province most union groups approached the masses on sociopolitical issues in an SR vein, but there were also zealous Social Democrats among union members.[35] In general SR sympathies appear to have been strong at the November congress. But when fifty delegates tried to push through a resolution formally endorsing the program of the PSR, this was rejected. It was argued that such a move would destroy the very essence of the union, alienating not only members of the "other party" (SDs) but also those "wavering elements" which felt comfortable only in a nonparty organization. Sakharov rebuked the SRs for having so soon forgotten the attempt by their socialist rivals to seize the union. Given the imminent Armageddon between the "democratic" forces in Russian society and supporters of the Old Regime, as well as the struggle for the hearts and minds of the narod, most delegates argued the need for cooperation among all progressive forces. As Vakhterov confidently stated, "struggle with the conditions which give rise to the black hundreds demands work in locales where no party has penetrated but where, surely, are representatives of the Teachers' and Peasant Unions."[36]

A majority of delegates at the Moscow congress were probably sympathizers, if not adherents, of the major socialist parties; likewise, a large percentage of Teachers' Union members had apparently moved in this direction during the course of 1905, if not before. But most teachers believed that the time for party differentiation had not yet arrived, particularly in the countryside, where peasants were little interested in the fine points of party doctrine. More basic tasks of political enlightenment were on the agenda in rural Russia, and these, teachers firmly believed, could best be met by broadly based organizations like the peasant unions, aided by kindred organizations of the rural intelligentsia.[37]

And teachers understood that tangible support for their own activities would have to come from organizations with mass support in the countryside and that the best chance for this was held out by the Peasant Union, not the political parties which, by and large, were still based in the towns. From Kaluga, L. F. Rvachev, a member of the Teachers' Union's Moscow Regional Bureau and a delegate to both congresses of the Peasant Union, recalled his and other teachers' affection for the PSR but also noted that while "the SRs were considered the peasant party, I must tell the truth that I never received a single tangible directive from them on how to unite peasants or how to work among them. The only reasonable directive concerned organization of peasant unions."[38] Therefore, as the correspondent for *Russkoe slovo* noted, the delegates' attention was riveted on the joint session with the Peasant Union Congress scheduled for the evening of November 8.[39]

Here teacher and peasant pledged mutual support: teachers promised to aid the growth of the Peasant Union through agitation at rural *skhody* and distribution of literature; peasant delegates promised to support activist teachers. A peasant from Chernigov put it in simple but dramatic fashion: "Let teachers not be afraid; if the government persecutes the teacher the *muzhik* will find a potato to sustain him."[40] Recognizing, in conclusion, that victory over the regime would be possible only through a combined effort of the peasantry, workers, and "laboring intelligentsia," the teacher and peasant delegates resolved to "struggle henceforth, hand in hand, for Russia's future, placing on their banner the demand of 'land and liberty' for all of the laboring narod."[41]

Teachers, Peasant Unions, and Rural Revolution

All sources agree that the post-October period saw the most intensive activity by teachers outside the classroom during the entire revolutionary period, from 1904 through Stolypin's coup d'état of June 3, 1907. Responding to peasants' heightened sensitivity to political developments, teachers explained the "freedoms" contained in the manifesto (and to some extent the content of the Manifesto of November 3 promising cancellation of redemption payments and increased activity by the Peasant Land Bank)[42] and helped interpret recent domestic news, not the least the Peasant Union Congress. Along with reports of peasant hostility toward the Liberation Movement and attacks on the intelligentsia, were many more instances in which peasants eagerly dispatched horses at communal expense to bring a *govorok* (that is, an informed teacher) to their village to conduct political discussions. Peasant interest in politics ran high, and school buildings were the scene of countless "meetings." Rural teachers were subjected to increased pressure to assume a political role in the village, and the teacher's stock was never higher.[43]

Following the lead of the Moscow Regional Congress of early November, teachers' organizations throughout the country endorsed the Peasant Union and called on their members to popularize its program among the rural masses. This was taken regardless of the political tendency of local groups or the affiliation of individual teachers. On November 20–21, for instance, an assembly of the Pskov Teachers' Society, in which SDs had considerable strength, donated 100 rubles to the local Peasant Union organization.[44] The Peasant Union was heartily endorsed on November 13 by a meeting of the Pokrov district (Vladimir) section of the VSU, which was one of the strongest in the country, boasting over one hundred members and most of the district's teaching personnel, with strong SR sympathies. At the meeting teachers were urged to return to their villages and agitate on the union's behalf—specifically, to induce peasants to adopt *prigovory* demanding confiscation of church, state, and, in part, private lands and free allotment of these to peasants on the basis of a "laboring norm"; introduction of a progressive income tax; abolition of political police and land captains; democratization of education; and convocation of a national assembly with full legislative powers. Concerning rural black hundreds, the Pokrov teachers resolved to "place themselves under the protection of conscious peasants and workers who understand that teachers are allies."[45] Similar considerations prompted teachers to endorse the Peasant Union in neighboring Iaroslavl, where at a teachers' congress in Rostov in mid-November a speaker assured his audience: "The Peasant Union is an invincible citadel; take refuge around it and you will be invincible."[46] The bureau of the Iaroslavl teachers' union urged all teachers to agitate in favor of the union and sent to all schools a sample communal *prigovor* outlining the Peasant Union's program.[47]

Vladimir and Iaroslavl lay in the Central Industrial Region, part of the northern non–Black Earth belt, where large-scale gentry farming was little developed and peasant land hunger and dependence on local estates was less pronounced than in the south. Here the peasant movement of 1905–6 generally assumed less destructive forms than it did in the arc of provinces stretching from the Volga, Central Agricultural Region, and Ukraine, which in autumn 1905 was the scene of widescale, largely spontaneous agrarian revolts directed primarily against *pomeshchik* property.[48] In the north activist teachers were primarily concerned with gathering popular support for the political and other demands of "progressive" society, as well as defense against the growing forces of political reaction in the countryside. Teachers therefore promoted the political demands of the Peasant Union, which they shared, as well as supported peasant tax protests and other tactics pursued by peasant organizations throughout the northern provinces.

Similar concerns motivated teacher support for peasant unions in the Black Earth region, but here the destructive nature of peasant revolution presented special problems and lent urgency to teachers' support of a "conscious" peasant movement.[49] In the south, as a consequence of intensified gentry agriculture and increasingly exploitative agrarian relations during the previous decade, peasant disorders, even insurrection, flared up in a majority of districts during autumn 1905, and teachers were compelled to face the issue of agrarian violence and its consequences. By and large, teachers were suspicious of spontaneous peasant activism for several reasons: it seemed fluid and unpredictable (peasant violence could be turned against the intelligentsia); it seemed counterproductive, inviting only massive government repression and jeopardizing the course of constitutional and other reforms.

The issue was joined in Ekaterinoslav province, where the Teachers' Union had struck deep roots and which was the scene of a sweeping agrarian movement in November-December 1905, much of it concentrated in Verkhnedneprovsk district, where sixty-six estates were razed. A meeting of the union's provincial organization was held on November 20 and attended by 175 persons. The SRs dominated the Ekaterinoslav union, and the issue of "agrarian terror" (spontaneous acts of violence such as arson) had evoked a good deal of controversy within the PSR. Like the majority of the SR leadership, the Ekaterinoslav teachers had strong reservations concerning the efficacy of such time-honored forms of peasant activism. The teacher Vazhnenko urged that teachers bend every effort to see that the peasant movement assume "cultured forms": "Agrarian terror is not needed as it leads to nothing except savage repression at the hands of government troops." Vazhnenko argued instead for further political enlightenment. Other teachers, pointing to the recent Peasant Union Congress in Moscow, suggested that teachers support the union's recommendations for "peaceful" struggle, for example, an agricultural boycott: "At the height of the agricultural season, when the *pomeshchik* is most in need of workers, no individual will be permitted to work . . . [thus] the landowner will be put in such a position that he will be unable to work more land than is possible for one person." These arguments were contested by Prokhor Diinega, the fiery SR railway school teacher who was destined to become a martyr to the Teacher's Union after being killed in late December in the armed insurrection along the Ekaterininskaia Railway. "One cannot speak of cultured, peaceful forms now," insisted Diinega; "if peasants refuse to pay taxes they will be suppressed by troops, and really, can the peasant who works one-fourth *desiatina* afford to sit and wait until things become difficult for the *pomeshchik?*" He argued that teachers work to organize peasant "cells" and prepare for "practical actions," in other words, organize the peasantry for insurrection. Diinega was immensely popular among the teachers of Ekaterinoslav, and his critical analysis of passive forms of peasant struggle and their consequences had much merit. Still, a majority of the

Ekaterinoslav teachers endorsed the more moderate tactics of the Peasant Union and resolved to promote its growth by all means.[50]

Likewise in Volchansk district (Kharkov) politically active teachers adhering to the VSU sought to promote peasant demands through enlightenment and organization. In his unpublished memoir, Fedor Nikol'skii recalled his trip back to his school from the district town where he had attended a teachers' meeting in early November. On the road he met a caravan of peasant carts loaded with grain and implements taken from the estate of the local gentry marshal, which they had also put to the torch. The teacher "burst out with a thunderous speech in which I pointed out to the crowd that the buildings had great value, as did the machinery, etc. But the peasants replied that these things could go the devil (*Da nu ikh k 'bisu'*)." Nikol'skii was dismayed at the destruction involved in the agrarian movement in Volchansk, which reached a high point in late November. Until his arrest in December and exile to Siberia, ironically for "incitement to agrarian disorders," he doggedly continued in his attempts to impart some form of organization to the peasant movement, traveling from village to village, persuading peasants to sign *prigovory* demanding radical agrarian reform to be enacted by a constituent assembly.[51] An activist from Poltava explained the rural intelligentsia's support for the Peasant Union in terms of its desire "to paralyze spontaneous outbursts and convince peasants of the efficacy of legal struggle," pointing out that this concern cut across a wide political spectrum. "Only in this way can one explain the heterogeneous leadership of local Peasant Unions, in terms of social, professional and political orientation, which included landowners, teachers, priests, doctors, Kadets, SDs, SRs and, above all, nonparty people."[52]

Most Peasant Union organizing at the village and volost level took place during November-December 1905. News of the November 6–10 congress filtered down to the locales (its sessions were widely reported in the press), and the arrest a few days later of the union's bureau merely served to enhance its authority among the rural population.[53] Throughout the country rural intelligenty, particularly teachers, played an important role in disseminating information about the union and in agitating for formation of local organizations.[54] Indeed, there was a strong correlation between involvement in this movement and in the Teachers' Union.[55] In Ekaterinoslav province, for example, a majority of the Teachers' Union activists also conducted propaganda on behalf of the Peasant Union. Of twenty-nine persons brought to trial for Peasant Union activity in Ekaterinoslav in autumn 1905, nine were rural teachers, seven of whom were peasants by origin.[56]

Ekaterinoslav was not unique in this regard. In the Peterhof district of Petersburg, teachers and medical personnel, according to the police, acted as the main propagandists of the Peasant Union. Here fourteen zemstvo teachers were indicted, and most were brought to trial in 1907 in the affair of the Northern Bureau of Assistance to the Peasant Union, an organization with close links to the VSU. Member of the Teachers' Union Central Bureau, Kir'iakov, Miakotin, and Charnoluskii, played leading roles in the Northern Bureau, where they directed much of the Peasant Union's publishing efforts.[57] In Volokalamsk (Moscow) rural teachers were primarily responsible for Peasant Union agitation,[58] and in Sumy district (Kharkov), where the union struck deep roots during 1905, the start of 1906 saw a full-scale purge of third element personnel which included the dismissal or arrest and exile of thirty-one rural teachers. Similar evidence comes from Voronezh province.[59] Lists of rural agitators slated for arrest during December in Vladimir province—most for Peasant Union activity—contain the names of peasants, zemstvo employees, the radical zemstvo activist and landowner S. V. Bunin, but especially teachers.[60]

Their prominence underlay official allegations that the Peasant Union, in fact, did not represent the interests of "genuine" peasants but of radical elements alien to the narod. As early as November 17, 1905, three days after the arrest of union leaders in Moscow, D. F. Trepov reported to Tsar Nicholas that the Peasant Union was clearly a revolutionary organization and constituted a grave threat to the regime. Nevertheless, in the same breath he asserted that its political program was alien to the peasantry, arguing that if the intelligenty activists of the union were sometimes successful in inducing peasants to sign statements adhering to this program, such was actually accomplished by deceit and exploitation of peasant illiteracy. On November 23, Minister of Interior P. N. Durnovo alerted governors to the "special danger" posed by the union as compared even with the revolutionary parties. Durnovo urged his lieutenants to issue proclamations to the rural population unmasking the Peasant Union as an organization of the "professional intelligentsia."[61]

There was little substance to these claims. The union struck roots in the countryside in a remarkably short time—estimates place membership at a minimum of 200,000 by year's end—and its program addressed a wide range of peasant interests. The success of the union can be ascribed to its program, which meshed vital peasant demands (above all, for a massive transfer of land into peasant hands) with the demands of the radical intelligentsia and liberal zemstvo activists for political reform: a constituent assembly, or at least national assembly, elected on a more democratic franchise than the government's projected Duma. Furthermore, the Peasant Union addressed many broad issues of interest to peasants and rural intelligenty as well as teachers: removal of various legal disabilities, fundamental democratization of local institutions (for example, zemstvos), diminution of bureaucratic controls (both peasant and teacher harbored keen hatred for various *nachal'stva*), and democratization of public education.[62] The Peasant Union offered a framework to bridge the cultural and social gulf, as well as suspicion, that often separated the narod and the intelligentsia. The Peasant Unions were not so much "nonpeasant," as Durnovo and Trepov alleged, as the nucleus of a progressive coalition of liberals, third element radicals, and "conscious" peasants, a rural Liberation Movement which had already begun to enlist a mass constituency. Teachers rallied behind them because of their potential, program, moderate tactics, and because the Peasant Unions seemed to embody the Russian teachers' movement's professional ethos of public activism.

Aside from branding the union as nonpeasant, the government went one step further, claiming that Peasant Union activists, teachers in particular, were responsible for widescale propaganda directed toward a forceful seizure of private landholdings and armed insurrection against the state. This point was driven home to local officials as early as November 30, 1905, in a coded telegram from MVD Durnovo to provincial governors. Durnovo issued a more urgent circular on December 16. In it he pointed out that in recent years the ranks of zemstvo employees had been increasingly filled with "politically unreliable" elements.

> These persons adhered to revolutionary organizations, and utilizing their proximity to the urban, and also the peasant and factory population, are occupied with strenuous antigovernment propaganda, not shrinking from any means, including armed insurrection. Undoubtedly, such activity must have a huge bearing on the successful appearance throughout the empire of strikes and also widespread peasant riots and agrarian disorders.

Durnovo instructed his deputies to pay special attention to the political activities of zemstvo statisticians, lower medical personnel, and teachers, recommending that local authorities apply the "most decisive measures" to remove from service third element personnel suspected of antigovernment activity.[63]

Such a view—that rural intelligenty and Peasant Union activists contributed significantly to the crescendo of agrarian disorders at the end of 1905—were strongly buttressed by most provincial governors, who singled out the Peasant Union and ascribed special significance to revolutionary agitation by teachers and medical personnel who were encouraged and protected by sympathetic liberals in the zemstvo boards.[64] Frightened landowners addressed urgent pleas to the government that seditious teachers be ferreted out and dealt with summarily. In response to one such appeal from Ekaterinoslav, Durnovo informed the newly appointed minister of education, I. I. Tolstoi, that "the widespread agrarian disorders in Bakhmut district have their roots in the criminal agitation of rural teachers, who, not meeting sufficient opposition from the inspectorate, strive to pursue among the peasantry the program of the revolutionary Peasant Union."[65]

From such reports comes an imposing degree of conservative and official consensus as to the revolutionary influence exerted by teachers on the rural masses after October, a consensus which, by the way, stands in marked contrast to the absence of reference to such influence in official evaluations of peasant unrest earlier in the year.[66] Reminiscent of the period immediately following the agrarian disorders of spring 1902, the rural teachers were considered "seditious" by definition, and even the most modest political activities, for example, reading and explaining the October Manifesto, fell under a cloud of suspicion. The result, as will be seen below, was a crushing wave of repression which affected thousands of teachers indiscriminately, officials failing to draw a distinction between acts as dissimilar as participation in peasant political meetings and open incitement to seize *pomeshchik* property.[67] Against the backdrop of agrarian disorders and consequent repression under martial law, *any* political activity on the part of rural intelligenty might be construed as *bunt*, and the historian must be wary of relying on official sources in characterizing teachers' activities during this period. Events in Tambov district provide a case in point.

As was true of much of the Central Black Earth region, Tambov was the scene of destructive peasant activism; troops were dispatched to put down disorders as early as late October. By the end of November some 130 estates had been sacked and looted (20 in Tambov district), including that of V. M. Petrovo-Solovovo, the local gentry marshal and zemstvo man who claimed losses of 130,000 rubles. The province was placed under martial law on December 9, 1905.[68] As elsewhere, the movement in Tambov was the result of various factors: a history of landowner-peasant conflict marked by exploitative lease arrangements and peasant land hunger, recent poor harvests, and news of revolutionary events in the cities.

There was little evidence, however, of revolutionary agitation by local teachers. Nevertheless, five zemstvo teachers in Tambov district were arrested and dismissed in November by overzealous authorities intent on stamping out sedition. The most damning evidence adduced against them was reading the October Manifesto during public readings in school on Sunday, and the fact that only five teachers suffered for such activity owed to the intercession of the local inspector, Tikhon E. Ostroumov, who resisted attempts by the regular administration to dismiss teachers on the flimsiest of evidence for political unreliability.[69]

For his efforts Ostroumov was himself exiled from Tambov on orders of Governor-General Klaver, and only after petitioning the minister of education and the tsar was he partially vindicated, securing a post in another province. The local zemstvo actively aided the authorities in their purge of rural teachers and resisted all attempts to restore the dismissed to their posts after their release from jail on lack of evidence. In his annual report to the Tambov district zemstvo assembly for 1905–6, which the zemstvo subsequently suppressed, Ostroumov recalled the situation in late 1905, vividly describing the countervailing pressures to which teachers were subjected during the revolution.

> For teachers the past year was one of exceptional trials. Part of society and the administration, seeing the troubles experienced as the result of ill-intentioned

> agitation by individuals, naturally cast its suspicious and hateful glance at the teacher. The teacher stands close to the dark narod and enjoys its trust. And so he is guilty because the narod incorrectly understood the manifesto and set off for the grain stores of the landowners. The agrarian disturbances resulted from agitation and the natural agitator among the peasants is the rural teacher. Thus the merciless persecution of teachers for the slightest cause, or without cause. They were charged with simply reading the precious words of the Tsar about freedom to the peasants, they were deprived of freedom for the fact that they talked about it with several adult peasants who came to the school, they all fell under grave suspicion for only their title (*zvanie*): teacher![70]

Repression for essentially moderate political activities, which seemed fully consistent with the October Manifesto, indeed discussion of the manifesto itself, was apparently widespread.[71] It was enough to prompt the acting head of the Petersburg school district, V. A. Latyshev, to complain to the Department of Police about the heavy-handed measures applied by local officials against teachers. Latyshev noted that at the "present difficult time of transition" peasants commonly approached teachers to help explain manifestoes "which undoubtedly contain ideas new and incomprehensible for rural dwellers, who at the same time are bombarded with revolutionary leaflets which appear everywhere." "Teachers," wrote Latyshev, "have not the slightest chance of avoiding the basic questions occasioned by the reforms," and by persecuting them for such activities the government was merely creating new recruits for the revolutionary movement.[72] In his unpublished reminiscences of his brief tenure as minister of education, I. I. Tolstoi noted that a significant minority of teachers, of both sexes, had been involved in the political ferment of the past year, "appearing naturally as interpreters (*istolkovateli*) of the ensuing liberation movement among the dark peasantry and sometimes as agitators of the most extreme socialist and anarchist teachings." But all teachers, noted Tolstoi, became suspect in the eyes of the authorities. Even the most innocent were subjected to dismissal and arrest, and local school officials were powerless to protect their charges from arbitrary actions by the regular administration.[73]

Tolstoi's assertion that many rural teachers acted as "interpreters" and purveyors of the radical tenets of the Peasant Union and the revolutionary parties finds support in the range of literature uncovered in police investigations of teacher-propagandists, as well as testimony by activists of the Teachers' Union.[74] Many teachers, certainly the majority of the Teachers' Union's membership, supported a radical solution to the land question and agitated on behalf of a transfer of large holdings into peasant hands, often without redemption to private owners. The prevalence of such agitation, as teachers moved leftward in late 1905, is incontestable, but the relationship between this agitation and peasant disorders is not as cut and dried as a Durnovo might have thought.

The Peasant Union was committed to radical land reform, but through nonviolent means. There had been considerable tension at the union's November congress over the question of tactics, with militants calling on the peasantry to "take up the cudgel" and seek a solution to the land question according to time-honored methods.[75] But a majority of delegates, while issuing the threat of peasant insurrection if a political solution to peasant land hunger could not be found, agreed on restraint. And the available evidence suggests that in the countryside the Peasant Union was actually a moderating influence, curbing spontaneous outbursts in favor of more organized tactics: nonpayment of taxes (including zemstvo levies), replacement of rural officials and police, agricultural strikes and boycotts of local landowners, including refusal to lease *pomeshchik* lands, and simply the compilation of communal *prigovory* adopting the union's program. One cannot rule out an indirect effect of Peasant Union agitation, or simply news of the organization's existence, on the incidence of agrarian disorders; after all, there were reports during this period that the October Manifesto's promise of "freedoms" was interpreted by peasants as freedom to settle old scores with neighboring landowners. But, in general, in those locales where the Peasant Union was strong there was a relative absence of destructive violence; indeed, cases of agrarian terror often increased *after* wholesale repression of local peasant organizations.[76]

Evidence from two provinces indicates that teachers supported continued political enlightenment, peasant organization, and nonviolent means of pressure against the government and ruling classes: Ekaterinoslav, an area of large estates in the rich Ukrainian steppe, and Vladimir, in the Central Industrial Region. In both provinces there had been considerable ferment among teachers since spring 1905 (the Teachers' Union was strong in each) and both witnessed intense political activity by teachers and other intelligenty at the end of 1905, mainly on behalf of the Peasant Union.

What makes Ekaterinoslav and Vladimir particularly interesting is that both were the scene of major, well-publicized trials of teachers and other Peasant Union agitators. Such political trials were rare; in most cases teachers were summarily dismissed, arrested, and often exiled on suspicion of "political unreliability," "antigovernment activity," "Peasant Union agitation," or "incitement to agrarian disorders."[77] The evidence brought to light at these trials provides a useful antidote to characterizations of teachers' activities contained in official reports, especially since the latter were often based on denunciations lodged by persons who had a personal interest in seeing activist teachers removed, such as village clerics or rural officials. Memoirs by teachers active in both provinces help round out the picture. If anything, one might expect these to inflate the "revolutionary" role of teachers during 1905; in fact, they strongly support the generalizations drawn above.

In both provinces official reports claimed a direct link between teacher agitation and peasant action against private property: in Ekaterinoslav looting and destruction of estates and in Vladimir theft of timber from private and state forests.[78] Evidence at the trials indicated otherwise. In the Ekaterinoslav Peasant Union trial, held in 1908, it was apparent that the accused (including teachers) had, in fact, worked energetically to head off "pogroms" of *pomeshchik* "nests," preferring to organize agricultural strikes and other forms of "passive resistance," as they were termed in the official indictment (for example, refusal to provide horses to police couriers). Teachers and other union activists urged peasants to await a final solution of the agrarian question through legislative channels, were directly responsible for averting cases of violence, and in at least one case, effected a return of property looted from a local estate. This activity seems consistent with decisions adopted by the Ekaterinoslav Teachers' Union organization. Testimony at the trial was compelling, and a majority of the accused was acquitted.[79]

Much the same resulted from a series of trials held in Vladimir in October 1906. Here prosecutors attempted to prove that Peasant Union agitation, much of it conducted by rural teachers, constituted an appeal for "subversion of the existing social and political system by force from below." The testimony of most witnesses indicated otherwise. Teachers and others had urged restraint. Property seizures were eschewed in favor of agitation for nonpayment of taxes and redemption payments (in some districts such campaigns were directed specifically against zemstvo taxes), as well as political organization. In each case the result was either acquittal or a very light sentence ranging from one and a half to six months, which in most instances had already been served.[80]

Other evidence from Ekaterinoslav and Vladimir supports the above generalizations concerning teachers' activities while providing further details. In Ekaterinoslav, for example, many rural teachers began to use the Ukrainian language in the classroom in direct contravention of officially approved curricula. In Pokrov district, Vladimir, Teachers' Union activists organized a successful strike of 4,000 textile workers; they forced concessions from factory owners and in general carried political agitation to remote locales "where [political] parties had never penetrated."[81] Neither province provides much evidence that local teachers' organizations or individual teachers sought to foment agrarian violence or prepare the ground for peasant insurrection. The message they carried to the rural masses was often radical, but their activities were relatively moderate and consistent with Peasant Union tactics in most places. That teachers' activity in other parts of the country was of a similar nature is indicated by a variety of sources, most notably the reports of provincial delegates to the Second Congress of the All-Russian Teachers' Union, where teachers tried to assess the political experience of recent months and brace themselves for the ensuing wave of reaction.

With the Narod: The Second Teachers' Union Congress

The Second Congress of the VSU was held clandestinely in Finland on December 26–29, 1905, after troops already had broken the back of the revolutionary movement in Russia's cities by putting down the Moscow insurrection and punitive detachments had restored a semblance of order in the countryside. Here, in a small Finnish resort hotel, the teacher-delegates, drawn disproportionately from the northern and central provinces,[82] described intensive and often successful agitation among the rural population in recent months, mainly in the spirit of the Peasant Union, but also of the political parties, especially the PSR. Many characterized this work in glowing terms, as did a delegate from Novgorod province. "Peasants are very interested in political questions; they invite teachers to assemblies and grumble about those teachers who do not share newspapers or do not explain anything . . . 'we once thought that you were with the lords (*s barami*), but now we see that you stand with us.' "[83] Other speakers likewise spoke of growing peasant receptivity to radical propaganda promising "land and liberty" and of the increasing moral authority enjoyed by activist teachers in the local community.

But other delegates reminded their comrades that there were still strong conservative elements among the narod—cases of popular reaction against radical teachers were recounted in harrowing detail—and that these were easily exploited by reactionary landowners, merchants, clerics, and officials. Nearly all delegates concurred that teachers had to be sensitive to the peasant's "world view," avoiding direct attacks against the tsar and the Orthodox faith, regardless of whether popular political and religious convictions ran counter to those of the intelligentsia.[84]

The assembled delegates condemned the revised Duma electoral of December 11, and local union groups in many cases agitated for a boycott of the elections since the new law retained multistaged elections (four, in the case of the peasant *soslovie*), voting by curiae, and limitations on preelectoral agitation. Although rural teachers and other third element employees of nonpeasant origins were now enfranchised, they were assigned to the urban curia and were thus apparently denied any influence in the electoral process in the village, in which they would naturally be most interested and where they could have the most impact.[85] Delegates reported widespread agitation by teachers against the Duma in favor of a constituent assembly elected on a four-tail franchise but admitted that the attitude of the peasantry toward the elections was mixed. Most peasant adherents of the Peasant Union favored a boycott, but they represented only a small part of the rural population; the remainder of the peasantry was either in favor of participation or indifferent to it. Nevertheless, teachers gave a cool reception to the arguments in favor of participation adduced by P. N. Miliukov, guest speaker for the Kadets. Instead, they resolved by an overwhelming majority to boycott the elections and "organize the forces of the narod in struggle for a constituent assembly," a decision consistent with the official position of the Peasant Union.[86]

As for the Peasant Union, the Second Teachers' Union Congress reaffirmed its members' commitment to it, pledging coordination of activities between the two organizations at both local and national levels; the delegates also endorsed an appeal to the armed forces not to take part in the government's suppression of the revolution issued by the Main Committee and Saratov organization of the Peasant Union.[87] This commitment to the organized, "conscious" elements of the peasantry, which had appeared so compelling in the weeks following the October Manifesto, now seemed desperately urgent, as activist teachers found themselves on the front lines of the campaign to bring the Liberation Movement to the countryside, dangerously exposed and highly vulnerable.

Nearly all delegates took note of the most significant change in provincial politics since October, the rightward movement of the zemstvos, which now cast a wary eye at teachers' political activity. Viewing restoration of order in the countryside as the highest priority and disturbed by radical propaganda, local zemstvos joined with school officials and school boards in demanding that teachers confine their activities to the classroom; a number of district zemstvos pointedly warned teachers not to use school buildings for "political meetings."[88] More often than not zemstvo boards followed the lead of the Tambov district zemstvo, acquiescing to administrative demands that suspect teachers be dismissed and in some cases initiating such action themselves. Only a handful of zemstvos, it seems, attempted to provide material assistance to teachers repressed for political activity, as the Teachers' Union had requested in its September appeal.[89]

Particularly sharp conflicts arose between zemstvos and teachers over peasant refusal to pay taxes. Some sixty-six districts were affected by tax protests in 1905, mainly in the non–Black Earth provinces; in many instances this protest was directed specifically at zemstvo taxes, commonly assessed at higher rates on peasant allotment land than private holdings.[90] Such action, while occasioned in part by recent poor harvests, no doubt reflected peasant discontent over these inequalities, as well as the *soslovie*-based representation of local self-government, which favored the gentry. Local zemstvos faced a fiscal crisis, as many landowners also ceased paying zemstvo levies.

Teachers and other Peasant Union activists supported peasant resistance to state and local taxes, a tactic in line with decisions taken by the November Congress of the Peasant Union. Local Teachers' Union groups waged antitax agitation which encompassed zemstvo levies. In one district (Tsarskoe Selo?) in Petersburg province the zemstvo board threatened that teachers would be issued only half of their salaries after Christmas if they persisted in such agitation.[91] The Semenov zemstvo (Nizhegorod) likewise blamed teachers' agitation for massive arrears, and in Pokrov district (Vladimir) the zemstvo curtly rejected petitions lodged by teachers who had been dismissed on orders of the governor for political unreliability. The teachers, all members of the Teachers' Union, asked for emergency relief for themselves and their families, but the executive board replied that the current year's budget (1906) was strained to the limit, something that could be explained "by the recent ferment among the peasant population, caused by propaganda of the program of the Peasant Union which had found adherents among the teaching personnel of Pokrov district."[92]

Zemstvo-teacher conflicts were especially bitter in Novgorod province. As early as November 2, 1905, the Staraia Russa zemstvo notified teachers that it had information that zemstvo teachers were urging peasants not to pay zemstvo taxes and other levies and warned that in those volosts where peasants refused to pay taxes teachers would not be issued salaries. The local Teachers' Union organization condemned this attempt to "interfere in the public activity of teachers" and demanded a voice at an emergency session of the zemstvo called to deal with the controversy. This was denied, and union members resigned their posts in protest.[93]

Similar conflicts arose in Beloozero[94] and Kresttsy districts,[95] but perhaps the sharpest disagreement in Novgorod province took place in Cherepovets. Here, according to Okhrana reports, revenues to zemstvo coffers had completely ceased by autumn 1905, as the result of agitation which informed peasants that two-thirds of arrears in zemstvo payments belonged to the gentry and other large property owners. Much of this agitation was apparently conducted by rural teachers led by Stepan Vinogradov and Il'ia Chumakov, both SRs and local Teachers' Union leaders who supported the program of the Peasant Union. The issue came to a head on November 17, when the zemstvo convened an extraordinary session to discuss the fiscal crisis. A large crowd of peasants led by Vinogradov and Chumakov burst into the assembly amid cries of "down with the zemstvo." The zemstvo session was forced to close, after which the zemstvo fired off a sharply worded telegram to Count Witte demanding that the government take strict measures against seditious teachers.[96] As early as May 1905 the Cherepovets Teachers' Union group had planned to conduct an antitaxation campaign among the population if the government failed to summon a national assembly elected on the basis of a four-tail franchise. Apparently, teachers such as Vinogradov and Chumakov, both graduates of the local teachers' seminary and of peasant origin, were able to make good on this pledge with considerable success.[97]

The Teachers' Union roundly condemned the Cherepovets zemstvo and other institutions of local self-government which sought to curb teachers' political activity. The very cautious criticism that had been leveled during the spring and summer at the zemstvos as undemocratic, *soslovie*-based organs unresponsive to teachers' needs, was now full blown. The Second Congress reiterated the union's demand that day-to-day management of schools be turned over to elected collegial organs which would include teachers' representatives and would be responsible for appointments and dismissals. Moreover, the delegates considered it the duty of every teacher to explain to the local population the inequities of the contemporary zemstvo and to actively agitate for its reform along the lines of the four-tail electoral formula. Boycotts, collective resignations, and other measures were threatened in case of zemstvo reprisals against teachers.[98]

Teachers still expressed the hope, though with little conviction, that "progressive" zemstvos (the delegates' reports suggested that these were becoming an endangered species) would continue to support them. Realistically, however, they sensed that the former alliance between zemstvo men and third element employees, which had played such an important part in the development of the teachers' movement and in zemstvo achievements in the field of education, had been seriously fractured. What politically active teachers now realized was that their former liberal patrons did not represent, at least in a political sense, the zemstvo rank and file, which teachers now openly assailed as "*pomeshchik*," "black hundred," or "bourgeois." In fact, this rank and file had already begun to turn against the liberal leadership which had set the tone in zemstvo affairs for the past decade; during the regular zemstvo sessions of autumn 1906, many of these liberals would be unceremoniously thrown from office and many of their programs and policies repudiated.[99]

The gentry-dominated zemstvos had considerably less patience for radical third element people who were blamed for various revolutionary manifestations in the countryside. This was especially true of teachers, who the average zemstvo man had always viewed with condescension and with whom he felt few ties, social, professional, or otherwise. During the era of liberal hegemony, it is true, the zemstvos often served teachers as useful allies. To one degree or another the zemstvos had opposed government attempts to maintain teachers in a state of professional isolation and to erect artificial barriers between teacher and peasant, on the one hand, and between teacher and society, on the other. In early 1905 some zemstvo men had even encouraged teachers' political mobilization as well as modest political activity among the narod. Zemstvo patronage, of course, was dictated by more than selfless idealism: after the Great Famine of the early 1890s zemstvo activists were increasingly cognizant of the imperatives of cultural enlightenment, and during 1905 many felt the urgent need to establish links with the masses, during a period of imminent political and social change. Teachers were obvious candidates for both tasks.

But in the wake of the revolutionary excesses of late 1905, the logic behind "enlightenment"—whether cultural or political—gave way to an overriding concern for the social and political order. Now many zemstvo men embraced the administration's long-held view of the teacher as a threat to that order and joined with the authorities in exacting vengeance upon them. The conservative zemstvo man from Samara, N. A. Naumov, no doubt speaking for many of his fellows, later excoriated teachers for "depraving young hearts and minds and arousing class hatred and criminal appetites with dreams of black repartition."[100] The result, as we will see, was a crushing wave of repression that affected thousands of teachers, altering the face and scarring the psyche of the profession and setting teachers' professional organization back nearly a decade.

Zemstvo reaction was triggered by, and in turn reinforced, teachers' open identification with popular demands, including tax protests and radical land reform. Indeed, such identification seemed almost a logical culmination of political processes unfolding during 1905, if not before. Tension had already marked the zemstvo-teacher relationship before 1905, and with the open rift in autumn 1905 it was inevitable that teachers would cast their lot with the more radical elements of society and with the narod. Such a stance was inherent in the logic of the revolutionary process, but also in that of the teachers' professional movement. After October this movement clearly needed a new powerful ally, first to survive, then to realize its own agenda. By 1905 activist teachers accepted that resolution of their own problems of status was possible only in the context of a general democratization of education management and of rural society (including the zemstvos) *and* of radical reforms at the national level. All were linked. Democratization of policymaking and professional autonomy were unlikely without an overhaul of local government. These and other changes, such as meaningful school reforms, seemed even less likely without constitutional reform based on a democratic four-tail franchise. Once reform, at both levels, had been repudiated by zemstvos and other moderate elements of society, teachers came to rely even more on peasant support and to gamble on organizations like the Peasant Union as viable engines of change.

Political processes in the village likewise reinforced teachers' identification with the peasantry and helped shape new post-October alignments. Delegates at the Second Congress of the Teachers' Union spoke of increased peasant receptivity to teachers' propaganda; indeed, peasants had exerted pressure upon intelligenty to play a political role in the village, a natural extension of the modest role of "interpreter" which many rural teachers had filled since the beginning of the year and the embodiment of a professional ethos as public activists which many had internalized on the eve of the revolution. At subsequent gatherings teachers spoke of strengthened ties with local communities and the growing "moral authority" of activist teachers. Delegates attending a congress of the Union's Moscow Regional Organization in late May 1906 concurred that a significant growth in peasant political consciousness had occurred since October 17. Teachers and others had helped popularize political concepts and tactics of struggle that were still foreign to many peasants and, to some extent, link peasant protest with the demands of the urban opposition. They certainly helped focus rural discontent against the government (though less so against the tsar) and thus helped politicize the peasant movement.

Teachers' status in the community had altered in the process. The peasantry, teachers noted, were now able to discern friend from foe. In the recent past teacher-propagandists who had tried to explain the "significance of current events" had been met by peasant suspicion, and some had even been physically assaulted in the name of "Tsar, Throne, and Fatherland." Such incidents had been amply documented at the last meeting of the Moscow Teachers' Union organization in early November 1905. Since that time, however, peasant attitudes toward the teacher had shifted from hostility to "trust," inasmuch as teachers had "by their actions demonstrated their dedication to the vital interests of the narod." In some cases, the delegates in Moscow pointed out, this trust translated into active peasant support of teachers in instances of conflict with the authorities: some communes refused to hand radical teachers over to the police, others compiled *prigovory* protesting the dismissal of teachers for political propaganda and boycotted their vacant posts.[101] During this period, the most dramatic indication of the growing bond between peasant and teacher and of teachers' contribution to raising peasant political consciousness was provided by the elections to the First Duma, which convened in April 1906.

In this light it is somewhat ironic that the Teachers' Union, along with the Peasant Union and revolutionary parties, had endorsed a boycott of the Duma elections. By and large this tactic seems to have broken down at the local level, where the peasantry remained unresponsive to calls for a boycott and still hopeful of a radical solution to the agrarian question and other issues by a national assembly. Sensitive to peasant perceptions, many local union groups as well as individual teachers, the evidence suggests, worked actively to support the election of progressive representatives in the multistaged electoral process.[102] Despite the fact that the Duma electoral law barred the majority of rural teachers (those not of the peasant *solslovie*, women, and those under twenty-five years of age) from participation in the electoral process, a good number of teachers' candidacies were put forward by the peasantry, and a number of teachers (or former teachers) of peasant origin were ultimately elected as deputies to the First Duma.[103] As was true of the majority of deputies elected by the peasantry, these intelligenty tended to gravitate toward the radical parliamentary fraction of Trudoviki, which enjoyed the support of Teachers' Union organizations throughout the short life of the First Duma, where it clashed with the government over the issue of radical land reform.[104]

Detailed information regarding the electoral process at the lower levels is sparse, but it is noteworthy that the elections to the Second Duma returned an even larger number (thirty-eight) of primary schoolteachers among the deputies. Most of these were rural teachers or former teachers, many had been active in politics during 1905 (often in the Peasant Unions), and most were affiliated with parties to the left of center: the Trudoviki and the major socialist parties which chose not to boycott the elections this time around.[105] These election results occurred despite the government's attempts to nullify the influence of rural intelligenty on elections in the countryside: a Senate "interpretation" of the electoral law designed to disqualify intelligenty of peasant origin (the so-called "householders" amendment) and a September 14, 1906, circular of the Council of Ministers barring zemstvo and other employees from membership in oppositional political parties, from (and including) the Kadets leftward.[106] Once again Teachers' Union organizations played an active role in the electoral campaign both in the towns and countryside, by and large supporting leftist candidates.[107] Few teachers were elected to the Third Duma, the result of growing reaction and wholesale purge of teaching personnel, as well as the government's revision of the electoral law (Stolypin's coup d'état).

Clearly, the prominence of intelligenty such as teachers in the Duma elections of 1905–7 is significant. Some fairly straightforward conclusions can be drawn. Peasants selected rural intelligenty to represent them in St. Petersburg for several reasons: many were of peasant origin and knew the village firsthand; they possessed literacy skills and the political savvy to defend peasant interests in competition with other groups, such as the gentry, in a national political forum. Most important, and this stands out in statements of teachers at various congresses of this period, teachers and others were perceived by peasants as having their interests at heart. Intelligenty, who in the course of 1905, or even earlier, had demonstrated their support for popular interests, often at considerable personal and professional risk, would not betray them.[108]

9. The Reaction and Its Consequences, 1906–1914

Teachers had tried to chart a course in the winter of 1905–6 between violent peasant revolution and vicious reaction, and in the Peasant Unions and Duma elections they had scored some notable successes. In a tragically ironic sense, however, the fragile vessel of the teachers' movement was dashed against both rocks. The Peasant Unions, which many teachers had supported, had exercised a moderating influence on the peasant movement. That it was not more successful owed to the familiar difficulties of peasant organizing, timing, and a situation of extreme social and political polarization not conducive to moderate solutions. Repudiated by moderate elements in society and subjected to fierce repression by the government, the tactics pursued by the Peasant Union proved unviable. The activities of the Peasant Union and its teacher adherents required some measure of toleration by the government in order to survive and flourish. Such was not forthcoming, as the regime and its supporters, including the zemstvo gentry, proved either incapable or, one suspects, unwilling to differentiate between modest political enlightenment—or even agitation for radical reform—and incitement to peasant insurrection. For teachers, therefore, a conscious peasant movement proved a slender reed, not the sheet anchor they had envisaged. Although there is little evidence that they were responsible for inciting peasants against gentry estates in 1905, the degree of repression meted out to teachers was staggering.

By late December the Teachers' Union had information concerning 450 teachers dismissed in recent weeks for political activity of one kind or another (of these, 250 had been arrested, 14 exiled, and 4 killed). These figures were incomplete. In Ekaterinoslav province alone union figures for early 1906 registered nearly 200 teachers dismissed (167 arrested), and in the backwater of Chistopol (Kazan) the local union group reported 16 dismissals (10 jailed) during the same period, affixing blame for this upon the local zemstvo which assumed that teachers were responsible for "all the disorder in the countryside."[1] Among non-union teachers in the Baltic and other borderlands, moreover, government repression was quite heavy.[2] Nikolai Chekhov estimated that by the beginning of 1906 the number of repressed teachers was closer to 2,000, and the purge continued steadily during the early months of that year, as is evident from even a cursory reading of teachers' professional journals, the general press, as well as the "chronicles" compiled by V. P. Obninskii, a Kadet and former chairman of the Kaluga zemstvo board. By mid-1906 the union's own very incomplete data counted over 1,500 teachers dismissed, arrested, and exiled, and the union's Commission to Aid Repressed Teachers (established on January 7, 1906) was deluged with requests for assistance from local groups and individuals.[3]

Some locales were swept by mass purges, particularly where teachers and other rural intelligenty had been relatively successful in helping organize Peasant Unions and had worked to avert agrarian violence: Novomoskovsk (Ekaterinoslav), Sudzha (Kursk), Sumy (Kharkov). In Lokhvitsa (Poltava) the third element purge was much heavier than in neighboring districts where there had actually been significant disorders but where Peasant Unions had exerted less influence and teachers had been less involved in political work.[4] In many areas the campaign assumed the character of a witch hunt with rural authorities, themselves barely literate, doing all they could to uncover seditious teachers. P. I. Kalashnikova recalled how the local police official burst into her school in Iaransk (Viatka) to "check the school library": "'Tell us honestly,' he said, 'whether you have any books with red covers here.'" Kalashnikova and a fellow teacher were dismissed for disseminating illegal literature and migrated to Perm, but as "unreliables" they were unable to secure teaching posts and wound up working as cashiers in a theater.[5]

In most cases it is impossible to determine which agency initiated action against teachers: school board, inspectorate, regular authorities, or zemstvos. Many dismissals took place under martial law, in effect in many parts of the empire in late 1905 and 1906. By and large, zemstvos and school boards, which under normal circumstances had the final say in matters of dismissal, supported repressive measures if they did not initiate them. The purge continued through 1906 and the school year 1906–7. In early September the Petersburg daily *Rus'* reported that some 20,000 teachers were out of work and under police surveillance. A Menshevik commentator claimed in 1908 that dismissals of third element personnel during 1905–7 totaled 22,000 zemstvo teachers, 3,000 doctors, 5,500 lower medical personnel, and 5,000 other employees. Finally in 1910, during education debates in the Third Duma, a rightist deputy, P. N. Krupenskii, lashed out at seditious teachers in secular schools, bolstering his support for clerical-run education with the revelation that 23,000 of these "seducers of youth" had been dismissed for political unreliability during the "liberation era."[6] If these figures have any validity they are awesome, since they relate to schools (including zemstvo) under the jurisdiction of the MNP, which in 1904 were staffed by an estimated 63,871 teachers empire-wide.[7] (The figure of 22,000 zemstvo teachers must be seriously doubted because in 1903 approximately 27,000 persons were laboring in 18,817 zemstvo-run schools, while as late as 1909–10 there were 39,651 zemstvo teachers in 25,047 schools.)[8]

Undoubtedly Russia's educational system, indeed rural culture, was dealt a severe blow. I. I. Tolstoi, the former minister of education, remarked that in 1906 "primary schools were nearly everywhere in the most pitiful state, since a significant percentage of teachers had been arrested and dismissed for antigovernment political activity, and nearly all had become suspect in the government's eye and at any moment could be deprived of their posts."[9] At the start of the 1906–7 school year *Birzhevye vedomosti* warned of a grave "teachers' crisis." Faced with empty coffers, many zemstvos closed their schools or failed to pay teachers' salaries during early 1906, and teachers drifted into the cities to seek employment.[10] Political considerations reinforced fiscal concerns. As in other zemstvo fields, liquidation of services reflected an inclination to settle scores with radical third element people, and cutbacks in education, which did not directly benefit the gentry, were directed against peasants who had refused to pay taxes. The Cherepovets zemstvo, where high arrears had been blamed on teacher agitators, voted in 1907 to close all 142 of its schools.[11]

But this crisis in education was also due in large measure, *Birzhevye vedomosti* pointed out, to the wave of repression which removed thousands of qualified personnel from a system which had always been plagued by a dearth of adequately trained teachers. Schools stood empty for months, either because replacements could not be found for dismissed personnel or because local Teachers' Union groups boycotted the positions. The union had agonized over the boycott issue, and, despite the short-term harm to the local community, many affiliates attempted to boycott the posts of repressed comrades.[12] In some cases they received the enthusiastic support of peasants who signed *prigovory* demanding the return of their old teachers,[13] and in a few instances local authorities acceded to the demands of local communities.[14] But such action was difficult to sustain given the absence of community control over schools and lack of solidarity among teachers. In Nolinsk district (Viatka) the local union pronounced the boycott a failure, "thanks to the low level of development of the mass of teachers," while a union activist from Grodno province, writing in the 1920s, recalled bitterly that the boycott was "not honored by the old, reactionary teachers who now receive pensions from the Workers' and Peasants' Government!"[15]

By 1908 the zemstvo fiscal crisis had lessened, and education budgets increased. Schools were staffed, networks expanded, and the half-decade before World War I saw impressive gains in mass education, with unprecedented numbers of school-age children acquiring the rudiments of literacy.[16] But the effects of government repression lingered, affecting the teaching profession's composition, organization, and morale. The purge of 1905–7 tended to accelerate the process of feminization that had already begun to alter the face of the profession by the turn of the century and which undoubtedly affected teachers' status within the village community. Disciplinary action fell disproportionately on male teachers. For example, in Ekaterinoslav province, Mariupol district, 2 of 17 dismissed teachers were women; in Aleksandrov 4 of 17; Verkhnedneprovsk, 2 of 15; Ekaterinoslav, 1 of 11; Novomoskovsk, 0 of 18; Bakhmut, 10 of 51. In Bakhmut local authorities subsequently reinstated 22 teachers, which included 8 of the 10 women dismissed.[17] These figures reflect greater involvement by men in rural politics during 1905 but also the official consensus that women would prove more docile candidates. During the war years military conscription, from which primary schoolteachers were not exempt, further speeded feminization.

The administrative purge of teaching personnel naturally had an adverse effect on qualifications, at least for the short term. Although Ben Eklof has demonstrated the success of the Russian rural school in providing basic schooling before 1914, the reaction tended to remove the cultural activists, those involved in adult education and other attempts to extend the teacher's mission beyond the classroom. Such commitment, which almost inevitably engendered political activity, invited official scrutiny, and so not surprisingly the post-1905 purge swept away many innovative and committed teachers who had begun to attain a broader cultural influence in the village. And what of teachers who survived the reaction and those who entered the profession in large numbers after 1905? It is true that this period marked the beginning of substantial state investment in popular schooling, including the goal of increasing teachers' salaries to a minimum of 360 rubles. Eklof has shown that these recruits were successfully teaching the basics and contributing to the evolution of a school system that would provide a firm basis for Soviet efforts.[18] But there is little evidence that the Tsarist government had been able to enlist rural teachers as active supporters of the regime within peasant society. Despite the valuable spadework they were performing in the classroom, evidence suggests that Russian teachers during the postrevolutionary reaction were a profession in a state of malaise, isolation, and unsure identity.

As early as November 1906 an anonymous teacher, writing in a Iaroslavl daily, described the depression and loss of élan that had overcome the profession:

> The repression of the past year cut deeply into teachers' ranks, casting out the most energetic and committed to popular improvement, and everywhere introduced demoralization. The terror that has overcome teachers is so great that one is confronted with a massive turn backward, even compared with the period that preceded the "epoch of freedoms." Some teachers, out of fear of reprisals, have ceased such legal and innocent endeavors as public readings with projectors, despite the fact that all materials have passed the censor, because they do not want to attract attention.[19]

The reaction had a particularly dramatic effect in stifling teacher association after 1905. Not surprisingly, the reaction dealt a severe blow to the Teachers' Union, as it did to all of the political-professional unions established in 1905. Union membership, which stood at from 12,000 to 13,000 in autumn 1905, declined steadily thereafter as local groups were decimated by arrests and as the more timid—often those who had joined after October 17—left its ranks, either under direct pressure from school officials and zemstvos or from fear of reprisals.[20] An organization representing mainly rural teachers was especially vulnerable to such pressure. Given the rightward shift of their former benefactors in the zemstvos, teachers' organizations, thrown upon their own meager resources, found it difficult to provide much in the way of material assistance to repressed members. The Central Bureau in Petersburg organized a mutual insurance fund, as well as a Commission to Find Employment for Repressed Union Members. The Union's regional organization in Moscow initiated similar services and was overwhelmed by teachers seeking any kind of work, and some local union organizations and mutual aid societies set up modest political funds.[21] Given the scope of repression, however, these resources were rapidly depleted. The union's failure to provide for its members in their hour of need, as with the failure of boycotts, stemmed from its inability to encompass the wide masses of teachers, and this provoked renewed debate over the union's platform.

Pressure to drop the union's political plank mounted in early 1906. With elections to the First Duma and increasing differentiation of Russian society into political parties, the SDs' arguments for a politically neutral platform gained support.[22] Furthermore, proponents of revision argued that exclusion of political aims might lead to legalization and thus open the union to the timid, politically inert mass of teachers. A purely professional organization would, according to its advocates, provide a valuable school for the growth of corporate consciousness among teachers as well as an estimable force behind the union's tactics of self-defense and professional struggle. An organization encompassing both SDs and "zemstvo rabbits" was an attractive prospect.[23]

By mid-year a majority of local groups, shaken by the reaction and eager for a rapprochement with the Social Democrats, inclined toward revision. At the Union's Third Congress, held in Finland, June 7-10, 1906, and attended by 179 delegates representing 109 local groups in 43 provinces, the issue was hotly debated and monopolized most of the discussion. By a vote of 95 to 79 with 13 abstentions the congress adopted a professional platform. V. M. Chernov, as official representative of the PSR, noted that his party favored retention of the political plank but would not apply any pressure on SR teachers in this regard. Despite the vote, however, the delegates then accepted an addendum (paragraph 23) which underscored the continued primacy of politics: union congresses could issue "tactical resolutions" on contemporary political issues, but individuals would be

Members of the Moscow Regional Bureau and other delegates to the Third Congress of the All-Russian Teachers' Union held in Iustila, Finland, June 7–10, 1906 (Nikolai Chekhov seated center, second row). Source: *Niva*, No. 26, July 1, 1906, p. 410.

free to follow the directives of their particular party when the latter conflicted with a union position.[24]

The congress then passed a number of political resolutions, including a pledge to support the parliamentary Duma fraction, the Trudoviki (*Trudovaia gruppa*), an organization close to the Peasant Union that enjoyed considerable support among the rural intelligentsia. Three former teachers, including Stepan Anikin, represented the Trudoviki at the Teachers' Congress. After the dissolution of the First Duma the VSU joined the Trudoviki, the revolutionary parties, and the more radical of the unions in issuing a "Manifesto to the Russian Peasantry." Declaring the final bankruptcy of the government, they called on the peasantry to seize control of the local administrative apparatus and, in an orderly fashion, take possession of all landholdings until a constituent assembly could resolve the question of final disposition.[25] During elections to the Second Duma the union's bureau urged all teachers to actively support the electoral efforts of leftist parties, and in Moscow the local union organization entered into an electoral bloc with SRs, SDs, Popular Socialists, and radical unions.[26]

Revision of the union's program resulted in a compromise with the Social Democrats, who entered the VSU as a special party "section." Debate over the inclusion of political tasks continued to rage after the Third Congress, with some affiliates splitting over the decision adopted in Finland. The SR-dominated Voronezh group demanded restoration of the political plank, while SDs succeeded in some locales in completely excluding political tasks.[27] All of this discussion came to a head at the Fourth (and last) Congress of the Teachers' Union held in Finland in June 1907. Here, after acrimonious debate between SDs and SRs, delegates adopted a resolution which further toned down the union's political agenda. But this discussion took place in a weirdly surreal atmosphere. Delegates passionately debated plans for a radical transformation of education, urged their fellows to wage vigorous agitation and expose the class nature of the zemstvos, and once again tackled the poisonous issue of whether a teachers' organization was, by definition, "petty-bourgeois," as some SDs continued to insist, or "democratic" and "toiling."[28] By this time the revolution was over, the reaction complete with Stolypin's coup d'état, and the union crushed.

The reaction was not kind to legal associations. As early as summer-autumn 1905 a number of mutual aid societies were closed on administrative order for political activity, generally for six to twelve months. Such closures continued in 1906 and 1907 and in some cases remained in effect for some time. The Nizhegorod Society and its district sections were not permitted to hold meetings until 1909; the Ekaterinoslav Society was closed on orders of the local governor-general in January 1906, resurrected in early 1907 and again liquidated at the end of that year; the Viatka Society, closed in 1907, was unable to resume activity until 1915.[29] For teachers these closures spelled the cutoff of vital services, such as aid to teachers' children studying in provincial towns.

Societies which did not suffer such a fate nonetheless fell on hard times. The more active members were often those first purged, and whole executive boards were swept away by arrest and exile.[30] Annual grants from zemstvos, which had occupied such a prominent place in the budgets of most teachers' societies, often dried up. Zemstvos usually pointed to their own bad fiscal straits in rejecting requests for aid, although the Orel zemstvo cut support when the local teachers' society issued a statement in favor of the Trudovik group in the Duma.[31] Zemstvos also cut off aid to teachers in subscriptions, which in Iaroslavl and elsewhere had increased steadily in recent years, while continuing allocations for upkeep of roads and other services untainted by politics. Where they had formerly served as patrons of teacher associations, many zemstvos now apparently embraced the government's view of the mutual aid societies as cradles of subversion, and zemstvo men who had served as officers in the societies now registered their disapproval of recent activities of these societies by leaving them.[32]

Most disturbing was a precipitous decline in the interest of teachers in the societies after 1905. Recently stirred by the prospect of transforming the societies into vibrant professional associations, as well as the excitement of the revolutionary year, many teachers were no longer satisfied with the pallid existence to which the government now intended to reduce them.[33] Perhaps more important was the long-term effect of the reaction on corporate activity. Not only did the repression of 1906–7 tend to remove the more activist elements, but in its ferocity it thoroughly "terrorized the mass of teachers, which retreated into rural isolation, lay dormant and dead."[34]

The life of teachers' societies, as all sources agree, reached a low point in 1908–9 when the government rejected a petition to hold a second national congress of societies' representatives and placed a ban on the opening of any new societies. A ministry report sharply criticized the past activities of the societies, which caused "disorder in the schools and among the peasant population" and in 1910 resurrected the Turau proposals to revise the "normal statute" and bring the societies firmly under official control.[35] Happily, this project was not put into effect, and after 1910 the societies began to slowly revive. In part this owed to a new solicitude on the part of the zemstvos as well as the government in the wake of renewed activity in primary education on the eve of World War I.[36] In 1912 the Ministry of Education revoked its ban on new societies, and during the Christmas recess of 1913–14 the government permitted the convocation of a second All-Russian Congress of Representatives of Teachers' Societies in St. Petersburg.[37] Teachers' interest in the societies increased, but their revival was slow, and the societies had not regained their former prominence when the Tsarist order collapsed in February 1917.

Beginning in 1908 the number of summer teachers' courses began to increase after a five-year lull, as zemstvos and government recognized the need to raise teachers' qualifications at a time when the school system was rapidly expanding. Organization of courses was still fraught with vexing administrative restrictions and plagued by official denial of zemstvo petitions. A more or less benevolent attitude was not evident in St. Petersburg until 1915 after the appointment of P. N. Ignat'ev as minister of education.[38] As for local teachers' congresses, sanctioned according to the "temporary rules" of 1899, these never were held with frequency before World War I. The reasons remained the same as before 1905: official suspicion and zemstvo indifference. Thus, few teachers benefited from these potentially invaluable gatherings. The fate of local congresses in Moscow district is instructive. A congress had been held there in 1901, the next not until 1914.[39] Given the normal rate of turnover in the profession and the postrevolutionary purge, it is unlikely that many of those who attended the 1901 congress were around for the second thirteen years later.

Not only teachers' associations suffered severe setbacks following the failed 1905 revolution. As was true of other liberationist groups, the reaction dealt a devastating blow to teachers, not only in terms of professional morale, but in the wider sense of rural culture. The immediate sense of depression and isolation has already been mentioned, and contemporaries agreed that the repression of 1906–8 left scars on teachers' collective psyche which lasted for the remainder of the Tsarist period. Nina Popova claimed that the mass of teachers had internalized the reaction, and Ivan Samokhvalov, writing in 1915, bemoaned the decline of "public spirit" among teachers. In his 1927 memoir Ivan Sergeini described the period between the two revolutions: "Twelve years of systematic persecution . . . the constant position of teachers under the 'Damocles sword' irrevocably altered the physiognomy of the schoolteacher, and from an optimist-public activist (*optimist-obshchestvennik*) rendered him passive, cowardly, isolated in his backwater."[40] Others remarked that the new teachers who staffed the expanding school system during the half decade before the war represented a new breed. Many of these were graduates of clerical institutions such as the diocesan schools, and these *eparkhial'ki*, aside from a meager educational background, were less committed to public enlightenment than those who had entered the profession during the decade before 1905. The personnel in zemstvo schools, these critics suggested, was now little distinguished from the inert, oppressed creatures who taught in church-run schools.[41]

Of course, these comments come from people who had been active in the teachers' movement of the previous decade and were active in 1905. For them the era of mundane "small deeds" that followed must have appeared dreary and their successors lacking in the sense of commitment and élan which had motivated them. Nevertheless, there is evidence that the reaction was a very real, daily phenomenon for those who remained in the profession or entered it during this period. Official supervision over teachers' activities increased. The staff of the school inspectorate was beefed up considerably in the years after the revolution: from 489 inspectors in 1907 to 784 in 1914. Although pedagogical consideration played a large part in this development—this was a period when the government finally began a serious financial commitment to develop primary education—those of a political nature cannot be ruled out. The inspector's role remained a dual one: educator and policeman. Political activity by teachers during the revolution, if not before, had tilted the balance decisively toward the latter's preoccupation with security. In Pokrov district (Vladimir), where teachers had been militant during 1905, a new inspector was added, a reactionary land captain who, according to one teacher, had no expertise in educational matters whatsoever.[42] And some evidence suggests that the school administration often pursued purely police functions, stamping out any hint of sedition among their charges and attempting to keep teachers in the classroom, inhibiting intercourse with the peasant population at large. Some inspectors issued special circulars warning teachers that they would be harshly disciplined if they appeared at village *skhody* or other peasant meetings. In 1914, under the stewardship of the reactionary Kasso, the Ministry of Education published a circular barring teachers from participation in any organizations aside from their own mutual aid societies, a move that was interpreted in the field as prohibiting their involvement in rural cooperatives and other endeavors.[43]

Although this evidence is admittedly slender, one can still understand how the rural teachers who met the revolutionary year 1917 were a different breed than those who welcomed the Revolution of 1905. Both the physiognomy and the psychology of the profession had changed. The wholesale purge of 1906–8 was followed by a period of reaction during which teachers' organizations were crushed, professional association hampered, and official supervision increased. Under these circumstances it is not at all surprising that the new recruits who entered the expanding school system at the time, increasingly women, kept to the classroom and displayed little of the "public spirit" of their predecessors.[44] Nor is it surprising that rural teachers in 1917 appear to have played little part in village politics. A Provisional Government survey of spring 1917 noted that peasants tended to avoid the election of teachers and other intelligenty to the new volost committees and other bodies: "Male teachers and especially female teachers, who had been vigilantly isolated from the peasants by the Old Regime, lack any link with the [population] and do not enjoy any authority."[45] In evaluating this turn of events it is necessary to note that the political situation in 1917 was much more polarized than had been the case twelve years earlier. Peasants were gravely disillusioned with the prospect of orderly, gradual reform, and popular patience had been exhausted by the war. As members of the resurrected Teachers' Union sadly admitted, class lines were sharply drawn and, more often than not, teachers were regarded by peasants, not only as "outsiders," but also as "bourgeois enemies of popular interests."[46] This turn of events stands in sharp contrast to 1905–7 when teachers exercised considerable influence in the countryside, as demonstrated most dramatically in the elections to the first two Dumas, when, according to activist teachers themselves, their authority among the peasantry had never been higher.

Conclusions

The fortunes of Russia's fledgling teaching profession fluctuated during the final decades of the Tsarist regime, a period of intense social and political conflict which found reflection in often conflicting efforts to define the rural teacher's position in society. Primary education was a battleground upon which state and society contested the difficult issues of Russia's development. Nothing less was at stake than the hearts and minds of the popular masses of town and countryside. Russia's ill-equipped and much-maligned rural teachers stood at the strategic frontier where its two societies, *obshchestvo* and narod, met and eyed each other uneasily. Teachers' professional status was thus vitally linked to wider conflicts between state and society and to the dynamics of rural politics under the Old Regime. This was no doubt true of other emerging professions in Tsarist Russia, but the very process of rural education, and hence teachers' connection to the village, was of central importance.

Better than any other group, rural teachers exemplified the problems faced by all rising professions in carving out a niche and asserting corporate claims in the face of Russia's traditional *soslovie*-based order and political institutions. The politicization of the professional intelligentsia in late Imperial Russia is well known. In the case of teachers the evidence suggests that Russia's social and political structures were not flexible enough to accommodate the natural and inevitable demands of new groups for recognition and autonomy, claims grounded on principles of expertise, social value, and mobility which were inherently inimical to traditional institutions. The inability of the Tsarist regime to accommodate and coopt activist teachers stands in sharp contrast to the experience of Prussia or the French Third Republic but parallels the Russian government's failure to incorporate another new social force that did not fit into the traditional order, namely, workers. Indeed, the restrictive and frustrating policies towards labor unions pursued by the Tsarist regime in the years leading up to 1914 resemble in certain respects those applied to the Russian teachers' movement, and, as Victoria Bonnell has shown, they yielded similar results. Study of Russian teachers, in this sense, casts doubt on the ability of the regime to generate reforms.[47] It also underscores the truly monumental problems involved in integrating Russia's peasant masses with the wider society, whether through dispersal of vital services in the countryside or efforts at rural political mobilization.

Both roles— teachers as cultural agents and as political activists—were eventually accepted by the teachers' professional movement. The major impetus behind the rise of a militant teachers' movement, we have argued, lay in teachers' striving to overcome their isolation (from both educated society and other teachers), their cultural deprivation, as well as their depressed legal status and material insecurity. The problems facing teachers were tightly wound: subordinate status within school administration and rural society, and poverty, reinforced limited access to cultural commodities (reading material), as well as dissociation.

But rural backwardness and poverty could not account wholly for the teacher's predicament. The fundamental contradiction in the Russian rural teacher's status—that between the ideal of a cultural pioneer charged with the almost sacred task of bringing enlightenment to the rural masses and the reality of the "civilized savage," a cultural agent divorced from the sources of modern secular culture—was, to a significant degree, shaped and perpetuated by the state. The government's education policies in general, and regarding teachers in particular, were ambivalent. On the one hand, the state had made a limited commitment to primary schooling, though given its industrialization priorities it was unable to allocate adequate funds. On the other hand, the government was concerned with security, namely, the potential threat schooling and the teacher posed to the traditional social order: peasant monarchism, deference, and religiosity. If Jeffrey Brooks is correct in his assessment of the impact of literacy on the Russian lower classes, schooling would inevitably generate increased demands for a more open society and responsive polity. The Tsarist autocracy could do little to arrest these processes. Nevertheless, the administration tried, pursuing policies aimed at cutting teachers off from radical influences, which official analyses located in urban Russia and educated society. The assumption that the rural teacher posed a threat to the Old Regime as a link between opposition groups and the peasantry dated from the Populist movement of the 1870s and henceforth remained an important component of official thinking. Thus, the government's approach to the profession had always been restrictive and often repressive. Professional and even intimate social gatherings of teachers had at various times been banned; rural teachers were not allowed to read materials cleared by censors for the general urban population; mutual aid societies were hampered by official regulations; teachers' courses and congresses were subject to a haphazard and often arbitrary petitioning process.

Several things can be said about the results of these policies. In the first place they were often successful. Candidates for teaching posts were closely screened and, once they arrived in the village, bureaucratic restrictions combined with the physical and social realities of rural life to isolate teachers and neutralize their potential as carriers of "harmful" ideas and values. Of course, the result of official success in isolating the rural teacher was that many of these people remained intellectually stunted and cowed "zemstvo rabbits," barely equipped to combat illiteracy in the classroom, let alone act as viable and authoritative cultural agents within the wider peasant community. We would suggest that these factors were more significant than teachers' social origins, or even sex, in inhibiting their potential as agents of enlightenment in the countryside. Official policy also contributed either directly or indirectly to the profession's instability, through turnover and flight, and thus hindered its overall effectiveness; the post-1905 purge represents a dramatic instance of a more general problem plaguing the profession. Nevertheless, one can conclude that official policy served the short-term security interests of the regime. The assertions of conservative officials and proponents of church schools to the contrary, the majority of teachers, even in the exceptional year 1905, eschewed politics and seemed barely aware of the pressing issues that concerned Russian educated society. One can argue, however, that the government's approach was ultimately shortsighted, since it failed to nurture a confident cadre of professionals, commanding authority in the village and asserting official ideology and values. In fact, just the opposite occurred.

What is really surprising is the number of teachers who broke their long silence and became involved in the Liberation Movement of 1905. The roots of this phenomenon, we have suggested, lay in the recent tortuous history of teachers' professional association. Given the inherent tension in state policy, its approach toward teachers' association was inconsistent, both within the bureaucracy (with the Ministry of Interior stressing security and the Ministry of Education more open to educational development) and over time. Relative toleration of teachers' professional activities reigned in the 1890s when teachers began to organize and internalized a professional ethos as cultural pioneers. When, in the wake of the agrarian disorders of 1902, official attitudes tilted toward preoccupation with security, the promising developments of recent years were cut short. The years 1902–4 saw steady erosion of legal means for professional association and improvement, part of a futile attempt to quarantine the village from mounting political opposition in the cities. In light of rising expectations and solidarity the result for many teachers was a high level of frustration, reflected in political opposition.

The history of the teachers' movement in Russia is not limited to the important relationship between state and teacher. As students of modern professions have pointed out, the expectations and perceptions of society at large have a profound influence on a given profession's status, identity, autonomy, and organization. This was especially so in Russia after the great famine of the early 1890s, when educated society demonstrated renewed interest in and commitment to popular education. Only then was the humble rural teacher rediscovered and teachers' status raised as a major social issue. Along with the resurgent campaign to foster popular enlightenment came material and moral support from zemstvos and other elements of *obshchestvo*. Given this new climate and modest concessions by the government, teachers gained new opportunities to come together and articulate their interests (at summer courses and in the mutual aid societies), as well as enter into a dialogue with educated society. Most important, teachers found allies who offered a positive image of their still unrealized potential—either the liberal *Kulturtrager* ethos of the zemstvo activists or the revolutionaries' vision of the rural teacher as a popular tribune and revolutionary conduit to the countryside—and the promise that through reform or revolution the contradictions in teachers' status would find resolution.

All of this stood in sharp contrast to previous decades when teachers remained virtually isolated and largely forgotten. And the results were rather remarkable. Whereas in 1895, at the Second Congress on Technical Education, teacher representatives had been silent, the following years witnessed a flurry of professional activity and discussion among teachers, culminating in the Moscow Congress of 1902–3 and the adoption of a comprehensive program combining broad education reform and specific professional demands with a sharp animus against bureaucratic rule and the old order.

The role of the zemstvos, in particular, was important in stimulating teachers' professional activity and abetting the growth of corporate consciousness, as well as politicizing the teachers' movement. By placing popular education high on their agendas, publicizing themselves as opponents of a reactionary bureaucracy which appeared to hamstring society's enlightenment campaign, and demonstrating renewed commitment to this campaign, zemstvo activists were able to forge an alliance with activist teachers which lasted until 1905. In terms of organizational and moral support this alliance was of inestimable value to teachers. Liberal zemstvo men, in particular, sought in rural teachers both instruments of zemstvo cultural policy, endorsing a multifaceted role for teachers in the village, and eventually political cadres which they hoped might help them garner a mass constituency during the hectic days of 1905. The relationship was a symbiotic one and reflects well the significance of the liberal *zemtsy*-radical intelligenty alliance for provincial politics during this period and the social and organizational bases of the all-nation Liberation Movement.

Prior to 1905 the cornerstone of the zemstvo-teacher partnership had been a shared commitment to educational progress, demands for greater local control over schools and the perception of a common foe in the government. A common program and joint struggle found their clearest reflection in the militant Thirty-Two Theses issued by the Moscow Congress, which called for removal of bureaucratic controls from both zemstvo school and teacher. But even before the revolution it was apparent that teacher and zemstvo views on the extent of reform had begun to diverge. As teachers gained an increased sense of their own competence, it was inevitable that they would demand a greater measure of autonomy as well as influence in the formulation of education policy and management of schools. In advancing demands for experimentation with collegial school commissions, as well as supporting the notion of a small zemstvo unit, teachers parted company with many zemstvo men, for whom the issue of local control over schools was mainly one of enhancing zemstvo prerogatives at the expense of the bureaucracy, rather than any democratization of zemstvo institutions. These incipient conflicts over local reform were eventually reflected in national politics during 1905 when rank-and-file zemstvo men refused to support a democratic franchise for a constitutional regime. As in local affairs zemstvo men believed themselves best suited, by virtue of education, culture, property, and experience, to represent the nation. Zemstvo opposition to teachers' demands revealed the intractability and undemocratic nature of local self-government, which, somewhat paradoxically, was antithetical to the autocracy but at the same time embedded in Tsarist political culture.

For teachers before 1905 the limitations of local government and realities of gentry domination were partially masked by the primacy of struggle against the government and the temporary ascendancy of a liberal minority within the zemstvos. Teachers' failure to secure autonomy through collegial management and local congresses, both modeled on initiatives undertaken by zemstvo physicians, was placed squarely at the government's door. Official harassment obscured the social and political foundations of local self-government. These realities became clarified only in 1905 when teachers and other third element employees concluded that their interests could not be accommodated within existing zemstvo institutions, just as they could not be accommodated within the institutions of autocracy. The very pressures generated by the teachers' professional movement, which zemstvos had helped foster, eventually helped fracture their alliance. During 1905 this conflict was rapidly overshadowed by another, deeper political rift, expressed in the rightward march of zemstvos from late summer and in the increasing identification of rural teachers with popular demands.

Teachers plunged into the swirling political waters of 1905 for a variety of reasons. The onset of revolution and bureaucratic disarray quickened the pace of teachers' professional mobilization and culminated in the organization of the All-Russian Union of Teachers, an organization dedicated to both professional and political struggle, particularly efforts to bring the Liberation Movement to the narod. Liberal and radical elements in society exhorted rural teachers to exert a political influence in the village. Even moderate zemstvo men, concerned with peasant monarchism and the specter of spontaneous rural violence, initially reached out to rural intelligenty as a link with the masses. Moreover, pressures "from below" propelled teachers into often unaccustomed political roles. We have examined this pattern of incipient rural political mobilization in some detail. Peasant interest in national events (war and revolution) and in the prospects for reform (the February Decree and October Manifesto) compelled many teachers to confront the issues of the day and assume a more active role in rural affairs, initially as decoders and interpreters of national political developments and subsequently as cadres. Teachers and peasants found a common ground in demands for access to education, democratization of local government, civil freedoms, and constitutional reform. And many teachers came to support popular demands for radical agrarian reform as long as these were pursued through organized, nonviolent forms of struggle. The Peasant Union movement of 1905 represented the logical outcome of this process.

Local Peasant Union activity demands a separate study, but our own evidence reveals much about the nature of peasant activism and the position of the rural intelligentsia in peasant society. It is generally believed that agrarian activism in 1905 (as in 1917) took traditional Russian forms: spontaneous, localized, violent risings without overt political aims and only tenuously linked to political currents in urban Russia and among other sectors of society. Local Peasant Union activity during 1905 reveals the existence of another, *organized* type of peasant movement seeking to effect agrarian and other reforms through political channels and in coalition with other groups like liberal zemstvo gentry and third element intelligenty. Here, in fact, was the germ of a more modern rural movement, which, if not for wholesale and indiscriminate official repression, might have helped integrate Russia's rural masses into national political and social structures. Failure to achieve such integration is generally recognized as a basic weakness of Imperial Russian society, responsible, in part, for the maximalist solutions of 1917. The Peasant Union experiment would have required some measure of official toleration to survive. Such was not forthcoming. Nevertheless, the Peasant Union's initial success indicates that conventional views stressing the isolation of the Russian peasantry during this period need to be revised.

The dynamic relationship that evolved during 1905 between teachers and peasant communities suggests much the same thing. Teachers and other rural intelligenty sometimes felt the full force of popular suspicion and conservatism. The violent anti-intelligentsia campaign of early 1905 strongly underscored teachers' isolation within the village and popular hostility to outsiders perceived as bearing an alien culture which threatened the fragile social ties and cultural norms of village life. More commonly, peasants simply ignored these "outsiders" living in their midst. But other teachers managed in the course of 1905 to carve out a niche of authority within the local community which was best reflected in teachers' participation in mass organizations like the peasant unions and in the elections to the Duma. Some "zemstvo rabbits" were transformed into popular spokespersons. That this happened says something about teachers' status and peasant relations with outsiders. Teachers' status within the village was not one of unremitting isolation. Peasants do seem to have responded pragmatically to stimuli and opportunities outside the narrow confines of the local community. Much as they had come to accept basic schooling for their children as a necessary means to cope with an increasingly complex world, peasants appeared willing to utilize potentially sympathetic outsiders to help them frame and press their interests.

The degree of political activism on the part of teachers in 1905 should not be overstressed. The majority apparently shunned politics. But activist elements did play a significant role in rural politics during 1905, in the main one that supported radical, but nonviolent change. Despite the assertions of officials and conservative gentry that teachers and other rural intelligenty incited the peasantry to agrarian violence, the evidence suggests that teachers exerted, whenever possible, a moderating influence in the countryside. Indeed, teachers distrusted spontaneous peasant activism as an uncontrollable tidal wave that might sweep all culture, schools included, away with gentry estates. Instead, they supported the growth of an organized "conscious" peasant movement pursuing fairly moderate tactics.

As we have suggested, such a solution was precluded by the ferocity of government repression after 1905, which failed to discriminate between moderate and revolutionary elements. The reaction fell with particular fury upon the Peasant Union and also upon rural teachers who occupied a highly exposed position. Much work needs to be done on the period of reaction, the war, and the Revolutions of 1917. They lie beyond the scope of this study. Nevertheless, one suspects that teachers' potential as a mediating influence between the narod and society during periods of crisis was effectively nullified during the post-1905 reaction when Russia's teaching profession was shaken up, intimidated, and driven back into the classroom, forced to abandon the modest position of authority which teachers had begun to consolidate in 1905. Ultimately, the social and political institutions of Old Regime Russia—both autocracy and gentry-dominated zemstvos—failed to enlist groups like teachers as effective mediators between the culture of privileged Russia and the masses. The fact that in 1917, after three years of wrenching war and increasing social polarization, such links were largely absent helps explain the rapid collapse of the old order and much of what was to follow.

Notes

1. Introduction

1. On the resilience of Russia's estate-based social order, with reference to the professions, see Gregory L. Freeze, "The *Soslovie* (Estate) Paradigm and Russian Social History," *American Historical Review,* 91 (February 1986), pp. 11–36.

2. On the Third Element, see N. M. Pirumova, *Zemskaia intelligentsiia i ee rol' v obshchestvennoi bor'be do nachale XX veka* (Moscow, 1986); V. R. Leikina-Svirskaia, *Intelligentsiia v Rossii vo vtoroi polovine XIX veka* (Moscow, 1971); Idem., *Russkaia intelligentsiia v 1900–1917 godakh* (Moscow, 1981); Nancy M. Frieden, *Russian Physicians in an Era of Reform and Revolution, 1856–1905* (Princeton, 1981); contributions by Frieden, Samuel C. Ramer, Jeffrey Brooks, and Robert E. Johnson in Terence Emmons and Wayne S. Vucinich, eds., *The Zemstvo in Russia: An Experiment in Local Self-Government* (Cambridge, 1982).

3. A. V. Ushakov, *Revoliutsionnoe dvizhenie demokraticheskoi intelligentsii v Rossii, 1895–1904* (Moscow, 1976). On the Union of Unions, see Jonathan E. Sanders, "The Union of Unions: Political, Economic, Civil and Human Rights Organizations in the 1905 Revolution," Ph.D. Dissertation, Columbia University, 1985.

4. Ben Eklof, "The Village and the Outsider: The Rural Teacher in Russia, 1864–1914," *Slavic and European Education Review,* No. 1 (1979), pp. 1–19; and Eklof, *Russian Peasant Schools: Officialdom, Village Culture and Popular Pedagogy, 1861–1914* (Berkeley, 1986).

5. Brief surveys of teachers' activity in 1905, mainly of the national union organization, exist: see Sanders, "Union of Unions," pp. 774–825; Ronald H. Hayashida, "The Unionization of Russian Teachers, 1905–1908: An Interest Group under the Autocracy," *Slavic and European Education Review,* No. 2 (1981), 1–16; John D. Morison, "Les instituteurs de village dans la revolution de 1905 en Russie," *Revue des Etudes Slaves,* (Fall 1986), pp. 205–19.

6. Terence Emmons, "The Zemstvo in Historical Perspective," in Emmons and Vucinich, eds., *The Zemstvo in Russia,* p. 427. In a more nuanced treatment that incorporates peasants' suspicion of carriers of external values corrosive of traditional rural society, Eklof concludes that "although teachers had the necessary skills to teach reading and writing, the quantitative evidence suggests that they remained outsiders, to be exploited and utilized, but not trusted." *Russian Peasant Schools,* p. 214

7. Teodor Shanin, *Russia, 1905–07: Revolution as a Moment of Truth* (New Haven, 1986).

8. See T. Leggatt, "Teaching as a Profession," in J. A. Jackson, ed., *Professions and Professionalization* (Cambridge, 1970), pp. 153–78; Amitai Etzioni, ed., *The Semi-Professions and Their Organization: Teachers, Nurses and Social Workers* (New York, 1969).

9. J. A. Jackson, "Professions and Professionalization—Editorial Introduction," in Jackson, ed., *Professions,* p. 14.

10. Ibid., p. 11.

11. Jeffrey Brooks, *When Russia Learned to Read: Literacy and Popular Literature, 1861–1917* (Princeton, 1985).

12. Allen Sinel, *The Classroom and the Chancellery: State Educational Reform in Russia under Count Dmitry Tolstoi* (Cambridge, Mass., 1973); Eklof, *Russian Peasant Schools,* chapter 4.

2. *Teachers and the Politics of Education in Russia*

1. The basic source here is *Statisticheskii vremennik Rossiiskoi imperii. Sel'skie uchilishcha v Evropeiskoi Rossii i Privislenskikh guberniiakh*, ed. A. V. Dubrovskii, Seriia III, vypusk 1 (St. Petersburg: izd. Tsent. Stat. Kom. Min. Vnut. Del, 1884). See G. Fal'bork and V. Charnoluskii, "Nachal'noe narodnoe obrazovanie," *Entsiklopedicheskii slovar'* Brokgauza-Efrona, 86 vols. (St. Petersburg, 1890–1907), 40, p. 761; L. K. Erman, "Sostav intelligentsii v Rossii v kontse XIX i nachale XX v.," *Istoriia SSSR,* No. 1 (1963), p. 175; Leikina-Svirskaia, *Intelligentsiia v Rossii,* chapter 6. For details of the 1880 census data, see G. Fal'bork and V. Charnoluskii, *Narodnoe obrazovanie v Rossii* (St. Petersburg, 1899), pp. 51–55 and appendixes (pp. 170–75). In addition, there were 12,566 teachers of catechism classes *(zakonouchitelia),* usually local clerics. A word of caution here: data on teachers sometimes lump the catechism teachers together with regular rural teachers, significantly inflating the totals. On this problem, see N. V. Chekhov, "Kak veliko chislo narodnykh uchitelei v Rossii," *Russkaia shkola,* No. 3, section 2 (1908), pp. 68–70. In general, catechism teachers comprise about one-third of such totals.

2. These schools accounted for nearly 70 percent of all rural primary schools in these provinces. This was before the major campaign by the Holy Synod to open church-run schools. See E. G. Kornilov, "Zemskaia demokraticheskaia intelligentsiia 70-kh godov XIX veka," in *Voprosy obshchestvennogo i sotsial'no-ekonomicheskogo razvitiia Rossii v XVIII–XIX vekakh (po materialam tsent. gub.)* (Riazan, 1974), pp. 94–95.

3. B. B. Veselovskii, *Istoriia zemstva za sorok let,* 4 vols. (St. Petersburg, 1909–1911), I, 485; Ben Eklof, *Russian Peasant Schools,* chapter 3 and "The Myth of the Zemstvo School: The Sources of the Expansion of Rural Education in Imperial Russia: 1864–1914," *History of Education Quarterly* (Winter 1984), pp. 561–84; Brooks, *When Russia Learned to Read,* chapters 1 and 2.

4. V. Farmakovskii, "Deiatel'nost' ministerstva narodnago prosveshcheniia v oblasti nachal'nago narodnago obrazovaniia v poslednee desiatiletie (1894–1903)," *Zhurnal ministerstva narodnago prosveshcheniia,* No. 4, section 2 (1904), pp. 11–12.

5. See, for example, the memoir of a future teacher, S. Anikin, "Kholernyi god," *Vestnik Evropy,* No. 1 (1913), pp. 98–126; V. I. Dmitrieva, "Po derevniam: iz zametok 'epidimicheskago vracha'," Ibid., 1896, No. 10, pp. 520–565; No. 11, pp. 131–76; S. Grin, "Voina s batsillami (iz zametok zhenshchiny-vracha)," Ibid., No. 5 (1900), pp. 589–654; Frieden, *Russian Physicians,* pp. 149–50.

6. E. O. Vakhterova, *V. P. Vakhterov, ego zhizn' i rabota,* (Moscow, 1961), p. 107. On the work of the committees, see Ibid., chapter 4; Veselovskii, III, 385–88; O. Kaidanova, *Ocherki po istorii narodnogo obrazovaniia v Rossii i SSSR na osnove lichnogo opyta i nabliudenii,* 2 vols. (Berlin, 1938), I, 515–16; P. N. Miliukov, *Ocherki po istorii russkoi kul'tury,* vol. II, part 2 (Paris, 1931), pp. 853–54; N. M. Pirumova, *Zemskoe liberal'noe dvizhenie: sotsial'nye korni i evoliutsiia do nachala XX veka* (Moscow, 1977), pp. 117–19; A. D. Stepanskii, "Liberal'naia intelligentsiia v obshchestvennom dvizhenii Rossii na rubezhe XIX-XX vv.," *Istoricheskie zapiski,* 109 (1983), pp. 66–68; in general, see Allen Sinel, "The Campaign for Universal Primary Education in Russia, 1890–1904," *Jahrbücher für Geschichte Osteuropas,* 30, No. 4 (1982), pp. 481–507, and Eklof, *Russian Peasant Schools,* chapter 4.

7. I. I. Ianzhul, "Shkol'nyi uchitel' pobedil," in *Ekonomicheskaia otsenka narodnago obrazovaniia,* 2nd ed. (St. Petersburg, 1899).

8. Cited in V. V. Kir'iakov, *Shag za shagom: K istorii ob"edineniia narodnykh uchitelei—iz lichnykh vospominanii i perezhivanii* (Moscow, 1914), p. 32.

9. V. P. Vologdin, "Zemskaia statistika narodnago obrazovaniia," in B. B. Veselovskii and Z. G. Frenkel', eds., *Iubileinyi zemskii sbornik, 1864–1914* (St. Petersburg, 1914), pp. 399–400; Veselovskii, III, 389.

10. Survey results were compiled and published in: M. Sobolev, "K voprosu o polozhenii uchashchikh v narodnoi shkole," *Russkaia mysl'*, No. 9, section 2 (1898), pp. 189–212; V. Gol'tsev, "K voprosu o polozhenii uchashchikh v narodnoi shkole," Ibid., 1897, No. 6, section 2, pp. 82–94; No. 12, section 2, pp. 61–78; V. Gol'tsev, "O polozhenii uchashchikh v shkolakh Vladimirskoi gubernii," *Obrazovanie*, No. 4 (1897), pp. 9–16. Much of this material is summarized in L. N. Blinov, "Narodnyi uchitel' v Rossii," in kn. D. I. Shakhovskoi, ed., *Vseobshchee obrazovanie v Rossii: sbornik statei* (Moscow, 1902), pp. 63–84.

11. A useful list of zemstvo statistical studies can be found in N. Bratchikov, "Uchebno-vospitatel'naia chast' v nachal'noi shkole," *Russkaia shkola*, No. 3 (1909), pp. 91–93; see also I. S. Samokhvalov, *Kratkii ukazatel' literatury po statistike narodnogo obrazovaniia v Rossii* (Moscow, 1920).

12. N. A. Skvortsov, "Nazrevshii vopros (polozhenie narodnykh uchitel'nits i uchitelei)," *Obrazovanie*, No. 2, section 2 (1897), pp. 19–25 (results of Nizhegorod Teachers' Society survey); D. N. Zhbankov, "O polozhenii narodnykh uchitelei v Smolenskoi gubernii," *Zhizn'*, No. 11 (1900), pp. 168–82 (Smolensk Teachers' Society).

13. Bratchikov, "Uchebno-vospitatel'naia chast'," *Russkaia shkola*, No. 2 (1909), p. 115. At this time (1899) there were some 37,000 schools under the jurisdiction of the MNP empire-wide (including urban and rural primary schools, as well as zemstvo schools). In these, according to Ministry figures, there were 57,200 teachers (32,100 men and 25,100 women). At the same time there were some 40,000 schools under the Holy Synod, the result of phenomenal growth and huge state subsidies from the mid-1880s. See Leikina-Svirskaia, *Intelligentsiia v Rossii*, pp. 166–67; Blinov, "Narodnyi uchitel' v Rossii," p. 63. Of the MNP schools in 1898, 16,400 were zemstvo schools. On the growth of zemstvo schools, see below, note 39.

14. S. I. Mitskevich, *Zapiski vracha-obshchestvennika, 1888–1918*, 2nd ed. (Moscow, 1969), p. 78; V. P. Akimov-Makhnovets, "Stroiteli budushchego," *Obrazovanie*, No. 5 (1907), p. 78.

15. For a good survey of the teacher as "outsider," see Eklof, "The Village and the Outsider," pp. 1–19, and also his *Russian Peasant Schools*, chapters 7 and 8.

16. Over 70 percent of students in state teachers' seminaries were of peasant origin: S. V. Rozhdestvenskii, *Istoricheskii obzor deiatel'nosti ministerstva narodnago prosveshcheniia. 1802–1902 gg.* (St. Petersburg, 1902), p. 724; *Vsepoddanneishii otchet ministra narodnago prosveshcheniia za 1903 god* (St. Petersburg, 1905), p. 462. On Tolstoi's preference for peasant students (and teachers), see Allen Sinel, "Educating the Russian Peasantry: The Elementary School Reforms of Count Dmitri Tolstoi," *Slavic Review*, 27, No. 1 (1968), p. 63.

17. In 1880 there were 7,369 teachers of peasant origin (30.2 percent of the total), and in 1911 there were 44,607 teachers of peasant origin in rural schools (40.8 percent): Erman, "Sostav intelligentsii," pp. 175–76. For data from individual provinces, see Bratchikov, "Uchebno-vospitatel'naia chast'," pp. 116–17; Leikina-Svirskaia, *Intelligentsiia v Rossii*, p. 163.

18. Bratchikov, "Uchebno-vospitatel'naia chast'," pp. 115–16.

19. *Nachal'noe narodnoe obrazovanie v Tul'skoi gubernii v 1896–1897 uchebnom godu* (Tula, 1898), chapter 5 (paginated separately), p. 4; *Polozhenie nachal'nago narodnago obrazovaniia v Novgorodskoi gubernii*, 4 vols. (Novgorod, 1901–4), I, 4; V. Shcherba, "K voprosu o podgotovke uchitel'skago personala," *Saratovskaia zemskaia nedelia*, No. 6–7, section 3 (1903), pp. 2–3; *Obzor sostoianiia nachal'nago narodnago obrazovaniia v*

Kurskoi gubernii za 5 let (1895/96–1900/01 uchebn. g.g.) (Kursk, 1902), pp. 106–9; O. S[mir]nov, "Itogi deiatel'nosti zemstv po narodnomu obrazovaniiu," *Narodnyi uchitel'*, No. 5 (1907), pp. 4–5, provides a provincial breakdown by sex. In only six zemstvo provinces did males predominate: S. Anikin, "Vystavka v Iaroslavle," *Saratovskaia zemskaia nedelia* No. 8 (1903), p. 103.

20. For example, in Kursk province over a five-year period, 1895/6–1900/1, the number of teachers in zemstvo schools increased by 236; the number of male teachers increased by only one and that of females nearly doubled during this period of rapid expansion. N. Tulupov, "Kurskaia vystavka po narodnomu obrazovaniiu," *Russkaia mysl'*, No. 8, section 2 (1902), p. 116.

21. N. Lozanov, "Ob otkrytii uchitel'skoi seminarii v gor. Saratove," *Saratovskaia zemskaia nedelia*, No. 2, section 3 (1903), pp. 53–54. Vas. Golubev. "Polozhenie narodnago obrazovaniia v Saratovskoi gubernii (po otzyvam mestnykh zhitelei)," *Saratovskaia zemskaia nedelia*, No. 2, section 3 (1902), p. 167. In one communal resolution adopted in 1905, among other demands for educational reform, peasants demanded that they be sent a well-informed teacher, stressing that such not be a woman: "Agrarnoe dvizhenie v Smolenskoi gubernii v 1905–1907 gg.," *Krasnyi arkhiv*, No. 1 (74), 1936, p. 110.

22. A 1911 empire-wide census of all primary schools (including those in urban areas) found a total of 154,177 teachers: 83,311 women and 70,866 men (that is, 54.1 percent were female). See B. Veselovskii, "Vserossiiskaia perepis' shkol," *Sovremennyi mir*, No. 7 (1911), p. 248.

23. Tulupov, "Kurskaia vystavka," p. 117.

24. I. P. Belokonskii, "Obzor deiatel'nosti zemstv po narodnomu obrazovaniiu za 1902 g.," *Russkaia shkola*, No. 2 (1903), p. 163; N. V. Tulupov, "Pervyi vserossiiskii s"ezd predstavitelei obshchestv vspomoshchestvovaniia litsam uchitel'skago zvaniia," *Russkaia mysl'*, No. 3, section 2 (1903), p. 130; see also Eklof, *Russian Peasant Schools*, pp. 206–11.

25. Sobolev, "K voprosu o polozhenii," pp. 191–92, 195, 201; V. Serebriakov, "Sovremennoe sostoianie russkoi derevni i eia nuzhdy, po otzyvam sel'skikh zhitelei," *Saratovskaia zemskaia nedelia*, No. 10–12, section 3 (1905), pp. 5–8; Vakhlin, "Narodnoe obrazovanie v Orekhovo-Zuevskom uezde do revoliutsii," in *Orekhovo-Zuevskii uezd, Moskovskoi gubernii: istoriko-ekonomicheskii sbornik* (Orekhovo-Zuevo, 1926), pp. 420–21; S. T. Semenov, *Dvadtsat' piat' let v derevne* (Petrograd, 1915), p. 163. Teachers complained of poor maintenance by local communes and that peasants skimped on firewood for the school, arguing that the pupils themselves would heat the building up, or that after eight o'clock in the evening peasants compelled teachers to sit without fire or light, since the *mir* itself went to sleep then: I. P. Kupchinov, *Krest'ianskoe samoupravlenie: ocherk zakonov, blizkikh k krest'ianskoi zhizni*, 2nd ed. (Moscow, 1905), pp. 143–44.

26. *Saratovskii listok*, No. 184, September 10, 1905, p. 3; No. 194, September 23, 1905, p. 3.

27. Compare the success of French teachers in acquiring such status: Barnett Singer, "The Teacher as Notable in Brittany, 1880–1914," *French Historical Studies*, 9 (1976), pp. 635–59; Eugen Weber, *Peasants into Frenchmen: The Modernization of Rural France, 1870–1914* (Stanford: Stanford University Press, 1976), pp. 317–18.

28. According to the Committee of Literacy survey, in thirty-three provinces, male teachers' salaries averaged 270 rubles and females' salaries 252 rubles: Blinov, "Narodnyi uchitel' v Rossii," p. 75.

29. Blinov, "Narodnyi uchitel' v Rossii," p. 82. A. I. Shingarev, "Osnovaniia zemskago sanitarnago nadzora za nachal'nymi shkolami," in Shakhovskoi, ed., *Vseobshchee obrazovanie v Rossii*, pp. 99–119.

30. Teachers were appointed by the institution maintaining the school (for example, zemstvos), subject to approval by the state school inspector and final con-

firmation by the local school board. Transfers and dismissals could be initiated by either the zemstvo or inspector (or requested by the teacher), with final decision by the school board. Inspectors also had the right to remove a teacher temporarily, until the next session of the board. For a review of the legislation (School Statute of 1874 and subsequent MNP circulars) regulating teacher hiring, transfer, and dismissal, see: O. N. Smirnov, "Zemstvo i biurokratiia v dele narodnago obrazovaniia," *Russkaia shkola,* No. 12 (1906), pp. 14–16; O. Smirnov, "Prava zemstv i uchitelei v dele narodnago obrazovaniia," in E. A. Zviagintsev, et al., *Shkola, zemstvo i uchitel': sbornik statei* (Moscow, 1911), pp. 117–19; V. Sokolov, "Pravovoe polozhenie uchitelei," *Saratovskaia zemskaia nedelia,* No. 6–7, section 3 (1905), pp. 35–37.

31. On Iablochkov, see N. V. Chekhov, "Moi vospominaniia o P. M. Shestakove," *Dlia narodnago uchitelia,* No. 1 (1915), 6–7; *Russkiia vedomstvo,* No. 333, December 7, 1897, p. 2 (zemstvo protest against inspectoral "rules" in Tver); see also E. A. Zviagintsev, *Inspektsiia narodnykh uchilishch (Russkoe obschestvo i uchebnoe vedomstvo v shkol'nom dele),* 2nd ed. (Moscow, 1914); Eklof, *Russian Peasant Schools,* chapter 5.

32. TsGAOR, f. 6862, op. 1, d. 80, 1. 29ob–31ob; A. L., "Vnutrennaia khronika," *Zhurnal dlia vsekh,* No. 5 (1904), p. 317; A. Ivashkin, "Iz vospominanii o narodnykh uchiteliakh," *Saratovskaia zemskaia nedelia,* No. 2, section 3 (1905), p. 42; A. Petrishchev, "Iz zametok shkol'nago uchitelia," *Russkoe bogatstvo,* No. 10 (1904), p. 91.

33. Gol'tsev, "O polozhenii uchashchikh," p. 16.

34. Skvortsov, "Nazrevshii vopros," p. 19.

35. One report claimed that the rate of attrition among male teachers was 38 percent in ten zemstvo provinces and 61 percent in three nonzemstvo provinces: "Khronika vnutrennei zhizni," *Russkoe bogatstvo,* No. 4, section 2 (1900), pp. 186–88; I. P. Belokonskii, "Derevenskiia vpechatleniia (iz zapisok zemskago statistika)," *Russkoe bogatstvo,* No. 9 (1898), p. 118. On the monopoly, see Theodore H. Von Laue, *Sergei Witte and the Industrialization of Russia* (New York, 1963), p. 103.

36. *Izvlechenie iz vsepoddanneishago otcheta ministra narodnago prosveshcheniia za 1900 god* (St. Petersburg, 1902), pp. 552–53. This report notes that during the 1880s when the rural police post of *uriadnik* was introduced many schools had to suspend operations due to teacher flight. In 1903 these officials received from 310 to 400 rubles per year, considerably more than most teachers: George L. Yaney, *The Systematization of Russian Government: Social Evolution in the Domestic Administration of Imperial Russia, 1711–1905* (Urbana, 1973), p. 335.

37. Veselovskii, *Istoriia zemstva,* I, 474, 514–15; also A. V. Peshekhonov, "Na ocherednye temy (zemskaia doroga)," *Russkoe bogatstvo,* No. 2 (1914), pp. 324–25; A. I. Novikov, *Zapiski zemskago nachal'nika* (St. Petersburg, 1899), p. 200; V. M. Khizhniakov, *Vospominaniia zemskago deiatelia* (Petrograd, 1916), pp. 193–97.

38. Sinel, *The Classroom and the Chancellery,* chapter 7.

39. Veselovskii, I, 475–76; III, 389; also see E. A. Zviagintsev, *Polveka zemskoi deiatel'nosti po narodnomu obrazovaniiu,* 2nd ed. (Moscow, 1917), p. 48, which gives the following figures for the growth of zemstvo schools: 1877: 10,100; 1894: 13,100; 1898: 16,400; 1903: 18,700; 1911: 35,000; 1914: over 40,000. Before 1880 the zemstvos opened an annual average of 800 rural schools, while in the period 1880–94 this figure was nearly cut in half. During this fourteen-year period the average number of pupils per school rose from 52.6 to 70.6, which, of course, placed additional burdens on teachers. Fal'bork and Charnoluskii, "Nachal'noe narodnoe obrazovanie," pp. 766–67.

40. Veselovskii, I, 567–68 (for a provincial breakdown, p. 569). Average annual zemstvo education budgets (in thousands of rubles for one province) increased as follows: to 1871 (8,500 rubles); 1871–80 (12,600); 1881–90 (5,900); 1891–95 (11,800); 1895–1901 (38,200); 1902–3 (41,600).

41. Veselovskii, I, 462–64, 467–68, 473, 527–33, 540–41, 585; Miliukov, *Ocherki po istorii russkoi kul'tury,* vol. II, part 2, p. 828. According to a survey conducted by the

Saratov zemstvo in 1902 covering 207 district zemstvos, zemstvos assumed total funding in the following areas: (a) teachers' salaries (in 75.4 percent of zemstvos); (b) textbooks, writing materials, and so on (77.7 percent); (c) repair of school buildings (23.3 percent); (d) so-called *khoziaistvennye* expenditures, that is, hiring school guard, fuel, lighting, and so on (14 percent): Bratchikov, "Uchebno-vospitatel'naia chast'," No. 3, p. 78. The latter item is significant, as teachers were still largely dependent upon local peasant officials for crucial necessities, a frequent source of conflict as well as cold classrooms and difficult working conditions. See V. V. Akimov, "Deiatel'nost' kurskago zemstva po narodnomu obrazovaniiu," *Zhurnal ministerstva narodnago prosveshcheniia*, No. 10, section 3 (1910), pp. 143–45.

42. See V. Charnoluskii, "Zemstvo i vneshkol'noe obrazovanie," in Veselovskii and Frenkel', eds., *Iubileinyi zemskii sbornik*, p. 376; Veselovskii, I, 547–54.

43. During the period 1893–96 the question of universal schooling was raised in twenty-four out of thirty-four provincial zemstvos: Ibid., p. 516; B. B. Veselovskii, "Vseobshchee obuchenie i zemstvo," in Veselovskii and Frenkel', eds., *Iubileinyi zemskii sbornik*, p. 392.

44. Veselovskii, I, 518–19; III, 389. According to a survey of the Vologda zemstvo in 1906, twenty-one provincial zemstvos had such commissions: V. I. Charnoluskii, ed., *Ezhegodnik narodnoi shkoly* (Moscow, 1908), p. 235.

45. Veselovskii, III, 680–81.

46. Pirumova, *Zemskoe liberal'noe dvizhenie*, p. 152; *Trudy mestnykh komitetov o nuzhdakh sel'skokhoziaistvennoi promyshlennosti*, 58 vols. (St. Petersburg, 1903), XXVIII (report of A. A. Stakhovich in the Orel committee), p. 439.

47. See S. N. Prokopovich, *Mestnye liudi o nuzhdakh Rossii* (St. Petersburg, 1904); M. S. Simonova, "Zemsko-liberal'naia fronda (1902–1903 gg.)," *Istoricheskie zapiski*, 91 (1973), pp. 150–216; N. L. Peterson, comp., *Svod trudov mestnykh komitetov po 49 guberniiam Evropeiskoi Rossii: Prosveshchenie* (St. Petersburg, 1904) and N. V. Chekhov, "Narodnoe obrazovanie," in *Nuzhdy derevni: po rabotam komitetov o nuzhdakh sel'skokhoziaistvennoi promyshlennosti*, 2 vols. (St. Petersburg, 1904), I, 382–85.

48. Prokopovich, *Mestnye liudi*, pp. 53–54; also A. V. Ososkov, *Voprosy istorii nachal'nogo obrazovaniia v Rossii (II pol. XIX- nach. XX vv.)*, 2 vols. (Moscow, 1974–75), II, 6–7; *Trudy mestnykh komitetov*, XXXVII, 608.

49. Cited in Pirumova, *Zemskoe liberal'noe dvizhenie*, p. 152; see also Eklof, "The Myth of the Zemstvo School," p. 566.

50. Veselovskii, I, 479; and especially the individual surveys of zemstvos in vol. IV of his *Istoriia zemstva*.

51. *Obozrenie zemskikh uchrezhdenii Tverskoi gubernii: otchet direktora Departamenta Obshchikh Del Ministerstva Vnutrennykh Del Gofmeistera Shtiurmera 1903 g.* (n. p., n. d.), pp. 20–21. MVD officials who audited other zemstvos likewise stressed the political intent of zemstvo educational efforts, for example, in Moscow: *Vestnik vospitaniia*, No. 7, section 2 (1904), pp. 94–95.

52. Veselovskii, IV, 334-36; I, 569; I. P. Belokonskii, "Obzor deiatel'nosti zemstv po narodnomu obrazovaniiu v 1903 g.," *Russkaia shkola*, No. 4 (1904), pp. 158–160; Vologdin, "Zemskaia statistika," pp. 401–3.

53. Akimov, "Deiatel'nost' kurskago zemstva," *ZhMNP*, No. 9, section 3 (1910), pp. 17–18; Zviagintsev, *Polveka zemskoi deiatel'nosti*, pp. 58–61; Akimov, "Deiatel'nost' kurskago zemstva," *ZhMNP*, No. 11 (1910), pp. 23–29.

54. Veselovskii, IV, 384–86.

55. Ibid., pp. 208–9, 278–80, 286–87; Pirumova, *Zemskoe liberal'noe dvizhenie*, p. 92.

56. N. Malinovskii, "O shkol'nom muzee Slavianoserbskago uezdnago zemstva," in *Otchet Obshchestva vzaimopomoshchi uchashchim i uchivshim v nachal'nykh uchilishchakh Slavianoserbskago uezda, s l-go sentiabria 1904 goda po l-e ianvaria 1907 goda (god 5-i i 6-i)*, (Lugansk, 1907), pp. 67–69.

57. Pirumova, *Zemskoe liberal'noe dvizhenie,* chapter 3; Roberta Thompson Manning, "Zemstvo and Revolution: The Onset of the Gentry Reaction, 1905–1907," in Leopold H. Haimson, ed., *The Politics of Rural Russia, 1905–1914.* (Bloomington: Indiana University Press, 1979), pp. 30–37, and especially, her *Crisis of the Old Order in Russia: Gentry and Government* (Princeton, 1982), chapter 3; Gary H. Hamburg, "The Russian Nobility on the Eve of the 1905 Revolution," *Russian Review,* 38, No. 3 (July 1979), pp. 323–38; Terence Emmons, "The Russian Landed Gentry and Politics," *Russian Review,* 33, No. 3 (July 1974), pp. 269–83.

58. Veselovskii, III, 466–67; Manning, "Zemstvo and Revolution," pp. 34–36; Pirumova, *Zemskoe liberal'noe dvizhenie,* pp. 87–93, and appendix, 232–82.

59. V. Chernov, *Zapiski sotsialista-revoliutsionera* (Berlin, 1922), p. 251. Incidentally, one can see a pattern of liberal leadership and zemstvo education activity in Tambov similar to the pattern described above for other provinces: Veselovskii, IV, 376–77; Terence Emmons, *The Formation of Political Parties and the First National Elections in Russia* (Cambridge, Mass., 1983), pp. 66–72.

60. Veselovskii, III, 385–88; K. Dikson and B. Ketrits, *S.-Peterburgskii komitet gramotnosti (1861–1911),* (St. Petersburg, 1912), pp. 22, 52–53; Pirumova, *Zemskoe liberal'noe dvizhenie,* pp. 117–19.

61. *Obozrenie zemskikh uchrezhdenii Tverskoi gubernii,* p. 75.

62. Akimov, "Deiatel'nost' kurskago zemstva," No. 9, pp. 14–15.

63. Veselovskii, III, 390–91; Pirumova, *Zemskoe liberal'noe dvizhenie,* p. 49; O. N. Smirnov, "Zemstvo i biurokratiia," p. 15. The addition of land captains to local school boards was a factor for teachers, who complained of their ill-informed meddling in the affairs of the school, particularly in holding the certificate examinations at the end of the third year of the school course (which reduced the term of military service for graduates): see *Iuzhnaia zaria* (Ekaterinoslav), No. 80, July 20/August 2, 1906, p. 4; *Vladimirets* (Vladimir), No. 89, April 27, 1907, p. 4.

64. *Svod vysochaishikh otmetok po Vsepoddanneishim otchetam za 1898 g. gubernatorov, voennykh gubernatorov i gradonachal'nikov* (St. Petersburg, 1901), p. 44; see also governors' protests of zemstvo education outlays: I. P. Belokonskii, *Zemstvo i konstitutsiia* (Moscow, 1910), p. 71 (Voronezh); Veselovskii, IV, 336 (Kursk); on the taxation issue, see Thomas S. Fallows, "The Zemstvo and the Bureaucracy," in Emmons and Vucinich, *The Zemstvo in Russia,* pp. 215–18.

65. N. V. Chekhov, *Narodnoe obrazovanie v Rossii s 60-kh godov XIX veka* (Moscow, 1912), pp. 191–92.

66. *Svod vysochaishikh otmetok po Vsepoddanneishim otchetam za 1895 g.* (St Petersburg, 1898), pp. 134, 160–61; E. A. Zviagintsev, "Zemstvo i uchebnoe vedomstvo" in Veselovskii and Frenkel', eds., *Iubileinyi zemskii sbornik,* pp. 363–64.

67. Pirumova, *Zemskoe liberal'noe dvizhenie,* p. 49; *Russkiia vedomosti,* No. 33, February 2, 1901, p. 3; Chekhov, *Narodnoe obrazovanie v. Rossii,* p. 190; I. P. Belokonskii, *Zemskoe dvizhenie,* 2nd ed. (Moscow, 1914), pp. 81–82; Veselovskii, III, 542–43.

68. Veselovskii, I, 492–95.

69. Veselovskii, I, 488; III, 540–43. Ben Eklof takes a more sanguine view of zemstvo-government relations in the area of public education before 1905, arguing that they were generally harmonious: *Russian Peasant Schools,* p. 66 and chapter 5.

70. Chekhov, *Narodnoe obrazovanie v Rossii,* pp. 192–95; Ososkov, *Voprosy istorii,* II, 5–10.

71. Belokonskii, *Zemstvo i konstitutsiia,* p. 125.

72. L. D. Briukhatov, "Nuzhdy narodnago uchitelia," *Russkiia vedomosti,* No. 265, October 10, 1905, p. 3.

73. This point was made by V. Mut'ev, the MNP official who directed the state pension fund for teachers: TsGIA, f. 733, op. 173, d. 127, 1. 13ob-14.

3. *Cultural Impoverishment and the Impulse to Associate*

1. Blinov, "Narodnyi uchitel," pp. 66–68; N. Bratchikov, "Uchebno-vospitatel'naia chast' v nachal'noi shkole," *Russkaia shkola,* No. 2 (1909), pp. 119–20; *Nachal'noe narodnoe obrazovanie v Tul'skoi gubernii v 1896–1897 uchebnom godu,* pp. 11–17 (section on teachers paginated separately). For brief descriptions of the institutions and their curricula, see A. I. Piskunov, ed., *Ocherki istorii shkoly i pedagogicheskoi mysli narodov SSSR: vtoraia polovina XIX v.* (Moscow, 1976).

2. TsGIA, f. 1278, op. 2 (1908), d. 542, 1. 3-3ob.; Shcherba, "K voprosu o podgotovke," pp. 3–4.

3. V. B., "K voprosu o podgotovke uchitel'skago personala," *Obrazovanie,* No. 4 (1902), p. 98–100; Blinov, "Narodnyi uchitel'," pp. 69–70; Allen Sinel, "Count Dmitrii Tolstoi and the Preparation of Russian School Teachers," *Canadian-American Slavic Studies,* 3, No. 2 (Summer 1969), pp. 252–53; N. Akhutin, "K voprosu o podgotovke narodnykh uchitelei," *Russkaia shkola,* No. 1 (1905), pp. 125–34.

4. On declining qualifications, see Bratchikov, "Uchebno-vospitatel'naia chast'," pp. 118–20; Shcherba, "K voprosu o podgotovke," p. 3; Leikina-Svirskaia, *Intelligentsiia,* p. 165; *Obzor sostoianiia nachal'nago obrazovaniia v Kurskoi gubernii za 5 let: 1895/96–1900/01 uchebn. gg.* (Kursk, 1902), p. 113; Tulupov, "Kurskaia vystavka," p. 116. Among those with "satisfactory" qualifications are graduates of the diocesan schools, which granted teaching certificates for primary schools but whose curriculum stood well below the women's gymnasium.

5. According to MNP figures more than one-third of those entering teaching posts in 1899 lacked specialized or complete secondary educations: Rozhdestvenskii, *Istoricheskii obzor,* p. 723; Farmakovskii, "Deiatel'nost' ministerstva narodnago prosveshcheniia," p. 20. Eklof makes a good case that by the 1900s, formal educations, certifying exams, and experience on the job insured that most teachers were competent "craftsmen," equipped to teach the rudiments to peasant children. This study focuses on teachers' potential influence outside the classroom, and, contrary to Eklof's conclusions, our evidence strongly suggests that in the years before 1905 many teachers aspired to play a more active role in the countryside and painfully felt their own lack of preparation to do so. See Eklof, *Russian Peasant Schools,* pp. 194–206.

6. V. V. Petrov, ed., *Voprosy narodnago obrazovaniia v Moskovskoi gubernii,* 4 vols. (Moscow, 1897–1901), II, 5–6, 8.

7. A. Odintsov, comp., *Uchitel'skii s"ezd* (Moscow, 1904), p. 56; N. Zapankov, *Uchitel' narodnoi shkoly* (SPB, 1906), p. 36.

8. TsGIA, f. 733, op. 173, d. 127, 1. 74-74ob.

9. A. A. Kovalev, "Ocherk vozniknoveniia i razvitiia uchitel'skikh kursov i s"ezdov v Rossii," *Russkaia shkola,* No. 12 (1905), p. 88.

10. K. Ia. Vorob'ev, "Narodnye otzyvy o tsenzure," *Russkiia vedomosti,* No. 182, July 8, 1905, p. 3.

11. V. D. Pupu, "Vospominaniia o revoliutsii 1905 goda," TsGAOR, f. 6862, op. 1, d. 86, 1. 52-52ob. He failed to heed this warning, and when in 1905 he related press reports on current events to the local population she turned her hunting dogs on him.

12. V. A. Samsonov, *Byt uchashchikh v Novgorodskoi gubernii* (Novgorod, 1907), p. 83; Blinov, pp. 72–73.

13. Pupu, "Vospominaniia," 1. 51ob.

14. Samsonov, *Byt uchashchikh v Novgorodskoi gubernii,* pp. 4–5.

15. Petrov, *Voprosy,* II, p. 22; Belokonskii, Derevenskiia vpechatleniia," pp. 114–15; Samsonov, *Byt uchashchikh v Novgorodskoi gubernii,* pp. 8–9.

16. Petrov, *Voprosy,* II, pp. 22–25; Samsonov, *Byt uchashchikh v Novgorodskoi guber-*

nii, p. 89; Odintsov, *Uchitel'skii*, p. 56; Vl. Ladyzhenskii, "Ocherki zemskago obrazovaniia v Penzenskoi gubernii," *Russkaia mysl'*, No. 11, section 2 (1904), p. 172. On zemstvo libraries at the zemstvo board, see Veselovskii, *Istoriia*, III, 479.

17. P. Shesternin, "Iz vospominanii sel'skago uchitelia," *Obrazovanie*, No. 9 (1898), p. 114.

18. Blinov, p. 73. Evidence correlating gender and reading habits is slim. A survey from Nizhegorod district (1905) found that male teachers tended to allocate a greater portion of their budgets to reading. Women tended to spend less to satisfy "cultural needs" than did male teachers with families: G. I. Sergeev, comp., *Narodnaia shkola v Nizhegorodskom uezde* (Nizhnii-Novgorod, 1905), p. 29.

19. V. Gol'tsev, "O polozhenii uchashchikh v shkolakh Vladimirskoi gubernii," *Obrazovanie*, No. 4 (1897), pp. 11–13; also a later survey by the Vladimir Teachers' Society cited in E. O. Vakhterova, "Umstvennye zaprosy narodnago uchitelia i ikh udovletvorenie," in *Trudy I-go vserossiiskago s"ezda predstavitelei obshchestv vspomoshchestvovaniia litsam uchitel'skago zvaniia*, ed. V. M. Evteev, 2 vols. (Moscow, 1907), I, 657–58.

20. Gol'tsev, "K voprosu o polozhenii," No. 12 (1897), pp. 66–67, 73–75; Gol'tsev, "K voprosu o polozhenii," No. 6 (1897), p. 91; Sobolev, "K voprosu o polozhenii," No. 9 (1898), pp. 191–92, 197.

21. Gol'tsev, No. 6 (1897), pp. 85–86; Sobolev, pp. 201–02.

22. Ibid., pp. 208–09. Concerning "teachers' libraries" at schools, of 2,103 replies received from 24 provinces by the Moscow Literacy Committee, a total lack of libraries was noted in 1,350 cases (a collection of ten books was considered a library): Vakhterova, "Umstvennye zaprosy," pp. 659–60.

23. A. A. Nikolaev, "Neskol'ko slov o biudzhete narodnago uchitelia," *Russkaia shkola*, No. 5–6 (1912), pp. 94–95.

24. Mirovich, "Obrazovatel'nye stremleniia uchitelia i lektsii v provintsii," *Zhurnal dlia vsekh*, No. 5 (1905), p. 302.

25. Ibid. In Kursk the zemstvo found that in 1904 out of 810 respondents, 430 teachers (53 percent) did not subscribe to a single periodical. Of the latter, 170 were able to borrow these from neighbors (priests, landowners), but 260 had no access whatsoever: I. P. Belokonskii, "Obzor deiatel'nosti zemstv po narodnomu obrazovaniiu za 1904 g.," *Russkaia shkola*, No. 4 (1905), p. 147; see also Petrov, *Voprosy*, II, 4–5; Bratchikov, "Uchebno-vospitatel'naia chast'," p. 126; M. F. Superanskii, *Byt uchashchikh v nachal'nykh shkolakh Simbirskoi gubernii* (Simbirsk, 1905), pp. 20–21; S. O. Seropolko, *Polozhenie uchashchikh v zemskikh shkolakh Tul'skoi gubernii* (Tula, 1904), pp. 7–9.

26. Samsonov, *Byt uchashikh v Novgorodskoi gubernii*, pp. 77–78; Sergeev, *Narodnaia shkola v Nizhegorodskom uezde*, p. 36.

27. A. V. Panov, "Voprosy narodnago obrazovaniia na gubernskom zemskom sobranii (pis'mo iz Saratova)," *Obrazovanie*, No. 2, section 3 (1902), p. 34.

28. A. A. L[okti]n, "Kakiia periodicheskiia izdaniia vypisyvaiut uchashchie nachal'nykh shkol v Iaroslavskoi gubernii," *Vestnik vospitaniia*, No. 3, section 2 (1904), pp. 85–87; Bratchikov, pp. 123–124.

29. Ibid., pp. 125–26.

30. *Niva*, the best-selling "thin" journal in Russia, was richly illustrated and included photographs; see Jeffrey Brooks, "Readers and Reading at the End of the Tsarist Era," in William Mills Todd III, ed., *Literature and Russian Society, 1800–1914* (Stanford: Stanford University Press, 1978), pp. 102–3.

31. Bratchikov, p. 127. S. V. Anikin wrote that among "Three-fourths of the Iaroslavl teachers circulate such periodicals that are barely read within the intelligentsia milieu": "Vystavka v Iaroslavle," p. 106; M. Tugan-Baranovskii, "Zemskii uchitel' v Lokhvitskom uezde," *Mir bozhii*, No. 12, section 2 (1903), p. 35.

32. *Privolzhskii krai*, No. 9, January 13, 1905, p. 3.

33. *Severnyi krai*, No. 51, February 25, 1904, p. 2; *Zhurnaly komissii po narodnomu obrazovaniiu pri gub. zemskoi uprave 21 i 22 noiabria 1905 goda* (Vladimir, 1905), pp. 42–43; Charnoluskii, ed., *Ezhegodnik narodnoi shkoly*, pp. 241, 245; Panov, "Voprosy," p. 32.

34. Veselovskii, *Istoriia*, I, 551; for a teacher's evaluation of these libraries, see Vakhlin, "Narodnoe obrazovanie v Orekhovo-Zuevskom uezde," p. 416.

35. A. A. Stakhovich, "O bibliotekakh pri uchilisch-uchenicheskoi i uchitel'skoi i o katalogakh dlia nikh," in *Trudy s"ezda pri upravlenii Moskovskago uchebnago okruga po voprosam narodnago obrazovaniia*, 2 vols. (Moscow, 1902), II, 103–4.

36. Vakhterova, "Umstvennye zaprosy," p. 658; Charnoluskii, *Ezhegodnik*, pp. 290–91.

37. *Russkiia vedomosti*, No. 359, December 27, 1902, p. 2; *Russkaia shkola*, No. 1, section 2 (1903), p. 58.

38. *Russkiia vedomosti*, No. 156, June 8, 1903, p. 2; L. F. Rvachev, "Iz proshlogo (Vospominaniia sel'skogo uchitelia o revoliutsii 1905 goda)," TsGAOR. f. 6862, op. 1, d. 86, 1. 89–90.

39. Vakhterova, "Umstvennye zaprosy," p. 672.

40. Stakhovich, "O bibliotekakh," pp. 106–07.

41. Rvachev, "Iz proshlogo," 1. 90.

42. Rozhdestvenskii, *Istoricheskii obzor*, pp. 723–24; also MNP, *Vsepoddanneishii otchet ministra narodnago prosveshcheniia za 1903 god* (SPB, 1905), pp. 524–25; V. V. Litvinov, *Voronezhskaia uchitel'skaia seminariia, 1875–1910* (Voronezh, 1911), pp. 64–65; *Dvadtsatipiatletie Kazanskoi zemskoi shkoly dlia obrazovaniia narodnykh uchitel'nits, 1871–1896*, comp. A. Ershov (Kazan, 1897), p. 143.

43. N. A. Feliksov, "Pedagogicheskie kursy i uchitel'skie s"ezdy," *Russkaia mysl'*, No. 10 (1896), pp. 38–41; Smirnov, "Zemstvo i biurokratiia," p. 4.

44. Feliksov, "Pedagogicheskie kursy," *Russkaia mysl'*, No. 11 (1896), p. 37.

45. M. F. Superanskii, *Nachal'naia narodnaia shkola v Simbirskoi gubernii* (Simbirsk, 1906), p. 200; N. K. Bunakov, *Izbrannye pedagogicheskie sobraniia* (Moscow, 1953), p. 341.

46. Kornilov, "Zemskaia demokraticheskaia intelligentsiia," p. 109; E. A. Zviagintsev, *Voprosy i nuzhdy uchitel'stva: sbornik statei*, 10 vols. (Moscow, 1909–11), I, 18; A. M. Vezhlev, "Uchitel'skie s"ezdy i kursy v Rossii (vtoraia polovina XIX veka)," *Sovetskaia pedagogika*, No. 7 (1958), p. 80.

47. A. Loktin, "Uchitel'skie kursy i s"ezdy," *Vestnik vospitaniia*, No. 6, section 2 (1904), pp. 77–78; K. Ch., "Sel'skii uchitel'," *Russkoe bogatstvo*, No. 4, section 2 (1898), p. 12.

48. D. I. Tikhomirov, "Iz zhizni zemskoi shkoly i uchitel'skikh kursov (po vospominaniiam za 35 let rukovoditel'stva)," in V. A. Vagner, et al., *Zemskie obshcheobrazovatel'nye kursy dlia narodnykh uchitelei* (SPB, 1906), pp. 10–18.

49. Zviagintsev, *Voprosy i nuzhdy uchitel'stva*, I, 18; V. Farmakovskii, "S"ezdy uchitelei nachal'nykh uchilishch prezhde i teper'," *ZhMNP*, No. 12, section 4 (1900), p. 73; I. Iakhontov, "Uchitel'skie kursy, s"ezdy i sobraniia," *Vestnik Novgorodskago zemstva*, No. 11 (1905), pp. 36–37.

50. See M. A. O- v, "Dva dnia na uchitel'skom s"ezde (iz vospominanii o 70-kh godakh)," *Russkaia shkola*, No. 5–6 (1913), pp. 54–55.

51. Allen Sinel, "Educating the Russian Peasantry: The Elementary School Reforms of Count Dmitri Tolstoi," *Slavic Review*, 27, No. 1 (1968), pp. 55–56; Eklof, *Russian Peasant Schools*, pp. 66–69.

52. Zviagintsev, *Voprosy*, I, 18–19; Farmakovskii, "S"ezdy uchitelei," p. 76; V. I. Charnoluskii, comp., *Sputnik narodnago uchitelia i deiatelia narodnago obrazovaniia* (SPB, 1908), pp. 223–27; Sinel, "Educating the Russian Peasantry," pp. 64–65.

53. Kovalev, "Ocherk vozniknoveniia i razvitiia uchitel'skikh kursov," p. 79; Feliksov, "Pedagogicheskie kursy," No. 10, p. 41.

54. V. Shcherba, "Uchitel'skie kursy i pravila o kursakh," *Vestnik Evropy,* No. 5 (1902), pp. 774–75; N. Karyshev, "Zemskie khodataistva," *Russkoe bogatstvo,* No. 2 (1899), p. 41; Feliksov, No. 10, pp. 44–56; No. 11, pp. 32–38.

55. Smirnov, "Zemstvo i biurokratiia," p. 20; Iakhontov, pp. 37–38.

56. E. G. Kornilov, "Zemskie uchitelia v revoliutsionnom dvizhenii 70-kh gg. XIX v.," *Uchenye zapiski Moskovskogo gos. ped. in-ta V. I. Lenina,* 439 (Moscow, 1971), p. 132; B. G. Mikhailov, "Revoliutsionnaia propaganda sredi krest'ian na Evropeiskom Severe Rossii v 70- e gody XIX v.," *Istoricheskie zapiski,* 106 (1981), pp. 348–68; Pirumova, *Zemskaia intelligentsiia,* pp. 78–84. Memoir literature attests that populists of the 1870s eagerly utilized the post of rural teacher: S. I. Mitskevich, *Na grani dvukh epokh: ot narodnichestva k marksizmu* (Moscow, 1937), p. 39; *Russkiia vedomosti, 1863–1913: sbornik statei* (Moscow, 1913), pt. II, p. 33 (autobiography of I. P. Belokonskii).

57. V. Kolpenskii, "Sel'skaia shkola posle krest'ianskoi reformy," *Arkhiv istorii truda v Rossii,* No. 6–7 (1923), p. 179; Vezhlev, "Uchitel'skie kursy," p. 84.

58. Zviagintsev, *Voprosy,* I, 19; *Sbornik postanovlenii zemskikh sobranii Novgorodskoi gubernii za 1886* (Novgorod, 1887), p. 201.

59. P. Shesternin, "Iz vospominanii sel'skago uchitelia," pp. 114, 116. The new rural police post of *uriadnik* reportedly attracted many male teachers.

60. Cited in *Russkiia vedomosti, 1863–1913,* p. 246.

61. Akimov, "Zemskaia rabota," No. 6, p. 129.

62. Gol'tsev, "O polozhenii uchashchikh," p. 11; Sobolev, "K voprosu o polozhenii," pp. 192, 203, 209.

63. Zviagintsev, *Polveka,* p. 22.

64. On local medical congresses, see Samuel C. Ramer, "The Zemstvo and Public Health," in Terence Emmons and Wayne S. Vucinich, eds., *The Zemstvo in Russia: An Experiment in Local Self-Government* (Cambridge, 1982), pp. 287–89, 300; Kornilov, "Zemskaia demokraticheskaia intelligentsiia," pp. 101–05; Veselovskii, *Istoriia,* I, 300–05; D. N. Zhbankov, *O deiatel'nosti sanitarnykh biuro i obshchestvenno-sanitarnykh uchrezhdenii v zemskoi Rossii: kratkii istoricheskii obzor* (Moscow, 1910), pp. 8–13. According to the latter, provincial doctors' congresses were held fairly frequently in this period and later: 70 during the 1870s, 96 during the 1880s, 94 during the 1890s, and 68 during the 1900s.

65. V. I. Charnoluskii, *Zemstvo i narodnoe obrazovanie,* 2 vols. (SPB, 1910–11), I, 53–57; Feliksov, No. 9, p. 7.

66. N. V. Chekhov, "K voprosu o letnykh uchitel'skikh kursakh," *Russkiia vedomosti,* No. 132, June 9, 1912, p. 5.

67. For example, the Kursk zemstvo (in 1896), which began to hold summer courses annually in 1897; *Tekushchaia shkolnaia statistika Kurskago gub. zemstva: god odinnadtsatyi 1906–1907 uchebnyi god* (Kursk, 1908), pt. 1, pp. 75–76.

68. Rozhdestvenskii, *Istoricheskii obzor,* pp. 723–24; "Vnutrennee obozrenie," *Zhizn',* No. 9 (1900), pp. 406–7.

69. Farmakovskii, "S"ezdy uchitelei," p. 79.

70. Loktin, "Uchitel'skie kursy," p. 77; Shcherba, "Uchitel'skie kursy," p. 775.

71. A. Prugavin, "Kak u nas ustraivalis' pedagogicheskie kursy," *Obrazovanie,* No. 9, section 2 (1902), pp. 68–69; Val. Denisov, "Znachenie uchitel'skikh kursov po otzyvam zemskikh uchitelei," *Obrazovanie* No. 7, section 2 (1904), pp. 40–41; P. Grigor'ev, "Zemskie pedagogicheskie kursy i pravila 1875 goda," *Russkaia shkola,* No. 3 (1903), pp. 131–33; Vakhterova, *V. P. Vakhterov,* pp. 145, 154–56.

72. Loktin, "Uchitel'skie kursy," pp. 77–78; somewhat different figures are given in Veselovskii, *Istoriia,* I, 505; "Pedagogicheskaia khronika," *Russkaia shkola,* No. 9, section 3 (1913), p. 65; Grigor'ev, "Zemskie," pp. 129–30.

73. Prugavin, "Kak u nas ustraivalis,'," p. 70; Grigor'ev, "Zemskie," p. 131.

74. F. Ch. [G. A. Fal'bork and V. I. Charnoluskii], "Otgoloski uchitel'skikh

s"ezdov, kursov i soveshchanii," *Vestnik vospitaniia*, No. 9, section 2 (1901), pp. 88–109.

75. Bunakov, *Izbrannye*, p. 371; "Khronika," *Obrazovanie*, No. 5–6, section 2 (1902), pp. 98–101.

76. D. A. Isakov, "Pedagogicheskie kursy dlia uchitelei narodnykh uchilishch," *Trudy s"ezda pri upravlenii Moskovskago uchebnago okruga*, II, 178; *Russkiia vedomosti*, No. 345, December 14, 1897, p. 2; *Russkaia shkola*, No. 9, section 3 (1913), pp. 67–68.

77. *Russkaia shkola*, No. 7–8, section 2 (1903), p. 100; teachers at pedagogical courses in Penza in 1903 likewise argued that general education courses were needed: I. P. Belokonskii, "Obzor deiatel'nosti zemstv po narodnomu obrazovaniiu za 1903 g.," *Russkaia shkola*, No. 4 (1904), p. 180.

78. V. B., "K voprosu o podgotovke narodnago uchitelia," pp. 100–1.

79. Panov, "Voprosy narodnago obrazovaniia," pp. 31–33.

80. *Otchet po revizii zemskikh uchrezhdenii Moskovskoi gubernii*, ed., N. A. Zinov'ev, 3 vols. (SPB, 1904), I, 276–77.

81. Chekhov, *Narodnoe obrazovanie*, pp. 118–20.

82. A. Nechaev, "Pamiati zemskikh obshcheobrazovatel'nykh kursov dlia narodnykh uchitelei," *Rus'*, No. 162, July 19, 1905, p. 5; Denisov, "Znachenie," pp. 57–58; *Niva*, No. 42 (1900), p. 844; *Russkaia shkola*, No. 9, section 3 (1913), pp. 69–70. The Irkutsk Teachers' Society funded members' trips to the Pavlovsk courses in 1902 (TsGAOR, f. 6862, op. 1, d. 74, 1. 44, memoir of A. Groshkov).

83. Grigor'ev, "Zemskie," p. 135. By contrast, in Saratov in 1901 at courses for teachers in church-run schools there was a heavy emphasis on applied subjects like agricultural skills; out of a total of 130 lessons, 66 were devoted to singing: F. Ch., "Otgoloski," pp. 88–89.

84. Denisov, "Znachenie," pp. 42–47. Much of this information from Saratov and elsewhere is surveyed in V. Vakhterov, "Zaprosy narodnykh uchitelei i obshcheobrazovatel'nye uchitel'skie kursy," in Vagner, *Zemskie obshcheobrazovatel'nye kursy*, pp. 34–52.

85. Sergeev, *Narodnaia shkola v Nizhegorodskom uezde*, pp. 36–37; Samsonov, *Byt uchashchikh v Novgorodskoi gubernii*, pp. 87–88.

86. Rvachev, "Iz proshlogo," 1. 119.

87. Sergeev, *Narodnaia shkola v Nizhegorodskom uezde*, p. 36.

88. A. M. Tiutriumov, "S"ezdy narodnykh uchitelei, kak obshchestvenno-pedagogicheskaia mera," *Russkaia shkola*, No. 5–6 (1894), pp. 163–77; *Russkiia vedomosti*, No. 345, December 14, 1897, p. 2.

89. Gol'tsev, "K voprosu o polozhenii," pp. 84–85, 89; G. O., "K voprosu o polozhenii," p. 76; V. Vasilevich [V. V. Kir'iakov], "K voprosu ob uchitel'skikh s"ezdakh," *Obrazovanie*, No. 5–6 (1898), pp. 194–95; Samsonov, *Byt uchashchikh v Novgorodskoi gubernii*, pp. 78–80.

90. *Russkiia vedomosti*, No. 32, February 1, 1898, pp. 3–4; *Otchet po revizii*, I, 274–75; Vasilevich, "K voprosu ob uchitel'skikh s"ezdakh," pp. 193–98, and V. V. Kir'iakov, "S"ezd uchitelei moskovskago uezdnago zemstva," *Russkoe bogatstvo*, No. 1 (1902), pp. 225–26. In 1898 the Kursk zemstvo also petitioned for new rules on teachers' congresses (Veselovskii, *Istoriia*, IV, 336).

91. Rozhdestvenskii, *Istoricheskii obzor*, p. 724; Akimov, "Zemskaia rabota," No. 6, pp. 130–31.

92. The 1899 rules are cited in *Narodnoe obrazovanie v Rossii* (Moscow, 1910), pp. 159–60.

93. *Russkiia vedomosti*, No. 281, October 11, 1903, p. 3; also K. Miagkova, *O polozhenii narodnykh uchitelei* (Velikii Ustiug, 1905), pp. 67–69.

94. This was pointed out by the Viatka zemstvo in a critique of the rules: *Otchet po revizii zemskikh uchrezhdenii Viatskoi gubernii*, 2 vols. (SPB, 1905), II, 315.

95. V. V. Kir'iakov, *Shag za shagom: K istorii ob"edineniia narodnykh uchitelei- iz lichnykh vospominanii i perezhivanii* (Moscow, 1914), pp. 51–52.

96. *Trudy mestnykh komitetov o nuzhdakh sel'skokhoziaistvennoi promyshlennosti*, XXVIII, 449–53; *Pravo*, No. 12, March 17, 1902, col. 620 (Saratov zemstvo).

97. *Trudy s"ezda pri upravlenii Moskovskago uchebnago okruga*, I, 171–80.

98. Reports on the Moscow district congress are: Kir'iakov, "S"ezd uchitelei," pp. 229–56; S. A. Volkov, "Pervyi s"ezd narodnykh uchitelei i uchitel'nits (zametki i vpechatleniia)," *Russkaia mysl'*, No. 10, section 2 (1901), pp. 208–18; *Russkiia vedomosti*, 1901, Nos. 227, 228, 229, 232, 233, 234, 235.

99. F. Ch., "Otgoloski," p. 100.

100. Kir'iakov, "S"ezd uchitelei," pp. 235–40; Moscow zemstvo, *Doklady s"ezda uchitelei i uchitel'nits Moskovskago uezda, avgust 1901* (n.p., n.d.), pp. 170–78.

101. Kir'iakov, "S"ezd uchitelei," p. 234, 247; Samsonov, *Byt uchashchikh v Novgorodskoi gubernii*, p. 84.

102. G. I. Chernov, "Pereklikaias' s minuvshim (ob uezdnom s"ezde narodnykh uchitelei v 1901 g)," *Nachal'naia shkola*, No. 1 (1970), pp. 91–93, and G. I. Chernov, *Stranitsy proshlogo* (Vladimir, 1970), pp. 163–66; *Saratovskaia zemskaia nedelia*, No. 4, section 2 (1902), pp. 73–84. The Aleksandrov congress supported the notion of zemstvo aid in subscriptions, and a favorable response came from the Vladimir provincial zemstvo: I. P. Belokonskii, "Obzor deiatel'nosti zemstv po narodnomu obrazovaniiu za 1902 g.," *Russkaia shkola*, No. 4 (1903), p. 177.

103. "S"ezd uchitelei Balashovskago uezda," *Saratovskaia zemskaia nedelia*, No. 4, section 2 (1903), pp. 1–2; also on congress held in Klin (Moscow) in 1904, see *Otchet po revizii*, I, 275.

104. N. Nardov, "V sumerkakh zhizni (iz zhizni dorevoliutsionnogo uchitel'stva)," *Natisk* (Gor'kii), No. 4–5 (1935), pp. 45–46; N. Iordanskii, comp., *Rezultaty soveshchanii uchashchikh Nizhegorodskago uezda po obsuzhdeniiu programmy s"ezda 15–21 maia 1903 goda* (Nizhnii-Novgorod, 1903); also Iordanskii's comments in *Trudy s"ezda pri upravlenii Moskovskago uchebnago okruga*, I, 171; *Russkiia vedomosti*, No. 264, September 26, 1903, p. 2.

105. Loktin, "Uchitel'skie kursy," p. 78; A ministry report lists only four congresses held in 1904 through January 1905: TsGIA, f. 733, op. 173, d. 8.

106. Akimov, "Zemskaia rabota," No. 6, p. 131.

107. Shakhovskoi's comments were made at the Moscow district conference: *Trudy s"ezda pri upravlenii*, I, 171–72; Smirnov, "Zemstvo i biurokratiia," p. 18.

108. For example, in four districts in Novgorod province in 1902: *Osvobozhdenie*, No. 6, September 2/15, 1902, pp. 91–92; TsGIA, f. 733, op. 175, d. 77, 1. 361–62.

109. E. Zviagintsev, "Uchitel'skie s"ezdy i soveshchaniia," in Zviagintsev, et al., *Narodnoe obrazovanie v zemstvakh: sbornik* (Moscow, 1914), p. 243.

110. Charnoluskii, *Ezhegodnik narodnoi shkoly*, p. 244.

111. *Polozhenie narodnago obrazovaniia vo Vladimirskoi gubernii po izsledovaniiu 1910 goda*, vyp. II (Vladimir, 1911), p. 46.

112. On "conflicts" before 1905 with doctors and statisticians, see A. Bel'skii, "Zemskaia biurokratiia," *Obrazovanie*, No. 2 (1905), pp. 1–12; A. V. Peshekhonov, "Krizis v zemskoi statistike," *Russkoe bogatstvo*, No. 12, section 2 (1901), pp. 167–89; Ushakov, *Revoliutsionnoe dvizhenie*, pp. 48, 100–4.

113. *Russkiia vedomosti*, No. 208, July 30, 1903, p. 2.

114. TsGIA, f. 1284, op. 188, d. 47, 1. 2–6ob. In 1903, in response to its petition that provincial congresses of teachers be allowed, the Kherson zemstvo received word from the MNP that the latter had already worked out new rules on congresses which would be put into effect in the near future: *Russkaia shkola*, No. 9, section 2 (1903), p. 50; Farmakovskii, "Deiatel'nost' ministerstva narodnago prosveshcheniia," pp. 30–31," hinted in 1904 at projected reforms in the rules on both courses and congresses.

115. Cited in V. S. Dzhanpoladian, "V. P. Vakhterov: vidnyi deiatel' dorevoliutsionnoi nachal'noi shkoly," kand. diss., Akademiia pedagogicheskikh nauk RSFSR (Moscow, 1954), p. 36.

116. S. Seropolko, "Kak voznik vserossiiskii uchitel'skii soiuz," *Dlia narodnago uchitelia*, No. 3 (1907), p. 5; K- v, "Pedagogicheskie kursy dlia uchitelei i uchitel'nits nachal'nykh shkol Iaroslavskoi gub.," *Severnyi krai*, No. 66, March 11, 1905, p. 3.

4. *Organization and Program*

1. Kir'iakov, *Shag za shagom*, p. 23.

2. Jacob Walkin, *The Rise of Democracy in Pre-Revolutionary Russia* (New York, 1962), chapter 6.

3. V. Murinov, "Obshchestva vzaimnago vspomoshchestvovaniia uchashchim i uchivshim," in Shakhovskoi, *Vseobshchee obrazovanie*, pp. 85–56; TsGIA, f. 733, op. 195, d. 623, 1. 88.

4. Murinov, pp. 85–86. In Moscow province teachers participated in both district teachers' societies and societies of mutual aid for zemstvo employees: see *Saratovskaia zemskaia nedelia*, No. 3, section 2 (1905), pp. 36–37; A. Rumiantsev, "K voprosu ob ob"edinenii uchitel'skikh obshchestv vzaimopomoshchi Moskovskoi gubernii," *Vestnik vospitaniia*, No. 5, section 2 (1905), p. 64.

5. Details on expenditures can be found in Murinov, pp. 90–92 and TsGIA, f. 733, op. 195, d. 623, 1. 89–89ob. The importance of being able to provide an education for the children of rural teachers was argued at many teacher gatherings, for example a local teachers' congress in Riazan in 1903; see Odintsov, *Uchitel'skii s"ezd*, pp. 54–55; *Russkaia shkola*, No. 10–11, section 2 (1903), pp. 33–36.

6. Murinov, pp. 87–88, 93; Khizhniakov, *Vospominaniia zemskago deiatelia*, p. 198. For the normal statute of 1894, see *Spravochnaia kniga uchitel'skikh obshchestv vzaimopomoshchi* (Moscow, 1905), pp. 73–79.

7. *Trudy I-go vserossiiskago s"ezda predstavitelei obshchestv vspomoshchestvovaniia litsam uchitel'skago zvaniia*, ed. V. M. Evteev, 2 vols. (Moscow, 1907), II, 1176; Seropol ko, "Kak voznik vserossiiskii," p. 5.

8. On the zemstvo pension funds, see Veselovskii, *Istoriia zemstva*, III, 494. The MNP in 1900 also set up a pension fund for teachers, but its terms were far from liberal and teacher participation was limited.

9. The Nizhegorod Society pioneered in the provision of such varied services; its statute, approved before the "normal statute," was fairly liberal; see M. I. Obukhov, *Itogi deiatel'nosti Obshchestva vzaimnago vspomoshchestvovaniia uchiteliam i uchitel'nitsam Nizhegorodskoi gubernii za 10 let sushchestvovaniia ego 1894–1904 g.* (Nizhnii-Novgorod, 1905). On legal aid, see *Mir bozhii*, No. 12, section 2 (1904), p. 41. The Akmolinsk Society (in Siberia where zemstvos did not exist) was able to organize summer courses in 1897: G. Furaev, *Ocherk po istorii professional'nogo ob"edineniia rabotnikov prosveshcheniia Omskoi gubernii 1895–1924* (Omsk, 1924). p. 6.

10. Murinov, pp. 89–90.

11. P. Zhulev, "Ob uchitel'skikh obshchestvakh vzaimopomoshchi," *Russkaia shkola*, No. 4 (1909), pp. 81–89.

12. N. V. Tulupov, "Osnovnye voprosy uchitel'skago byta," *Russkaia mysl'*, No. 12, section 2 (1902), p. 90. This situation compares favorably with membership in workers' trade unions: Victoria E. Bonnell, *Roots of Rebellion: Workers' Politics and Organizations in St. Petersburg and Moscow, 1900–1914* (Berkeley: University of California Press, 1983), pp. 134–38, 203–9.

13. Samsonov, *Byt uchashchikh v Novgorodskoi gubernii*, pp. 93–94; Tulupov, "Osnovnye voprosy," p. 90; *Zhurnaly VI ocherednago obshchego sobraniia chlenov Obshchestva vzaimnago vspomoshchestvovaniia uchashchim i uchivshim Chernigovskoi gubernii 26 iiulia 1904 goda* (Kiev, 1905), pp. 11, 69–70.

14. *Kratkii obzor deiatel'nosti Obshchestva popecheniia ob uluchshenii byta uchashchikh v nachal'nykh uchilishchakh g. Moskvy za 1895–1901 g.g.* (Moscow, 1903), pp. 6, 33.

15. A good summary of the problems involved in organizing teachers can be found in Tulupov, "Osnovnye voprosy," pp. 90–92. The Vladimir Society delegated certain teachers as regional "agents," responsible for collecting membership dues, and so on. One agent complained that all correspondence between himself and the executive board had ceased for two years; the latter replied that notices had been sent out to rural teachers, concluding that the "fault lies with those who run the mails." *Severnyi krai,* No. 122, May 12, 1905, p. 2.

16. Samsonov, *Byt uchashchikh v Novgorodskoi gubernii,* pp. 94–95.

17. Prior to 1905 only twenty-two of eighty teachers in Lokhvitsa district (Poltava) were members of the district society, which the board ascribed to the cost to rural teachers of getting to town: *Sbornik postanovlenii po narodnomu obrazovaniiu uezdnykh zemskikh sobranii Poltavskoi gubernii za 1905 goda* (Poltava, 1907), pp. 96–97.

18. E. Tomashevich, *Istoricheskii ocherk deiatel'nosti Tul'skago Obshchestva vzaimopomoshchi uchashchim i uchivshim za istekshee desiatiletie 19 sentiabria 1895–18 sentiabria 1905 gg.* (Tula, 1907), p. 4; the statute for district societies, issued on September 18, 1903, can be found in *Spravochnaia kniga,* pp. 79–82.

19. *Zhurnaly VI ocherednago obshchego sobraniia,* p. 70; also P. Abakumov, "Indifferentizm uchashchikh k obshchestvam vzaimopomoshchi," *Tavricheskii narodnyi uchitel',* No. 14–15 (1907), pp. 7–9.

20. Sergeev, *Narodnaia shkola v Nizhegorodskom uezde,* p. 29.

21. N. Kapralov, "Iz istorii ob"edineniia rabotnikov prosveshcheniia v Nizhegorodskoi gubernii," TsGAOR, f. 6862, op. 1, d. 89, 1. 16–17.

22. S. Zolotarev, "Ocherk po istorii uchitel'skago ob"edineniia v Rossii," *Professional'nye uchitel'skiia organizatsii na Zapade i v Rossii: sbornik statei* (Petrograd, 1915), pp. 253–54; A. A. Nikolaev, "Soiuz narodnykh uchitelei i deiatelei po narodnomu obrazovaniiu," *Vestnik znaniia,* No. 7 (1905), pp. 114–15; N. Chekhov, "Blestiashchaia stranitsa v istorii russkago uchitel'stva," *Zhizn' i shkola,* No. 11 (1907), pp. 3–4.

23. Nikolaev, "Soiuz," pp. 112–13.

24. *Spravochnaia kniga,* pp. 62–63; Tomashevich, *Istoricheskii ocherk,* pp. 7–9; Nikolaev, "Soiuz," pp. 114–15.

25. *Mir bozhii,* No. 12, section 2 (1904), p. 41.

26. The following discussion of the Iaroslavl Society is based on the following sources: V. K. Burtsev, "Professional'no-politicheskoe dvizhenie Iaroslavskogo uchitel'stva za 20 let (1898–1917 gody)," TsGAOR, f. 6862, op. 1, d. 21; TsGIA, f. 733, op. 195, d. 623; A. A. Loktin, "Iz Iaroslavlia," *Saratovskaia zemskaia nedelia,* No. 8, section 2 (1905), pp. 99–110; *Ocherk deiatel'nosti obshchestva vzaimnago vspomoshchestvovaniia uchashchim i uchivshim v nachal'nykh uchilishchakh Iaroslavskoi gubernii za 10 let sushchestvovaniia, 1902–1912 gg.* (Iaroslavl, 1913); *Iskra,* No. 5, June, 1901, p. 2; *Severnyi krai,* No. 72, March 17, 1904, p. 3.

27. Burtsev, 1. 271.

28. The advisory school commissions at the provincial zemstvo level were generally composed of zemstvo deputies and third element specialists, but rarely teachers; they should not be confused with the district zemstvo organs to be discussed below.

29. Burtsev, 1. 272.

30. V. I. Gurko, *Features and Figures of the Past,* trans. Laura Matveev (Stanford: Stanford University Press, 1939), p. 185.

31. TsGIA, f. 733, op. 195, d. 623, 1. 116; T. K. Gladkov, M. A. Smirnov, *Menzhinskii* (Moscow, 1969), pp. 62–63.

32. V. V. Sokolov, *Semen Aleksandrovich Musin-Pushkin* (Iaroslavl, 1907), pp. 3–4; TsGIA, f. 733, op. 195, d. 623, 1. 116.

33. Veselovskii, *Istoriia,* IV, 458–60.

34. Pirumova, *Zemskoe liberal'noe dvizhenie;* Emmons, *The Formation of Political Parties.*

35. During its first year (1900) the Ekaterinoslav Society encompassed 500 teachers, but by 1905 had only 277 active members (one-sixth of the teachers in the province): *Vestnik iuga,* No. 920, April 26, 1905, p. 2.

36. Von Laue, *Sergei Witte and the Industrialization of Russia,* p. 132; N. Rumiantseva, "Desiatiletie deiatel'nosti nizhegorodskago obshchestva vzaimopomoshchi uchashchim," *Mir bozhii,* No. 1, section 2 (1904), pp. 32–36.

37. Kapralov, "Iz istorii ob'edineniia," 1. 17–18; Kir'iakov, *Shag za shagom,* pp. 25–28.

38. N. Suprunenko, "Iz nedavnego proshlogo: istoriia organizatsii uchitel'skikh obshchestv," *Rabotnik prosveshcheniia,* No. 13–14 (1924), p. 48.

39. One teacher recalled: "By day we darted around the exhibition, by night we gathered together under threat of the police baton, when there were heated discussions about the tasks of the school ('rearing the critically thinking personality'), new teaching methods, and compilation of a catalog of books for self-education." TsGAOR, f. 6862, op. 1, d. 87, 1. 83; also Vakhterova, *V. P. Vakhterov,* pp. 127–29.

40. N. A. Malinovskii, *Narodnyi uchitel' v revoliutsionnom dvizhenii* (Moscow, 1926), p. 37.

41. S. K. Govorov, "Istoricheskaia zapiska o sozyve v Moskve I-go vserossiiskago s"ezda," in *Trudy I-go vserossiiskago s"ezda,* ed. V. M. Evteev, 2 vols. (Moscow, 1907), I, 1–12; TsGIA, f. 733, op. 195, d. 623, 1. 89ob–90ob.

42. Ibid., 90ob–91, 127ob; S. Zolotarev, "Ocherk po istorii uchitel'skago ob"edineniia v Rossii," p. 246.

43. TsGIA, f. 733, op. 195, d. 623, 1. 91; V. V. Vasilevich [V. V. Kir'iakov], *Moskovskii s"ezd predstavitelei uchitel'skikh obshchestv vzaimopomoshchi* (Moscow, 1905), p. 23.

44. *Vsepoddanneishii otchet ministra narodnago prosveshcheniia za 1903 god* (St. Petersburg, 1905), pp. 523–24.

45. TsGIA, f. 733, op. 195, d. 623, 1. 93.

46. Veselovskii, *Istoriia zemstva,* IV, 332–39; *1905 god v Kurskoi gubernii* (Kursk, 1925), p. 49; reportedly, Dolgorukov's wife was a former rural teacher: I V. Gessen, *V dvukh vekakh* (Berlin, 1937), p. 161.

47. On the Kursk commission, see "Khronika", *Russkaia shkola,* No. 1, section 2 (1904), pp. 38–48; I. P. Belokonskii, "Obzor deiatel'nosti zemstv po narodnomu obrazovaniiu za 1903 g.," Ibid., No. 4 (1904), pp. 158–161; Kurskoe Zemstvo, *Otchet po revizii proizvedennoi v 1904 godu senatorom N. A. Zinov'evym,* 2 vols. (St. Petersburg), I, 333.

48. See Simonova, "Zemsko-liberal'naia fronda," pp. 164–65.

49. Descriptions of the exhibition can be found in I. B., "Pervaia vystavka po narodnomu obrazovaniiu," *Russkiia vedomosti,* 1902, Nos. 133–138, 142, 150, 173, 175, 186; N. Tulupov, "Kurskaia vystavka," pp. 108–26; I. P. Belokonskii, *Zemskoe dvizhenie,* pp. 136–39; Veselovskii, *Istoriia zemstva,* III, 570–571; TsGIA, f. 733, op. 195, d. 623, 1. 93.

50. Chekhov, *Narodnoe obrazovanie v Rossii,* pp. 119–20; also Zolotarev, "Ocherk po istorii," p. 244.

51. TsGIA, f. 733, op. 195, d. 623, 1. 93–95.

52. Kir'iakov, *Shag za shagom,* pp. 22–25; V. Kir'iakov and S. Akramovskii, *Golos narodnago uchitelia. Otchet o Moskovskom s"ezde predstavitelei uchitel'skikh obshchestv vzaimopomoshchi 28. XII. 1902- 6.I. 1903 g.* (Moscow, 1903), pp. 9–10.

53. Shmuel Galai, *The Liberation Movement in Russia, 1900–1905* (New York, 1973), pp. 111–12; *Osvobozhdenie,* No. 6, September 2/15, 1902, p. 95.

54. E. E. Kerekesh, *Prazdnik narodnago uchitelia (pervaia vystavka po narodnomu obrazovaniiu, sostoiavshaias' v 1902 godu v Kurske),* (Chernigov, 1903); also S.

Zinov'evskii, "Pervaia zemskaia vystavka po narodnomu obrazovaniiu v g. Kurske," *Vestnik Vladimirskago zemstva,* No. 19–20 (1902), p. 40–48; Chekhov, *Narodnoe obrazovanie v Rossii,* p. 119; TsGIA, f. 733, op. 195, d. 623, 1. 93, 127ob.

55. Ibid., 1. 97–98; Vasilevich, *Moskovskii s"ezd,* p. 25. More detailed information on the delegates is provided by N. V. Tulupov and P. M. Shestakov, *Pervyi vserossiiskii s"ezd predstavitelei obshchestv vzaimopomoshchi litsam uchitel'skago zvaniia* (Moscow, 1903), pp. 14–15.

56. TsGIA, f. 733, p. 195, d. 623, 1. 98ob; TsGAOR, f. 63, op. 12, d. 1304, 1. 112–116ob.

57. TsGAOR, f. 6862, op. 1, d. 20, 1. 11–12, 77–78; this is a manuscript by Tsvetkov written in the mid-1920s and apparently intended to be a history of the teachers' movement through 1917; the archive contains only drafts of the first chapters.

58. TsGIA, f. 733, op. 195, d. 623, 1. 98ob; *Russkiia vedomosti,* No. 357, December 28, 1905, p. 3; Malinovskii, *Narodnyi uchitel',* p. 40.

59. A. G. Karneev, *O moskovskom s"ezde* (Mogilev, 1904), pp. 6–7. Vasilevich, *Moskovskii s"ezd,* pp. 47, 76–77; Vakhterova, *V. P. Vakhterov,* p. 158; TsGIA, f. 733, op. 195, d. 623, 1. 99–100ob; one delegate admitted as much: M. I. Obukhov, *Pervyi Vserossiiskii s"ezd predstavitelei obshchestv vzaimopomoshchi uchashchikh* (Nizhnii-Novgorod, 1903), p. 2.

60. TsGAOR, f. DP 00, op. 241, d. 75, 1. 4; *Trudy I-go vserossiiskago s"ezda,* I, 69–77; *Russkiia vedomosti,* No. 258, December 29, 1902, p. 3.

61. TsGAOR, f. DP 00, op. 241, d. 75, 1. 4.

62. N. V. Tulupov, "Pervyi vserossiiskii s"ezd predstavitelei obshchestv vspomoshchestvovaniia litsam uchitel'skago zvaniia," *Russkaia mysl',* No. 3 (1903), p. 129.

63. Ushakov, *Revoliutsionnoe dvizhenie demokraticheskoi intelligentsii,* p. 18.

64. S. V. Anikin, "O material'noi i iuridicheskoi neobezpechennosti russkago narodnago uchitelia," *Trudy I-go vserossiiskago s"ezda,* I, 255–265; TsGAOR, f. DP 00, op. 241, d. 75, 1. 8; Lozovoi was arrested and exiled later in 1903 and again in late 1905 for revolutionary agitation among the peasantry in Novooskol district (Kursk): S. M. Dubrovskii and B. Grave, eds., *Agrarnoe dvizhenie v 1905–1907 gg.* (Moscow, 1925), pp. 243, 259.

65. *Trudy I-go vserossiiskago s"ezda,* I, 97; Tulupov and Shestakov, *Pervyi vserossiiskii s"ezd,* p. 238.

66. *Trudy I-go vserossiiskago s"ezda,* I, 83.

67. Ibid., pp. 80–85, *Russkiia vedomosti,* No. 360, December 31, 1902, p. 3.

68. Cited in Tulupov, "Pervyi vserossiiskii s"ezd," p. 132.

69. *Trudy I-go vserossiiskago s"ezda,* I, 101–02.

70. Ibid., p. 100, 105; Tulupov, "Pervyi vserossiiskii," 129; TsGAOR, f. DP OO, op. 241, d. 75, 1. 8–8ob.

71. Ibid., p. 189–90; TsGAOR, f. DP OO, op. 241, d. 75, 1. 9; *Trudy I-go vserossiiskago s"ezda,* I, 191–92; according to police reports chairman Dolgorukov echoed the above statements, remarking that there were already enough bureaucrats standing over the peasantry and over the zemstvos: TsGIA, f. 733, op. 195, d. 623, 1. 104.

72. Teodor Shanin, *The Awkward Class: Political Sociology of Peasantry in a Developing Society: Russia, 1910–1925* (Oxford, 1972), p. 178.

73. Ibid., I, 678–81, II, 779–80, 821, 1136; N. Zapankov, "O samoobrazovanii narodnago uchitelia," *Russkaia shkola,* No. 1 (1904), pp. 89–105; Tulupov, "Pervyi," pp. 118–25.

74. Karneev, *O moskovskom s"ezde,* p. 7.

75. Vakhterova's detailed report, "Umstvennye zaprosy narodnago uchitelia," is

in *Trudy I-go vserossiiskago s"ezda,* I, 655–77 and also *Russkaia shkola,* No. 1 (1903), pp. 142–59.

76. TsGIA, f. 733, op. 195, d. 623, 1. 100ob–101; *Trudy I-go vserossiiskago s"ezda,* I, 619; the police report is in TsGAOR, f. DP OO, op. 241, d. 75, 1. 5.

77. TsGAOR, f. DP OO, op. 241, d. 75, 1. 7–7ob.

78. Ibid., II, 1020–1021; I, 389–90, 395 (Lozovoi report); Petrishchev, "Iz zametok shkol'nago uchitelia," pp. 83–90.

79. Ibid., I, 298–311.

80. These reports are M. T. Shaternikov, "On School Councils at the Zemstvo Board" (Ibid., I, 279–81); M. K. Chernogubova, "On the Organization of Management-Pedagogical Councils of Teachers at the Zemstvo Board," (Ibid., I, 284–88); S. I. Akramovskii, "On the Participation of Primary Schoolteachers in Zemstvo Assemblies and in Conferences at Zemstvo Boards in the Area of Education," (Ibid., I, 372–73); the citation is in Ibid., I, 284.

81. Ibid., I, 110–11, 372–73; N. V. Tulupov, "Osnovnye voprosy," pp. 92, 95. See chapter 5 for an evaluation of these and subsequent experiments.

82. Tulupov, "Pervyi vserossiiskii s"ezd," pp. 15–17; Tulupov, "Osnovnye voprosy," pp. 92–93; TsGIA, f. 733, op. 195, d. 623, 1. 103–103ob.

83. TsGAOR f. DP OO, op. 241, d. 75, 1. 7ob–8; on the Pirogov Society, see Frieden, *Russian Physicians,* pp. 118–22.

84. Police reports were especially sensitive to such statements. One delegate complained about teacher dependence on the "dregs" *(podonki)* of the peasant community, that is peasant communal officials (Ibid., 1. 6). For a summary of discussion of legal status at the congress, see V. M. Sokolov, "Pravovoe polozhenie uchitelia," *Saratovskaia zemskaia nedelia,* No. 6–7 (1905), pp. 35–49.

85. *Trudy I-go vserossiiskago s"ezda,* I, 274.

86. Ibid., I, 386–88, 395.

87. Tulupov, "Pervyi vserossiiskii s"ezd," p. 130.

88. *Trudy I-go vserossiiskago s"ezda,* I, 273; Vagner had taught (and been dismissed) in various provinces since the mid-1890s; police reports describe her as being a close follower of Tolstoi and active in support of the Dukhobors. In 1905 she was active in both Teachers' and Peasant Union organizing in Kromy district, Orel province: TsGAOR, f. DP OO, op. 5, d, 999, ch. 45, 1. 134ob–136ob; TsGAOR, f. 63, op. 12, d. 1304, 1. 647; Vakhterova, *V. P. Vakhterov,* p. 165.

89. TsGIA, f. 733, op. 195, d. 623, 1. 103ob–104. Aside from Sakharov the members were: V. P. Vakhterov (major figure in teachers' movement); M. M. Borisovskii (from Saratov, police record/arrest, future SD); E. A. Frenkel' (Tver province, probably an SR); N. V. Chekhov (zemstvo specialist, Tver; active in 1905 teachers' organization); S. I. Akramovskii (SR, central figure in pre-1905 revolutionary teachers' union, long history of arrests); E. D. Vagner (Tolstoyan, under police surveillance); S. A. Spasskii (Tver, member of one of revolutionary parties); A. A. Sokolov (zemstvo employee, Moscow district; former teacher); N. P. Rumiantseva (St. Petersburg city teacher, sister of Bolshevik, herself an SD by 1905); P. A. Bobrinskii (radical zemstvo man, Tula); M. I. Obukhov (Nizhnii-Novgorod city teacher, active in union movement in 1905; secretary of Legal Commission); A. G. Sobol'ev (SR, Perm); V. D. Samsonov (activist in Novgorod Teachers' Society).

90. "Doklad komissii po vyiasneniiu pravovago polozheniia uchitelei, dolozhennyi v zasedanii 1-i sektsii s"ezda delegatov obshchestv vzaimopomoshchi uchitelei, 4 ianvaria 1903 goda," *Pravo,* No. 6 (1903), col. 364–70.

91. "Doklad komissii," col. 367–68.

92. Ibid., col. 368.

93. Ibid., col. 368–69. Teachers were granted immunity from corporal punishment by law in 1863: Frieden, *Russian Physicians,* p. 185, note 20. The issue of

corporal punishment had been raised by liberals in various zemstvo assemblies and elsewhere in recent years: Pirumova, *Zemskoe liberal'noe dvizhenie*, p. 154.

94. Chekhov's review of the Congress' *Trudy* appeared in *Russkaia shkola*, No. 1, section 2 (1908), p. 31; Mikhailovskii's remarks are recorded in Anna Akramovskaia's biographical sketch of her husband Sergei Ivanovich: TsGAOR, f. 6862, op. 1, d. 174, 1. 3 (paginated separately).

95. TsGAOR, f. 63, op. 12, d. 1304, 1. 306–306ob; TsGIA, f. 733, op. 195, d. 623, 1. 105ob–106; *Trudy I-go vserossiiskago s"ezda*, I, 205–206; Tulupov and Shestakov, *Pervyi vserossiiskii s"ezd*, pp. 178–79.

96. TsGIA, f. 733, op. 195, d. 623, 1. 100; TsGAOR, f. 63, op. 12, d. 1304, 1. 306ob–307ob.

97. *Trudy I-go vserossiiskago s"ezda*, I, 212; TsGAOR, f. 63, op. 12, d. 1304, 1. 302.

98. *Russkaia shkola*, No. 1, section 2 (1908), p. 29; Vakhterova, *V. P. Vakhterov*, p. 166.

99. TsGIA, f. 733, op. 195, d. 623, 1.108ob–109.

100. Karneev, *O moskovskom s"ezde*, p. 24; TsGIA, f. 733, op. 195, d. 623, 1. 109; *Russkiia vedomosti*, No. 7, January 7, 1903, p. 2; Tulupov, "Pervyi vserossiiskii s"ezd," p. 111; a report in the emigre *Osvobozhdenie*, of course, stressed the solidarity between teachers and local self-government: Z., "Uchitel'skii s"ezd," No. 19, March 19/April 1, 1903, pp. 334–35.

101. TsGIA, f. 733, op. 195, d. 623, 1. 108ob; TsGAOR f. DP OO, op. 241, d. 75, 1. 3, 13–13ob, 14g; TsGIA, f. 733, op. 195, d. 623, 1. 109ob; *Iskra*, No. 36, March 15, 1903, p. 5; a participant from Tver province recalled private meetings of teachers arranged by local SR and SD organizations ("Kratkii ocherk uchitel'skogo dvizheniia i soiuza rabotnikov prosveshcheniia Tverskoi gubernii," TsGAOR, f. 6862, op. 1, d. 21, 1. 137ob).

102. TsGIA, f. 733, op. 195, d. 623, 110ob; TsGAOR, f. DP OO, op. 241, d. 75, 1. 24ob. For a survey of attempts to publish the materials, see P. Sh[estako]v, "Sud'ba otchetov o pervom vserossiiskom s"ezde uchitelei," *Russkiia vedomosti*, No. 244, September 8, 1905, p. 3; *Russkoe slovo*, No. 241, September 5, 1905; also letter of S. I. Lisenko on futile attempt to publish resolutions in Odessa (GBL-RO, f. 218, N. V. Tulupov, No. 375, p. 30). The government's prohibition was not totally effective, however, as the Nizhegorod Society managed to publish a report on the congress which included the thirty-two legal theses (Obukhov, *Pervyi Vserossiiskii s"ezd)*, passing the local censor in March–April 1903; the two books are N. V. Tulupov and P. M. Shestakov, *Pervyi vserossiiskii s"ezd predstavitelei obshchestv vspomoshchestvovaniia litsam uchitel'skago zvaniia* (Moscow, 1903); S. Akramovskii and V. Kir'iakov, *Golos narodnago uchitelia: otchet o Moskovskom s"ezde predstavitelei uchitel'skikh obshchestv vzaimopomoshchi 28. XII. 1902–6. I. 1903 g.* (Moscow, 1903). Copies located in the Public Library (Saltykov-Shchedrin), Leningrad.

103. Pleve's statement is in L. M. Dobrovol'skii, *Zapreshchennaia kniga v Rossii 1825–1904; arkhivo-bibliograficheskie razyskaniia* (Moscow, 1962), p. 241.

104. Loktin, "Iz Iaroslavlia," pp. 105–7; Suprunenko, "Obshchestvo vzaimopomoshchi uchashchikh," 1. 48–49.

105. TsGIA, f. 733, op. 195, d. 623, 1. 122ob–124; *Russkaia shkola*, No. 12, section 2 (1904), p. 116.

106. N. Malitskii, "Professional'noe dvizhenie vo Vladimirskoi gubernii v 1905–1907 g.g.," in *O rabochem dvizhenii i sotsial'-demokraticheskoi rabote vo Vladimirskoi gubernii v 900-kh godakh*, vypusk 1, ed. A. N. Asatkin (Vladimir, 1926), pp. 58–60.

107. *Saratovskii listok*, No. 111, May 29, 1903, pp. 2–3; TsGAOR, f. DP OO, op. 5 (1905), d. 80, ch. 5, 1. 4–5.

108. A. Ivanov, "Iz istorii soiuza vo Vladimire," *Rabotnik prosveshcheniia*, No. 13–14 (1924), p. 84; *Osvobozhdenie*, No. 56, September 7/20, 1904, p. 112.

109. TsGIA, f. 733, op. 195, d. 623, 1. 127ob–130ob.

110. Belokonskii, *Zemskoe dvizhenie*, 2nd ed., p. 173; L. D. Briukhatov, "Znachenie 'tret'iago elementa' v zhizni zemstva," in B. B. Veselovskii and Z. G. Frenkel', eds., *Iubileinyi zemskii sbornik: 1864–1914* (St. Petersburg, 1914), p. 204; also Pleve's comments on Third Element in conversation with M. P. Kolobov, chairman of the Tambov provincial zemstvo board: *Revoliutsionnaia Rossiia*, No. 30, August 20, 1903, p. 11.

111. Vasilevich, *Moskovskii s"ezd*, p. 23.

5. *The Turn to Activism*

1. *Osvobozhdenie*, No. 11 (35), November 12/25, 1903, pp. 194–95; I. P. Belokonskii, *Zemstvo i konstitutsiia* (Moscow, 1910), p. 106.

2. George Fisher, *Russian Liberalism: From Gentry to Intelligentsia* (Cambridge, MA, 1958); Galai, *The Liberation Movement in Russia;* Pirumova, *Zemskoe liberal'noe dvizhenie;* Manning, *The Crisis of the Old Order.*

3. Maureen Perrie, *The Agrarian Policy of the Russian Socialist-Revolutionary Party from Its Origins through the Revolution of 1905–1907* (New York, 1976); David Lane, *The Roots of Russian Communism: A Social and Historical Study of Russian Social Democracy 1898–1907* (Assen, 1969).

4. *Svod vysochaishikh otmetok po vsepoddanneishim otchetam za 1902 g. general-gubernatorov, gubernatorov, voennykh gubernatorov i gradonachal'nikov* (St. Petersburg, 1905), pp. 53–54, 42–43; *Vestnik Vladimirskago gubernskago zemstva*, No. 13–14, section 1 (1905), pp. 36–37.

5. TsGIA, f. 1278, op. 2, d. 542 (1908 g.), 1. 30ob; also A. L., "Vnutrennaia khronika," *Zhurnal dlia vsekh*, No. 5 (1904), p. 317.

6. *Vsepoddaneishii otchet ministra narodnago prosveshcheniia za 1903 god* (St. Petersburg), p. 463.

7. *Svod vysochaishikh otmetok po vsepoddanneishim otchetam za 1903 i 1904 g. g.*, pp. 31–32; the existence of radical circles among the Cherepovets Seminary students is confirmed by the memoirs of former students: V. G., "Cherepovetskaia uchashchaiasia molodezh' v 1905 godu," *1905 god: Sbornik statei i vospominanii uchastnikov revoliutsii 1905 goda v Cherepovetskom uezde* (Cherepovets, 1925), pp. 39–54; P. Izmailov, "Marksistskii kruzhok v Cherepovetse," *Katorga i ssylka*, No. 1, 14 (1925), pp. 175–76. According to a former student at the Kirzhache (Vladimir) seminary both SR and SD circles existed among the seminarists during the early 1900's: G. I. Chernov, *Stranitsy proshlogo* (Vladimir, 1970), p. 6. In an effort to protect the seminarists from radical currents the government tended to establish the teachers' seminaries in district towns or even more remote rural settlements, which as some critics pointed out made it difficult to attract good instructors: see *Severnyi krai*, No. 199, August 15, 1905, p. 3; TsGAOR, f. 6862, op. 1, d. 86, 1. 18 (seminary in Kukarka, Viatka).

8. *Svod vysochaishikh otmetok po vsepoddanneishim otchetam za 1895* (St. Petersburg, 1897), p. 187; I. G. Drozdov, *Agrarnye volneniia i karatel'nye ekspeditsii v Chernigovskoi gubernii v gody pervoi revoliutsii 1905–1906 g. g. (po neopublikovannym arkhivnym dannym byvshego Chernigovskogo gub. zhandarmskogo upravleniia, a takzhe po drugim arkhivnym materialam)* (Moscow-Leningrad, 1925), p. 20.

9. Volosatyi, "Politicheskie aresty narodnykh uchitelei," *Osvobozhdenie*, No. 3 (27), July 19, 1903, pp. 47–48; see also *Ibid.*, No. 8 (32), October 15, 1903, p. 143 and No. 19, 1903, p. 344; on repression against former participants of the Moscow Congress, see I. P. Belokonskii, "Zemskoe dvizhenie do obrazovaniia partii narodnoi svobody," *Byloe*, No. 9 (1907), pp. 229–30; see also V. P. Iakovlev, "Revoliutsionnoe dvizhenie v Peterburgskoi gubernii nakanune i v gody pervoi russkoi

revoliutsii," *Voprosy istorii Rossii XIX-nachala XX veka: mezhvuzovskii sbornik*, ed., V. V. Mavrodin, et al. (Leningrad, 1983), p. 115.

10. *Osvobozhdenie*, No. 4, August 2/15, 1902, p. 57; *Obozrenie zemskikh uchrezhdenii Tverskoi gubernii*, pp. 37–38; *Revoliutsionnaia Rossiia*, No. 8, June 15, 1902, p. 22; also TsGIA, f. 1405, op. 521, d. 521, d. 457 and 458; TsGIA, f. 733, op. 201, d. 6, 1. 32.

11. *Svod vysochaishikh otmetok po vsepoddanneishim otchetam za 1902 g.*, p. 17; *Revoliutsionnaia Rossiia*, No. 10, August 15, 1902, pp. 24–25; Belokonskii, *Zemskoe dvizhenie*, pp. 143–44; *Osvobozhdenie*, No. 8 (32), October 2/15, 1903, p. 148; D. N. Shipov, *Vospominaniia i dumy o perezhitom* (Moscow, 1918), p. 182.

12. *Osvobozhdenie*, No. 4 (28), August 2/15, 1903, p. 61 and No. 11 (35), November 12/25, p. 193.

13. Loktin, "Uchitel'skie kursy i s"ezdy," pp. 77–78; O. Smirnov, "O narodnykh uchiteliakh," *Syn otechestva* (Petersburg), No. 124, July 12, 1905, pp. 1–2; TsGAOR, f. 812, op. 1, d. 7, 1. 3–3ob. Veselovskii notes that five courses were held in 1904 but provides no specifics or sources of information (*Istoriia zemstva*, I, 505). My own research contradicts some of Loktin's information; for example, courses were held in Voronezh in 1903, while in Kherson the local zemstvo's plans for courses were unsuccessful, owing to ministerial quibbling over the proposed program: see *Russkaia shkola*, No. 3 (1904), pp. 151–52; No. 9, section 2 (1904), 93.

14. Prugavin, "Kak u nas ustraivalis'," pp. 54–55; I. Stepnoi [I. S. Samokhvalov], "Zhivotvoriashchii dukh," *Dlia narodnago uchitelia*, No. 5 (1915), pp. 2–3; *Tekushchaia shkol'naia statistika Kurskago gub. zemstva. God odinnadtsatyi, 1906–1907 uchebyni god* (Kursk, 1908), p. 76; Belokonskii, "Obzor deiatel'nosti zemstv po narodnomu obrazovaniiu za 1903 g., " *Russkaia shkola*, No. 4 (1904), p. 162; Denisov, "Znachenie uchitel'skikh kursov," p. 42.

15. For details of zemstvo petitions and their rejection by the MNP in 1904, see Ia. Abramov, "Khronika narodnago obrazovaniia," *Russkaia shkola*, No. 9, section 2 (1904), pp. 22–31; Belokonskii, "Obzor deiatel'nosti zemstv po narodnomu obrazovaniiu za 1904 g.," Ibid., No. 3 (1905), p. 183 (Chernigov); A. Nechaev, "Pamiati uchitel'skikh kursov," *Rus'* (Petersburg), No. 162, July 19/August 1, 1905, p. 5; *Pravo*, No. 20, May 16, 1904, col. 1125.

16. TsGIA, f. 733, op. 173, d. 56, 1. 280; *Russkiia vedomosti*, No. 206, July 26, 1904, p. 2. School authorities subsequently reported that political discussions took place at the Kostroma courses. Iu. A. Spasskii, a liberal zemstvo man and chairman of the local Pushkin Society for the Spread of Public Education, reportedly made speeches critical of the government's education policies and distributed illegal proclamations among the teachers: TsGIA, f. 733, op. 173, d. 55, 1. 32ob; Spasskii and the Pushkin Society were also accused of stocking teachers' libraries with books published under the general censorship (TsGIA, f. 733, op. 195, d. 623, 1. 117ob). An openly antigovernment meeting of forty teachers was held near the city on July 15 (cited from archive in Ushakov, *Revoliutsionnoe dvizhenie demokraticheskoi intelligentsii*, p. 38) and at least one teacher, N. P. Lapshin, was dismissed for participation in political discussions at the courses: *Severnyi krai*, No. 91, April 6, 1905, p. 2.

17. *Chastnoe soveshchanie zemskikh deiatelei proiskhodivshee 6, 7, 8 i 9 noiabria 1904 goda v S.-Peterburge* (Moscow, 1905), pp. 108–9.

18. TsGIA f. 1284, op. 188, d. 97, 1. 1–1ob; see *Russkiia vedomosti*, Nos. 160 and 225 (1905), and *Pravo*, No. 23, June 12, 1905, col. 1912 on the zemstvo's petition.

19. *Russkiia vedomosti*, No. 225, August 20, 1905, p. 1. No zemstvo courses were permitted in 1906 (*Khar'kovskaia zhizn'*, No. 80, May 24, 1906, p. 3), but some were held in Vologda and Viatka that summer under the guise of public lectures under new government rules on assembly issued in March 1906.

20. On the PSR's shift toward renewed faith in the revolutionary potential of the peasantry, see Perrie, *Agrarian Policy*, chapters 6–7.

21. S. Nechetnyi [S. N. Sletov], "K voprosu o postanovke raboty v derevne

(pis'mo v redaktsiiu)," *Revoliutsionnaia Rossiia*, No. 35, November 1, 1903, p. 7; "K voprosu o roli narodnykh uchitelei v sotsial'no-revoliutsionnom dvizhenii," Ibid., No. 40, January 15, 1904, p. 6; see also Manfred Hildermeier, *Die Sozialrevolutionäre Partei Russlands: Agrarsozialismus und Modernisierung im Zarenreich (1900–1914)* (Cologne, 1978), p. 117.

22. "K voprosu o roli narodnykh uchitelei," p. 7.

23. "Iz partiinoi deiatel'nosti," *Revoliutsionnaia Rossiia*, No. 30, August 20, 1903, p. 20.

24. N. Malinovskii, *Narodnyi uchitel'*, p. 37; the term *gastrolery* was also used in a report from the governor of Tula province to describe teachers from other provinces visiting local courses: *Osvobozhdenie*, No. 11 (35), November 12/25, 1903, p. 193. On Malinovskii, see Kaidanova, *Ocherki po istorii*, I, 193–196.

25. On the Saratov courses, see chapter 3; on the strength of the local PSR organization, see Perrie, *Agrarian Policy*, chapter 4; Scott J. Seregny, "Politics and the Rural Intelligentsia in Russia: A Biographical Sketch of Stepan Anikin, 1869–1919," *Russian History*, 7, No. 1–2 (1980), pp. 173–177.

26. On the courses in Perm, see K., "Pis'mo iz Permi," *Osvobozhdenie*, No. 2, July 2/15, 1902, pp. 31–32; V. Trapeznikov, "V strane nevoli," *Katorga i ssylka*, No. 6 (19), (1925), pp. 203–4; Malinovskii, *Narodnyi uchitel'*, p. 47; also F. Ch. [G. Fal'bork and V. Charnoluskii], "Otgoloski uchitel'skikh kursov," *Vestnik vospitaniia*, No. 9 (1901), p. 105, on the educational issues discussed at the Perm courses.

27. TsGIA, f. 733, op. 195, d. 623, 1. 95ob–96ob.

28. *Tambovskii golos*, No. 23, June 15, 1905; F. Ch., "Otgoloski uchitel'skikh kursov," pp. 95, 98; *Pamiati Stepana Nikolaevicha Sletova* (Paris, 1916), p. 8. On Sletov and the significance of his pamphlet in the evolution of SR theory, see Perrie, *Agrarian Policy*, pp. 49–50; V. Chernov, *Zapiski sotsialista-revoliutsionera* (Berlin, 1922), p. 268.

29. See, for example, *Iskra*, No. 1, December 1900, pp. 4–5; no. 46, August 15, 1903, p. 3; and No. 29, December 1, 1902, p. 7.

30. On Perm, see M. A. Chulkina, "Bor'ba bol'shevikov Urala za vovlechenie demokraticheskoi intelligentsii i uchashcheisia molodezhi v revoliutsionnoe dvizhenie v gody pervoi russkoi revoliutsii (1905–1907 gg.)," Candidate's dissertation, Moscow State Pedagogical Institute, 1969, p. 85. On Tver, see V. V. Malinovskii, "Iz istorii bor'by iskrovskikh organizatsii na mestakh za vovlechenie narodnogo uchitel'stva v revoliutsionnoe dvizhenie (1900–1903 gg.)," in *Iz proshlogo i nastoiashchego Kalininskoi oblasti* (Moscow, 1965), p. 158; *Rzhev v 1905 godu: Sbornik* (Rzhev, 1925), p. 7; Lane, *Roots of Russian Communism*, p. 152.

31. TsGIA, f. 733, op. 195, d. 623, 1. 95ob; Baum, "Neskol'ko faktov," pp. 164–166; see his autobiographical sketch in *Katorga i ssylka*, No. 32, 1927, p. 162, and N. Rozhkov and A. Sokolov, *O 1905 gode: Vospominaniia* (Moscow, 1925), p. 5.

32. Malinovskii, *Narodnyi uchitel'*, p. 47; A. I. Spiridovich, *Partiia Sotsialistov-Revoliutsionerov i ee predshestvenniki, 1886–1916*, 1st ed. (Petrograd, 1916), p. 99, dated the formation of the union to May 1903. Aside from Spiridovich's the only treatment of the union is Perrie, *Agrarian Policy*, pp. 83–88. Since she relies exclusively on the published materials of the PSR Central Committee in *Revoliutsionnaia Rossiia*, Perrie's information on the union, like that of the party leadership, is incomplete.

33. "K voprosu o roli narodnykh uchitelei," p. 6.

34. A large contingent of delegates to the congress had police records or were under Okhrana surveillance: TsGAOR, f. 63, op. 12, d. 1304, 11. 112–116ob.

35. The nonparty union's appeal was printed, with critical commentary, in "Ob"edinitel'naia popytka," *Revoliutsionnaia Rossiia*, No. 37, December 1903, pp. 3–4. It was issued some time later in 1903 (A. Nasimovich, "Vospominaniia o 1905 g.," *Narodnyi uchitel'*, No. 11, 1925, p. 37).

36. TsGAOR, f. 63, op. 12, d. 1304, 11. 647–49, 659; Malinovskii, *Narodnyi uchitel'*, p. 42; E. O. Vakhterova, *V. P. Vakhterov*, p. 167. According to Olga Kaidanova,

Malinovskii was elected a member in absentia, though he does not mention the fact (*Ocherki po istorii*, I, 194).

37. TsGAOR, f. 6862, op. 1, d. 174, 11. 1–7 (a sketch by Akramovskii's widow); also Malinovskii's testimony at a "memoir evening" in 1925: TsGAOR, f. 6862, op. 1, d. 69, 11. 22–23; TsGAOR, f 63, op. 12, d. 1304, 1. 114ob.

38. A. Nasimovich, "Iz vospominanii," TsGAOR, f. 6862, op. 1, d. 84, 1. 119.

39. Nasimovich, "Vospominaniia," TsGAOR, f. 6862, op. 1, d. 82, 1. 2 (a variant of memoir cited in note 38). *Iskra*'s agent in Moscow, A. G. Orlov, in a letter to the editorial board of February 1903, mentioned that the local SD committee had recently made contact with a group of teachers formed after the Moscow congress which planned to circulate revolutionary literature and asked Orlov to provide it with SD material (*Perepiska V. I. Lenina i redaktsii gazety "Iskra" s sotsial-demokraticheskimi organizatiiami v Rossii 1900–1903 gg.*, vol. 3 [Moscow, 1970], pp. 291–92).

40. Nasimovich, "Vospominaniia," 1. 2. On the congress, see *Osvobozhdenie*, No. 17 (41), February 5/18, 1904, pp. 309–11, and I. P. Belokonskii, *Zemskoe dvizhenie*, (Moscow, 1914), pp. 184–88. Pleve described the congress as an "antigovernment mob": TsGIA, f. 1405, op. 539 (1904), d. 346, 1. 1.

41. Nasimovich, "Vospominaniia," 1. 2. The arrests are reported in *Revoliutsionnaia Rossiia*, No. 43, March 15, 1904, p. 14. Mentioned in this "SR Affair" are the arrests of Akramovskii, Nikiforov, and Filatov. I have identified Nikiforov as an SR member of the union's "bureau," but Filatov, a city teacher, was an SD (a number of rural teachers are also named).

42. Nasimovich, "Iz vospominanii," 1. 120; note from Dmitriev to I. L. Tsvetkov (1925) in TsGAOR, f. 6862 op. 1, d. 84, 1. 235; TsGAOR, f. 6862, op. 1, d. 56, 1. 14–15 (police report on Akramovskii's arrest).

43. "Iz partiinoi deiatel'nosti," *Revoliutsionnaia Rossiia*, No. 30, August 20, 1903, p. 20; "K voprosu o roli uchitelei," p. 6.

44. "Otchet Komiteta Soiuza narodnykh uchitelei Partii Sotsialistov-Revoliutsionerov," *Revoliutsionnaia Rossiia*, No. 40, January, 1904, p. 22; *Revoliutsionnaia Rossiia*, No. 43, March 15, p. 22; No. 45, April 15, p. 20; No. 54, October 30, 1904, p. 22.

45. Malinovskii, "K istorii zarozhdeniia," p. 36.

46. TsGAOR, f. 6862, op. 1, d. 174, 11. 3–4; N. Speranskii, ed., *1905 god v Samarskom krae: materialy po istorii R. K. P. (b) i revoliutsionnogo dvizheniia* (Samara, 1925), p. 619.

47. Rvachev, "Iz proshlogo," 1. 91. S. N. Dmitriev, an SD member of the non-party union's bureau, later wrote that the vast majority of teachers could not make sense of the "bitter struggle between Bolsheviks, Mensheviks and SRs." TsGAOR, f. 6862, op. 1, d. 84, 1. 235.

48. "Kratkii ocherk uchitel'skogo dvizheniia i soiuza rabotnikov prosveshcheniia Tver'skoi gubernii," TsGAOR, f. 6862, op. 1, d. 21, 1. 144 (on the Iaroslavl exhibition); Baum, "Neskol'ko faktov," pp. 164–65; Kaidanova, *Ocherki*, vol. 1, pp. 189–90; *Osvobozhdenie*, No. 12 (36), November 24/December 3, 1903, pp. 203–06 (on the Kursk courses).

49. *Osvobozhdenie.*, No. 8 (32), October 2/15, p. 143; No. 11 (35), November 19/25, 1903, pp. 194–195 (Kursk); *Revoliutsionnaia Rossiia*, No. 43, March 15, pp. 22–24; No. 44, April 1, pp. 20–21; No. 45, April 15, 1903, p. 14 (Saratov); TsGIA, f. 733, op. 195, d. 623, 1. 119 (Tula); *Revoliutsionnaia Rossiia*, No. 49, 1904, p. 20 (Tambov); Smirnov, "O narodnykh uchiteliakh," pp. 1-2.

50. K. F. Shatsillo, "Formirovanie programmy zemskogo liberalizma i ee bankrotstvo nakanune pervoi russkoi revoliutsii (1901–1904 gg.)," *Istoricheskie zapiski*, 97 (1976), p. 76; I. I. Petrunkevich, *Iz zapisok obshchestvennogo deiatelia* (Berlin 1934), p. 313.

51. S. I. Mitskevich, *Revoliutsionnaia Moskva. 1888–1905* (Moscow, 1940), pp. 341–

342; T. Galynskii, *Ocherki po istorii agrarnoi revoliutsii Serdobskogo uezda, Saratovskoi gubernii* (Serdobsk, 1924), p. 57; S. Anikin, "Za 'pravednoi zemlei' (pamiati I. M. Igoshina)," *Vestnik Evropy*, No. 3 (1910), pp. 97–98; Spiridovich, *Partiia Sotsialistov-Revoliutsionerov*, p. 98; Maureen Perrie, "The Social Composition and Structure of the Socialist-Revolutionary Party before 1917," *Soviet Studies*, vol. 24 (1972), pp. 238–39.

52. Nechetnyi, "K voprosu o postanovke," p. 8.

53. There is one case recorded of teachers leaving the SDs for the SRs over the agrarian question, in Ekaterinoslav: E. Kogan, "Iz istorii selian'skogo dvizheniia na Ekaterinoslavshchine nakanune 1905 g.," *Letopis' revoliutsii*, No. 5 (1926), pp. 107–10, cited in Lane, *Roots of Russian Communism*, pp. 164–65.

54. Nechetnyi, "K voprosu o postanovke," p. 8.

55. Rvachev, "Iz proshlogo," 1. 98, 107.

56. M. N. Pokrovskii, "K uchitel'skomu s"ezdu," *Na putiakh k novoi shkole*, No. 1, (1925), p. 5.

57. Veselovskii, *Istoriia zemstva* I, 475–85; *Russkaia shkola*, No. 1, section 2 (1904), p. 42; Charnoluskii, *Ezhegodnik narodnoi shkoly*, p. 239; Brooks, "Zemstvo and Education," pp. 263–65.

58. *Russkiia vedomosti*, No. 287, October 19, 1903, p. 2, and *Russkaia mysl'*, No. 11, section 2 (1903), p. 101; A. Bagil'dinskii, "Iz Atkarska," *Saratovskaia zemskaia nedelia*, No. 6–7, section 2 (1905), pp. 33–40.

59. *Russkaia shkola*, No. 1, section 2 (1904), p. 95; surveys of zemstvo resolutions on salaries in 1903–4 can be found in Ia. Abramov, "Khronika narodnago obrazovaniia," *Russkaia shkola*, No. 12, section 2 (1904), pp. 47–49.

60. "Begstvo narodnykh uchitelei," *Russkaia shkola*, No. 1, section 2 (1904), p. 107; *Syn otechestva*, No. 11, November 28, 1904, p. 5; the number of teachers in Suzdal is taken from *Zhurnal zasedanii komissii po narodnomu obrazovaniiu pri gub. zemskoi uprave 21 i 22 noiabria 1905 g.* (Vladimir-na-Kliazme, 1905), p. 34; on this problem in general, see also Shipov, *Vospominaniia i dumy*, pp. 40-41.

61. See *Morshanskoe uezdnoe zemskoe sobranie ocherednoi sessii 1907 g.: zhurnal* (Morshansk, 1908), pp. 286–87; on regional variations, see also Anikin, "Vystavka v Iaroslavle," p. 103.

62. See, for example, Samsonov, *Byt uchashchikh v Novgorodskoi gubernii*, pp. 65–76; Sergeev, *Narodnaia shkola v Nizhegorodskom uezde*, pp. 27–29; *Sbornik postanovlenii po narodnomu obrazovaniiu uezdnykh zemskikh sobranii Poltavskoi gub. za 1905 god* (Poltava, 1907), pp. 99–100.

63. Superanskii, *Byt uchashchikh v nachal'nykh shkolakh*, p. 4; *Russkiia vedomosti*, No. 287, October 19, 1903, p. 2.

64. Chekhov, *Narodnoe obrazovanie v Rossii*, p. 64; E. A. Zviagintsev, "Zemstvo i uchebnoe vedomstvo," in *Iubileinyi zemskii sbornik*, p. 363; Akimov, "Deiatel'nost' kurskago zemstva," pp. 12–13; Brooks, "Zemstvo and Education," pp. 251–52; Eklof, *Russian Peasant Schools*, pp. 126–38.

65. On this and the general organization of zemstvo school management, see D. Rozanov, "Ob organizatsii zavedeniia delom narodnago obrazovaniia pri obshchestvennykh samoupravleniiakh," *Vestnik vospitaniia*, No. 8 (1908), pp. 103–32.

66. E. G. Kornilov, "Zemskaia demokraticheskaia intelligentsiia," pp. 101–06; B. B. Veselovskii, *Istoricheskii ocherk deiatel'nosti zemskikh uchrezhdenii Tverskoi gubernii (1864–1913 gg.)* (Tver, 1914), p. 68; Veselovskii, *Istoriia zemstva*, I, 308–9; III, 395; I. D. Strashun, "Polveka zemskoi meditsiny (1864–1914)," *Ocherki istorii russkoi obshchestvennoi meditsiny (k stoletiiu zemskoi meditsiny): sbornik statei*, ed. P. I. Kaliu (Moscow, 1965), p. 51; Ramer, "The Zemstvo and Public Health," p. 300; Frieden, *Russian Physicians*, pp. 87–96, 140–43, 159. On conflicts, see Ushakov, *Revoliutsionnoe*

dvizhenie demokraticheskoi intelligentsii, p. 48; A. Bel'skii, "Zemskaia biurokratiia," *Obrazovanie,* No. 5 (1905), pp. 8–9.

67. N. V. Chekhov, "Uezdnye uchilishchnye komissii," *Russkaia shkola,* No. 9 (1906), pp. 104–5; V. Ia. Kanel', "Obshchestvennaia meditsina v sviazi s usloviiam zhizni naroda," *Istoriia Rossii v XIX veke,* 9 vols. (St. Petersburg, 1907–11), VIII, 178–83; S. I. Mitskevich, *Na grani dvukh epokh: ot narodnichestva k marksizmu* (Moscow, 1937), p. 108; Briukhatov, "Znachenie 'tret'iago elementa'," p. 194.

68. Chekhov, "Uezdnye uchilishchnye komissii," p. 104; MVD officials who conducted inspections of zemstvos in the early 1900's agreed as to the significance and influence wielded by local medical sovety: Kurskoe zemstvo, *Otchet po revizii,* II, 153–54; *Otchet po revizii zemskikh uchrezhdenii Moskovskoi gubernii,* I, 211–19; Charnoluskii, *Zemstvo i narodnoe obrazovanie,* II, 253–54.

69. S. I. Igumnov, *Zemstvo i tret'ii element* (Kharkov, 1914), pp. 4–5.

70. For example, the Moscow district congress in 1901 (see chapter 3) and at assembly of the Mozhaisk Society: *Otchet po revizii,* I, 271; Vasilevich, *Moskovskii s"ezd,* pp. 89–90; *Resoliutsii III-go s"ezda russkikh deiatelei po tekhnicheskomu i professional'nomu obrazovaniiu v Rossii 1903–1904 g.g.* (St. Petersburg, 1906); *Russkiia vedomosti,* No. 1, January 1, 1905, appendix (survey of 1904), pp. 48–49.

71. A. V. Panov, "Shag vpered: zasedanie uchilishchnoi komissii Saratovskago uezdnago zemstva pri uchastii uchitelei," *Obrazovanie,* No. 12, section 2 (1901), pp. 31–42; also G. S., "Soveshchanie shkol'noi komissii Saratovskago uezdnago zemstva s uchiteliami zemskikh shkol," *Vestnik Vladimirskago gub. zemstva,* No. 19 (1901), pp. 15–19. Eklof cites the provincial and district zemstvo school commissions as a way zemstvos gained increased control over schooling from the 1890s but plays down the extent to which this generated conflict with the government and does not deal with the question of teacher participation: *Russian Peasant Schools,* pp. 147–48.

72. *Zhurnaly uchilishchnoi komissii Saratovskago uezdnago zemstva pri uchastii gg. uchashchikh zemsko-obshchestvennykh uchilishch Saratovskago uezda* (Saratov, 1901); *Spravochnaia kniga po nizshemu obrazovaniiu, God tret'ii (svedeniia za 1905 god),* comp. S. I. Antsyferov (St. Petersburg, 1908), part II, pp. 261–62. In late 1908 the Saratov district commission was still operating, and teachers and zemstvo men were discussing issues relating to school textbooks and construction of new buildings (*Dlia narodnago uchitelia,* No. 4 [1909], p. 29). The relative success of the Saratov experiment is all the more interesting in that some of its members were conservative zemtsy who played a visible role in the post-1905 reaction (for example, Iseev, K. N. Grimm). I have examined the zemstvo assembly records for 1905–7; although there were attacks on individual teachers for radical political activity, the usefulness of the commission seems never to have been questioned.

73. In the ultraliberal Novotorzhok zemstvo in 1900, and in Vesegon in 1901: Veselovskii, *Istoricheskii ocherk,* p. 69; *Sistematicheskii svod ukazov Pravitel'stvuiushchego Senata, posledovavshikh po zemskim delam,* comp. N. I. Kuznetsov, vol. 9 (1912 g.), Voronezh, 1913, p. 310; in Borovichi and Tikhvin districts: Tulupov, "Osnovnye voprosy," p. 92; Charnoluskii, *Ezhegodnik narodnoi shkoly,* p. 361; Samsonov, *Byt uchashchikh v Novgorodskoi gubernii,* p. 86. In 1901 the Kursk provincial zemstvo assembly endorsed the idea of district school commissions with teachers. The response from the districts was lukewarm at best; only the Shchigry zemstvo voted to expand its existing commission to include teachers: Akimov, "Deiatel'nost' kurskago zemstva," pp. 14–15, 29–30. By 1905 the Kursk zemstvo had turned sharply to the right and rejected in principle the idea of teachers' involvement in school management: *Tekushchaia shkol'naia statistika Kurskago gubernskago zemstva: god odinnadtsatyi 1906–1907 uchebnago goda,* part 1, pp. 52–56.

74. *Russkaia shkola,* No. 10–11, section 2 (1903), pp. 38–39; No. 12, section 2 (1903), pp. 35–36; *Otchet po revizii zemskikh uchrezhdenii Moskovskoi gubernii,* I, 219–22, 272.

75. TsGAg.M, f. 459, op. 4, d. 3592, 1, 1–3ob., 6–7; *Otchet po revizii,* I, 221–22; K.

K. Arsen'ev, "Moskovskoe gubernskoe zemstvo i administrativnaia reviziia," *Vestnik Evropy* No. 9 (1904), pp. 340–41; *Russkiia vedomosti,* No. 239, August 28, 1904, p. 3; *Vestnik vospitaniia,* No. 7 (1904), section 2, p. 94. On the conferences of chairmen, see Veselovskii, *Istoriia zemstva,* III, 447, 548; Shipov and other Moscow zemstvo men had attended the Moscow Congress which the local zemstvo helped fund.

76. *Otchet po revizii,* I, 222–23; Veselovskii, *Istoriia zemstva,* IV, 541; *Zhurnal dlia vsekh,* No. 10 (1904), p. 637.

77. TsGIA, f. 733, op. 195, d. 623, 1. 121–121ob; Charnoluskii, *Ezhegodnik narodnoi shkoly,* p. 234; *Spravochnaia kniga po nizshemu obrazovaniiu. God tret'ii,* p. 171. In 1904 the Smolensk provincial zemstvo planned a "conference" on education, but of the forty-eight persons invited only twenty showed up; not one teacher appeared and pressure from their superiors can only be assumed: Belokonskii, "Obzor deiatel'nosti zemstv po narodnomu obrazovaniiu za 1904 g.," *Russkaia shkola,* No. 7–8 (1905), p. 274.

78. Charnoluskii, *Ezhegodnik narodnoi shkoly,* p. 243; *Russkiia vedomosti,* No. 260, September 22, 1905, p. 2: Veselovskii, IV, 505. Until 1906 the Bogorodits zemstvo was sharply oppositional.

79. *Russkiia vedomosti,* No. 305, November 5, 1904; Veselovskii, IV, 377–78; on Vladimir, *Russkiia vedomosti,* No. 312, November 12, 1904; Veselovskii, IV, 480–81; *Zhurnaly ocherednogo Kovrovskogo uezdnago zemskago sobraniia 1905 goda* (Vladimir, 1905) pp. 18–20.

80. *Kalendar'-spravochnik 1908/09 uchebnyi god,* comp. O. N. Smirnov (Kiev, 1908), p. 131; the zemstvo article can be found in Charnoluskii, *Sputnik narodnago uchitelia,* pp. 12–13.

81. *Otchet po revizii zemskikh uchrezhdenii Viatskoi gubernii,* 2 vols. (St. Petersburg, 1905), I, 229–31 (on school commissions set up in 1903 at the Urzhum and Nolinsk zemstvos); *Otchet po revizii zemskikh uchrezhdenii Moskovskoi gubernii,* I, 220, 224; "Vespoddaneishii raport tovarishcha ministra vnutrennykh del, senatora, tainago sovetnika Zinov'eva," *Pravo,* No. 27, July 4, 1904, col. 1449–1457; Kurskoe zemstvo, *Otchet po revizii,* II, 153–56.

82. Pirumova, *Zemskaia intelligentsiia,* pp. 193–94; Thomas Fallows, "The Zemstvo and the Bureaucracy, 1890–1904," in Emmons and Vucinich, *The Zemstvo in Russia,* pp. 218–26.

83. Veselovskii, IV, 345–46; Belokonskii, "Obzor deiatel'nosti zemstv po narodnomu obrazovaniiu za 1904 g.," *Russkaia shkola,* No. 4 (1905), pp. 156–157; TsGIA, f. 733, op. 195, d. 623, 1. 117ob.

84. Ibid., 1. 118; *Pravo,* No. 8, February 22, 1904, col. 537–538; TsGAg.M, f. 459, op. 4, d. 3421, 1. 1–2ob.

85. TsGIA, f. 733, op. 195, d. 623, 1. 118; *Pravo,* No. 44, October 31, 1904, col. 3059–3060; A. Stakhovich, "O doverii obshchestva k uchebnoi administratsii i obratno," *Russkiia vedomosti,* No. 303, October 31, 1904, p. 4. The Elets sovet, on which teachers had full voting rights and elected their own representatives, apparently functioned until 1906, when liberal zemstvo men were thrown out of office in the regular zemstvo elections: Charnoluskii, *Ezhegodnik narodnoi shkoly,* p. 234.

86. Pirumova, *Zemskoe liberal'noe dvizhenie,* pp. 266–72; on the earlier period and the roots of liberalism among the Tver gentry, see Terence Emmons, *The Russian Landed Gentry and the Peasant Emancipation of 1861* (Cambridge, 1968); *Obozrenie zemskikh uchrezhdenii Tverskoi gubernii,* p. 59, Veselovskii, IV, 567–68.

87. Kornilov, "Zemskie uchitelia v revoliutsionnom dvizhenii," pp. 119–22; *Obozrenie zemskikh uchrezhdenii,* pp. 48–50; according to an unpublished MS on the teachers' movement in Tver, during the period 1890–1902 in the chancellery of the governor, despite considerable loss of archival materials, were thirty-one files concerning 120 teachers, many of whom were dismissed, arrested, or placed under

police surveillance: "Kratkii ocherk uchitel'skogo dvizheniia," 1. 137; see also Pirumova, *Zemskaia intelligentsiia*, pp. 200–7.

88. N. Malinovskii, "O shkol'nom muzee Slavianoserbskago uezdnago zemstva," *Otchet Obshchestva vzaimopomoshchi uchashchikh i uchivshikh v nachal'nykh uchilishchakh Slavianoserbskago uezda, s 1-go sentiabria 1904 goda po 1-e ianvaria 1907 goda (god 5-i i 6-i)*, (Lugansk, 1907), pp. 69–71; *Obozrenie zemskikh uchrezhdenii*, p. 52; "Kratkii ocherk uchitel'skogo dvizheniia," 1. 137ob; TsGIA, f. 733, op. 195, d. 623, 1. 113–133ob. In July 1903 elections the leading liberals in Slavianoserbsk were defeated, and conservative forces turned against radical teachers. According to the PSR eight teachers who had attended the Moscow Congress were forced to resign and others were transferred to inferior posts; the school commission ceased functioning (*Revoliutsionnaia Rossiia*, No. 32, September 15, 1903, p. 10; Malinovskii, "O shkol'nom muzee," pp. 73–74). In 1904 the MVD audited the Slavianoserbsk zemstvo, which ended in a mass resignation of teachers (over 50!) and dismissals: see school director's report in *Otchet Ekaterinoslavskoi gub. zemskoi upravy za 1904 god: narodnoe obrazovanie* (Ekaterinoslav, 1905), pp. 156, 171; Belokonskii, "Obzor deiatel'nosti zemstv po narodnomu obrazovaniiu za 1904 g.," *Russkaia shkola*, No. 2 (1905), p. 166–67.

89. TsGIA, f. 733, op. 195, d. 623, 1. 112ob–114ob; *Obozrenie zemskikh uchrezhdenii*, pp. 52–53. The commission included teachers who had participated in the Moscow Congress: Spasskii, Frenkel', Andreev, Sokol'skii, Pukhlimskii, Mitropol'skii.

90. TsGIA, f. 733, op. 195, d. 623, 1. 112ob–113ob; Belokonskii, *Zemskoe dvizhenie*, 2nd ed., p. 195; *Obozrenie zemskikh uchrezhdenii*, p. 63; A. Belov, "Ocherk revoliutsionnogo dvizheniia v Tverskoi gubernii," *1905 god v Tverskoi gubernii* (Tver, 1925), p. 27.

91. *Russkaia shkola*, No. 10–11, section 2 (1904), p. 38; *Russkiia vedomosti*, No. 55, September 17, 1903, p. 2; *Obozrenie zemskikh uchrezhdenii*, pp. 66–67; "Kratkii ocherk uchitel'skogo dvizheniia, 1. 138, 145–46; Belokonskii, *Zemskoe dvizhenie*, pp. 195–96; Mestnyi, "Razgrom novotorzhskago zemstva (pis'mo iz Torzhka)," *Osvobozhdenie*, No. 23 (47), May 2/15, 1904, pp. 410–12; "Iz russkoi zhizni," Ibid., No. 59, November 10/October 28, 1904, p. 151; M. V. Sedel'nikova, *N. V. Chekov: vidnyi deiatel' narodnogo prosveshcheniia* (Moscow, 1960), p. 55; Veselovskii, III, 550–51.

92. *Spravochnaia kniga po nizshemu obrazovaniiu, God tret'ii*, pp. 65–67, 168–72, 261–62, 314–15, 372–73, 418–19, 468; also, review, of this source by V. Charnoluskii in *Vestnik vospitaniia*, No. 1, section 2 (1909), pp. 16–17; *Spravochnaia kniga po nizshemu obrazovaniiu. God chetvertyi (svedeniia za 1906 god)*, comp. A. I. Antsyferov, (St. Petersburg, 1908), part 2, pp. 30–31, 149–50, 270–72, 360, 497–98; Charnoluskii, *Ezhegodnik narodnoi shkoly*, p. 234; as late as 1914 teachers participated in zemstvo school commissions in only a handful of district zemstvos: Akimov, "Zemskaia rabota po podgotovke," *ZhMNP*, No. 6 (1915), p. 144.

93. Zemets, "Zemstvo i vrachi," p. 281; Sh. [A. I. Shingarev?], "Po povodu stat'i g. 'Zemtsa'-'Zemstvo i vrachi'," *Zhurnal Obshchestva russkikh vrachei v pamiat' N. I. Pirogova*, No. 1–2 (1904), p. 178.

94. *Obozrenie zemskikh uchrezhdenii*, pp. 67–76.

95. V. U. S., "Kratkii ocherk istorii Vserossiiskago soiuza uchitelei i deiatelei po narodnomu obrazovaniiu," *Narodnyi uchitel'*, No. 4 (1906), p. 12.

96. Cited in K. F. Shatsillo, "Formirovanie programmy zemskogo liberalizma," p. 76.

6. *The Teachers' Movement and Revolutionary Politics in 1905*

1. Ia. Kapanadze, *Golos sel'skago uchitelia* (n. p., n. d.), p. 6.

2. Among others returned from exile were G. A. Fal'bork, V. I. Charnoluskii

(exiled for their part in the Third Technical Education Congress), V. P. Vakhterov, the Kursk teacher F. Lozovoi, and others. For details on the amnesty, see Belokonskii, *Zemskoe dvizhenie*, p. 208.

3. Terence Emmons, "Russia's Banquet Campaign," *California Slavic Studies*, 10 (1977), p. 53.

4. For general background, see Belokonskii, chapter 8; Galai, *The Liberation Movement in Russia*, chapters 8–10; Fischer, *Russian Liberalism*, chapters 4–5.

5. On the zemstvo address campaign, see Manning, "Zemstvo and Revolution," pp. 37–38; on the banquets, see Emmons, "Russia's Banquet Campaign," pp. 45–86; Sanders, "Union of Unions," pp. 204–43.

6. "Zemtsy-konstitutsionalisty o konstitutsionno-demokraticheskoi partii: zhurnal s"ezda gruppy zemtsev konstitutsionalistov 9–10 iulia 1905 goda v Moskve," Prilozhenie k No. 78/79 "Osvobozhdeniia," p. 9.

7. *Pravo*, No. 13, March 30, 1905, col. 1047; V. Zelenko, "Uchitel' nizshei shkoly," *Vestnik znaniia*, No. 8 (1905), p. 96.

8. Vl. Ladyzhenskii, "Melkoe raskreposhchenie," *Russkiia vedomosti*, No. 86, (March 30, 1905), p. 4; see also Ibid., No. 64, (March 8, 1905), pp. 2–3.

9. Sel'skii Uchitel', "Zametki," *Vestnik iuga* (Ekaterinoslav), No. 908, (April 11, 1905), pp. 2–3 (emphasis in original).

10. Uchitel' Shchipakin, "Pochemu molchit narodnyi uchitel'?," *Syn otechestva* (St. Petersburg), No. 34, March 28, 1905, p. 1.

11. Malinovskii, *Narodnyi uchitel' v revoliutsionnom dvizhenii*, p. 49.

12. I. Samokhvalov, "Otryvki iz vospominanii o 1905 gode," *Narodnyi uchitel'*, No. 11 (1925), p. 51.

13. On the Saratov "banquets," see Seregny, "Politics of the Rural Intelligentsia," pp. 177–78. On teachers at the Orel banquet: E. A. Zviagintsev, *Inspektsiia narodnykh uchilishch* (Moscow, 1914), p. 67; *Russkiia vedomosti*, No. 23, January 28, 1905, p. 2; Emmons, "Russia's Banquet Campaign," pp. 64–65. Teachers' participation in city meetings was apparently widespread enough to prompt the inspector of schools in Saratov district to issue a circular to all volost boards in early December 1904 advising rural officials to insure regular attendance by teachers in school and charging them to inform the school administration of any absences by teachers from their place of service: *Russkiia vedomosti*, No. 350, December 17, 1904, p. 3.

14. N. Sokolov, "Kratkii ocherk istorii Vserossiiskago soiuza," *Vestnik Soiuza uchitelei i deiatelei po narodnomu obrazovaniiu*, No. 2 (1905), p. 3.

15. L. Menzhinskaia, "Peterburgskoe uchitel'stvo v 1905 g.," *Narodnyi uchitel'*, No. 11 (1925), p. 39. For the text of the resolution, see "Rezoliutsiia S.-Peterburgskago Pedagogicheskago Obshchestva vzaimnoi pomoshchi uchashchim," *Osvobozhdenie*, No. 62, December 31 (18), 1904, p. 216.

16. N. Suprunenko, "Iz nedavnego proshlogo: istoriia organizatsii uchitel'skikh obshchestv," *Rabotnik prosveshcheniia*, No. 13–14 (1924), p. 53; also *Nizhegorodskii listok*, No. 276, October 13, 1905, p. 1.

17. N. Kapralov, "Iz istorii ob"edineniia rabotnikov prosveshcheniia v Nizhegorodskoi gubernii," TsGAOR, f. 6862, op. 1, d. 89, 1. 19ob (Nizhegorod); TsGIA, f. 733, op. 173, d. 56, 1. 215 (Tauride); *Russkiia vedomosti*, No. 15, January 17, 1905, p. 3; *Nasha zhizn'*, No. 55, January 1, 1905, p. 4 (article by S. Seropolko).

18. *Privolzhskii krai*, No. 11, January 20, 1905, p. 2; *Russkiia vedomosti*, No. 15, January 17, 1905, p. 3 (Simbirsk); *Severnyi krai*, No. 5, January 6, 1905, pp. 3–4; TsGIA, f. 733, op 173, d. 55, 1. 21–22; *Russkiia vedomosti*, No. 19, January 21, 1905, p. 2. On Florovskaia and the local PSR organization, see TsGAOR, f. 102, DP OO (1905), d. 1800, ch. 54, 1. 1.

19. N. Rumiantseva, "Politicheskaia zabastovka gorodskogo uchitel'stva Peterburga v 1905 g.," TsGAOR, f. 6862, op. 1, d. 87, 1. 77.

20. TsGAOR, f. DP, 7-oe deloproizvodstvo, d. 27, 1. 13–13ob; TsGIA, f. 733, op.

173, d. 57, 1. 97–97ob; *Kaluzhskaia guberniia v 1905 godu: sbornik statei, vospominanii i materialov* (Kaluga, 1925), p. 440. In March the society's board was arrested for holding this meeting: *Russkiia vedomosti,* No. 85, March 29, 1905, p. 2 (Kaluga); TsGIA, f. 733, op. 173, d. 55, 1. 11–13ob, 102–03 (Voronezh).

21. A. Groshkov, "K istorii Irkutskogo uchit. o-va za 1-e desiatiletie," TsGAOR, f. 6862, op. 1, d. 74, 1. 44ob-45; "Uchastie Samarskikh uchitelei v osvoboditel'nom dvizhenii" (unsigned MS.), TsGAOR, f. 6862, op. 1, d. 88, 1. 1; TsGIA, f. 733, op. 173, d. 56, 1. 245.

22. See "Narodnyi uchitel' v Germanii," *Russkiia vedomosti,* No. 357, December 25, 1902, p. 4; also N. Tulupov and P. Shestakov, *Germanskii uchitel'skii soiuz* (Moscow, 1905).

23. N. Popova, "K istorii vserossiiskago uchitel'skago soiuza (Moskovskaia oblastnaia organizatsiia)," *Vestnik vospitaniia,* No. 4–5 (1917), p. 98; N. Popova, "Moskovskaia oblastnaia organizatsiia Vserossiiskogo Uchitel'skogo Soiuza," *Narodnyi uchitel',* No. 11 (1925), p. 46; Zolotarev, pp. 258–59.

24. At this time there were more than 350 city schools in the capital, with 500 separate classes and 25,000 pupils. The city government demanded high qualifications from its teachers; for the most part men with higher education preferred to teach in secondary schools, where they were better paid and enjoyed the prerogatives of state service: see Rumiantseva, "Politicheskaia zabastovka," 1. 76–77 and Iu. N. Lavrinovich, *Narodnoe obrazovanie v Peterburge* (St. Petersburg, 1902), p. 1.

25. TsGAOR, f. 518, op. 1, d. 76, 1. 10–15ob; Sokolov, "Kratkii ocherk," p. 4; Menzhinskaia, "Peterburgskoe uchitel'stvo," pp. 39–40; testimony of Ivan Tsvetkov and Menzhinskaia at a "memoir evening" of April 26, 1925, in TsGAOR, f. 6862, op. 1, d. 69, 1. 6, 35.

26. N. Tulupov and P. Shestakov, *K voprosu ob ustroistve vserossiiskago uchitel'skago soiuza* (Moscow, 1905), pp. 9–11. The *zapiska* was widely printed in the press: *Syn otechestva,* No. 26, March 20, 1905, p. 2; *Vestnik iuga* (Ekaterinoslav), No. 906, April 9, 1905, p. 2; *Pravo,* No. 12, March 27, 1905, col. 922–24.

27. The composition of the Petersburg Bureau is not clear but it likely included such well-known education experts as Charnoluskii, Fal'bork, Ia. I. Dushechkin (who taught in an upper-level city school), V. A. Gerd, P. A. Miakotin and others involved in the Petersburg Teachers' Society. Further discussion of the union issue took place at a session of the Ushinskii Commission on March 19, where a report, "The History of the German Teachers' Union and the Embryonic Russian Union," was read: *Syn otechestva,* No. 27, March 21, 1905.

28. Authorities from all ends of the empire reported the appearance of the *zapiska,* either in envelopes of the Ushinskii Commission or of the Imperial Free Economic Society: TsGAOR, f. DP OO (1905), d. 999, ch. 1, tom I, 1, 5–13ob, 19–21, 55, 89, 99, 109–109ob. The *zapiska* also arrived in Russian Poland where it helped spark the formation of a Polish Teacher's Union, autonomous from the Russian body: Michal Szulkin, *Strajk szkolny 1905 roku* (Wroclaw, 1959), pp. 165–68. Some zemstvo chairmen turned the *zapiska* over to the authorities, for example in Mtsensk and Kromy districts in Orel province, TsGAg.M, f. 459, op. 4, d. 3969, 1. 1–2, 5–6.

29. Sokolov, "Kratkii ocherk," p. 5; TsGAOR, f. DP OO (1905), d. 999, ch. 1, tom I, 1. 6–6ob, 20.

30. These efforts were described at a "memoir evening" in 1925 commemorating the April conference in which Chekhov and Popova took part: TsGAOR, f. 6862, op. 1, d. 69, 1. 16–17, 30–32, 38; on this twentieth anniversary gathering, see Iv. Tsvetkov, "Pervyi vecher Istprofa (K godovshchine uchitel'skogo dvizheniia 1905 g.)," *Rabotnik prosveshcheniia,* No. 10 (1925), p. 6; on the "lecture group" see S. Mitskevich, "Lektorskaia gruppa pri M. K. v 1905–07 gg.," *Proletarskaia revoliutsiia,* No. 9 (44), 1925, pp. 49–61.

31. See A. L. Savich, "Pedagogicheskoe obshchestvo pri Moskovskom univer-

sitete," *Vestnik Moskovskogo universiteta,* No. 10 (1953), pp. 131–36; Rozhkov and Sokolov, *O 1905 g.*, pp. 6–8; E. A. Morokhovets, "Kratkie biograficheskie svedeniia o N. A. Rozhkove," pp. 10–11, and M. M. Bogoslovskii, "Iz vospominanii o N. A. Rozhkove," pp. 144–45, both in a memorial volume on Rozhkov: Institut istorii (RANION), *Uchenye zapiski,* 5 (Moscow, 1928); Nasimovich, "Iz vospominanii," TsGAOR, f. 6862, op. 1, d. 84, 1. 121–122.

32. I. Ia. Gerd, "Ob uchrezhdenii vserossiiskago soiuza lits, zanimaiushchikhsia pedagogicheskim delom," *Russkiia vedomosti,* No. 37, February 8, 1905, p. 3; also No. 40, February 11, 1905, p. 3.

33. *Russkiia vedomosti,* No. 76, March 21, 1905, p. 3. Dubovka was a large settlement with a population (in 1897) of 16,521; in 1906 it had ten primary schools and a women's gymnasium: M. A. Vodolagin, *Ocherki istorii Volgograda, 1589–1967* (Moscow, 1968), pp. 145–46.

34. *Russkiia vedomosti,* No. 62, March 6, 1905, p. 3; S. Seropolko, "Kak voznik vserossiiskii uchitel'skii soiuz," *Dlia narodnago uchitelia,* No. 3 (1907), p. 7. Felitis was an instructor at the Moscow Teachers' Institute (Nasimovich, "Iz vospominanii," 1. 115).

35. Popova, "K istorii vserossiiskago," p. 100. Chekhov later recalled contacts with V. A. Gerd and Dushechkin from the Petersburg organization to plan the congress (TsGAOR, f. 6862, op. 1, d. 69, 1. 17), as does Rozhkov (*O 1905 g.*, p. 12). M. N. Popov noted that a joint group was formed (just when is not clear) which included him and his wife, Dushechkin, A. Ia. Zaks, Gerd, Chekhov, Ia. Ia. Gurevich, Pokrovskii, L. A. Voskresenskaia, and O. N. Markovskaia: TsGAOR, f. 6862, op. 1, d. 175 (his autobiography, paginated separately).

36. Of the seventy-one primary teachers in attendance, it is not possible to separate rural from urban teachers; fifty-two participants were secondary school instructors and twenty-nine were other "activists" in education: "Vserossiiskii uchitel'skii soiuz," *Russkiia vedomosti,* No. 106, April 21, 1905, p. 4; Popova, "K istorii vserossiiskago," pp. 99–100. Police intercepted a letter from Chekhov to Seropolko of the Tula Teachers' Society asking him to popularize the idea of a union among teachers and to see that rural teachers in particular were represented at the Moscow gathering: TsGAOR, f. DP, OO (1905), d. 999, ch. 1, tom I, 1. 59–59ob.

37. S. R. Popova, "Donskoe uchitel'stvo (Po vospominanii uchastnitsy)," *Uchitel'stvo Severnogo Kavkaza v 1905 godu* (Rostov-on-Don, 1925), p. 31; Burtsev, "Professional'no-politicheskoe dvizhenie," 1. 276–276ob.

38. *Russkiia vedomosti,* No. 106, April 21, 1905, p. 4; Tulupov and Shestakov, *K voprosu ob ustroistve,* pp. 18–20.

39. See Emmons, "Russia's Banquet Campaign," p. 79; Petr Struve, "Zemstvo i demokratiia," *Osvobozhdenie,* No. 69–70, May 7/20, 1905, pp. 330–31; Sanders, "Union of Unions," chapter 3.

40. "Organizatsionnyi vopros," *Revoliutsionnaia Rossiia,* No. 69, June 15, 1905, p. 2–5 (Perrie attributes this unsigned article to Viktor Chernov: *The Agrarian Policy of the Socialist-Revolutionary Party,* pp. 107–108); Karmeliuk, "O liberalizme, voobshche, i o russkikh liberalakh v chastnosti i v osobennosti," *Volnyi diskussionyi listok* (Geneva), No. 2 (1905), p. 10; Dikii, "Na zlobu dnia: o 'soiuzakh' i 'partiiakh'," *Revoliutsionnaia Rossiia,* No. 69, June 15, 1905, pp. 7–10.

41. "Otchet o Moskovskom soveshchanii uchitelei i deiatelei po narodnomu obrazovaniiu 11–13 aprelia 1905 g.," *Vestnik Soiuza uchitelei i deiatelei po narodnomu obrazovaniiu,* No. 2 (December, 1905), pp. 16–18, 20.

42. S. I. Mitskevich, *Revoliutsionnaia Moskva, 1888–1905* (Moscow, 1940), pp. 336, 340–50; TsGAOR, f. 6862, op. 1, d. 69, 1. 36; G. M. Ameshina, "Ivan Ivanovich Skvortsov-Stepanov (8 marta 1870–8 oktiabria 1928)," *Istoriia i istoriki: 1971* (Moscow, 1972), p. 387; Vakhterova, *V. P. Vakhterov,* pp. 173–75.

43. Rozhkov and Sokolov, *O 1905 g.*, p. 12; "Vechera vospominanii," in *Materialy*

po istorii professional'nogo dvizheniia v. Rossii, 5 vols. (Moscow, 1924–27), IV, 40–42; the Moscow SD committee issued a special leaflet "K narodnym uchiteliam" before the congress: Ososkov, *Voprosy istorii*, II, 24–25.

44. "Osvobozhdentsy za rabotoi (Pis'mo iz Moskvy)," *Proletarii* No. 8, July 17/4, 1905, pp. 3–4. On this article, see I. A. Slonimskaia, *Meditsinskie rabotniki v revoliutsii 1905–1907 gg.* (Moscow, 1955), pp. 28–30; Mitskevich, *Revoliutsionnaia Moskva*, pp. 338, 341.

45. J. L. H. Keep, *The Rise of Social Democracy in Russia* (Oxford, 1963), p. 193.

46. "Otchet o Moskovskom soveshchanii," p. 15; Frumkina, delegated to the Moscow gathering by the Minsk Society for the Spread of Enlightenment among Russian Jews, pointed out that teachers in Minsk could not grasp her argument against the union adopting a political platform: TsGAOR, f. 6862, op. 1, d. 69, 1. 18–19.

47. "V soiuze uchitelei (iz stat'i M. Pokrovskogo 'Literatorskaia gruppa M. K. v 1905 g.' po povodu vospominanii tov. S. I. Mitskevicha)," TsGAOR, f. 6862, op. 1, d. 84, 1. 72ob.

48. "Otchet o Moskovskom soveshchanii," pp. 15–19.

49. Elena Shchepot'eva, "Ob"edinenie ili raskol?," *Syn otechestva*, No. 92, June 4, 1905, p. 1. This and Rozkhov's articles were part of a series by various individuals on the issue of the political-professional unions and their place in the revolution. For a summary of the debate, see V. Agafonov, "Professional'nye soiuzy," *Mir bozhii*, No. 6, section 2, (1905), pp. 124–129; P. N. Miliukov, *God bor'by* (St. Petersburg, 1907), pp. 34–53; Sanders, "Union of Unions," pp. 880–99.

50. "Otchet o Moskovskom soveshchanii," pp. 19, 21; Sokolov, "Kratkii ocherk," p. 5; TsGAOR, f. 6862, op. 1, d. 69, 1. 17 (Chekhov).

51. Menzhinskaia, "Peterburgskoe uchitel'stvo," p. 41; "V soiuze uchitelei," 1. 72ob–73ob; TsGAOR, f. 63, op. 14, d. 787, 1. 4–5ob.

52. Burtsev, "Professional'no-politicheskoe dvizhenie," 1. 277–277ob; "Organizatsiia burzhuaznoi demokratii," *Iskra*, No. 103, June 21, 1905, pp. 1–2.

53. Mitskevich, *Revoliutsionnaia Moskva*, pp. 349–50; clear reference to wavering among local party members (probably in Moscow) on this issue is found in "Liberal'nye soiuzy i sotsial'demokratiia," *Proletarii*, No. 18, September 26/13, 1905, p. 2; P. Strel'skii, "Raznochintsy v 1905 g.," *Obrazovanie*, No. 5 (1906), p. 22.

54. "V soiuze uchitelei," 1. 72–72ob; Uchitel', "Professional'naia intelligentsiia i sotsial'-demokraty (Pis'mo v redaktsiiu)," *Proletarii*, No. 13, August 22/9, 1905, p. 3. Lenin's comment follows as an editorial note; Ivan Tsvetkov, "Pervyi vecher Istprofa," p. 6 and his autobiographical sketch in TsGAOR, f. 6862, op. 1, d. 175.

55. Iv. Sergeini, "Ternistym putem (K 20 letiiu uchitel'skogo professional'nogo ob"edineniia)," TsGAOR, f. 6862, op. 1, d. 74, 1. 26.

56. Groshkov, "K istorii Irkutskogo uchit. o-va," 1. 46; R. Olenin, "Krest'iane i intelligentsiia," *Russkoe bogatstvo*, No. 1 (1907), pp. 254–55.

57. A third decree, a manifesto, issued on the same day gave a contradictory signal, calling on all patriotic Russians to rally to the defense of the Fatherland and throne against both external foes and internal sedition. Not surprisingly, this document was largely ignored by those calling for reform. On the February 18 acts, see Belokonskii, *Zemskoe dvizhenie*, 2nd ed., pp. 263–67; E. D. Chermenskii, *Burzhuaziia i tsarizm v pervoi russkoi revoliutsii*, 2nd ed. (Moscow, 1970), pp. 54–61; Galai, *The Liberation Movement*, pp. 242–43; V. A. Maklakov, *Vlast' i obshchestvennost' na zakate staroi Rossii*, 3 vols. (Paris, 1936), III, 359–60.

58. *Severnyi krai*, No. 81, March 27, 1905, p. 2; *Syn otechestva*, No. 34, March 28, 1905, p. 3.

59. TsGIA, f. 733, op. 173, d. 55, 1. 90–90ob, 103–103ob, 226–226ob; *Iskra*, No. 93, March 10, 1905, p. 5; *Syn otechestva*, No. 26, March 20, 1905, p. 5.

60. TsGIA, f. 733, op. 173, d. 55, 1. 104, 124.

61. Immediately after publication of the *ukaz* the Iaroslavl Society formed a "legal commission" which became the nerve-center of the society; it was in this commission that the idea of a Teachers' Union was first discussed, and the commission expended considerable energies to provide rural teachers with current political literature (on this, see the following chapter): *Ocherk deiatel'nosti obshchestva*, p. 6; Burtsev, "Professional'no-politicheskoe dvizhenie," 1. 275ob-276; "Zasedenie pravovoi komissii obshchestva vzaimopomoshchi uchitelei Iaroslavskoi gub. 10 aprelia," *Severnyi krai*, No. 105, April 22, 1905, p. 3.

62. The text of the MVD circular is in Belokonskii, *Zemskoe dvizhenie*, 2nd ed., pp. 264–67; TsGIA, f. 733, op. 173, d. 56, 1. 96; Shipov, *Vospominaniia i dumy*, p. 296; Chermenskii, *Burzhuaziia i tsarizm*, p. 61.

63. TsGAOR, f. 63, op. 14, d. 787, 1. 29, 33–34ob (list of addresses), 45–45ob.

64. *Nizhegorodskii listok*, No. 94, April 8, 1905, p. 2; No. 104, April 21, 1905, p. 3.

65. TsGAg.M, f. 459, op. 4, d. 3966, 1. 3, 5–5ob; *Nizhegorodskii listok*, No. 105, April 22, 1905, p. 3; Kapralov, "Iz istorii ob"edineniia rabotnikov prosveshcheniia v Nizhegorodskoi gubernii," 1. 19ob.

66. *Nizhegorodskii listok*, No. 116, May 4, 1905, p. 4; No. 130, May 18, 1905, p. 4; No. 140, May 29, 1905, p. 4. The district was divided into three regional union groups, each sending a delegate (the doctor I. I. Zakharov, and teachers I. S. Samokhvalov and V. I. Vogau): TsGAOR, f. 518, op. 1, d. 76, 1. 173–173ob.

67. *Rabochee i professional'noe dvizhenie v Nizhegorodskom krae, 1869–1917*, ed. V. T. Illarionov (N-Novgorod, 1923), p. 208–10; *Nizhegorodskii listok*, No. 153, June 11, 1905, p. 3 and No. 155, June 13, 1905, p. 4.

68. TsGIA, f. 733, op. 173, d. 55, 1. 273–74; *Tambovskii golos*, No. 3, May 19, 1905, p. 4; *Russkiia Vedomosti*, No. 128, May 20, 1905, p. 3; in Morshansk district the union was endorsed by the local chairman of the school board and gentry marshal, A. N. Gruzinov and other zemstvo activists, undoubtedly a factor in its rapid growth (fifty-six members by late spring): *Tambovskii golos*, No. 24, June 16, 1905, p. 3. A local group was also organized in Kozlov in early May: TsGAOR, f. DP OO (1905), d. 999, ch. 1, tom I, 1. 118.

69. *Spravochnaia kniga uchitel'skikh obshchestv*, pp. 19–20; Sergeini, "Ternistym putem," 1. 23; "Stat'i (neizvestnykh avtorov) ob organizatsii i deiatel'nosti professional'nogo soiuza narodnykh uchitelei Ekaterinoslavskoi gub. za 1905–1922 g. g.," (dated 1925), TsGAOR, f. 6862, op. 1, d. 78, 1. 5; for membership data, see L. Rodnev, "Storinka z istorii vchitel'stva na Katerinoslavshchini (Tovaristvo vzaemnoi dopomogi vchiteliv narodnykh shkil na Katerinoslavshchini z 1898–1908 r.)," *Robitnik osviti* (Kharkov), No. 7 (1925), p. 46; *Vestnik iuga* (Ekaterinoslav), No. 920, April 26, 1905, p. 2.

70. *Pridneprovskii krai* (Ekaterinoslav), No. 2426, February 19, 1905, p. 4; *Vestnik iuga*, No. 872, March 5, 1905 (letter of S. F. Samoilenko); *Pridneprovskii krai*, No. 2437, March 3, 1905 (article by I. Odinokovskii); Ibid., No. 2454, March 20, 1905 (article by N. Emel').

71. *Zhurnal Obshchego sobraniia 22 aprelia 1905 goda*, izd. Ekaterinoslavskago gub. ob-va vzaimopomoshchi narodnykh uchitelei (Ekaterinoslav, 1905), pp. 4, 7–9; *Vestnik iuga*, No. 920, April 26, 1905, pp. 2–3; No. 927, May 4, 1905, p. 3.

72. Sergeini, "Ternistym putem," 1. 27; *Vestnik iuga*, No. 1016, August 24, 1905, pp. 2–3; *Zhurnal obshchego sobraniia*, pp. 11–13, 19–20.

73. *Vestnik iuga*, No. 918, April 24, 1905, p. 3; No. 943, May 21, p. 3 and No. 1016, August 24, 1905, pp. 2–3; TsGIA, f. 733, op. 173, d. 57, 1. 45ob-46; *Syn otechestva*, No. 169, August 31, 1905, p. 4; Sergeini, "Ternistym putem," 1. 29; their posts were subsequently boycotted by the Union: *Vestnik iuga*, No. 1087, November 30, 1905, p. 2. The society was finally closed under conditions of martial law by governor-general Sandetskii on January 28, 1906, and only reopened in 1907: "Stat'i (neizvestnykh avtorov)," 1. 12–13; Rodnev, "Storinka z istorii," p. 48.

74. Teachers in railway and factory-mining schools in Ekaterinoslav province (concentrated in Bakhmut district and elsewhere) were in a comparably better situation than those in zemstvo schools. Aside from residing in larger settlements with better communications they received higher salaries and taught in multiclass schools (therefore with more than one teacher), contributing to contacts and corporate activity. They were better educated (in Bakhmut 83.6 percent had secondary and specialized educations), and men predominated over women, in contrast to the situation in zemstvo schools: see *Otchet inspektora narodnykh uchilishch o sostoianii uchilishch, podvedomstvennykh inspektsii narodnykh uchilishch Bakhmutskago uezda Ekaterinoslavskoi gubernii, za 1905 god* (Bakhmut, 1905), 25–30.

75. D. Protopopov, "Iz nedavnego proshlogo (Samara v 1904–1905 gg.)," *Russkaia mysl'*, No. 11, section 2 (1907), pp. 32–33; *Samarskaia gazeta*, No. 91, May 22, 1905, p. 2; No. 99, June 1, p. 2 and No. 100, June 2, p. 3.

76. *Nasha zhizn'*, No. 100, May 24/June 6, 1905, p. 4; "Uchastie Samarskikh uchitelei," 1. 1–2; *Samarskaia gazeta*, No. 85, April 29, 1905, p. 2 (declaration of a group of teachers from Stavropol district).

77. TsGIA, f. 733, op. 173, d. 56, 1. 245ob–246; *Nasha zhizn'*, No. 100; *Russkiia vedomosti*, No. 116, May 9, 1905, p. 4; *Privolzhskii krai*, No. 101, May 25, 1905, p. 2.

78. In advance of the May 26 assembly, school officials sent notices calling on all teachers loyal to tsar and country to turn out to protest the actions of radicals in the society and to revise the organization's charter to exclude nonteachers from membership; *Syn otechestva*, No. 84, May 25, 1905, p. 3; "Uchastie Samarskikh uchitelei," 1. 6ob; Trepov's note to MNP Glazov is in TsGIA, f. 733, op. 173, d. 56, 1. 209ob; for details on the May 26 assembly, see V. M., "Iz Samary," *Saratovskaia zemskaia nedelia*, No. 6–7, section 2 (1905), pp. 45–52.

79. *Samarskaia gazeta*, No. 99, June 1, 1905, p. 2; TsGIA, f. 733, op. 173, d. 56, 1. 168–168ob, 290ob–211, 238; *Russkiia vedomosti*, No. 145. June 1, 1905, p. 2; Klafton was a major figure in radical politics in Samara; a former collaborator in the Marxist *Samarskii vestnik*, in November 1905 he was elected chairman of the Samara section of the Union of Unions: I. Blumental, "Sotsial'-demokratiia i revoliutsionnoe dvizhenie 1905 goda v Samarskom krae," *1905 god v Samarskom krae: materialy po istorii R. K. P. (b.) i revoliutsionnogo dvizheniia*, ed. N. Speranskii (Samara, 1925), p. 160, 238.

80. TsGIA, f. 733, op. 195, d. 720, 1. 49–ob. Arkhangel'skii was soon dismissed from government service. In his memoirs A. N. Naumov, who was marshal of nobility in Novouzensk, and thus chairman of the school board, complains bitterly that Arkhangel'skii used his inspectoral powers to place radical teachers in the schools under his jurisdiction, disregarding the wishes of the school board: A. N. Naumov, *Iz utselevshikh vospominanii, 1868–1917*, 2 vols. (New York, 1954–55), I, 331–33.

81. "Uchastie Samarskikh uchitelei," 1. 3–6; *Samarskaia gazeta*, No. 93, May 25, 1905, p. 3; authorities later described the origins of political agitation among the district's peasantry to this gathering: TsGIA, f. 733, op. 175, d. 76, 1. 33.

82. Neposed, "Pis'mo iz Vladimira," *Severnyi krai*, No. 109, April 27, 1905, p. 3; *Syn otechestva*, No. 63, April 30, 1905, p. 6; TsGIA, f. 733, op. 173, d. 55, 1. 246ob–247.

83. Along with other materials the board distributed copies of *Severnyi krai* (No. 109), which, along with an account of the April 23 assembly, contained a report on the Moscow April conference with the projected union statute: *Syn otechestva*, No. 68, May 5, 1905, p. 4; *Severnyi krai*, No. 118, May 7, p. 3 and No. 138, May 28, 1905, p. 3; TsGIA, f. 733, op. 173, d. 55, 1. 247–247ob.

84. TsGIA, f. 733, op. 173, d. 56, 1. 1–2 on the volost gatherings; also *Severnyi krai*, No. 136, May 29, 1905, p. 2; *Nasha zhizn'*, No. 107, May 31; and No. 109, June 2, 1905, p. 6 on inspectoral circulars and prohibitions on meetings in certain locales.

On the governor's ban, see *Severnyi krai*, No. 126, May 17, p. 2 and No. 129, May 20, 1905, p. 3. On the May 22 meetings, see Malitskii, "Professional'noe dvizhenie vo Vladimirskoi gubernii," p. 66 and Ivanov, "Iz istorii Soiuza vo Vladimire," p. 86. For the society's closure for one year, see *Pravo*, No. 35, September 4, 1905, col. 1904.

85. Malitskii, "Professional'noe dvizhenie," pp. 78–80; "Vospominaniia t. A. I. Skobennikova ob uchitel'skom soiuze," *O rabochem dvizhenii i sotsial'-demokraticheskoi rabote vo Vladimirskoi gubernii v 900-kh godakh*, vyp. 1. (Vladimir, 1926), p. 201.

86. Viatka Society (April 22): TsGAOR, f. DP OO (1905), d. 999, ch. 1, tom 5, 1. 42ob; Tomsk Society (April 10): TsGIA, f. 733, op. 173, d. 56, 1. 4–5; *Severnyi krai*, No. 101, April 16, 1905, p. 2.

87. Sources on the spring movement, from mid-May, are as follows: *Voronezh* (May 12 and June 24): TsGIA, f. 733, op. 173, d. 56, 1. 7–13, 270–274ob; TsGAOR, DP OO (1905), d. 999, ch. 1, tom I, 1. 148–149ob; *Syn otechestva*, No. 83, May 24, p. 4, No. 85, May 26, 1905, p. 3, and No. 123, July 9, 1905, p. 5; *Russkiia vedomosti*, No. 138, May 22, 1905, pp. 3–4. *Kostroma* (May 22): TsGIA, f. 733, op. 173, d. 56, 1. 279–286ob; *Syn otechestva*, No. 89, May 31, 1905, p. 4; *Russkiia vedomosti*, No. 243, September 7, 1905, p. 3; *Pravo*, No. 36, September 11, 1905, col. 2976–77. *Irkutsk* (May?): *Syn otechestva*, No. 83, May 24, 1905. *Kaluga* (the society did not hold a regular assembly but distributed union materials among teachers; a "private" teachers' assembly was held sometime in May): TsGIA, f. 733, op. 173, d. 57, 1. 146b; TsGAOR, f. 63, op. 14, d. 787, 1. 12–12ob; *Russkiia vedomosti*, No. 232, August 15, 1905, p. 2. *Kazan* (May 22): *Volzhskii listok* (Kazan), No. 193, May 31, 1905, p. 4 and *Volzhskii vestnik* (Kazan), No. 21, June 2, 1905, p. 2; also the assembly of the Chistopol district section of the society (June 3): TsGIA, f. 733, op. 173, d. 57, 1. 77–77ob; *Volzhskii listok*, No. 358, January 19, 1906, p. 3. *Iaroslavl* (May 22, August 29): TsGIA, f. 733, op. 173, d. 57, 1. 10–13ob; *Severnyi krai*, No. 135, May 28, 1905, p. 3; No. 216, September 3, p. 3 and No. 217, September 4, 1905, p. 3; *Syn otechestva*, No. 87, May 28, 1905, p. 4. *Yalta* (May 15): *Syn otechestva*, No. 83, May 24, 1905, p. 1. *Pskov* (May 22): *Syn otechestva*, No. 107, June 20, 1905, p. 3; *Pravo*, No. 23, June 12, 1905, col. 1899. *Penza* (June 12–13): *Russkiia vedomosti*, No. 171, June 17, 1905, p. 2. *Kursk* (June 12): *Syn otechestva*, No. 106, June 19, 1905, p. 4; TsGIA, f. 733, op. 173, d. 56, 1. 299–301ob, 310–310ob. *Saratov* (May 29–31): TsGAOR, f. DP OO (1905), d. 999, ch. 1, tom I, 1. 155–159; TsGIA, f. 733, op. 173, d. 56, 1. 35–36ob, 133–133ob, 195–208ob; *Saratovskii dnevnik*, No. 108, May 31, p. 2 and No. 110, June 2, p. 2; *Saratovskii listok*, No. 107, June 2, 1905, p. 2; *Privolzhskii krai*, No. 104, May 31, 1905, p. 3. *Tula* (May 29): TsGIA, f. 733, op. 796, d. 166, 1. 90–90ob.

88. *Chernigov* (scheduled for June 8): TsGAOR, f. DP OO (1905), d. 999, ch. 1, tom I, 1. 160–161ob; TsGAOR, f. 518, op. 1, d. 76, 1. 205. *Perm: Syn otechestva*, No. 118, July 3, 1905, p. 3; *Severnyi krai*, No. 219, September 8, 1905, p. 2; TsGAOR, f. DP OO (1905), d. 999, ch. 1, tom I, 1. 200–203 and tom II, 1. 32–33; TsGIA, f. 733, op. 175, d. 65, 1. 103f. *Arkhangel: Severnyi krai*, No. 119, May 8, 1905, p. 2; *Syn otechestva*, No. 121, July 7, 1905, p. 3: TsGIA, f. 733, op. 196, d. 52, 1. 213–213ob; *Otchet o deiatel'nosti Obshchestva Vzaimnago Vspomoshchestvovaniia uchashchim i uchivshim v narodnykh uchilishchakh Arkhangel'skoi gubernii* (Arkhangel'sk, 1906).

89. *Smolensk* (August 29): *Nasha zhizn'*, No. 263, September 13, 1905; *Russkiia vedomosti*, No. 236, August 31, 1905, p. 2; TsGAOR, f. 518, op. 1, d. 76, 1. 196ob–197 (assembly decision that teachers be given the right to meet and discuss professional needs and to explain to the population the significance of popular representation). *Novgorod* (August 15): *Volkhovskii listok*, Nos. 572, 573, 575, 1905. *Tver* (September 14): *Russkiia vedomosti*, No. 251, September 17, 1905. *Vologda* (?): TsGAOR, f. 518, op. 1, d. 76, 1. 198–199.

90. *Syn otechestva*, No. 178, September 9, 1905, p. 4 (Kherson district); *Russkiia vedomosti*, No. 129, May 12, 1905, p. 2 (Rostov-on-Don); Ibid., No. 133, May 17, p. 4 (Kuznetsk, Saratov); TsGAOR, f. DP OO (1905), d. 999, ch. 1, tom II, 1. 51–51ob

(Beloozero, Novgorod); 26–26ob, 53–53ob (Valuiki, Voronezh); TsGIA, f. 733, op. 195, d. 720, 1. 2–3ob (Orenburg); *Russkiia vedomosti,* No. 176, July 1, 1905, p. 2 (Sumy, Kharkov); No. 186, July 12, p. 2 (Kozlov, Tambov); *Nasha zhizn',* No. 107, May 31/June 13, 1905, p. 3 (Sudzha, Kursk); *Syn otechestva,* No. 76, May 15, 1905, p. 6 (Kirillov, Novgorod); *Russkiia vedomosti,* No. 223, August 18, 1905, p. 2 (Novocherkassk); Malitskii, "Professional'noe dvizhenie," p. 66 (Kovrov, Vladimir); Oniani, *Bol'shevistskaia partiia i intelligentsiia v pervoi russkoi revoliutsii* (Tiflis, 1970), pp. 132–33 (Odessa).

91. P. Zhulev, "Ob uchitel'skikh obshchestvakh vzaimopomoshchi," *Russkaia shkola,* No. 4 (1909), p. 83; *Otchet pravleniia obshchestva vzaimnago vspomoshchestvovaniia uchashchim i uchivshim v nachal'nykh shkolakh Chernigovskoi gubernii za 1904, 1905 i 1906 gody* (Chernigov, 1907), p. 5, 45; Zolotarev, "Ocherki," pp. 276–77.

92. TsGIA, f. 733, op. 173, d. 57, 1. 10ob–11.

93. TsGIA, f. 733, op. 173, d. 56, 1. 205–205ob.

94. See, for example, the 21 point resolution drawn up by the Kostroma Society: Ibid., 1. 282–283ob.

95. Ibid., 1. 15–16. In some instances, as in Belebei district (Ufa), teachers demanded humane treatment and boycotted school officials who addressed them with the familiar Russian "you" and diminutive first names like "Stepka" instead of polite address: *Kliazma,* No. 31, February 2, 1906, p. 3.

96. *Russkiia vedomosti,* No. 222, August 17, 1905, p. 1 and sources on these societies cited in note 87.

97. TsGIA, f. 733, op. 173, d. 56, 1. 280ob–281 (zemstvo activist Iu. A. Spasskii at May 22 meeting of the Kostroma Society).

98. A., "Uchitel' i shkola (pis'mo iz Ialty)," *Syn otechestva,* No. 83, May 24, 1905, p. 1; also Iaroslavl Society: TsGIA, f. 733, op. 173, d. 57, 1. 12ob.

99. TsGAOR, f. DP OO (1905), d. 999, ch. 1, tom I, 1. 157ob.

100. TsGIA, f. 733, op. 173, d. 56, 1. 202–202ob.

101. This was particularly true at assemblies held later during the summer; Voronezh Society (June 24) and Iaroslavl Society (August 29): *Severnyi krai* No. 217, September 4, No. 3 and No. 221, September 11, 1905, p. 3.

102. Cited in L. M. Gordeeva, "Deiatel'nost' bol'shevikov sredi narodnykh uchitelei v gody pervoi russkoi revoliutsii," Candidate dissertation, Gor'kii State University (Gor'kii, 1970), p. 175.

103. *Syn otechestva,* No. 85, May 26, 1905, p. 3.

104. Ibid., No. 83, May 24, 1905, p. 3; *Russkiia vedomosti,* No. 126, May 8, 1905, p. 4; V. A. Zelenko, "Iz perezhitogo (Vospominaniia o revoliutsionnoi deiatel'nosti uchitel'stva)," *Dela i dni: istoricheskii zhurnal,* No. 3 (1922), pp. 99–120, Tsvetkov, "Istoriia professional'nogo ob"edineniia," col. 654.

105. On Kaluga, see TsGAOR, f. 63, op. 14, d. 787, 1. 12–12ob; on Pskov, see *Syn otechestva,* No. 107, June 20, 1905, p. 3; a union was established in Pskov in August: TsGAOR, f. 518, op. 1, d. 76, 1. 209–210ob.

106. V. Anan'in, "Uchitel'stvo moskovskikh gorodskikh shkol v 1905 godu (Vospominaniia moskovskogo uchitelia)," TsGAOR, f. 6862, op. 1, d. 84, 1. 224; Popova, "K istorii," p. 103; Menzhinskaia, "Peterburgskoe uchitel'stvo," p. 41; also her testimony in 1925 that in the elections of delegates to the Finland Congress from St. Petersburg a majority were SDs (although members of the Petersburg Bureau attended ex officio): TsGAOR, f. 6862, op. 1, d. 69, 1. 36.

107. *Vestnik uchitelei,* No. 2 (April 1906), p. 82; it is possible that this was the motivation behind dissent over the political platform in the Kazan and Tver Societies. Popova later claimed that in the provinces SD agitation for a professional union met sympathy, by and large, among the more conservative teachers who feared politics and expected only material benefits from the Union: "K istorii Vserossiiskago," p. 103.

108. Sanders, "Union of Unions," chapter 8; Henry Reichman, *Railwaymen and Revolution: Russia, 1905* (Berkeley: University of California Press, 1987), chapter 6.

109. Zolotarev, "Ocherki," p. 261; V. Charnolusskii, "Iz vospominanii ob Uchitel'skom Soiuze," *Narodnyi uchitel'*, No. 11 (1925), p. 60.

110. Samokhvalov, "Otryvki iz vospominanii," p. 52; see also E. Vakhterova, "O vserossiiskom uchitel'skom soiuze v iiune 1905 g.," (undated ms.), TsGAOR, f. 6862, op. 1, d. 72, 1. 4; S. Seropolko, "Pervye tri s"ezda Vserossiiskago uchitel'skago soiuza," *Dlia narodnago uchitelia*, No. 4 (1907), p. 7.

111. "Protokoly Vserossiiskago s"ezda delegatov uchitelei nizshei i srednei shkoly i deiatelei po vneshkol'nomu obrazovaniiu sostoiavshagosia v Peterburge 7–10 iiunia 1905 g.," *Vestnik Vserossiisskago soiuza uchitelei i deiatelei po narodnomu obrazovaniiu*, No. 2 (December 1905), p. 27.

112. Ibid., pp. 22–23, 26 (reference to deputation of June 6 to Nicholas II from the Zemstvo Congress of late May which adopted resolutions considered overly moderate by much of the radical intelligentsia: no overt constitutional demands or the four-tail franchise).

113. Ibid., p. 23–24, 26, 28.

114. Ibid., pp. 27–28; on SD efforts, see Menzhinskaia, "Peterburgskoe uchitel'stvo," p. 42; *Bor'ba* (St. Petersburg), No. 2, November 29, 1905. In Viatka at a provincial congress held August 6–9, 1905, the clauses of the union statute on political tasks were accepted unanimously and local sections were formed in all districts; in Slobodsk and Glazov these were led by SRs, but in Viatka, Urzhum, and Sarapul local sections were led by SDs: I. Mirov, "Professional'nye soiuzy v Viatskoi gubernii v period pervoi russkoi revoliutsii," *1905 god v Viatskoi gubernii* (Viatka, 1925), p. 219.

115. For the secondary school controversy, see "Protokoly Vserossiiskago s"ezda," pp. 31–34; on this union, see Zolotarev, "Ocherki," pp. 263–64; Tsvetkov, "Istoriia professional'nogo ob"edineniia," col. 654; Alston, *Education and the State*, pp. 179f. Some secondary instructors (for example, M. N. Popov) remained members of both unions.

116. "Protokoly Vserossiiskago s"ezda," pp. 35–36; the appeal was issued in early September (see chapter 7). The composition of the Central Bureau elected at the congress was as follows: V. I. Charnoluskii (SPB), G. A. Fal'bork (SPB), N. V. Chekhov (Moscow), V. V. Kir'iakov (Moscow), Ia. I. Dushechkin (SPB), P. A. Miakotin (SPB), V. A. Gerd (SPB), N. M. Sokolov (SPB), E. F. Proskuriakova (SPB), V. V. Vodovozov (SPB), O. A. Dobiash (SPB), A. A. Nikolaev (Pskov), V. P. Vakhterov (listed as Novgorod, but residing in Moscow), I. N. Sakharov (Moscow), V. P. Kondrateva (Kharkov).

117. "Protokoly," p. 36.

118. "Protokoly," pp. 37–38; both speeches and other advice on tactics were sent out to union members in the form of a hectographed "Vyborka po voprosam taktiki" by the Central Bureau, probably later during the summer: TsGIA, f. 733, op. 195, d. 23, 1. 131–133ob; also TsGIA, f. 1405, op. 530, d. 1052, 1. 32–33ob.

119. On closure of teachers' societies in the summer 1905, see TsGIA, f. 733, op. 173, d. 56, 1. 214–215ob (Voronezh, Vladimir, Tauride); *Pravo*, No. 29, July 24, col. 2400 (Saratov); other societies suffered the same fate at the end of 1905 and in 1906.

120. TsGIA, f. 733, op. 195, d. 720, 1. 15–16, 34–34ob; *Russkiia vedomosti*, No. 222, August 17, p. 1; No. 230, August 25, 1905, p. 3; *Severnyi krai*, No. 203, August 20, 1905, p. 2; *Pravo*, No. 32, August 15, 1905, col. 2620.

121. *Pravitel'stvennyi vestnik*, No. 73, April 14, 1905, p. 3; *Russkiia vedomosti*, No. 89, April 2, p. 2; No. 96, April 10, 1905, p. 1; *Syn otechestva*, No. 94, June 5, 1905, pp. 3–4; *Birzhevye vedomosti* (morning edition), June 5, p. 3 and Nos. 8847, 8851, 8853; *Novoe vremia*, June 9/22, 1905.

122. *Severnyi krai*, No. 237, September 30, p. 3; No. 283, November 29, 1905, p. 2.

Musin-Pushkin had just returned from Western Europe where he had studied primary and secondary schools; he was appointed curator of the Odessa school district in January 1905. Latyshev had previously served as chairman of the Petersburg provincial Teachers' Society and in 1905, as acting curator (Izvol'skii had gone abroad due to illness) he attempted to defend teachers suspected of sedition (see chapter 8).

123. TsGIA, f. 733, op. 173, d. 127, 1. 9–16, 50–57ob, 58–66, 69–73, 81ob–82, 86–94.

124. Musin-Pushkin's final report is in Ibid., 1. 78–79ob; on the MNP directives, see *Iuzhnye zapiski*, no. 32, August 7, p. 62; No. 35, August 28, 1905, p. 65.

7. *Teachers in the Countryside*

1. For a good survey of the teacher as "outsider," see Eklof, "The Village and the Outsider," pp. 1–19. The "small zemstvo unit" and similar prescriptions were endorsed by the Moscow Congress of 1902–3: see S. Bleklov, "Vopros o melkoi zemskoi edinitse v zemstvakh, komitetakh o sel'sko-khoziaistvennoi promyshlennosti i obshchestvennykh sobraniiakh za 1902 g. i nachalo 1903 g.", in *Melkaia zemskaia edinitsa v 1902–03 gg.: sbornik statei*, vypusk 2 (St. Petersburg, 1903), pp. 200–1; Vasilevich, Moskovskii s"ezd, pp. 93–94; *Trudy*, I, 289–94.

2. Positive peasant response was indicated by the classic study undertaken in Voronezh in the 1890s under the direction of the zemstvo statistician Shcherbina: for a summary of this and other materials, see Gr. Shreider, "Melkaia zemskaia edinitsa v usloviiakh russkoi zhizni," in *Melkaia zemskaia edinitsa*, p. 36; Miliukov, *Ocherki*, II, part 2, pp. 837–39, 859–60. For similar material, and with a critical analysis of what peasants expected of literacy and schooling, see Ben Eklof, "Peasant Sloth Reconsidered: Strategies of Education and Learning in Rural Russia before the Revolution," *Journal of Social History*, 14, No. 3 (1981), pp. 355–80.

3. V. Serebriakov, "Sovremennoe sostoianie russkoi derevni i eia nuzhdy, po otzyvam sel'skikh zhitelei," *Saratovskaia zemskaia nedelia*, No. 10–12, section 3 (1905), pp. 5–8.

4. Pupu, "Vospominaniia o revoliutsii 1905-go goda," 1. 55ob–57ob; Vakhlin, "Narodnoe obrazovanie," p. 421. It may be worth noting that in terms of educational background clerics seem to have had lower qualifications than teachers. Of 1,910 clerics in the Kazan diocese in 1906, more than half had only lower or "home" schooling: *Volzhskii kur'er*, No. 176, September 23, 1906, p. 3.

5. *Volzhskii vestnik*, No. 13, November 23, p. 4; No. 35, December 20, 1905, p. 4; *Privolzhskii krai*, No. 31, February 13, p. 2; No. 187, September 19, 1905, p. 2.

6. Tomashevich, *Istoricheskii ocherk deiatel'nosti Tul'skago Obshchestva*, p. 8.

7. *Pravo*, No. 11, March 20, 1905, col. 824–25, and especially the zemstvo's report on these events in "Polozhenie zemstva Saratovskoi gubernii," *Russkiia vedomosti*, No. 91, April 4, 1905, p. 3; also Voskresenskii, "Narodnoe obrazovanie na uezdnykh sobraniiakh sessii 1905 goda," *Saratovskaia zemskaia nedelia*, No. 10–12, section 2 (1905), pp. 41–42; *Pravo*, No. 12, March 27, 1905, col. 946–47.

8. I. Nikolaev, "Povtoritel'nye zaniatiia so vzroslymi," *Saratovskaia zemskaia nedelia*, Nos. 6–7, section 2 (1904), pp. 35–67; Panov, "Voprosy narodnago obrazovaniia," pp. 35–37; "Polozhenie zemstva Saratovskoi gubernii," p. 3; "Iz khroniki zemskikh shkol v Saratovskoi gub.," *Saratovskaia zemskaia nedelia*, No. 2, section 2 (1905), pp. 23–26.

9. *Pravo*, No. 28, July 17, 1905, col. 2329–30; *Zhurnaly ekstrennago Saratovskago Gubernskago Zemskago sobraniia 15–20 marta 1905 goda* (Saratov, 1905), pp. 117–18.

10. "Iz khroniki zemskikh shkol," pp. 24–25; *Russkiia vedomosti*, No. 76, March 20, 1905, p. 3; *Pravo*, No. 12, March 27, 1905, col. 946.

11. *Pravo,* No. 11, March 20, 1905, col. 852–53; *Russkiia vedomosti,* No. 63, March 7, 1905, p. 2. School officials sent a similar warning at the start of the new school year: *Saratovskii listok,* No. 194, September 23, 1905, p. 2.

12. Sergeev, *Narodnaia shkola v Nizhegorodskom uezde,* p. 39; *Russkiia vedomosti,* No. 92, April 5, 1905, p. 3.

13. Ibid., No. 102, April 15, 1905, p. 3; *Pravo,* No. 12, col. 1144; *Syn otechestva,* No. 91, June 2, 1905, p. 4; *Severnyi krai,* No. 114, May 3, 1905, p. 2; also John S. Curtiss, *Church and State in Russia* (New York, 1940), pp. 245–46, 261.

14. *Russkiia vedomosti,* No. 73, March 17, p. 3 and No. 133, May 20, 1905, p. 4; *Privolzhskii krai,* No. 35, February 18, 1905, p. 2.

15. *Nizhegorodskii listok,* No. 113, April 30, 1905, p. 2; *Pravo,* No. 18, May 8, 1905, col. 1501–1502.

16. P. Zorev, *Perelom: obzor pervago perioda osvoboditel'nago bor'by* (Moscow, 1907), pp. 265–67; Maslov, *Agrarnyi vopros,* II, 217–18; TsGIA, f. 733, op. 195, d. 720, 1. 43–46ob; TsGAOR, f. DP OO (1905), d. 999, ch. 1, t. I, 1. 70–71ob; *Russkiia vedomosti,* No. 133, May 20, 1905, p. 5.

17. Chermenskii, *Burzhuaziia i tsarizm,* 2nd ed., p. 58; Galai, *The Liberation Movement,* pp. 242–43. The manifesto and *ukaz* both appeared in *Pravitel'stvennyi vestnik* on February 15, the former in large type in the first column, the latter in regular type in the third column.

18. "Polozhenie zemstva Saratovskoi gubernii," p. 3; R. Olenin, "Krest'iane i intelligentsiia (K kharakteristike osvoboditel'nago dvizheniia v Malorossii)," *Russkoe bogatstvo,* No. 2 (1907), p. 138; K. V. Sivkov, "Krest'ianskie prigovory 1905 goda," *Russkaia mysl',* No. 4, section 2 (1907), p. 26.

19. Based on his observations in Poltava the writer Korolenko claimed that the war was unpopular from the very start since local peasants believed that victory in the Far East would result in new laws on resettlement to Siberia rather than substantive agrarian reform at home: V. G. Korolenko, "Zemli, zemli," *Golos minuvshego,* No. 2 (1922), pp. 134–35. Stepan Anikin, on the other hand, notes that among the peasants of Saratov the notion was widespread that victory against Japan would result in a favorable solution to the land question: S. V. Anikin, "Za 'pravednoi zemlei'," p. 96.

20. Kl. Vorob'ev, "Narodnye otzyvy o tsenzure," *Russkiia vedomosti,* No. 182, July 8, 1905, p. 2; also K. Sidorov, "Krest'ianskoe dvizhenie Viatskoi gubernii v 1905–1906 gg.," in *1905 god v Viatskoi gubernii* (Viatka, 1925), pp. 83–84; Kn. P. Dolgorukov, "Agrarnaia volna," *Pravo,* No. 1, January 9, 1906, col. 32; Brooks, *When Russia Learned to Read,* pp. 28–29.

21. On these events and the agrarian movement in general, see Teodor Shanin, *Russia, 1905–1907: Revolution as a Moment of Truth* (New Haven, 1986); Geroid T. Robinson, *Rural Russia under the Old Regime* (New York, 1932); B. B. Veselovskii, *Krest'ianskii vopros i krest'ianskoe dvizhenie v Rossii, 1902–1906 gg.* (St. Petersburg, 1907); Maslov, *Agrarnyi vopros,* vol. II; Maureen Perrie, "The Russian Peasant Movement of 1905–1907: Its Social Composition and Revolutionary Significance," *Past and Present,* No. 57 (1972), pp. 123–55.

22. *Statisticheskii ezhegodnik Moskovskoi gubernii za 1905 g.,* as cited in N. Miliutin, *Nakanune pervoi revoliutsii v Moskve* (Moscow-Leningrad, 1926), p. 163; "Gazeta v derevne," in *Statisticheskii ezhegodnik Moskovskoi gubernii za 1906* (Moscow, 1907), part 1, pp. 209–19; this is supported by evidence from other locales: *Iuzhnaia zaria,* No. 28, May 19, 1906, p. 4; *Vladimirets,* No. 58, March 16, 1907, p. 3; Olenin, "Krest'iane i intelligentsiia," *Russkoe bogatstvo,* No. 1 (1907), p. 265.

23. *Statisticheskii ezhegodnik Moskovskoi gubernii za 1906,* pp. 212–13; Olenin, "Krest'iane i intelligentsiia," No. 2, p. 137; *Russkiia vedomosti,* No. 171, June 17, 1905, p. 2 (reports at assembly of Penza Teachers' Society); *Severnyi krai,* No. 97, April 12, 1905, p. 2 (Vladimir).

24. See Anikin, "Za 'pravednoi zemlei,'" p. 96. It is worth noting that literacy rates were not high among rural officials at the head of the communal administration. A study conducted in Kazan province in 1904 determined that only 18.2 percent of the village elders *(starosta)* in the province were literate: *Vestnik vospitaniia,* No. 4, section 2 (1905), p. 78.

25. *Syn otechestva,* No. 91, June 2, 1905, p. 4; *Zhurnal dlia vsekh,* No. 6 (1904), p. 380.

26. Pupu, "Vospominaniia o revoliutsii 1905-go goda," 1. 52ob. He had earlier been threatened by drunken peasant recruits who called him a *sitsilist* ("socialist" in peasant parlance) and complained that he had criticized the tsar.

27. *Russkiia vedomosti,* No. 261, October 6, 1905, p. 3; No. 33, February 7, 1905, p. 2. In his report for 1905 the governor of Novgorod remarked that peasant interest in newspapers was sparked by the war and that rural teachers served as the primary conduit for the radical press in the countryside. Representing the "extremist parties," he charged, teachers cunningly exploited peasant interest in the war to conduct revolutionary propaganda dealing with domestic issues: TsGIA, f. 1284, op. 194, d. 87, 1. 8ob-9.

28. *Russkiia vedomosti,* No. 245, September 9, 1905, p. 3; *Syn otechestva,* No. 91, June 2, 1905, p. 4 (Odessa): "Protokoly Vserossiiskago s"ezda," p. 38.

29. Chermenskii, *Burzhuaziia i tsarizm,* 2nd ed., pp. 57, 60–61; A. V. Shestakov, *Krest'ianskaia revoliutsiia 1905–1907 gg. v. Rossi* (Moscow-Leningrad, 1926), p. 59.

30. Sivkov, "Krest'ianskie prigovory," pp. 25–26, 30–31; *Russkiia vedomosti,* No. 146, June 2, 1905, p. 3.

31. Olenin, "Krest'iane i intelligentsiia," p. 146.

32. Shanin, *Russia,* pp. 131–34; Veselovskii, *Krest'ianskii vopros,* pp. 58–62. Many of the peasant petitions found their way into the progressive press, and the best digest of these is Sivkov, "Krest'ianskie prigovory," pp. 24–48.

33. TsGIA, f. 1284, op. 194, d. 87, 1. 6–6ob; "Iz istorii bor'by s agrarnym dvizheniem 1905–1906 gg.," *Krasnyi arkhiv,* 39 (1930), p. 90.

34. Olenin, "Krest'iane i intelligentsiia," pp. 138–39; "Protokoly Vserossiiskago s"ezda," p. 38; Sokolov, "Kratkii ocherk," p. 9.

35. As cited in circular of Vladimir governor in *Severnyi krai,* No. 115, May 4, 1905, pp. 2–3. A short digest of these reports from land captains is in N. Lavrov, "Krest'ianskie nastroeniia vesnoi 1905 goda," *Krasnaia letopis',* No. 3 (14), 1925, p. 26–47.

36. Veselovskii, *Krest'ianskii vopros,* p. 65; on Balashov see, *Pravo,* No. 21, May 29, 1905, col. 1766; also correspondence of teacher A. A. Shchipakin to Union's Central Bureau in TsGAOR, f. 518, op. 1, d. 76, 1. 299–299ob and d. 77, 1. 48–49ob; on Vesegon, see *Russkiia vedomosti,* No. 167, June 23, 1905, p. 2. Gorshechnikov, who taught in Deledino, was a member of the local Vesegon group of the VSU formed on June 8, 1905: TsGAOR, f. DP OO (1905), d. 999, ch. 1, t. IV, 1. 205–205ob; on Tiraspol, see *Pravo,* No. 19, May 15, 1905, col. 1619; TsGAOR, f. DP OO (1905), d. 999, ch 1, t. II, 1. 66.

37. *Nasha zhizn',* No. 104, May 28/June 10, 1905, p. 4. Skrynnikov was later active in the peasant union movement in Sumy and was dismissed along with other teachers for this activity.

38. *Severnyi krai,* No. 205, August 23, 1905, p. 2; *Rus',* No. 201, August 27/September 9, 1905, p. 5; TsGIA, f. 733, op. 175, d. 77, 1. 363–363ob; A. I. Ivanov, *Krest'ianskoe dvizhenie vo Vladimirskoi gubernii v 1905–1906 gg.* (Vladimir, 1923), pp. 7–8.

39. *Russkiia vedomosti,* No. 190, July 16, p. 2; No. 217, August 12, p. 2; No. 222, August 17, p. 1; No. 240, September 1905, p. 3; *Pravo,* No. 32, August 14, 1905, col. 2585 (Kherson); *Mir bozhii,* No. 10, section 2 (1905), p. 141 (Vladimir); E.

Zviagintsev, "Sovremennye usloviia deiatel'nosti zemskikh uchrezhdenii," *Saratovskaia zemskaia nedelia,* No. 6–7, section 3 (1905), p. 71.

40. Olenin, "Krest'iane i intelligentsiia," p. 139.

41. I. G. Drozdov, "Petitsii Novozybkovskikh krest'ian v 1905 g.," *Proletarskaia revoliutsiia,* No. 11 (1925), pp. 124–51; Sivkov, "Krest'ianskie prigovory," pp. 31–32.

42. A report on the teachers' movement in Vologda stresses that teachers became active in politics only *after* the peasantry became affected by the "contemporary ferment" and turned to teachers for guidance; teachers then had to educate themselves: *Narodnyi uchitel',* No. 8 (1907), p. 21.

43. B. I. Syromiatnikov, "Letnye uchitel'skie kursy v Moskve," *Russkiia vedomosti,* No. 137, June 14, 1908, p. 4.

44. On Iaroslavl, see Burtsev, "Professional'no-politicheskoe dvizhenie," 1. 275ob–276, 277ob; *Ocherk deiatel'nosti obshchestva vzaimnago vspomoshchestvovaniia uchashchim i uchivshim v narodnykh uchilishchakh Iaroslavskoi gubernii,* pp. 6–7; "Protokoly Vserossiiskago s"ezda," p. 38. On Nizhegorod, see chapter 6, note 65 and Gordeeva, "Deiatel'nost' bol'shevikov sredi narodnykh uchitelei," pp. 171–72. On Klin, see V. I. Orlov, *1905 god v Klinskom uezde* (Moscow-Leningrad, 1931), p. 10; *Nasha zhizn',* No. 305, October 11/24, 1905, pp. 3–4; *Nizhegorodskii listok,* No. 266 (Oct. 3), p. 2 and No. 270 (Oct. 7), p. 2.

45. TsGIA, f. 733, op. 175, d. 77, 1. 56–60. Sivkov was of local peasant origin and subsequently took part in Peasant Union organization in Nolinsk; similar activities were undertaken by section of VSU in Shenkursk (Arkhangel): TsGAOR, f. 518, op. 1, d. 76, 1. 229–230ob.

46. *Vestnik uchitelei,* No. 1 (April 2, 1906), pp. 30–31; Popova, "K istorii Vserossiiskago," p. 110. In 1906 the Moscow Organization compiled a list of literature accessible to peasants: *Severnaia Rossiia,* No. 8, May 14, 1906, p. 8; *Ukazatel' obshchedostupnykh knig po obshchestvenno-politicheskim voprosam* (St. Petersburg, 1906). This work was compiled by the VSU's Literary Commission, one of the more active members of which was V. V. Kir'iakov (an SR), who was also active in a committee which issued many of the official publications of the Peasant Union.

47. Manning, *Crisis of the Old Order,* chapters 1–3; Terence Emmons, "The Russian Landed Gentry and Politics," *Russian Review,* 33, No. 3 (July 1974), pp. 269–83; G. M. Hamburg, "The Russian Nobility on the Eve of the 1905 Revolution," *Russian Review,* 38, No. 3 (July 1979), pp. 323–38; Thomas S. Fallows, "The Russian Fronde and the Zemstvo Movement: Economic Agitation and Gentry Politics in the Mid-1890s," *Russian Review,* 44, No. 2 (April 1985), p. 119–38. The latter includes a comprehensive list of relevant works.

48. On this deputation and its background, see Belokonskii, *Zemstvo i konstitutsiia,* pp. 167–73 and Chermenskii, *Burzhuaziia i tsarizm,* pp. 66–71. On the Union of Unions and its congresses in May and early June 1905, see Sanders, "Union of Unions," chapter 8; Galai, *The Liberation Movement,* pp. 248–49, 252–53, 258–59; "Soiuz soiuzov o proekte Bulygina," *Osvobozhdenie,* No. 75, August 19/6, 1905, pp. 428–29 (decision at meeting of July 1–3 to boycott Duma elections).

49. There had been earlier discussion of such tactics in February within the Beseda Circle: Terence Emmons, "The Beseda Circle, 1899–1905," *Slavic Review,* 32 (September 1973), p. 481; see Chermenskii, *Burzhuaziia i tsarizm,* pp. 90–95; Smith, "The Constitutional-Democratic Movement in Russia, 1902–1906," Ph.D. dissertation, University of Illinois, 1958, pp. 419–26; "Dokumenty zemskago s"ezda," *Osvobozhdenie,* No. 75, August 19/6, 1905, pp. 426–27. For full discussions at the congress, see "Iul'skii zemskii s"ezd," *Osvobozhdenie,* No. 76, September 15/2, 1905, pp. 447–60; Zemets-konstitutsionalist, "S zemskikh s"ezdov 6–8 i 9–10 iiulia," *Osvobozhdenie,* No. 75, p. 433. The moderate liberal Shipov considered this turn to the narod a risky venture, capable of inciting the destructive class interests of the "dark" peasantry: Shipov, *Vospominaniia i dumy,* pp. 394–97.

50. "Zemtsy-konstitutsionalisty," Prilozhenie k No. 78/79 "Osvobozhdeniia," p. 10; E. D. Chermenskii, *Burzhuaziia i tsarizm v pervoi russkoi revoliutsii,* 1st ed. (Moscow, 1939), p. 114.

51. Zviagintsev, "Sovremmennye usloviia," pp. 71–73; Veselovskii, *Krest'ianskii vopros,* pp. 42–44; *Vestnik vospitaniia,* No. 7–8, section 2 (1905), pp. 105–11; *Pravo,* No. 32, August 14, 1905, col. 2586–2587; *Russkiia vedomosti,* Nos. 172 (June 28), p. 3; 202 (July 28), p. 3; 235, August 30, 1905, p. 2; Sivkov, "Krest'ianskie progovory," p. 28.

52. *Russkiia vedomosti,* No. 182, July 8, 1905, p. 2; *Severnyi krai,* No. 140, June 3, 1905, p. 2 and No. 246, October 11, 1905, p. 2; *1905. Sbornik statei o revoliutsionnom dvizhenii 1905–1907 g.g. v Vologodskoi gubernii* (Vologda, 1925), p. 73. By the same token some school officials urged teachers to subscribe to reactionary newspapers: *Russkiia vedomosti,* No. 233, August 28, 1905, p. 3.

53. *Spravochnaia kniga po nizshemu obrazovaniiu. God tret'ii (svedeniia za 1905 god),* comp. S. I. Antsyferov (St. Petersburg, 1908), part II, pp. 94–95, 210, 282, 332, 440, 479. In 1906, with the onset of the zemstvo reaction, such allocations dropped off markedly (see *Spravochnaia kniga . . . svedeniia za 1906).*

54. TsGIA, f. 733, op. 173, d. 56, 1. 208–208ob.

55. TsGAOR, f. DP 00 (1905), d. 999, ch. 8, 1. 42; and ch. 1, t. II, 1. 66–66ob; TsGAOR, DP 00 (1905), d. 999, ch. 45, 1. 26–31.

56. TsGIA, f. 733, op. 173, d. 57, 1. 78–81ob; d. 56, 1. 243–44.

57. N. Karpov, ed., *Krest'ianskoe dvizhenie v revoliutsii 1905 goda v dokumentakh* (Leningrad, 1926), pp. 141, 202–04, 205 (Kharkov, Voronezh, Orel); TsGAOR, f. DP 00 (1905), d. 1800, ch. 38, 1. 4ob–5ob (Novgorod); ch. 29, 1. 67–67ob (Saratov); *1905. Sbornik statei o revoliutsionnom,* pp. 45–47, 72–74 (Vologda).

58. TsGAOR, f. DP 00 (1905), d. 999, ch. 1, t. II, 1. 26–26ob; Ibid., ch. 45, 1. 64, 110–111, 127–128ob, 145–147ob.

59. See Dolgorukov's testimony in the First Duma: *Gosudarstvennaia Duma. Stenograficheskie otchety, 1906,* 2 vols. (St. Petersburg, 1906), II, 1365–1366. On Shirkov's activities: TsGAOR, f. DP 00 (1905), d. 999, ch. 45, 1. 45ob, 49–49ob; *1905 god v Kurskoi gubernii,* p. 50; Chermenskii, *Burzhuaziia i tsarizm,* 2nd ed., p. 96; *Russkiia vedomosti,* No. 263, October 8, 1905, p. 3. The Lgov zemstvo also repudiated the recent Zemstvo Congress (Ibid., No. 260, Oct. 5, 1905, p. 2). Shirkov was elected to the First Duma as a Kadet.

60. TsGAOR, f. DP 00 (1905), d. 999, ch. 45, 1. 48–48ob, 82; *Rus',* No. 192, August 18, p. 5 and No. 201, August 27, 1905, pp. 4–5. The Teachers' Union threatened a boycott of schools in Shchigry if any teachers were dismissed by the zemstvo over this affair: *Vestnik Vserossiiskago soiuza uchitelei,* No. 1 (November 1905), p. 10 and TsGAOR, f. 6862, op. 1, d. 27, 1. 23–23ob. Markov attained national stature as a rightist Duma deputy and in 1904 figured prominently in attacks within the Kursk provincial zemstvo against the third element (see Pirumova, *Zemskoe liberal'noe dvizhenie,* p. 123).

61. TsGAOR, f. 6862, op. 1. d. 54, 1. 72ob–74, 125–128ob. That some degree of support from liberal zemstvo activists could be a factor in the growth of local union groups is indicated by a letter from a teacher in Mozhaisk (Moscow) to the Bureau: "The formation of a union group here is meeting significant obstacles. In this district the chairman of the zemstvo board, Count Uvarov, a reactionary, holds sway *(vladychestvuet).* He exerts influence on the selection of teaching personnel and intimidates it. It is not surprising that teachers are isolated and do not trust each other . . . As of now only six members have signed up and they are not very active." TsGAOR, f. 518, op. 1, d. 76, 1. 248–249.

62. For example, in Voronezh province police noted significant teacher involvement in Peasant Union organizing in districts with fairly liberal zemstvos (Valuiki, Bobrov, Zemliansk) but not in districts like Zadonsk where reactionary zemstvo

men had recruited docile teaching personnel: *1905 god v Voronezhe,* 4 vols. (Voronezh, 1925), III, 22–27, 34–41.

63. Sokolov, "Kratkii ocherk," p. 9–10. According to authorities the union appeal was sent to 1,697 points throughout the empire in official envelopes of the Free Economic Society and was compiled by the bureau member Dushechkin: TsGIA, f. 1405, op. 530, d. 1052, 1. 33ob–34ob; TsGIA, f. 733, op. 195, d. 720, 1. 32–32ob, 36–37ob. The appeal also appeared in the press: *Russkiia vedomosti,* No. 253, September 17, 1905, p. 1; *Syn otechestva,* No. 187, September 18, 1905, p. 3; *Severnyi krai,* No. 228, September 21, 1905, p. 1.

64. N. Suprunenko, untitled MS. (dated 1926), in TsGAOR, f. 6862, op. 1, d. 90, 1. 3; *Vestnik Vserossiiskago soiuza uchitelei,* No. 3 (December 1905), p. 12; *Vestnik uchitelei,* No. 1 (1906), pp. 25–26; TsGAOR, f. DP 00 (1905), d. 999, ch. 1, t. II, 1. 57–57ob, 62–74, 103–104; *Russkiia vedomosti,* No. 268, October 13, 1905, p. 2; *Samarskaia gazeta,* No. 203, Oct. 28, 1905, p. 3; *Zhizn' i shkola,* No. 16, January 28, 1907, p. 3 (on district zemstvos in Simbirsk); TsGAOR, f. DP 00 (1905), d. 999, ch. 1, t. V (Viatka).

65. For example, Kirillov (Novgord), Gorodnia (Chernigov), Sumy, Sudzha, Berdiansk. The Kaluga provincial zemstvo board sent a note of sympathy to the union for which it was sharply censured by the zemstvo assembly in early December: V. D., "Iz Kalugi," *Saratovskaia zemskaia nedelia,* No. 10–12, section 2 (1905), pp. 105–107.

66. *Nasha zhizn',* No. 304, October 11/24, 1905, p. 4; *Zhurnaly ocherednago Kovrovskago uezdnago zemskago sobraniia 1905 goda,* pp. 10, 123–26; *Russkiia vedomosti,* No. 296, November 10, 1905, p. 3. The decision of 1905 was apparently overturned by a new, conservative board elected in 1906: *Vladimirets,* No. 203, September 21, 1907, p. 3; on local liberals, see Pirumova, *Zemskoe liberal'noe dvizhenie,* pp. 232–33.

67. M. T. [ikhomir]ov, "Uchitel'skii soiuz i Vladimirskoe gub. zemstvo," supplement to *Kliazma,* No. 19, January, 21, 1906. A handful of zemstvos, twenty-seven, did agree to include teachers in school commissions, mainly in response to petitions from mutual aid societies: *Vestnik vospitaniia,* No. 1, section 2 (1909), pp. 16–17; *Severnyi krai,* No. 141, June 4, 1905, p. 3 (petition of Iaroslavl Society); *Russkiia vedomosti,* No. 271, October 16, 1905, p. 1 (Biriuch district, Voronezh); V. I. Charnoluskii, *Itogi obshchestvennoi mysli v oblasti obrazovaniia* (St. Petersburg, 1906), p. 21.

68. *Nasha zhizn',* No. 263, September 13, 1905, p. 3; a similar petition elicited little zemstvo support in 1904. Only two zemstvos responded favorably to the 1905 plea in Smolensk province: see *Spravochnaia kniga . . . za 1905,* p. 171.

69. *Burzhuaziia i tsarizm,* 2nd ed., pp. 113–20; Manning, *Crisis,* pp. 133–37.

70. On these developments, see S. Bleklov, "Krest'ianskii soiuz," *Pravo,* No. 38, September 25, 1905, col. 3143–3144; E. I. Kiriukhina, "Vserossiiskii Krest'ianskii Soiuz v 1905 g.," *Istoricheskie zapiski,* 50 (1955), pp. 97–98; Maslov, *Agrarnyi vopros,* II, 219–20; A. V. Shestakov, "Vserossiiskii krest'ianskii soiuz," *Istorik-marksist,* No. 5 (1927), pp. 97–98; Miliutin, *Nakanune,* pp. 167–71.

71. TsGAOR, f. 102, 00, op. 5, d. 999, ch. 45, 1. 45–45ob (July 3, 1905 gathering in Kursk); Kiriukhina, "Vserossiiskii," p. 126; Scott J. Seregny, "A Different Type of Peasant Movement: Peasant Unions in the Russian Revolution of 1905," *Slavic Review,* No. 1 (1988), pp. 55–60.

72. See Veselovskii, *Krest'ianskii vopros,* pp. 45–51; Maslov, *Agrarnyi vopros,* II, 199–203; Manning, *Crisis of the Old Order,* pp. 122–27; Seregny, "Politics and the Rural Intelligentsia," pp. 181–82.

73. A. Smirnov, "Ekonomicheskii sovet pri kovrovskoi zemskoi uprave," *Russkiia vedomosti,* No. 240, September 4, pp. 3–4 and No. 245, Sept. 9, 1905, p. 4; Ivanov, *Krest'ianskoe dvizhenie,* pp. 5–6. The Kovrov *sovet* was subsequently closed by the MVD (*Russkiia vedomosti,* No. 229, August 24, 1905, p. 2).

74. Olenin, "Krest'iane i intelligentsiia," No. 2, p. 139; Seregny, "A Different Type of Peasant Movement," pp. 58–59.

75. For further details and sources on this episode, see Seregny, "Politics and the Rural Intelligentsia," pp. 181–83.

76. The identities of delegates are difficult to determine. At least two were teachers (and members of the VSU) of peasant origin: Rvachev from Tarussa district, Kaluga and Burtsev from Iaroslavl (Rvachev, "Iz proshlogo," 1. 154 and Burtsev, "Professional'no-politicheskoe dvizhenie," 1. 169). V. G. Tan-Bogoraz asserted that intelligenty at the congress were mainly rural teachers, volost clerks and zemstvo activists (*Russkiia vedomosti*, No. 278, October 23, 1905, p. 4). On the congress, see Veselovskii, *Krest'ianskii vopros*, pp. 68–69; Kiriukhina, "Vserossiiskii," pp. 102–10; Perrie, *The Agrarian Policy*, pp. 108–11; Robinson, *Rural Russia*, pp. 160–63.

77. Bleklov, "Krest'ianskii soiuz," col. 3147.

78. On the November congress, see *Materialy k krest'ianskomu voprosu: otchet o zasedaniiakh delegatskago s"ezda Vserossiiskago Krest'ianskago Soiuza 6–10 noiabria 1905 g.* (Rostov-na-Donu, 1905); Shanin, *Russia*, pp. 115–17, 122–27; Kiriukhina, "Vserossiiskii," pp. 115–25; Perrie, *The Agrarian Policy*, pp. 114–17; Robinson, *Rural Russia*, pp. 170–73. Mitskevich asserted that calls for moderation at the congress came mainly from teachers, zemstvo statisticians, and so on rather than rank-and-file peasant delegates (*Revoliutsionnaia Moskva*, p. 426).

79. Cited in Kiriukhina, "Vserossiiskii," p. 114; *Russkiia vedomosti*, No. 247, September 11, 1905, p. 3.

80. TsGAOR, f. 518, op. 1, d. 76, 1. 233–233ob.

81. *Iaroslavl' v pervoi russkoi revoliutsii*, ed. P. N. Gvuzdev, et al. (Iaroslavl, 1925), pp. 167–69, 175.

82. *Russkiia vedomosti*, No. 149, June 15, 1905, p. 2, which includes figures for other components of the Union of Unions: Office workers and bookkeepers (6,000); Academics (1,500); Lawyers (2,500); Women's Rights (1,000); Engineers and Technicians (3,500); Pharmacists (760); Secondary Teachers (280); Railway Employees (6,000); Jewish Emancipation (5,000). Sokolov, "Kratkii ocherk," p. 6. In early November the VSU had 7,500 members organized into 462 locals; by way of comparison, the Medical Union had 1,500 and the Secondary Teachers more than 300 members (TsGAOR, f. 518, op. 1, d. 11, 1. 4ob; *Severnyi krai*, No. 272, November 17, 1905). E. O. Vakhterova gives the following figures for VSU membership: 4,070 (early June 1905), 6,803 (September 1), 7,244 (October 10): "O vserossiiskom uchitel'skom soiuze," *Vestnik vospitaniia*, No. 1, section 2 (1906), p. 135. Later figures are 12,036 (March, 1906), 12,256 (April, 1906): *Vestnik uchitelei*, No. 2 (1906), pp. 92–93.

83. The bureau claimed that half of its correspondence was confiscated by the police: *Vestnik uchitelei*, No. 1 (1906), pp. 24–25; Sokolov, "Kratkii ocherk," p. 7. In September 1905 the bureau issued an appeal to local groups urging dispatch of members' dues, stating that the union's treasury was empty since of 7,000 members only 450 had sent their dues: TsGAOR, f. 63, op. 14, d. 787, 1. 227.

84. TsGAOR, f. 518, op. 1, d. 76, 1. 294ob. A teacher from Perm explained his and other teachers' refusal to join the union in a letter of July 1905: "the material insecurity of teachers with families and the absolute impossibility of finding suitable work of any kind in a backwater district town, in case one loses his post, is a primary obstacle in the way of adherence to such a highly sympathetic union." Ibid., 1. 159–69, and a series of letters in Ibid., d. 77, 1. 295–307.

85. Untitled MS. in TsGAOR, f. 6862 op. 1, d. 88, 1. 138–140; see also A. I. Senin, "V derevne," *Iuzhnaia zaria*, No. 68, July 6/19, 1906, p. 2.

8. October and Its Aftermath

1. According to the calculations of a Soviet historian there were 155 incidents of peasant unrest in August; 71 in September; 219 in October; 796 in November, and 575 in December: S. M. Dubrovskii, *Krest'ianskoe dvizhenie v revoliutsii 1905–1907 gg.* (Moscow, 1956), p. 42.

2. See Veselovskii, *Krest'ianskii vopros,* p. 84. In response to the bad harvest, affecting twenty-one provinces, and the threat of famine, the Teachers' Union joined with other unions and public organizations which pledged to aid in famine relief and declared their lack of faith in the government's ability to deal with the situation: *Russkiia vedomosti,* No. 238, September 2, p. 3; No. 246, September 10, p. 3, and No. 263, October 8, 1905, p. 3; *Nasha zhizn',* No. 298, October 7/20, 1905, p. 3.

3. At its Third Congress in early July a majority of the unions comprising the Union of Unions came out in favor of a boycott; three (writers, professors, secondary schoolteachers) voted against a boycott and four (Peasant, Jewish Equality, Veterinarians, and Teachers) abstained. The Zemstvo-Constitutionalists and Railwaymen were not represented. See S. D. K[irpichnikov], "Soiuz soiuzov," in *Sputnik izbiratelia na 1906 g.* (St. Petersburg, 1906), pp. 146–47; L. K. Erman, *Intelligentsiia v pervoi russkoi revoliutsii* (Moscow, 1966), pp. 107–8.

4. Sokolov, "Kratkii ocherk istorii," p. 11; *Nasha zhizn',* No. 298, October 7/20, 1905, p. 3; male teachers of peasant origin could take part and be elected from the peasant curia and, as it turned out, a number of teachers and other third element people were elected to the First Duma in this way (see below).

5. TsGAOR, f. 518, op. 1, d. 76, 1. 191–191ob; also L. M. Ivanov, "Boikot bulyginskoi dumy i stachka v Oktiabre 1905 g.," *Istoricheskie zapiski,* 83 (1969), p. 149.

6. See Reichman, *Railwaymen,* chapter 7; I. M. Pushkareva, *Zheleznodorozhniki Rossii v burzhuazno-demokraticheskikh revoliutsiiakh* (Moscow, 1975); Walter Sablinsky, "The All-Russian Railroad Union and the Beginning of the General Strike in October, 1905," in Alexander Rabinowitch, et al., eds., *Revolution and Politics in Russia: Essays in Memory of B. I. Nicolaevsky,* (Bloomington: Indiana University Press, 1972), pp. 113–33 and Shmuel Galai, "The Role of the Union of Unions in the Revolution of 1905," *Jahrbücher für Geschichte Osteuropas,* 24, No. 4 (1976), pp. 512–525.

7. The feasibility of teachers' strikes had been discussed at the June congress, where it was noted that such action would probably be feasible only in the cities: "Protokoly Vserossiiskago s"ezda," pp. 38–39; M. I. Akhun, V. A. Petrov, *Peterburg v 1905–1907 gg. (khronika sobytii),* Leningrad, 1930, p. 72; Menzhinskaia, "Peterburgskoe uchitel'stvo," pp. 42–43; Rumiantseva, "Politicheskaia zabastovka gorodskogo uchitel'stva," 1. 78–79; "Uchitel'skaia zabastovka v Peterburge v dni 14–21 okt. 1905 g.," *Vestnik Vserossiiskago soiuza,* No. 1 (November, 1905), pp. 11–13; L. K. Erman, "Uchastie demokraticheskoi intelligentsii vo vserossiiskoi oktiabr'skoi politicheskoi stachke," *Istoricheskie zapiski,* 49 (1955), pp. 374–377.

8. *Russkiia vedomosti,* No. 269, October 14, pp. 2–3 and No. 276, October 21, 1905, p. 3; according to Vakhterova all Moscow schools were affected: "O vserossiiskom uchitel'skom soiuze," *Vestnik vospitaniia,* No. 1, section 2 (1906), pp. 139–40; Rumiantseva, "Politicheskaia zabastovka," 1. 79; *Nasha zhizn',* No. 238, November 8, 1905, p. 5; *Syn otechestva,* No. 223, November 9, 1905, p. 3; *Russkiia vedomosti,* No. 295, November 9, 1905, p. 3. Some 231 primary teachers took part in the November strike; the Secondary Teachers' Union did not. On other cities affected by teachers' strikes, see V. G. Zemskii [V. I. Charnoluskii], "Vtoroi delegatskii s"ezd vserossiiskago soiuza uchitelei i deiatelei po narodnomu obrazovaniiu," *Vestnik vospitaniia,* No. 3, section 2 (1906), p. 131; V. P. Antonov-Saratovskii, *Krasnyi god,* pt. 1 (Moscow-Leningrad, 1927) p. 113 (on Saratov).

9. John Bushnell, *Mutiny amid Repression: Russian Soldiers in the Revolution of 1905–1906* (Bloomington: Indiana University Press, 1985), chapter 4.

10. Olenin, "Krest'iane i intelligentsiia," *Russkoe bogatstvo,* No. 2, pp. 147–148; on October 20 a directive was issued to local officials to the effect that existing laws should be applied "in the spirit" of the manifesto: TsGIA, f. 733, op. 175, d. 78, 1. 100–100ob.

11. *Syn otechestva,* No. 220, November 6, 1905, p. 3; *Severnyi krai,* No. 264, November 9, 1905, p. 1.

12. TsGIA, f. 733, op. 195, d. 720, 1. 47–47ob.

13. See chapter 7 for membership figures. In Grodno province, and generally in the western borderlands, there was little activity before October 17, but union organizing went on quickly from late October, teachers viewing the manifesto as providing legal sanction: *Prosveshchenie,* No. 5 (1907), pp. 46–47.

14. *Russkiia vedomosti,* No. 301, November 15, 1905, p. 2 (similarly in Elets, Orel: Ibid., No. 277, October 22, 1905, p. 3); Olenin, "Krestiane i intelligentsiia," p. 163. Rusinov had been a member of the liberal zemstvo "Beseda" circle before 1905 (see Pirumova, pp. 256–57 and Emmons, "The Beseda Circle," p. 490). It should be pointed out that in Lokhvitsa where the peasant union movement was widespread there was very little destructive violence against local estates during 1905: Kiriukhina, "Vserossiiskii krest'ianskii soiuz," p. 135; Karpov, *Krest'ianskoe dvizhenie,* p. 12.

15. *Protokoly vtorogo delegatskago s"ezda Vserossiiskago Soiuza uchitelei i deiatelei po narodnomu obrazovaniiu 26–29 dekabria 1905 goda* (St. Petersburg, 1906), p. 8; *Russkoe slovo,* No. 293, November 7/20, 1905, p. 3; TsGAOR, f. 6862, op, 1, d. 89, 1. 2 (untitled memoir of teacher P. I. Kalashnikova, Iaransk district, Viatka).

16. A Menshevik observer remarked that there existed an ominous fluidity between spontaneous peasant activism against gentry estates and popular reaction against the intelligentsia and political opposition: V. Voitinskii, *Gody pobed i porazhenii,* 2 vols. (Berlin-Petersburg-Moscow, 1923–24), I, 279.

17. TsGAOR f. 63, op. 14, d. 787, 1. 240; *Russkiia vedomosti,* No. 276, October 21, 1905, p. 1; Popova, "K istorii Vserossiiskago uchitel'skago soiuza," p. 104; Vakhterova, "O vserossiiskom uchitel'skom soiuze," p. 137.

18. *Russkiia vedomosti,* No. 277, October 22, 1905, p. 3 ("Oblastnoi s"ezd delegatov uchitel'skago soiuza").

19. For delegates' reports, see Ibid., No. 278, October 23, 1905, p. 4. For the congress's resolution, see Ibid., No. 281, October 26, 1905, p. 4. The delegates also called for the dismissal of Trepov from the post of police chief and removal of Cossacks from cities.

20. Ibid., No. 277, p. 3 and No. 278, p. 4. Tan's speech lauding the *soiuzy* drew a caustic response from Nikolai Rozhkov in the Bolshevik press. Insisting on the hegemony of the proletariat in the opposition movement against Tsarism, Rozhkov argued that the majority of the intelligenty unions were politically powerless (all the Teachers' Union had achieved was its "pitiful" circular to the zemstvos), and only political parties could constitute a real force. Following the line of thought advanced at the June congress by the SDs, Rozhkov insisted that the union should concern itself with the professional needs of its members: N. Rozhkov, "G. Tan i 'mobilizatsiia obshchestvennykh i narodnykh sil'," *Novaia zhizn'* (St. Petersburg), No. 2 (1905), pp. 5–6, and Tan's reply in Ibid., No. 3 (1905), p. 8.

21. *Russkoe slovo,* No. 293, November 7/20, 1905, p. 3 ("Uchitel'skii s"ezd"); *Russkiia vedomosti,* No. 289, November 5, 1905, p. 3. This second regional congress was held in the home of V. A. Morozova. Some of the delegates simultaneously held

mandates to attend the Peasant Union congress from local groups of that organization.

22. Olenin, "Krest'iane i intelligentsiia," p. 147; Aleksei Smirnov, "Manifesty v derevne," *Istina* (Moscow), No. 2 (January, 1906), pp. 25–26 (Vladimir); *Severnyi krai*, No. 258, November 3, 1905, p. 3 (Kostroma); *Russkiia vedomosti*, No. 303, November 17, 1905, p. 3.

23. Ibid., No. 295, November 8, 1905, p. 3; Vakhterova, "O vserossiiskom uchitel'skom soiuze," p. 142.

24. At the same time (November 6–13) in Moscow a congress of zemstvo activists was held, reflecting to some degree the rightward shift of these institutions; symbolically, there was no communication between this meeting and the teachers' congress: see *Russkaia mysl'*, No. 12 (1905), pp. 188–89; Chermenskii, *Burzhuaziia i tsarizm*, 2nd ed., pp. 160–61.

25. *Russkoe slovo*, No. 293, November 7/20, 1905, p. 3.

26. Ibid.; *Russkiia vedomosti*, No. 293, November 7, 1905, p. 4; Popova, "K istorii," p. 106; O. Vitten, "Nekotorye etapy," *Vestnik uchitelei*, No. 1 (April 2, 1906), pp. 11–14.

27. *Syn otechestva*, No. 243, November 30, 1905, p. 3; No. 227, November 13, 1905, p. 3; *Severnyi krai*, No. 269, November 14, 1905, p. 2; *Nasha zhizn'*, No. 335, November 16/29, 1905, p. 2; *Russkiia vedomosti*, No. 279, October 24, 1905, p. 2.

28. *Saratovskii listok*, No. 240, December 3, 1905, pp. 2–3; *Samarskaia gazeta*, No. 208 (November 3), p. 5; No. 210 (November 5), p. 5; No. 219 (November 19), p. 2 and No. 224 (November 25), 1905, p. 4 (Chlen uchitel'skago soiuza, "Po povodu obsharovskago pogroma").

29. Semenov, *Dvadtsat' piat' let*, pp. 212–17.

30. S. I. Kudriavtsev, "Uchitel' i naselenie Bronnitskogo uezda v 1905 godu (Vospominaniia)," TsGAOR, f. 6862, op. 1, d. 84, 1. 205–13; *Russkiia vedomosti*, No. 303, November 17, 1905, p. 3. Similar phenomena were noted by delegates at the November congress of the Peasant Union: *Materialy k krest'ianskomu voprosu*, p. 38 (Voronezh), p. 55 (Moscow). Other incidents are noted in V. Ivanovich, "Khronika," *Vestnik vospitaniia*, No. 2, section 2 (1906), pp. 114–21; V. Efimovskii, "Krest'ianskoe dvizhenie na Chernigovshchine v 1905 godu," *Letopis' revoliutsii* (Kharkov), No. 2 (11), 1925, p. 191. Untitled MS. by F. G. Nikol'skii (TsGAOR, f. 6862, op. 1, d. 88, 1. 141). Black hundred manifestations continued in certain locales in December: see *Nizhegorodskii listok*, No. 326, December 4, p. 4 and No. 338, December 19, 1905, p. 3.

31. *Vestnik Vserossiiskago soiuza*, No. 3 (December, 1905), p. 3.

32. Vakhterova, "O vserossiiskom uchitel'skom soiuze," p. 141; Samokhvalov, "Otryvki iz vospominanii," pp. 53–54. Samokhvalov returned to his native district, Pokrov (Vladimir) where he was active in the Peasant Union movement, apparently abandoning his teaching post in Nizhegorod province.

33. *Russkoe slovo*, No. 294, November 8/21, 1905, p. 2; also statement of delegate from Voronezh (*Russkiia vedomosti*, No. 295). Many of the delegates were upset by a statement by N. V. Chekhov who saw as a "great sin" of the intelligentsia that it had failed to instill in the narod a sense of toleration and regard for the opinions of others. Chekhov had been an eyewitness to a pogrom against zemstvo employees in the town of Tver (*Russkoe slovo*, No. 293).

34. Vakhterova, "O vserossiiskom uchitel'skom soiuze," pp. 143–44; *Russkoe slovo*, No. 295, November 9, 1905, pp. 3–4; *Vestnik Evropy*, No. 12 (1905), p. 792.

35. *Russkiia vedomosti*, No. 280, October 25, p. 4 and No. 281, October 26, 1905, p. 4 (report of N. Popova); *Russkoe slovo*, No. 293, p. 3.

36. Ibid., No. 294, p. 2; No. 293, p. 3.

37. See *Russkiia vedomosti*, No. 281, p. 4 and *Russkoe slovo*, No. 294, p. 2 (Tan's speech on the Peasant Union); also on this issue, see Olenin, "Krest'iane i intelligentsiia," p. 149; Seregny, "Politics and the Rural Intelligentsia," p. 200.

38. Rvachev, "Iz proshlogo," 1. 153.

39. *Russkoe slovo*, No. 295, November 9, 1905, pp. 3–4.

40. On the joint session, see *Russkiia vedomosti*, No. 296, November 10, 1905, p. 3; *Russkaia mysl'*, No. 12 (1905), p. 187; Samokhvalov, "Otryvki iz vospominanii," p. 54; Popova, "K istorii," pp. 107–8. Sometime after the November congress the Moscow Okhrana warned that the Teachers' Union had "resolved by all means in its power to spread among the peasant population the criminal ideas of the Peasant Union, which at present is being fulfilled with unconditional success by schoolteachers." (TsGAOR, f. 63, op. 14, d. 787, 1. 267ob).

41. Cited in Popova, "K istorii," pp. 107–8.

42. The November 3 manifesto also contained an appeal to the peasantry to remain loyal and calm. In Vladimir province it was reported that in many villages peasants heard about the November decree before the October Manifesto since the authorities were more eager to disseminate the former document in order to head off unrest: Smirnov, "Manifesty v derevne," p. 24.

43. *Russkoe slovo*, No. 293, November 7/20, 1905, p. 3; Vakhterova, "O vserossiiskom uchitel'skom soiuze," p. 140; also *Protokoly vtorogo delegatskago s"ezda*, pp. 9, 17; *Russkii vrach*, No. 50 (1905), p. 1589. A similar campaign of political education was conducted by urban groups of the union, for example in Nizhnii Novgorod, among workers and the urban lower classes: *Rabochee i professional'noe dvizhenie v Nizhegorodskom krae*, pp. 206–9; Suprunenko, "Obshchestvo vzaimopomoshchi," 1. 53–54; Dubrovskii and Grave, *Agrarnoe dvizhenie*, pp. 38–39.

44. *Syn otechestva*, No. 239, November 26, 1905, p. 4. Also other organizations, for example, the Saratov union of medical personnel: *Russkii vrach*, No. 49 (1905), p. 1553.

45. TsGAOR, f. DP OO (1905), d. 999, ch. 1, t. II, 1. 130–131ob, 135–135ob; *Syn otechestva*, No. 233, November 19, 1905, p. 5; *Kliazma* (Vladimir), No. 3, January 4, 1906, p. 3; also general Okhrana statement on local teachers' unions' support for the Peasant Union: TsGAOR, f. DP OO, op. 233, d. 1800, ch. 43, 1. 7ob.

46. *Novaia zhizn'*, No. 23, November 27, 1905, cited in E. I. Kiriukhina, "Mestnye organizatsii Vserossiiskogo Krestianskogo Soiuza v 1905 godu," *Uchenye zapiski Kirovskogo pedagogicheskogo instituta*, 10 (1956), p. 91. See also discussion at St. Petersburg Regional Congress of the Teachers' Union of November 20–21, 1905; *Nasha zhizn'*, No. 342, November 24/December 7, 1905, p. 5.

47. *Severnyi krai*, No. 280, November 26, 1905, p. 4; Burtsev, "Professional'no-politicheskoe dvizhenie," 1. 278; see also R-n, "Krest'ianskii soiuiz i narodnyi uchitel'," *Vestnik Vserossiiskago soiuza*, No. 3 (December, 1905), pp. 1–3.

48. For property losses ranked by province, see Veselovskii, *Krest'ianskii vopros*, pp. 86–87.

49. See A. I. Senin, "V derevne," *Iuzhnaia zaria*, No. 68, July 6/19, 1906, p. 2 (Senin was a leader of the Teachers' Union in Mariupol district, Ekaterinoslav).

50. *Vestnik iuga*, No. 1082, November 24, 1905, p. 2. On the agrarian movement in the province, see Veselovskii, *Krest'ianskii vopros*, p. 92. For SR discussion of "agrarian terror," see Perrie, *The Agrarian Policy*, pp. 91–97; also SR commentary on the disorders in Saratov province: *Volzhskii vestnik*, No. 14, November 21, 1905, p. 3 (from *Syn otechestva*).

51. TsGAOR, f. 6862, op. 1, d. 88, 1. 142–143. The agrarian movement in Volchansk in late October involved the destruction of some thirty estates (Veselovskii, *Krest'ianskii vopros*, p. 92). Nikol'skii and a neighboring teacher, Stepanenko, were exiled (TsGIA, f. 733, op. 175, d. 76, 1. 82–82ob).

52. Olenin, "Krest'iane i intelligentsiia," No. 2, pp. 149–50. This author explained the popularity of the Peasant Union among the masses by its agrarian program and the fact that its political agenda was less radical than that of the revolutionary parties (it did not demand a republic or direct attacks on religion).

53. Kiriukhina, "Vserossiiskii," p. 133, and "Mestnye organizatsii," p. 132; Olenin, "Krest'iane i intelligentsiia," p. 151.

54. Kiriukhina, "Mestnye organizatsii," p. 138, provides incomplete data on the backgrounds of 127 Peasant Union agitators at the local level: peasants (30), kulaks (3), village and volost elders (9); teachers (43), doctors (13), rural clerks (7), clerics (2); students (9), SRs (6), SDs (5).

55. In some locales, like Iaroslavl province and Beloozero district (Novgorod), Teachers' Union groups were directly responsible for initiating peasant unions. In Slobodsk (Viatka) the SR teacher Iu. N. Makushina was a leading figure in the local teachers' union, while her brothers, local peasants, were major figures in the local peasant union: *Protokol pervago severnago oblastnogo s"ezda Vserossiiskago krest'ianskago soiuza 29–30 dekabria 1905 goda* (St. Petersburg, 1906), p. 16; Mirov, "Professional'nye soiuzy v Viatskoi gubernii," p. 219.

56. Sergeini, "Ternistym putem," 1. 27–29; Pupu, "Vospominaniia o revoliutsii 1905-go goda," 1. 52–53ob; report of Ekaterinoslav delegate to Second VSU Congress: *Protokoly vtorogo delegatskago s"ezda*, p. 13; *Iuzhnaia zaria*, No. 539, February 20/ March 4, 1908, p. 3. The large percentage of intelligenty brought to trial no doubt reflected an attempt by the government to mask the genuine peasant nature of the Peasant Union: Novopolin, "Iz istorii tsarskikh rasprav (Krest'ianskii soiuz na Ekaterinoslavshchine)," *Katorga i ssylka*, No. 5 (1931), p. 119.

57. *Uchitel'* (Moscow), No. 4, March 15, 1907, p. 3; "Delo o Vserossiiskom krest'ianskom soiuze," *Pravo*, No. 48 (1907), col. 3104–3118; Kiriukhina, "Vserossiiskii," p. 127. A police search of ten of the indicted teachers (seven of whom were peasants by *soslovie*) yielded a wide range of political literature: SR, SD, Peasant Union, and VSU publications: TsGAOR, f. DP 7-oe deloproizvodstvo (1905), d. 6826, 1. 6–10ob.

58. Cited in S. P. Mazurenko, ed., *Vserossiiskii krest'ianskii soiuz pered sudom istorii* (Poltava, 1926?), p. 31; P. I. Klimov, *Revoliutsionnaia deiatel'nost' rabochikh v derevne v 1905–1907 gg.* (Moscow, 1960), pp. 166–67.

59. *Russkiia vedomosti*, No. 33, February 3; No. 34, February 4, 1906, p. 3; L. G. Chigovskaia, "Deiatel'nost' bol'shevikov Ukraini po vovlecheniiu demokraticheskoi intelligentsii v massovoe revoliutsionnoe dvizhenie 1905–1907 godov," Candidate dissertation, Kievskii gosud. universitet im. T. G. Shevchenko (Kiev, 1974), p. 152; *1905 god v Voronezhe*, III, 22–27, 34–41.

60. Ivanov, *Krest'ianskoe dvizhenie vo Vladimirskoi gubernii*, pp. 36–37; also provincial governors' reports: TsGIA, f. 1284, op. 194, d. 61, 1 5ob (Voronezh); d. 87, 1. 7–7ob (Novgorod).

61. "K istorii revoliutsionnogo dvizheniia v Rossii (Oktiabr'-noiabr' 1905 goda)," *Istoricheskii arkhiv*, No. 1 (1955), p. 123; TsGAOR, f. 102, DP OO, op. 5 (1905), d. 2250, 1. 3–5.

62. Among other reforms in primary education endorsed by the Peasant Union was the demand that teachers not be responsible for instruction in agriculture and trades: Bleklov, "Krest'ianskii soiuz," col. 3151.

63. Cited in Ivanov, *Krest'ianskoe dvizhenie vo Vladimirskoi gubernii*, p. 33–34. Durnovo raised the issue of third element activity in the countryside at the Palace Conference deliberations over revisions in the electoral law for the Duma in December 1905. Arguing against a democratic franchise, Durnovo claimed that landowners would not enter a Duma filled with "medical aids, zemstvo statisticians and so forth, individuals who recently had been marshals of predatory gangs raiding their estates" (cited from Ann K. Healy, *The Russian Autocracy in Crisis* (Hamden, Conn., 1976), p. 96).

64. A. V. Shebalov, "K istorii krest'ianskikh besporiadok v 1905 godu," *Arkhiv istorii truda v Rossii*, No. 6–7 (1923), pp. 190–93; also Karpov, *Krest'ianskoe dvizhenie*,

pp. 20–22, 94, 202–3, 258–59; "Agrarnoe dvizhenie v 1905 g. po otchetam Dubasova i Panteleeva," *Krasnyi arkhiv,* No. 4–5 (11–12), 1925, p. 188; TsGAOR, f. 1284, op. 194.

65. TsGIA, f. 733, op. 175, d. 76, 1. 21–22ob; see also Ibid., 1. 33–34 (Samara), 54 (Tula gentry assembly); *Novoe vremia,* No. 10671, November 29, 1905, p. 5 (Voronezh); Manning, *Crisis of the Old Order,* pp. 189–95, 275–76.

66. Lavrov, "Krest'ianskie nastroeniia," pp. 26–47.

67. Durnovo's circulars played some role in galvanizing local authorities to take action against teachers and other "agitators" as well as Peasant Union members, whereas in the weeks immediately following the October Manifesto many officials had taken a wait-and-see attitude, uncertain of shifting political winds: see Olenin, "Krest'iane i intelligentsiia," pp. 162–63; T. Asin, "K statistike arestovanykh i ssyl'nykh," *Russkoe bogatstvo,* No. 10, sec. 2 (1906), p. 6; *Russkiia vedomosti,* No. 35, February 5, 1906, p. 3 (Kursk).

68. M. Kolobov, "Agrarniia volneniia," *Russkiia vedomosti,* No. 311, November 25, 1905, p. 3; Dubrovskii and Grave, *Agrarnoe dvizhenie,* pp. 371–73.

69. *Tambovskii golos,* No. 138, October 14, 1906, pp. 3–4. Ostroumov was a liberal inspector who had played an active part in general education teachers' courses held in Tambov in 1901.

70. TsGIA, f. 733, op. 175, d. 77, 1. 263–265; d. 78, 1. 87–100ob; d. 79, 1. 71–73ob; his report is bound in Ibid., d. 78 as *list* 95 and paginated separately (see p. 4).

71. *Volzhskii vestnik,* No. 6, November 14, 1905, p. 4 (Chistopol, Kazan); *Saratovskii dnevnik,* No. 16, January 21, 1906, p. 3 (Novouzensk, Samara); *Russkiia vedomosti,* No. 309, November 23, 1905, p. 3 (Moscow district); *Vestnik uchitelei,* No. 1, April 2, 1906, pp. 37–38 (Pskov); TsGAOR, f. 518, op. 1, d. 76, 1. 217–217ob (Volynia): TsGAOR, f. 6862, op. 1, d. 47, 1. 13ob (Morshansk, Tambov): *Severnaia mysl',* No. 18, April 9, 1906, p. 2.

72. TsGAOR, f. DP OO (1905), d. 999, ch. 1, t. III, 1. 6–9. Latyshev, who was acting as curator in the absence of the ill P. P. Izvol'skii, was an official with extensive knowledge of teachers and their problems, having served as chairman of the Petersburg Teachers' Society and as a member of the Mut'ev commission on teachers' status.

73. Ivan I. Tolstoi, "Vospominaniia ego za vremia upravleniia Ministerstvom narodnogo prosveshcheniia, 1906 g.," Gosudarstvennaia Publichnaia Biblioteka (Leningrad), Rukopisnyi Otdel, f. 781. No. 568, 1. 134. Tolstoi received many complaints by MVD officials concerning the lack of resolve shown by local school officials in curbing teachers' political activities (TsGIA, f. 733, op. 175, d. 76, 1. 36–36ob, 64–65ob).

74. *Protokoly vtorogo delegatskago s"ezda,* pp. 11, 16, 23; see also note 57.

75. In their evaluations of the Peasant Union the government tended to latch on to these speeches, thus inflating (perhaps not unconsciously) its danger: see Mazurenko, *Vserossiiskii krest'ianskii soiuz,* pp. 31–32; Olenin, "Krest'iane i intelligentsiia," p. 162; also sources cited in note 61.

76. Aside from the articles by Kiriukhina, see Maslov, *Agrarnyi vopros v Rossii,* II, 234–40, 248–51; Shanin, *Russia,* pp. 101–14; Seregny, "A Different Type of Peasant Movement," pp. 61–64.

77. The MNP archive contains a partial list of teachers exiled during this period. Most were sentenced to three years for any one of these activities (TsGIA, f. 733, op. 175, d. 76).

78. TsGAOR, f. DP, OO, op. 233 (1905), d. 1800, ch. 12, 1. 138 (Ekaterinoslav okhrana report), and note 65. For Vladimir, see Ivanov, *Krest'ianskoe dvizhenie,* pp. 20–21.

79. Detailed coverage of the proceedings can be found in *Iuzhnaia zaria,* 1908, Nos. 539 (February 20/March 4), p. 3; 540–44; also Novopolin, "Iz istorii tsarskikh rasprav," pp. 101–19; E. Kogon, "Krest'ianskoe dvizhenie v. Ekaterinoslavskom

uezde," *Letopis' revoliutsii* (Kharkov) No. 6 (1928), pp. 169–229; O. Aleksandrov, *Selians'ka spilka pered tsarskim sudom* (Kharkov, 1931); *Pravo*, No. 2 (1906), col. 149; aside from the memoirs of Sergeini and Pupu, in TsGAOR, f. 6862, see M. Stasiuk, "Krest'ianskii soiuz v 1905 g.," in *Materialy po istorii Ekaterinoslavskoi sotsial-demokraticheskoi organizatsii bol'shevikov i revoliutsionnykh sobytii 1904, 1905, 1906 gg.* (Ekaterinoslav, 1924), pp. 285–91.

80. For the Vladimir trials, see *Vladimirets*, 1906, Nos. 60 (October 12), p. 2; 61 (Oct. 13) p. 3; 64 (Oct. 17), p. 3; 65 (Oct. 19), p. 3; 66 (Oct. 20), p. 3; 69 (Oct. 24), p. 3; 72 (Oct. 27), p. 3, and on the trial of S. V. Bunin and Co. Nos. 62, 75, 79, 80, 86, 87. See also *O rabochem dvizhenii i sotsial-demokraticheskoi rabote vo Vladimirskoi gubernii*, vypusk 1, pp. 263–66.

81. *Protokoly vtorogo delegatskago s"ezda*, p. 13; Popova, "K istorii Vserossiiskago," pp. 112–13; Vakhlin, "Narodnoe obrazovanie v Orekhovo-Zuevskom uezde," p. 423; TsGAOR, f. 518, op. 1, d. 77, 1. 19–19ob. One scholar points to evidence of teachers inciting agrarian disorders, but this is based on a few citations from police archives which must be used with caution: Morison, "Les instituteurs de village," pp. 212–13.

82. Estimates of the number of delegates range from 100 to 150: see "Vtoroi delegatskii s"ezd vserossiiskago soiuza uchitelei," *Viatskaia zhizn'*, No. 16, January 13, 1906, p. 2; V. G. Zemskii [V. I. Charnoluskii], "Vtoroi delegatskii s"ezd vserossiiskago soiuza uchitelei i deiatelei po narodnomu obrazovaniiu," *Vestnik vospitaniia*, No. 3, section 2 (1906), p. 122; E. R., "Vtoroi delegatskii s"ezd Vserossiiskago Soiuza uchitelei i deiatelei po narodnomu obrazovaniiu (Vospominaniia uchastnika)," *Vestnik uchitelei*, No. 1 (1906), p. 16. For security reasons the names of delegates are not given in the official record of the congress. Invited representatives of the major political parties took part in the discussions as did delegates from national minority teachers' organizations which had been established during 1905.

83. *Protokoly vtorogo delegatskago s"ezda*, pp. 11f, 93; also E. R., "Vtoroi delegatskii s"ezd," *Vestnik uchitelei*, No. 2 (1906), p. 65; Kiriukhina, "Mestnye organizatsii," p. 139; Zemskii, "Vtoroi delegatskii s"ezd," p. 123.

84. *Protokoly*, pp. 4, 11, 23–24; also Ivanov-Razumnik, "Chto dumaet derevnia? (vpechatleniia ochevidtsa)," *Russkoe bogatstvo*, No. 5, section 2 (1906), p. 9; Shanin, *Russia*, pp. 144–45.

85. *Protokoly*, pp. 29–30. A similar criticism of the December 11 law was leveled at the Northern Regional Congress of the Peasant Union which met at the end of December in Finland. *Protokol pervago severnago oblastnogo s"ezda*, pp. 34–35.

86. *Protokoly vtorogo delegatskago s"ezda*, pp. 29–60; E. R. "Vtoroi delegatskii s"ezd," pp. 59–64 (the resolution, however, was not binding on local groups).

87. *Protokoly*, pp. 62, 92–94; E. R., "Vtoroi delegatskii s"ezd," p. 65.

88. *Protokoly*, pp. 3–4, 23–24; also *Nasha zhizn'*, No. 342, November 24, 1905, p. 5 (report of Petergof district delegate to Northern Regional Congress of Teachers' Union, November 20–21, 1905); Ivanovich, "Khronika," *Vestnik vospitaniia*, No. 2, section 2 (1906), p. 121. In Urzhum district (Viatka) peasant political meetings were held in schools during November 1905 (discussion of a constituent assembly, four-tail zemstvo elections, and so on). The local zemstvo resolved to close schools to such meetings, a decision that drew an angry retort from the local teachers' organization. As recently as summer 1905 the Urzhum zemstvo leaders had exhorted teachers to carry constitutionalist propaganda to the peasantry (see chapter 7): *Volzhskii listok*, No. 326, December 4, 1905, p. 6; *Viatskaia gazeta*, No. 4, January 26, 1906, col. 136; also *Nizhegorodskii listok*, No. 8, January 9, 1906, p. 3 (local school board notice); *Budushchee* (Kharkov), No. 3, February 6, 1906, p. 3 (Valki).

89. The liberal Sudzha zemstvo board (Kursk), led by Dolgorukov, decided to give arrested teachers three months' salary, but such decisions appear to have been

rare: see "O zhizni mestnykh grupp," *Narodnyi uchitel'*, No. 17–18 (December 15, 1906), p. 9; Veselovskii, *Istoriia zemstva*, IV, 61–62; *Pravo*, No. 8 (1906), col. 735 (Moscow district zemstvo). On January 18, 1906 MVD Durnovo issued a circular instructing zemstvos not to issue salaries to employees who had been dismissed on orders of the authorities: *Saratovskii dnevnik*, No. 51, March 5, 1906, p. 3.

90. Veselovskii, *Istoriia zemstva*, IV, pp. 26–31; Olenin, "Krest'iane i intelligentsiia," p. 144; Dorothy Atkinson, "The Zemstvo and the Peasanty," in Emmons and Vucinich, eds., *The Zemstvo in Russia*, pp. 108–10.

91. Klimov, *Revoliutsionnaia deiatel'nost' rabochikh*, pp. 166–67; Popova, "K istorii Vserossiiskago," p. 112; *Protokoly*, p. 10.

92. Veselovskii, *Istoriia zemstva*, IV, p. 29; *Zhurnal chrezvychainago Pokrovskago uezdnago zemskago sobraniia 21 marta 1906 goda vmeste s dokladami upravy* (Vladimir-na-Kliazme, 1906), pp. 27–28.

93. The circular is printed in the Bolshevik daily *Novaia zhizn'*, No. 21, November 25, 1905. Details of the affair can be found in Union archival materials: TsGAOR, f. 518, op. 1, d. 76, 1. 273–278, and d. 77, 1. 149–149ob; also TsGAOR, f. DP OO (1905), d. 999, ch. 1, t. II, 1. 142–142ob.

94. Orest' Smirnov, "Minuvshii god v zhizni narodnoi shkoly," *Narodnyi uchitel'*, No. 1 (1907), p. 3; *Zhurnal ocherednago Belozerskago uezdnago zemskago sobraniia 1906 g.* (typed proceedings in Public Library, Leningrad) p. 23–24. At this September 1906 assembly peasant-deputies signed a declaration protesting the zemstvo's attempt to blame nonpayment of taxes on teachers, insisting that there were deeper causes to the movement, namely the undemocratic nature of local self-government. According to S. S. Kholopov, former chairman of the Beloozero board, the degree of peasant nonpayment of zemstvo taxes in 1905 was unprecedented, registering only 37 percent of estimated revenue. Peasant communes, according to Kholopov, had always been the most reliable group of taxpayers. His comments were in response to the questionnaire of the Imperial Free Economic Society on the agrarian movement of 1905–6: *Agrarnoe dvizhenie v Rossii v 1905–1906 gg. III otdelenie imperatorskago VEO ottisk Trudov I. V. E. O.*, 2 vols. (St. Petersburg, 1908), I. 269.

95. *Novgorodskaia nedelia*, No. 43, October 1, 1906, p. 8; No. 45, October 8, 1906, p. 8.

96. TsGAOR, f. DP OO (1905), d. 1800, ch. 38, 1. 6ob, 20ob–21; TsGAOR, f. DP OO (1905), d. 2540, t. II, 1. 7ob-8; *Nasha zhizn'*, No. 342, November 24, 1905, p. 5.

97. TsGAOR, f. 518, op. 1., d. 76, 1. 109–110ob (letter from Stepan Vinogradov to Ia. I. Dushechkin of the Union's Bureau). On the zemstvo tax crisis in the district, see *Severnaia rech'*, No. 11, July 2, 1906, p. 3.

98. Zemskii, "Vtoroi delegatskii s"ezd," pp. 130–33.

99. Manning, "Zemstvo and Revolution," p. 46; Veselovskii, *Istoriia zemstva*, IV, 55–57; Manning, *Crisis of the Old Order*, pp. 272–78.

100. Naumov, *Iz utselevshikh vospominanii*, p. 332. Even I. I. Petrunkevich in his memoirs remembered rural teachers as radical "half-intelligentsia," fanatical, doctrinaire adherents of the socialist parties: "Iz zapisok obshchestvennago deiatelia," pp. 311–13.

101. *Russkiia vedomosti*, No. 144, June 3, 1906, p. 4; Popova, "K istorii Vserossiiskago," pp. 112–13; *Russkiia vedomosti*, No. 29, January 29, 1906, p. 2 (case of Teachers' Union activist L. F. Rvachev). On the relative success of such actions, see the following chapter.

102. Popova, "K istorii Vserossiiskago," pp. 111–12; also Seregny, "Politics and the Rural Intelligentsia," pp. 185–188.

103. B. V., "Pedagogicheskii mir i Gosudarstvennaia Duma," *Russkaia shkola*, No. 4 (1906), pp. 128–38.

104. Popova, "K istorii Vserossiiskago," pp. 114–15; *Severnaia Rossiia*, No. 14, June

4, 1906, p. 4 (Iaroslavl Teachers' society vote of support for the Trudoviki, but not for the Kadets in the Duma).

105. See "Narodnye-uchitelia-izbranniki naroda (biografii)," *Narodnyi uchitel'*, No. 8 (1907), p. 14–19; V., "Predstaviteli pedagogicheskago mira v tret'ei Gosudarstvennoi Dume," *Russkaia shkola*, No. 11 (1908), p. 111.

106. See Seregny, "Politics and the Rural Intelligentsia," pp. 194–95; on this circular and its application in the locales, see *Vestnik vospitaniia*, No. 1, section 2 (1907), pp. 83–85; *Vladimirets*, 1906, Nos. 71 (October 26), p. 3; 76 (November 1), p. 4; 85 (Nov. 11), p. 1; *Iuzhnaia zaria*, No. 173, November 9, 1906, p. 3.

107. TsGAOR, f. DP OO (1905), d. 999, ch. 1, t. IV, 1. 8–8ob (reports at conference of VSU representatives in Petersburg on January 3, 1907); Popova, "K istorii Vserossiiskago," pp. 118–19; also discussion at the Fourth Congress of Moscow Regional Organization in March 1907 (see *Prosveshchenie*, No. 6 (March 31, 1907), p. 185).

108. Seregny, "Politics and the Rural Intelligentsia," pp. 169–200.

9. *The Reaction and Its Consequences*

1. Stoian, "Iz uchitel'skoi zhizni," *Volzhskii vestnik*, No. 112, April 20, 1906, p. 3; S. Seropolko, "2-i i 3-i s"ezdy Vserossiiskago uchitel'skago soiuza," *Dlia narodnago uchitelia*, No. 5 (1907), pp. 7–8; *Vestnik uchitelei*, No. 2 (May 7, 1906), p. 95; TsGIA, f. 733, op. 210, d. 38–50.

2. Zelenko, "Iz perezhitogo," pp. 119–120.

3. N. Chekhov, "Tiazhelye dni narodnoi shkoly," *Russkaia shkola*, No. 1 (1906), pp. 142–48; V. Obninskii, *Polgoda russkoi revoliutsii: sbornik materialov k istorii russkoi revoliutsii (oktiabr' 1905-aprel' 1906 gg.)*, vypusk 1 (Moscow, 1906), and *Mery protiv pechati, tiurma i ssylka, karatel'nye ekspeditsii, smertnaia kazn': khronika, aprel'-iul' 1906 g.* (Moscow, 1907); "Khronika (iz uchitel'skikh pis'em)," *Vestnik uchitelei*, No. 2 (May 7, 1906), pp. 72–74; *Narodnyi uchitel'*, No. 14–15, October 31, 1906, pp. 15–18; Ibid., No. 4 (1907), pp. 15–16. Such requests continued through late 1906: TsGAOR, f. DP OO (1905), d. 999, ch. 1, t. III, 1. 79.

4. Obninskii, *Mery protiv pechati*, pp. 69–70; *Pravo*, No. 5 (1906), col. 459; *Russkiia vedomosti*, No. 51, February 22, 1906; No. 49, February 20, 1906, p. 2; Obninskii, *Polgoda*, p. 145; *Budushchee*, No. 3, February 6, 1906, p. 4; *Pravo*, No. 1, col. 53; No. 2 (1906), col. 142; Olenin, "Krest'iane i intelligentsiia," No. 2, p. 165–66.

5. TsGAOR, f. 6862, op. 1, d. 89, 1. 2–2ob.

6. *Rus'* cited in *Vladimirets*, No. 196, September 12, 1907, p. 2; N. Iordanskii, "Voprosy tekushchei zhizni: krizis intelligentsii," *Sovremennyi mir*, No. 2, section 2 (1908), p. 84; *Gosudarstvennaia Duma. Stenograficheskie otchety*, Tret'ii sozyv, sessiia IV, zasedanie 6, vol. I, col. 414. To make his case in favor of church-run schools, Krupenskii claimed that only 150 teachers in these schools were dismissed for political unreliability in 1905–7. In 1906–7, as gentry marshal in Khotin district, Bessarabia, Krupenskii campaigned zealously against any political activity by teachers: *Vestnik vospitaniia*, No. 1, section 2 (1907), p. 84. His figure has been accepted by Tsvetkov, "K istorii uchitel'skogo dvizheniia," p. 170; *Rabotnik prosveshcheniia*, No. 19–20 (1925), p. 37. Indeed, one Soviet scholar believes Krupenskii's figure is an underestimate: Ososkov, *Voprosy istorii nachal'nogo*, II, p. 5

7. N. V. Chekhov, "Kak veliko chislo narodnykh uchitelei v Rossii," *Russkaia shkola*, No. 3, section 2 (1908), pp. 68–70; TsGAOR, f. 1278, op. 2, d. 138, 1. 13.

8. O. S[mir]nov, "Itogi deiatel'nosti zemstv po narodnomu obrazovaniiu," *Narodnyi uchitel'*, No. 5 (1907), pp. 4–5; B. B. Veselovskii, "Narodnoe obrazovanie i Gosudarstvennaia duma," *Sovremennyi mir*, No. 1 (1911), p. 313.

9. Tolstoi, "Vospominaniia ego za vremia," 1. 48.

10. Reprinted in *Viatskaia gazeta,* No. 39, September 28, 1906, col. 1218; *Russkoe slovo,* No. 26, February 2, 1907, p. 3 (letter of V. P. Vakhterov); *Dlia narodnago uchitelia,* No. 17 (1915), pp. 45–47 (obituary of teacher G. I. Orekhov); Chekhov, "Kak veliko chislo," p. 68.

11. Veselovskii, *Istoriia zemstva* IV, 29. The decision was protested and overturned by the governor. In Nolinsk district (Viatka) the local zemstvo in 1907 resolved to cut teachers' salaries. Remnants of the Teachers' Union tried to organize a strike against the zemstvo, but without success: "Svedeniia o zhizni i deiatel'nosti Nolinskoi gruppy," TsGAOR, f. 6862, op. 1, d. 27, 1. 5–5ob. On liquidation of services and zemstvo reaction against the third element generally, see Manning, *Crisis,* pp. 187–95; Veselovskii, *Istoriia zemstva,* IV, 60–75.

12. *Pravo,* No. 10 (1906), col. 957; TsGAOR, f. DP 00 (1905), d. 999, ch. 1, t. III, 1. 22–22ob (Mariupol, Ekaterinoslav); *Pravo,* No. 5 (1906), col. 456 (Pokrov, Vladimir); Ibid., No. 10 (1906), col. 957 (Lokhvitsa, Poltava; 16 schools remained empty); *Tambovskii golos,* No. 40.

13. *Saratovskii dnevnik,* No. 36, February 15, 1906, pp. 3–4; *Volzhskii vestnik,* December 8, 1905, No. 25, p. 4; *Volzhskii listok,* No. 329, December 9, 1905, p. 3 (Chistopol district); *Russkaia shkola,* No. 2, section 2 (1908), pp. 81–82 (Sormovo factory school, Balakhnia, 22 of 35 teachers dismissed, followed by workers' petition to zemstvo for their reinstatement); Vakhlin, "Narodnoe obrazovanie v Orekhovo-Zuevskom uezde," p. 423; *1905 god v Voronezhe,* vypusk 3 (Voronezh, 1925), p. 15. The Peasant Union had pledged to support teachers in school boycotts: *Protokol pervago severnago oblastnogo s"ezda,* p. 60. At the Third VSU Congress in June 1906 it was apparent that boycotts had usually been successful only with the support of the local population, as was the case in Ekaterinoslav, where, despite the presence of 70 candidates for 3 positions, the latter remained unoccupied: "Tretii delegatskii s"ezd," *Narodnyi uchitel',* No. 9–10 (July 31, 1906), p. 5; also testimony at a provincial congress of union activists in Viatka in August 1907: TsGAOR, f. 6862, op. 1, d. 38, 1. 3ob.

14. *Kozlovskaia zhizn',* No. 3, May 5, 1906; *Russkiia vedomosti,* No. 225, September 12, 1906, p. 3.

15. "Svedeniia o zhizni i deiatel'nosti Nolinskoi gruppy," 1. 4ob; TsGAOR, f. 6862, op. 1, d. 86, 1. 41ob (untitled ms. by S. S. Sergeev); also N. K. Popov, "1905 god v g. Nikol'ske, Severo-Dvinskoi gubernii (Vospominaniia narodnogo uchitelia)," TsGAOR, f. 6862, op. 1, d. 88, 1. 57.

16. On these developments, see A. V. Ososkov, *Bor'ba za vseobshchee nachal'noe obuchenie v dorevoliutsionnoi Rossii (1911-fevral' 1917 gg.),* Moscow, 1970, and especially Eklof, *Russian Peasant Schools.* Repression, coupled with the growth in schools after the Revolution of 1905–7, affected tenure. The January 1911 census of schools found that of rural teachers (in all types of primary schools), 42.6 percent of the men and 53.4 percent of women had been teaching less than five years (for example, since 1906): *Odnodnevnaia perepis' nachal'nykh shkol Rossiiskoi imperii, proizvedennaia 18 ianvaria 1911 g.,* ed., V. I. Pokrovskii, XVI (Petrograd, 1916), p. 97.

17. TsGIA, f. 733, op. 175, d. 76, 1. 68–116ob; TsGIA, f. 733, op. 201, d. 46, 1. 13–28; *Vestnik uchitelei,* No. 2 (May 7, 1906), p. 72.

18. Bratchikov, "Uchebno-vospitatel'naia chast'," No. 2, p. 120; Ben Eklof, "The Adequacy of Basic Schooling in Rural Russia: Teachers and Their Craft, 1880–1914," *History of Education Quarterly,* 26 (Summer 1986), pp. 199–224; and especially Eklof, *Russian Peasant Schools,* chapters 4 and 10.

19. *Severnaia rech',* No. 94, November 17, 1906, p. 1.

20. O. Vitten, "III delegatskii s"ezd V. S. U.," *Russkaia shkola,* No. 5–6, section 2 (1906), p. 77. Local authorities buttressed their agitation against the union by reference to a government circular of November 1905 (printed in No. 287 of *Pravitel'stvennyi vestnik*) barring membership of any state employees, including

zemstvo employees, in antigovernment unions: *Saratovskii dnevnik,* No. 32, February 10, 1906, p. 3.

21. Sokolov, "Kratkii ocherk," pp. 11–13; V. Ivanovich [Charnoluskii], "Tret'ii s"ezd vserossiiskago soiuza i deiatelei po narodnomu obrazovaniiu," *Vestnik vospitaniia,* No. 7, section 2 (1906), pp. 125–26; on the Moscow Regional Organization's activity, see Popova, "K istorii Vserossiiskago," p. 110; E. O. Vakhterova, "Bezrabotnye uchitelia v Moskve," *Vestnik vospitaniia,* No. 7, section 2 (1908), pp. 159–64; TsGAOR, f. 63, op. 14, d. 787, 1. 272–272 ob; on local activities, see *Russkiia vedomosti,* No. 239, September 3, 1905, p. 3; *Viatskaia zhizn',* No. 13, January 10, 1906, p. 3; *Narodnyi uchitel',* No. 1 (1906), p. 7; *Vladimirets,* No. 44, September 21, 1906, p. 4; *Severnaia rech',* No. 7, June 27, 1906, p. 3; *Iuzhnaia zaria,* No. 130, September 19, 1906, pp. 3–4.

22. Zemskii, "Vtoroi delegatskii s"ezd," pp. 137–38; *Protokoly vtorogo delegatskago s"ezda,* pp. 27–28; see, for example, discussion at a gathering of union members in Nizhegorod district in March 1906: *Nizhegorodskii listok,* No. 95, April 10, 1906, p. 3. Also provincial congress of union activists in Iaroslavl in April: *Severnaia mysl',* No. 23, April 15, 1906, p. 3.

23. "Po povodu proekta vserossiiskago professional'nago uchitel'skago soiuza," *Viatskaia zhizn',* No. 50, February 24, 1906, pp. 2–3; Raznochinets, "Ob intelligentskikh professional'nykh soiuzakh," *Saratovskii dnevnik,* No. 80, April 16, 1906, pp. 2–3; *Viatskaia zhizn',* No. 101, June 1, 1906, p. 3; No. 107, June 8, 1906, p. 3 (discussion at meetings of union members in Viatka); Chlen soiuza, "K voprosu o neitral'nosti soiuzov," *Saratovskii dnevnik,* No. 75, April 11, 1906, p. 2 and No. 81, April 18, 1906, p. 2.

24. *Narodnyi uchitel',* No. 7–8 (1906) p. 24. For summaries of the congress, see Ivanovich, "Tret'ii s"ezd," pp. 123–145; Vitten, "III delegatskii s"ezd," pp. 75–84. For details, see *Protokoly III-go s"ezda Vserossiiskago soiuza uchitelei i deiatelei po narodnomu obrazovaniiu 7–10 iiunia 1906 g.* (St. Petersburg, 1906). A list of local groups (including size) represented at the congress is in the VSU archive: TsGAOR, f. 518, op. 1, d. 75, 1. 46–49.

25. Ivanovich, "Tret'ii s"ezd," pp. 137–138; *Krasnoe znamia* (Paris), No. 4, July 1906, pp. 154–156; Charnoluskii, "Vserossiiskii soiuz uchitelei," ms. in TsGAOR, f. 6862, op. 1, d. 75, 1. 25. The manifesto was issued by the VSU, Trudoviki, PSR, RSDRP, Peasant and Railway Unions.

26. TsGAOR, f. DP 00 (1905), d. 999, ch. 1, t. III, 1. 89; Popova, pp. 118–119.

27. A. N. Tatarchukov, *Istoricheskii ocherk professional'nogo dvizheniia v Voronezhskoi gubernii,* vypusk 1 (Voronezh, 1921), pp. 49–50; *Narodnyi uchitel',* No. 11 (1906), p. 10.

28. On the Fourth VSU Congress, see *Narodnyi uchitel',* No. 10 (1907), pp. 11–13; No. 11 (1907), pp. 14–17.

29. N. K[apralo]v, "Proshloe i nastoiashchee Obshchestva vzaimnago vspomoshchestvovaniia uchiteliam i uchitel'nitsam Nizhegorodskoi gub.," *Dlia narodnago uchitelia,* No. 14 (1909), p. 19; Sergeini, "Ternistym putem" 1. 35; *Izvestiia Viatskago uchitel'stva,* No. 1, October 1, 1917, pp. 9–10; TsGAOR, f. DP 00 (1905), d. 999, ch. 1, t. V, 1. 42ob–43 (meetings of the Viatka Society had already been suspended in February 1906). The Tver and Kostroma Societies' meetings were suspended until 1909: *Dlia narodnago uchitelia,* No. 4 (1909), p. 29; No. 9 (1909) p. 25.

30. Sergeini, "Ternistym putem," 1. 31 (Mariupol Society); *Severnaia mysl',* No. 16, April 7, 1906, p. 3 (Iaroslavl Society); *Tambovskii golos,* No. 30, May 24, 1906, p. 4 (Borisoglebsk Society).

31. Veselovskii, *Istoriia zemstva,* IV, 69, 350; Zhulev, "Ob uchitel'skikh obshchestvakh," pp. 84–85; *Nizhegorodskii listok,* No. 48, February 19, 1906, p. 2 (Nizhegorod); *Saratovskii dnevnik,* No. 21, January 22, 1906, p. 3 and No. 4, January 5, 1906, p. 3. The Ekaterinoslav Society's petition was rejected by the provincial zemstvo and all district zemstvos: *Postanovleniia Ekaterinoslavskago gub. zemskago*

sobraniia XLII ocherednoi 1907 goda (Ekaterinoslav, 1908); *Iuzhnaia zaria*, No. 589, 1908, p. 3; see also *Otchet obshchestva vzaimopomoshchi uchashchim i uchivshim Samarskoi gub. za 1905, 1906 i perv. pol. 1907 g.* (Samara, 1907), p. 5.

32. Chekhov, "Khronika narodnago obrazovaniia v Rossii," *Russkaia shkola*, No. 2, section 2 (1908), p. 43; Zhulev, "Ob uchitel'skikh obshchestvakh," p. 89; A. Mezier, "Neskol'ko slov ob uchitel'skikh obshchestvakh vzaimopomoshchi (po povodu otcheta uchitel'skago ob-va vzaimopomoshchi Vologodskoi gub.)," *Russkaia shkola*, No. 1 (1908), p. 85.

33. *Nizhegorodskii listok*, No. 202, September 1, 1906, p. 2; *Ocherk deiatel'nosti obshchestva . . . Iaroslavskoi gub.*, p. 7; Groshkov, "K istorii Irkutskogo uchit. o-va," 1. 46; *Volzhskii kur'er*, No. 162, September 5, 1906, p. 3 and No. 163, p. 3; Burtsev, "Professional'no-politicheskoe dvizhenie," 1. 278ob–282; K[apralo]v, "Proshloe i nastoiashchee," p. 19; P. Zhulev, "Ob uchitel'skikh obshchestvakh," *Russkaia shkola*, No. 1 (1912), pp. 4–6.

34. N. Kapralov, "Deiatel'nost' Obshchestva vzaimopomoshchi uchashchikh Nizhegorodskoi guvernii s 1905 g. do 1918 g.," TsGAOR, f. 6862, op. 1, d. 89, 1. 10.

35. *Russkiia vedomosti*, No. 1, January 1, 1910 (supplement for year 1909, p. 10); Popova, "K istorii Vserossiiskago," pp. 128–129; E. A. Zviagintsev, "Khronika," *Vestnik vospitaniia*, No. 8, section 2 (1910), pp. 67–68; No. 7, section 2 (1912), pp. 140–41.

36. Kapralov, "Iz istorii ob"edinenii," 1. 19ob–20; Kapralov, "Deiatel'nost' Obshchestva," 1. 11–13; Burtsev, "Professional'no-politicheskoe dvizhenie," 1. 278–81, 283–85.

37. See *Trudy vtorogo vserossiiskago s"ezda imeni K. D. Ushinskago*, ed., V. A. Zelenko, 3 vols. (St. Petersburg, 1914–15). At the same time was held in the capital a national congress on education, attended by some 6,000 teachers: see Ososkov, *Bor'ba za vseobshchee nachal'noe obuchenie*, pp. 38–45. In 1910 (law of June 1) the government approved a Duma project that significantly improved the state pension fund for teachers, which according to its old statute (of July 12, 1900) had been singularly unattractive to teachers: Zviagintsev, "Khronika," *Vestnik vospitaniia*, No. 8, section 2 (1910), pp. 63–67.

38. N. Chekhov, "K voprosu o letnykh uchitel'skikh kursakh," *Russkiia vedomosti*, No. 132, June 9, 1912, p. 5; E. Zviagintsev, "Letnye uchitel'skie kursy," *Vestnik vospitaniia*, 1912, No. 1, pp. 115–55; No. 2, pp. 71–92; I. Stepnoi [I. S. Samokhvalov], "Zhivotvoriashchii dukh," *Dlia narodnago uchitelia*, No. 5 (1915), pp. 1–4.

39. E. Zviagintsev, "Pervyi zemsko-uchitel'skii s"ezd uezdnyi v Moskve," *Vestnik vospitaniia*, No. 5, section 2 (1914), pp. 69–94.

40. Sergeini, "Ternistym putem," 1. 36–37; Popova, "K istorii Vserossiiskago," p. 126; Stepnoi, "Zhivotvoriashchii dukh," p. 4.

41. A. A. Parshinskii, "Uchitel'stvo za gody pervoi revoliutsii i reaktsii," *Otrazhenie pervoi russkoi revoliutsii v S.-Dvinskoi gubernii: sbornik statei* (Velikii Ustiug, 1926), p. 79; M. G. Zavoloka, *Zagal'noosvitnia shkola Ukraini v kintsi XIX–na pochatka XX st.* (Kiev, 1971), p. 40.

42. Zviagintsev, "Zemstvo i uchebnoe vedomstvo," pp. 263–64; N. P. Lapshin, *Iz istorii russkoi dorevoliutsionnoi inspektsii narodnykh uchilishch (1869–1917)*, Elabuga, 1963, pp. 12–13; Vakhlin, "Narodnoe obrazovanie v Orekhovo-Zuevskom uezde," p. 421. The latter source also notes an increase in spying and denunciations by clerics after 1905, especially against women teachers.

43. Parshinskii, "Uchitel'stvo," pp. 78–79; I. Zhilkin, "Provintsial'noe obozrenie," *Vestnik Evropy*, No. 5 (1914), pp. 376–77. In his diary in late 1910 the Third Duma deputy I. S. Kliuzhev mentions a recent secret circular issued by the MVD to the effect that rural teachers should be removed from the field of adult education altogether. Kliuzhev found out about this in a conversation with a Ministry of

Education official, and this writer has not been able to confirm the existence of such a circular: TsGIA, f. 669, op. 1, d. 4.

44. A teacher from Novgorod remarked that in 1917 and after most teachers, especially "daughters of clergy" *(popovskie dochen'ki)*, took little part in "public activity," not going beyond the walls of the school: TsGAOR, f. 6862, op. 1, d. 87, 1. 18.

45. *Krasnyi arkhiv*, No. 2 (15), 1926, p. 42; also Orlando Figes, "Towards an Understanding of Village Social Relations in the Agrarian Revolution (1917–18): A Study of the Middle Volga," unpublished paper delivered at Conference on the Peasantry of European Russia, 1800–1917, University of Massachusetts, Boston, August 19–22, 1986.

46. N. V. Chekhov, "Russkii uchitel' i revoliutsii," *Narodnyi uchitel'*, No. 5–6 (1918), pp. 3–5; E. Vakhterova, "Iz zhizni," *Uchitel'*, No. 1 (1918), pp. 29–31.

47. Bonnell, *Roots of Rebellion*.

Bibliography

The following list is not intended to be a comprehensive recounting of all works consulted and cited in this study. Much of this study is based on materials in Soviet archives and contemporary periodicals; a list of these is included, as well as the more important memoirs and other unpublished manuscripts housed in the archives (largely in TsGAOR, f. 6862). As for published books and articles, only the most pertinent, or those frequently cited, are included. For other materials, particularly those not dealing specifically with teachers and primary education (for example, on the medical profession, Peasant Union, or more general works on the 1905 revolution), readers should consult the footnotes.

Archives:

Tsentral'nyi Gosudarstvennyi Istoricheskii Arkhiv SSSR, Leningrad (TsGIA)
Fond 733 Ministerstvo narodnago prosveshcheniia, Departament narodnago prosveshcheniia.
Fond 1284 Ministerstvo vnutrennykh del, Departament obshchikh del.

Tsentral'nyi Gosudarstvennyi Arkhiv Oktiabr'skoi Revoliutsii SSSR, Moscow (TsGAOR)
Fond 63 Moskovskoe okhrannoe otdelenie.
Fond 102 Departament politsii, Osobyi otdel.
Fond 518 Soiuz soiuzov.
Fond 812 V. I. Charnoluskii.
Fond 6862 Komissiia po izucheniiu istorii professional'nogo dvizheniia pri Ts. K. profsoiuza rabotnikov prosveshcheniia

Tsentral'nyi Gosudarstvennyi Arkhiv g. Mosky, Moscow (TsGAg.M)
Fond 459 Kantselariia popechitelia Moskovskogo uchebnogo okruga.

Gosudarstvennaia Publichnaia Biblioteka: Rukopisnyi Otdel, Leningrad, (GPB–RO)
Fond 781 I. I. Tolstoi.

Gosudarstvennaia Biblioteka imeni V. I. Lenina: Rukopisnyi Otdel, Moscow (GBL–RO)
Fond 46 V. P. Vakhterov.
Fond 218 N. V. Tulupov.

Unpublished Memoirs, Histories, and Dissertations:

Anan'in, V. "Uchitel'stvo Moskovskikh gorodskikh shkol v 1905 godu (Vospominaniia moskovskogo uchitelia)." TsGAOR, f. 6862, op. 1, d. 84, 1. 223–226.

Burtsev, V. K. "Professional'no-politicheskoe dvizhenie Iaroslavskogo uchitel'stva za 20 let (1898–1917 gody)." TsGAOR, f. 6862, op. 1, d. 21, 1. 271–289.

Charnoluskii, V. I. "Vserossiiskii soiuz uchitelei i deiatelei po narodnomu obrazovaniiu," TsGAOR, f. 6862, op. 1, d. 75 (irregular pagination).

Chigovskaia, L. G. "Deiatel'nost' bol'shevikov Ukraini po vovlecheniiu demokraticheskoi intelligentsii v massovoe revoliutsionnoe dvizhenie 1905–1907 godov." Dissertation, Kievskii gosud. universitet im. T. G. Shevchenko, Kiev, 1974.

Chulkina, M. A. "Bor'ba bol'shevikov Urala za vovlechenie demokraticheskoi intelligentsii i uchashcheisia molodezhi v revoliutsionnoe divizhenie v gody pervoi russkoi revoliutsii (1905–1907 gg.)." Dissertation, Moskovskii gosud. ped. institut im V. I. Lenina, Moscow, 1968.

Dzhanpoladian, V. S. "V. P. Vakhterov: vidnyi deiatel' dorevoliutsionnoi nachal'noi shkoly." Dissertation, Akademiia ped. nauk RSFSR, Moscow, 1954.

Fallows, Thomas S. "Forging the Zemstvo Movement: Liberalism and Radicalism on the Volga, 1890–1905." Ph.D. Dissertation, Harvard University, 1981.

Gordeeva, L. M. "Deiatel'nost' bol'shevikov sredi narodnykh uchitelei v gody pervoi russkoi revoliutsii." Dissertation, Gor'kovskii gosud. universitet im N. I. Lobachevskogo, Gorkii, 1970.

Groshkov, A. "K istorii Irkutskogo uchitel'skogo obshchestva za l-e desiatiletie." TsGAOR, f. 6862, op. 1, d. 74, 1. 43–46ob.

Kapralov, N. "Iz istorii ob"edineniia rabotnikov prosveshcheniia v Nizhegorodoskoi gubernii." TsGAOR, f. 6862, op. 1, d. 89, 1. 14–20.

"Kratkii ocherk uchitel'skogo dvizheniia i soiuza rabotnikov prosveshcheniia Tverskoi gubernii." (no author). TsGAOR, f. 6862, op. 1, d. 21, l. 133–151ob.

Kudriavtsev, S. I. "Uchitel' i naselenie Bronnitskogo uezda v 1905 godu (Vospominaniia)." TsGAOR, f. 6862, op. 1, d. 84, l. 199–213ob.

Nasimovich, A. "Iz vospominanii." TsGAOR, f. 6862, op. 1, d. 84, l. 110–133.

Nikol'skii, F. G. Untitled MS. TsGAOR, f. 6862, op. 1, d. 88, l. 137–149.

Pokrovskii, M. N. "V soiuze uchitelei." TsGAOR, f. 6862, op. 1, d. 84, 1. 72–74.

Popov, Nik. K. "1905 god v g. Nikol'ske Severo-Dvinskoi gubernii (Vospominaniia narodnogo uchitelia)." TsGAOR, f. 6862, op. 1, d. 88, l. 44–70.

Popova, N. "Iz vospominanii o korporatsii Moskovskikh gorodskikh uchitelei v 1905 g." TsGAOR, f. 6862, op, 1, d. 84, 1. 5–8.

Pupu, V. D. "Vospominaniia o revoliutsii 1905-go goda." TsGAOR, f. 6862, op. 1, d. 86, 1. 48–61ob.

Rvachev, L. F. "Iz proshlogo (Vospominaniia sel'skogo uchitelia o revoliutsii 1905 goda)." TsGAOR, f. 6862, op. 1, d. 86, l. 76–167.

Rumiantseva, N. "Politicheskaia zabastovka gorodskogo uchitel'stva Peterburga v 1905 g." TsGAOR, f. 6862, op. 1, d. 87, l. 76–80.

Sanders, Jonathan E. "The Union of Unions: Political, Economic, Civil and Human Rights Organizations in the 1905 Revolution." Ph.D. Dissertation, Columbia University, 1985.

Sergeini, Iv. "Ternistym putem (K 20 letiiu uchitel'skogo prof. ob"edineniia)." TsGAOR, f. 6862, op. 1, d. 74, l. 17–39.

"Stat'i (neizvestnykh avtorov) ob organizatsii i deiatel'nosti professional'nogo soiuza narodynkh uchitelei Ekaterinoslavskoi gub. za 1905–1922 g.g.," TsGAOR, f. 6862, op. 1, d. 78, l. 5–35.

Suprunenko, N. "Obshchestvo vzaimopomoshchi uchashchikh i uchivshikh v nachal'nykh uchilishchakh Lubenskogo uezda Poltavskoi gub. 1905–1907 gody." TsGAOR, f. 6862, op. 1, d. 74, l. 47–55.

Tolstoi, I. I. "Vospominaniia ego za vremia upravleniia Ministerstvom narodnogo prosveshcheniia, 1906 g." Gosudarstvennaia Publichnaia Biblioteka: Rukopisnyi Otdel, f. 781, No. 568.

Tsvetkov, I. L. Untitled MS. TsGAOR, f. 6862, op. 1, d. 20, l. 1–85.

"Uchastie Samarskikh uchitelei v osvoboditel'nom dvizhenii." (no author). TsGAOR, f. 6862, op. 1, d. 88, l. 1–9ob.

Vakhterova, E. "O Vserossiiskom uchitel'skom soiuze v iiune 1905 g." TsGAOR, f. 6862, op. 1, d. 72, l. 1–28.

Newspapers and periodicals (years consulted):

Biuletten' Vserossiiskago soiuza uchitelei i deiatelei po narodnomu obrazovaniiu (occasional, 1905–8).
Dlia narodnago uchitelia (Moscow, 1907–17).
Iuzhnaia zaria (Ekaterinoslav, 1906–8).
Kliazma (Vladimir, 1906).
Narodnyi uchitel' (Kishinev-Kiev-Moscow, 1906–18).
Nasha zhizn' (St. Petersburg, 1904–5).
Nizhegorodskii listok (Nizhnii-Novgorod, 1905–6).
Obrazovanie (St. Petersburg, 1892–1908).
Osvobozhdenie (Paris-Stuttgart, 1902–5).
Pedagogicheskii listok (Moscow, 1905–7).
Pravo (St. Petersbrug, 1902–8).
Pridneprovskii krai (Ekaterinoslav, 1905).
Privolzhskii krai (Saratov, 1905).
Prosveshchenie (Moscow, 1907).
Revoliutsionnaia Rossiia (Geneva-Paris, 1902–5).
Rus' (St. Petersburg, 1905).
Russkaia shkola (St. Petersburg, 1890–1917).
Russkiia vedomosti (Moscow, 1902–8).
Russkoe slovo (Moscow, 1905–7).
Samarskaia gazeta (Samara, 1905).
Saratovskaia zemskaia nedelia (Saratov, 1900–5).
Saratovskii dnevnik (Saratov, 1905–6).
Saratovskii listok (Saratov, 1903–5).
Severnaia mysl' (Iaroslavl, 1906).
Severnaia rech' (Iaroslavl, 1906).
Severnyi krai (Iaroslavl, 1903–5).
Syn otechestva (St. Petersburg, 1904–5).
Tambovskii golos (Tambov, 1905–6).
Uchitel' (St. Petersburg, 1907).
Vestnik iuga (Ekaterinoslav, 1905).
Vestnik uchitelei (St. Petersburg, 1906).
Vestnik vospitaniia (Moscow, 1890–1917).
Vestnik Vserossiiskago soiuza uchitelei i deiatelei po narodnomu obrazovaniiu (St. Petersburg, 1905).
Viatskaia gazeta (Viatka, 1906).
Viatskaia zhizn' (Viatka, 1905–6).
Vladimirets (Vladimir, 1906–7).
Volzhskii kur'er (Kazan, 1906).
Volzhskii listok (Kazan, 1905–6).
Volzhskii vestnik (Kazan, 1905–6).
Zadachi obnovlennoi shkoly (St. Petersburg, 1908).
Zhizn' i shkola (St. Petersburg, 1907–8).

Published articles:

Aizenberg, A. Ia. "Pedagogicheskoe obshchestvo pri Moskovskom universitete v period revoliutsii 1905–1907 gg." *Sovetskaia pedagogika*, No. 1 (1955): 67–79.

Akhutin, N. "K voprosu o podgotovke narodnykh uchitelei." *Russkaia shkola*, No. 1 (1905): 122–45.

Akimov, V. "Zemskaia rabota po podgotovke narodnykh uchitelei." *Zhurnal ministerstva narodnago prosveschcheniia*, 1915, No. 4: 145–83; No. 5: 1–25; No. 6: 129–67.

Anikin, S. "Vystavka v Iaroslavle." *Saratovskaia zemskaia nedelia*, No. 8 (1903): 93–112.

B. V. "Pedagogicheskii mir i Gosudarstvennaia Duma." *Russkaia shkola*, No. 4 (1906): 122–38.

Baum, Ia. D. "Neskol'ko faktov iz biografii N. A. Rozhkova." *Katorga i ssylka*, No. 6, 43, (1928): 168–69.

Belokonskii, I. P. "Derevenskiia vpechatleniia (iz zapisok zemskago statistika)." *Russkoe bogatstvo*, No. 9 (1898): 108–19.

Belokonskii, I. P. "Obzor deiatel'nosti zemstv po narodnomu obrazovaniiu." *Russkaia shkola* (continuing survey, 1901–5).

Blinov, L. N. "Narodnyi uchitel' v Rossii." in kn. D. I. Shakhovskoi, ed., *Vseobshchee obrazovanie v Rossii: sbornik statei*. Moscow, 1902, pp. 63–84.

Bratchikov, N. "Uchebno-vospitatel'naia chast' v nachal'noi shkole (po dannym zemskoi shkol'noi statistiki)." *Russkaia shkola*, 1909, No. 1: 89–118; No. 2: 107–131; No. 3: 78–93.

Briukhatov, L. D. "Nuzhdy russkago uchitelia." *Russkiia vedomosti*, No. 259, September 23, p. 4; No. 265, October 10, 1905, pp. 3–4.

Briukhatov, L. D. "Znachenie 'tret'iago elementa' v zhizni zemstva," in B. B. Veselovskii and Z. G. Frenkel', eds., *Iubileinyi zemskii sbornik, 1864–1914*. St. Petersburg: O. N. Popova, 1914, pp. 186–205.

Brooks, Jeffrey. "The Zemstvo and the Education of the People," in Terence Emmons and Wayne S. Vucinich, eds., *The Zemstvo in Russia: An Experiment in Local Self-Government*. Cambridge, 1982, pp. 243–78.

Charnoluskii, V. I. "Iz khroniki nachal'nago narodnago obrazovaniia." *Vestnik vospitaniia*, No. 1, section 2 (1907): 83–106.

Charnoluskii, V. I. "Iz vospominanii ob Uchitel'skom Soiuze epokhi pervoi russkoi revoliutsii." *Narodnyi uchitel'*, No. 11 (1925): 57–61.

Charnoluskii, V. I. "Nachal'noe obrazovanie vo vtoroi polovine XIX stoletiia," in *Istoriia Rossii v XIX veke*. Vol. VII. St. Petersburg: Granat, n. d., pp. 109–69.

Charnoluskii, V. I. "Zemstvo i vneshkol'noe obrazovanie," in Veselovskii and Frenkel', eds. *Iubileinyi zemskii sbornik*, pp. 370–90.

Chekhov, N. V. "Kak veliko chislo narodnykh uchitelei v Rossii." *Russkaia shkola*, No. 3, section 2 (1908): 68–70.

Chekhov, N. V. "Khronika narodnago obrazovaniia v Rossii." *Russkaia shkola*, No. 2, section 2 (1908): 42–52.

Chekhov, N. V. "Tiazhelye dni narodnoi shkoly." *Russkaia shkola*, No. 11, (1906): 142–148.

Chekhov, N. V. "Uezdnye uchilishchnye komissii." *Russkaia shkola*, No. 9 (1906): 103–11.

Chernov, G. I. "Pereklikaias' s minuvshim (Ob uezdnom s"ezde narodnykh uchitelei v 1901 g.)." *Nachal'naia shkola*, No. 1 (1970): 91–93.

Denisov, Val. "Znachenie uchitel'skikh kursov po otzyvam zemskikh uchitelei." *Obrazovanie*, No. 7, section 2 (1904): 39–67.

Drozdov, I. G. "Petitsii novozybkovskikh krest'ian v 1905 godu." *Proletarskaia revoliutsiia*, No. 11, (1925): 124–51.

Eklof, Ben. "The Myth of the Zemstvo School: The Sources of the Expansion of Rural Education in Imperial Russia: 1864–1914." *History of Education Quarterly* (Winter 1984): 561–84.

Eklof, Ben. "Peasant Sloth Reconsidered: Strategies of Education and Learning in

Rural Russia before the Revolution." *Journal of Social History*, 14, No. 3 (1981): 355–85.

Eklof, Ben. "The Village and the Outsider: The Rural Teacher in Russia, 1864–1914." *Slavic and European Education Review*, No. 1 (1979): 1–19.

Emmons, Terence. "Russia's Banquet Campaign." *California Slavic Studies*, 10 (1977): 45–86.

Erman, L. K. "Bor'ba bol'shevikov za vovlechenie narodnykh uchitelei v revoliutsionnoe dvizhenie v 1905 g." *Sovetskaia pedagogika*, No. 4 (1955): 60–80.

Erman, L. K. "Sostav intelligentsii v Rossii v kontse XIX i nachale XX v." *Istoriia SSSR*, No. 1 (1963): 161–76.

Erman, L. K. "Uchastie demokraticheskoi intelligentsii vo vserossiiskoi oktiabr'skoi politicheskoi stachke." *Istoricheskie zapiski*, 49 (1955): 352–78.

F[al'bork, G. A.] and Ch[arnoluskii, V. I.]. "Otgoloski uchitel'skikh s'ezdov, kursov i soveshchanii." *Vestnik vospitaniia*, No. 9, section 2 (1901): 88–109.

Farmakovskii, V. "Deiatel'nost' ministerstva narodnago prosveshcheniia v oblasti nachal'nago narodnago obrazovaniia v poslednee desiatiletie (1894–1903)." *Zhurnal ministerstva narodnago prosveshcheniia*, No. 4, section 2 (1904): 1–61.

Farmakovskii, V. "S"ezdy uchitelei nachal'nykh uchilishch prezhde i teper'." *Zhurnal ministerstva narodnago prosveshcheniia*, No. 12, section 4 (1900): 72–93.

Feliksov, N. A. "Pedagogicheskie kursy i uchitel'skie s"ezdy." *Russkaia mysl'*, 1896, No. 9, section 2: 1–28; No. 10, section 2: 38–56; No. 11, section 2: 32–56.

Galai, Shmuel. "The Role of the Union of Unions in the Revolution of 1905." *Jahrbücher für Geschichte Osteuropas*, 24, No. 4 (1976): 512–25.

Godnev, D. "Samarskaia uchashchaiasia molodezh' i uchitel'stvo v revoliutsii 1905 goda," in *1905 god: sbornik vospominanii uchastnikov revoliutsionnogo dvizheniia v byvshikh Samarskoi i Simbirskoi guberniiakh*. Moscow-Kuibyshev, 1935, pp. 161–80.

Gol'tsev, V. "K voprosu o polozhenii uchashchikh v narodnoi shkole." *Russkaia mysl'*, 1897, No. 6, section 2: 82–94; No. 12, section 2: 61–78.

Gol'tsev, V. "O polozhenii uchashchikh v shkolakh Vladimirskoi gubernii." *Obrazovanie*, No. 4 (1897): 9–16.

Grigor'ev, P. "Zemskie pedagogicheskie kursy i pravila 1875 goda." *Russkaia shkola*, No. 3 (1903): 129–39.

Hayashida, Ronald H. "The Unionization of Russian Teachers, 1905–1908: An Interest Group under the Autocracy." *Slavic and European Education Review*, No. 2 (1981), pp. 1–16.

Iakhontov, I. "Uchitel'skie kursy, s"ezdy i sobraniia." *Vestnik Novgorodskago zemstva*, 1905, No. 11: 31–40; No. 12: 46–52.

Iordanskii, N. "Voprosy tekushchei zhizni: krizis intelligentsii." *Sovremennyi mir*, No. 2, section 2 (1908): 67–84.

Ivanov, A. "Iz istorii Soiuza vo Vladimire." *Rabotnik prosveshcheniia*, Nos. 13–14 (1924): 84–94.

Ivanov-Razumnik. "Chto dumaet derevnia? (vpechatleniia ochevidtsa)." *Sovremmenost'*, No. 2, section 2 (1906): 50–76; *Russkoe bogatstvo*, No. 5, section 2 (1906): 1–14.

Ivanovich, V. [Charnoluskii]. "Tretii s"ezd vserossiiskago soiuza uchitelei i deiatelei po narodnomu obrazovaniiu." *Vestnik vospitaniia*, No. 7 (1906): 122–145.

K. Ch. "Sel'skii uchitel'." *Russkoe bogatstvo*, No. 4, section 2 (1898): 1–14.

Kir'iakov, V. V. "Organizatsiia khoziaistvennoi chasti v zemskikh shkolakh Moskovskoi gubernii." *Saratovskaia zemskaia nedelia*, Nos. 6–7, section 3 (1904): 164–78.

Kir'iakov, V. V. "S"ezd uchitelei moskovskago uezdnago zemstva." *Russkoe bogatstvo*, No. 1, section 2 (1902): 224–56.

Kiriukhina, E. I. "Mestnye organizatsii Vserossiiskogo Krest'ianskogo Soiuza v 1905 godu." *Uchenye zapiski Kirovskogo pedagogicheskogo instituta*, 10 (1956): 83–157.

Kiriukhina, E. I. "Vserossiiskii Krest'ianskii Soiuz v 1905 g." *Istoricheskie zapiski*, No. 50 (1955): 95–141.

Kolpenskii, V. "Sel'skaia shkola posle krest'ianskoi reformy." *Arkhiv istorii truda v Rossii*, No. 5 (1922): 36–46; Nos. 6–7 (1923): 173–82.

Kornilov, E. G. "Zemskaia demokraticheskaia intelligentsiia 70-kh godov XIX veka," in *Voprosy obshchestvennogo i sotsial'no-ekonomicheskogo razvitiia Rossii v XVIII–XIX rekakh (po materialam tsent. gub.)*. Riazan, 1974, pp. 89–112.

Kornilov, E. G. "Zemskie uchitelia v revoliutsionnom dvizhenii 70-kh gg. XIX v." *Uchenye zapiski Moskovskogo gos. ped. in-ta im. V. I. Lenina*, 439 (1971): 116–35.

Kovalev, A. A. "Ocherk vozniknoveniia i razvitiia uchitel'skikh kursov i s"ezdov v Rossii." *Russkaia shkola*, No. 12 (1905): 71–94.

Latyshev, V. A. "Uchitel'skie obshchestva vzaimopomoshchi." *Zhurnal ministerstva narodnago prosveshcheniia*, No. 12, section 2 (1909): 213–21.

Loktin, A. A. "Iz Iaroslavlia." *Saratovskaia zemskaia nedelia*, No. 8, section 2 (1905): 99–110.

Loktin, A. A. "Uchitel'skie kursy i s"ezdy." *Vestnik vospitaniia*, No. 6, section 2 (1904): 77–78.

Lozanov, N. "Ob otkrytii uchitel'skikh seminarii v gor. Saratove." *Saratovskaia zemskaia nedelia*, No. 2, section 3 (1903): 50–74.

Malinovskii, N. "K istorii zarozhdeniia vserossiiskogo soiuza uchitelei." *Narodnyi uchitel'*, No. 11 (1925): 24–36.

Malitskii, N. "Professional'noe dvizhenie vo Vladimirskoi gub. v. 1905–1907 g. g.," in *O rabochem dvizhenii i sotsial'-demokraticheskoi rabote vo Vladimirskoi gubernii v 900-kh godakh*, vypusk 1, ed. A. N. Asatkin. Vladimir, 1926, pp. 53–128.

Manning, Roberta Thompson. "Zemstvo and Revolution: The Onset of the Gentry Reaction, 1905–1907," in Leopold H. Haimson, ed., *The Politics of Rural Russia, 1905–1914*. Bloomington, Ind., Indiana University Press, 1979, pp. 30–66.

Menzhinskaia, L. "Peterburgskoe uchitel'stvo v 1905 g." *Narodnyi uchitel'*, No. 11 (1925): 38–45.

Mikhailovskaia, A. "Uchitel'skii soiuz v 1905 goda." *Narodnyi uchitel'*, Nos. 7–8 (1925): 131–34.

Mirov, I. "Professional'nye soiuzy v Viatskoi gubernii v period pervoi russkoi revoliutsii," in *1905 god v Viatskoi gubernii*. Viatka: "Truzhenik," 1925, pp. 206–27.

Mirovich, "Obrazovatel'nye stremleniia uchitelia i lektsii v provintsii." *Zhurnal dlia vsekh*, No. 5 (1905): 302–05.

Mitskevich, S. I. "Lektorskaia gruppa pri M. K. v 1905–1907 gg." *Proletarskaia revoliutsiia*, No. 9 (44), 1925: 49–61.

Morison, John D. "Education and the 1905 Revolution in the Russian Countryside." *Slavic and European Education Review*, No. 2 (1984): 46–57.

Morison, John D. "Les institutеurs de village dans la revolution de 1905 en Russie." *Revue des Etudes Slaves* (Fall 1986): 205–19.

Murinov, V. "Obshchestva vzaimnago vspomoshchestvovaniia uchashchim i uchivshim," in Shakhovskoi, ed, *Vseobshchee obrazovanie v Rossii*, pp. 85–98.

Nardov, N. N. "V sumerkakh zhizni (Iz zhizni dorevoliutsionnogo uchitel'stva)." *Natisk* (Gorkii), Nos. 4–5 (1935): 42–50.

"Narodnye uchitelia v pervoi russkoi revoliutsii." *Uchitel'skaia gazeta*, No. 101 (December 21, 1955): 4.

Nasimovich, A. "Vospominaniia o 1905 g." *Narodnyi uchitel'*, No. 11 (1925): 38–40.

Nikolaev, A. A. "Neskol'ko slov o biudzhete narodnago uchitelia." *Russkaia shkola*, Nos. 5–6 (1912): 89–95.

Nikolaev, A. A. "Soiuz narodnykh uchitelei i deiatelei po narodnomu obrazovaniiu." *Vestnik znaniia*, No. 7 (1905): 110–18.

O—v, M. A. "Dva dnia na uchitel'skom s"ezde (iz vospominanii o 70-kh godakh)." *Russkaia shkola*, Nos. 5–6 (1913): 54–77.

Olenin, R. "Krest'iane i intelligentsiia (K kharakteristike osvoboditel'nago dvizheniia v Malorossii)." *Russkoe bogatstvo*, 1907, No. 1: 246–68; No. 2: 135–69.

Ososkov, A. V. "Borba za vseobshchee obuchenie v gody pervoi russkoi revoliutsii." *Sovetskaia pedagogika*, No. 3 (1975): 119–26.

Panov, A. V. "Shag vpered: Zasedanie uchilishchnoi komissii Saratovskago uezdnago zemstva pri uchastii uchitelei." *Obrazovanie*, No. 12, section 2 (1901): 31–42.

Panov, A. V. "Voprosy narodnago obrazovaniia na gubernskom zemskom sobranii (pis'mo iz Saratova)." *Obrazovanie*, No. 2, section 3 (1902): 30–38.

Parshinskii, A. A. "Uchitel'stvo za gody pervoi revoliutsii i reaktsii," in *Otrazhenie pervoi russkoi revoliutsii v Severo-Dvinskoi gubernii: sbornik statei*. Velikii Ustiug, 1926, pp. 69–80.

Petrishchev, A. "Iz zametok shkol'nago uchitelia." *Russkoe bogatstvo*, 1904, No. 9: 59–85; No. 10: 80–115.

Pirumova, N. M. "Zemskaia intelligentsiia v 70–80-e gody XIX v." *Istoricheskie zapiski*, 106 (1981), pp. 127–61.

Popova, N. "K istorii Vserossiiskago uchitel'skago soiuza (Moskovskaia oblastnaia organizatsiia)." *Vestnik vospitaniia*, Nos. 4–5 (1917): 97–130.

Popova, N. "Moskovskaia oblastnaia organizatsiia Vserossiiskogo Uchitel'skogo Soiuza." *Narodnyi uchitel'*, No. 11 (1925): 45–51.

Prugavin, A. "Kak u nas ustraivalis' pedagogicheskie kursy." *Obrazovanie*, No. 9, section 2 (1902): 54–81.

Ramer, Samuel C. "The Zemstvo and Public Health," in Emmons and Vucinich, *Zemstvo in Russia*, pp. 279–314.

Rodnev, L. "Storinka z istorii vchitel'stva na Katerinoslavshchini (Tovaristvo vzaemnoi dopomogi vchiteliv narodnikh shkil na Katerinoslavshchini z 1898–1908 r.)." *Robitnik osviti*, No. 7 (1925): 45–49.

Rozanov, D. "Ob organizatsii zavedeniia delom narodnago obrazovaniia pri obshchestvennykh samoupravleniiakh." *Vestnik vospitaniia*, No. 8 (1908): 103–32.

Rumiantsev, A. "K voprosu ob ob"edinenii uchitel'skikh obshchestv vzaimopomoshchi Moskovskoi gubernii." *Vestnik vospitaniia*, No. 5, section 2 (1905): 64–71.

Samokhvalov, I. "Otryvki iz vospominanii o 1905 gode." *Narodnyi uchitel'*, No. 11 (1925): 51–56.

Serebriakov, V. "Sovremennoe sostoianie russkoi derevni i eia nuzhdy, po otzyvam sel'skikh zhitelei," *Saratovskaia zemskaia nedelia*, 1905, No. 5, section 3: 91–110; Nos. 10–12, section 3: 1–32.

Seregny, Scott J. "A Different Type of Peasant Movement: The Peasant Unions in the Russian Revolution of 1905." *Slavic Review*, 47, No. 1 (Spring 1988): 51–67.

Seregny, Scott J. "Politics and the Rural Intelligentsia in Russia: A Biographical Sketch of Stepan Anikin, 1869–1919." *Russian History*, 7, Nos. 1–2 (1980): 169–200.

Seregny, Scott J. "Revolutionary Strategies in the Russian Countryside: Rural Teachers and the Socialist Revolutionary Party on the Eve of 1905." *Russian Review*, 44, No. 3 (1985), pp. 221–38.

Seropolko, S. "Kak voznik vserossiiskii uchitel'skii soiuz." *Dlia narodnago uchitelia*, No. 3 (1907): 5–8.

Seropolko, S. "2-i i 3-i s"ezdy Vserossiiskago uchitel'skago soiuza." *Dlia narodnago uchitelia*, No. 5 (1907): 7–11.

Seropolko, S. "Pervye tri s"ezda Vserossiiskago uchitel'skago souiza." *Dlia narodnago uchitelia*, No. 4 (1907): 7–10.

Shcherba, V. "K voprosu o podgotovke uchitel'skago personala." *Saratovskaia zemskaia nedelia*, Nos. 6–7, section 3 (1903): 1–13.

Shcherba, Vl. "Uchitel'skie kursy i pravila o kursakh." *Vestnik Evropy*, No. 10 (1902): 773–781.

Shesternin, P. "Iz vospominanii sel'skago uchitelia." *Obrazovanie,* No. 9 (1898): 107–16.

Sinel, Allen, "Educating the Russian Peasantry: The Elementary School Reforms of Count Dmitrii Tolstoi." *Slavic Review,* 27, No. 1 (1968): 49–70.

Sinel, Allen, "The Campaign for Universal Primary Education in Russia, 1890–1904." *Jahrbücher für Geschichte Osteuropas,* 30, No. 4 (1982), pp. 481–507.

Sivkov, K. V. "Krest'ianskie prigovory 1905 goda." *Russkaia mysl',* No. 4, section 2 (1907): 24–48.

Skvortsov, N. A. "Nazrevshii vopros (polozhenie narodnykh uchitelei i uchitel'nits)." *Obrazovanie,* No. 2 (1897): 17–25.

S[mir]nov, O. "Itogi deiatel'nosti zemstv po narodnomu obrazovaniiu." *Narodnyi uchitel',* 1907, No. 4: 3–4; No. 5: 4–5.

Smirnov, O. N. "Zemstvo i biurokratiia v dele narodnago obrazovaniia." *Russkaia shkola,* No. 12 (1906): 1–27.

Sobolev, M. "K voprosu o polozhenii uchashchikh v narodnoi shkole." *Russkaia mysl',* No. 9, section 2 (1898): 189–212.

Sokolov, N. "Kratkii ocherk istorii Vserossiiskago soiuza." *Vestnik Vserossiiskago soiuza uchitelei,* No. 2 (1905): 3–14.

Sokolov, V. "Pravovoe polozhenie uchitelei." *Saratovskaia zemskaia nedelia,* Nos. 6–7, section 3 (1905): 35–49.

Stepnoi, I. [Samokhvalov, I. S.]. "Zhivotvoriashchii dukh." *Dlia narodnago uchitelia,* No. 5 (1915): 1–4.

Suprunenko, N. "Iz nedavnego proshlogo: istoriia organizatsii uchitel'skikh obshchestv." *Rabotnik prosveshcheniia,* Nos. 13–14 (1924): 47–53.

Tiutriumov, A. M. "S"ezdy narodnykh uchitelei, kak obshchestvenno-pedagogicheskaia mera." *Russkaia shkola,* 1894, Nos. 5–6: 163–177; Nos. 7–8: 118–135; No. 9–10: 250–261.

Tsvetkov, I. "Istoriia professional'nogo ob"edineniia rabotnikov prosveshcheniia," in *Pedagogicheskaia entsiklopediia,* ed. A. G. Kalashnikov. Moscow, 1927–29, III, col. 649–666.

Tsvetkov, I. L. "K istorii uchitel'skogo dvizheniia v Rossii," in A. A. Korostelev, ed., *Uchitel' i revoliutsiia: sbornik statei i materialov.* Moscow: "Rabotnik prosveshcheniia," 1925, pp. 153–78.

Tsvetkov, Iv. "Uchitel'skoe dvizhenie 1905 goda." *Narodnyi uchitel',* No. 11 (1925): 20–24.

Tugan-Baranovskii, M. "Zemskii uchitel' v Lokhvitskom uezda (pis'mo iz Lokhvitsy)." *Mir bozhii,* No. 12, section 2 (1903): 33–37.

Tulupov, N. "Kurskaia vystavka po narodnomu obrazovaniiu." *Russkaia mysl',* No. 8, section 2 (1902): 108–26.

Tulupov, N. V. "Osnovnye voprosy uchitel'skago byta (K predstoiashchemu s"ezdu)." *Russkaia mysl',* No. 12, section 2 (1902): 86–96.

Tulupov, N. V. "Pervyi vserossiiskii s"ezd predstavitelei obshchestv vspomoshchestvovaniia litsam uchitel'skago zvaniia." *Russkaia mysl',* No. 3, section 2 (1903): 111–35.

V. B. "K voprosu o podgotovke narodnago uchitelia." *Obrazovanie,* No. 4 (1902): 96–101.

Vakhlin. "Narodnoe obrazovanie v Orekhovo-Zuevskom uezde do revoliutsii," in *Orekhovo-Zuevskii uezd, Moskovskoi gubernii: istoriko-ekonomicheskii sbornik.* Orekhovo-Zuevo, 1926, pp. 398–441.

Vakhterova, E. "Bezrabotnye uchitelia v Moskve." *Vestnik vospitaniia,* No. 7, section 2 (1908): 159–64.

Vakhterova, E. "O vserossiiskom uchitel'skom soiuze." *Vestnik vospitaniia,* No. 1, section 2 (1906): 119–47.

Vasilevich, V. [Kir'iakov, V. V.]. "K voprosu ob uchitel'skikh s"ezdakh." *Obrazovanie,* Nos. 5–6 (1898): 193–98.

Vezhlev, A. M. "Uchitel'skie s"ezdy i kursy v Rossii (vtoraia polovina XIX veka)." *Sovetskaia pedagogika,* No. 7 (1958): 79–88.

Volkov, S. A. "Pervyi s"ezd narodnykh uchitelei i uchitel'nits (zametki i vpechatleniia)." *Russkaia mysl',* No. 10, section 2 (1901): 208–18.

Volkov, V. I. "Bor'ba bol'shevikov za uchashchuiusia molodezh' i uchitel'stvo v period revoliutsii 1905–1907 gg." *Sovetskaia pedagogika,* No. 1 (1951): 10–30.

Zelenko, V. A. "Iz perezhitogo (Vospominaniia o revoliutsionnoi deiatel'nosti uchitel'stva)." *Dela i dni: istoricheskii zhurnal,* No. 3 (1922): 99–120.

Zelenko, Vasili. "Uchitel' nizshei shkoly." *Vestnik znaniia,* No. 8 (1905): 96–105.

Zemskii, V. G. [Charnoluskii]. "Vtoroi delegatskii s"ezd vserossiiskago soiuza uchitelei i deiatelei po narodnomu obrazovaniiu." *Vestnik vospitaniia,* no. 3, section 2 (1906): 121–38.

Zhulev, P. "Ob uchitel'sikh obshchestvakh vzaimopomoshchi." *Russkaia shkola,* No. 4 (1909): 81–89; No. 1 (1912): 1–20.

Zolotarev, S. "Ocherk po istorii uchitel'skago ob"edineniia v Rossii," in *Professional'nye uchitel'skie organizatsii na Zapade i v Rossii: sbornik statei.* Petrograd, 1915, pp. 233–293.

Zviagintsev, E. A. "Zemstvo i uchebnoe vedomstvo," in Veselovskii and Frenkel', eds., *Iubileinyi zemskii sbornik,* pp. 359–69.

Books and pamphlets:

Alston, Patrick L. *Education and the State in Tsarist Russia.* Stanford: Stanford University Press, 1969.

Apletin, Mikh. *Etapy i formy prosveshchenskogo soiuznogo dvizheniia za piat' let (1917–1922 g.g.).* Moscow: "Rabotnik prosveshcheniia," 1923.

Belokonskii, I. P. *Zemstvo i konstitutsiia.* Moscow: "Obrazovanie," 1910.

Belokonskii, I. P. *Zemskoe dvizhenie.* 2d ed., Moscow: "Zadruga," 1914.

Brooks, Jeffrey. *When Russia Learned to Read: Literacy and Popular Literature, 1861–1917.* Princeton: Princeton University Press, 1985.

Bunakov, N. F. *Izbrannye pedagogicheskie sochineniia.* Moscow: Akademiia pedagogicheskikh nauk RSFSR, 1953.

Bushnell, John. *Mutiny amid Repression: Russian Soldiers in the Revolution of 1905–1906.* Bloomington: Indiana University Press, 1985.

Charnoluskii, V. I., ed. *Ezhegodnik narodnoi shkoly.* Moscow: I. D. Sytin, 1908.

Charnoluskii, V. I. *Itogi obshchestvennoi mysli v oblasti obrazovaniia.* St. Petersburg: Tovarishchestvo "Znanie," 1906.

Charnoluskii, V. I., comp. *Sputnik narodnago uchitelia i deiatelia narodnago obrazovaniia. Sbornik zakonov i svedenii po vsem voprosam shkol'nago, vneshkol'nago i doshkol'nago obrazovaniia.* St. Petersburg: "Znanie," 1908.

Charnoluskii, V. I. *Zemstvo i narodnoe obrazovanie.* 2 vols. St. Petersburg: "Znanie," 1910–11.

Chekhov, N. V. *Narodnoe obrazovanie v Rossii s 60-kh godov XIX veka.* Moscow: "Pol'za," 1912.

Chekhov, N. V., comp. *Uchitel'skie obshchestva, ikh zadachi i organizatsiia.* Moscow: I. D. Sytin, 1904.

Chermenskii, E. D. *Burzhuaziia i tsarizm v pervoi russkoi revoliutsii.* 2d ed., Moscow: "Mysl'," 1970.

Chernov, G. I. *Stranitsy proshlogo (Iz istorii dorevoliutsionnoi shkoly Vladimirskoi gubernii).* Vladimir, 1970.

Dvadtsatipiatletie kazanskoi zemskoi shkoly uchitel'nits, 1871–1896 gg. Comp. A. Ershov, Kazan: izd. Kazanskoi gub. zemstva, 1897.

Eklof, Ben. *Russian Peasant Schools: Officialdom, Village Culture and Peasant Pedagogy, 1861–1914*. Berkeley: University of California Press, 1986.

Emmons, Terence. *The Formation of Political Parties and the First National Elections in Russia*. Cambridge, Mass.: Harvard University Press, 1983.

Erman, L. K. *Intelligentsiia v pervoi russkoi revoliutsii*. Moscow: "Nauka," 1966.

Fal'bork, G. and Charnoluskii, V. *Narodnoe obrazovanie v Rossii*. St. Petersburg: O. N. Popova, 1899.

Fischer, George. *Russian Liberalism: From Gentry to Intelligentsia*. Cambridge, Mass.: Harvard University Press, 1958.

Frieden, Nancy M. *Russian Physicians in an Era of Reform and Revolution, 1856–1905*. Princeton: Princeton University Press, 1981.

Furaev, G. *Ocherk po istorii professional'nogo ob"edineniia rabotnikov prosveshcheniia Omskoi gubernii (1895–1924 g.)*. Omsk: Soiuz rabotnikov prosveshcheniia, 1924.

Galai, Shmuel. *The Liberation Movement in Russia, 1900–1905*. Cambridge: Cambridge University Press, 1973.

Golos narodnago uchitelia: sbornik l. Ed. D. I. Koleno. St. Petersburg: izd. uchitelei Bakhmutskago uezda Ekaterinoslavskoi gub., 1907.

Iaroslavl' v pervoi russkoi revoliutsii: sbornik materialov po istorii revoliutsii 1905 goda v Iaroslavskoi gubernii. Ed. P. N. Gvuzdev et al. Iaroslavl: "Sovetskii rabochii i Iaroslavskaia derevnia," 1925.

Igumnov, S. *Zemstvo i tretii element*. Kharkov, 1914.

Ivanov, A. I. *Krest'ianskoe dvizhenie vo Vladimirskoi gubernii v 1905–1906* gg. Vladimir: Vladimirskoe knigoizdatel'stvo, 1923.

Ivanov, A. I. *Professional'nyi soiuz rabotnikov prosveshcheniia Vladimirskoi gubernii (Kratkii istoricheskii ocherk)*. Vladimir: Vladimirskoe knigoizdatel'stvo, 1924.

Izvlechenie iz vsepoddanneishago otcheta ministra narodnago prosveshcheniia za 1900 god. St. Petersburg: izd. MNP, 1902.

Johnson, William H. E. *Russia's Educational Heritage*. Pittsburgh: Carnegie Press, 1950.

Kaidanova, O. *Ocherki po istorii narodnogo obrazovaniia v Rossii i SSSR na osnove lichnogo opyta i nabliudenii*. 2 vols. Berlin: Speer & Schmidt, 1938.

Kalendar'-spravochnik 1908/9 uchebnyi god. Comp. O. N. Smirnov. Kiev: "Narodnyi uchitel'," 1908.

Kapanadze, Ia. *Golos sel'skago uchitelia s "zapiskoi deiatelei po narodnomu obrazovaniiu."* n. p., n. d.

Karpov, N., ed. *Krest'ianskoe dvizhenie v revoliutsii 1905 goda v dokumentakh*. Leningrad: Gos. izdat., 1926.

Kerekesh, E. E. *Prazdnik narodnago uchitelia (pervaia vystavka po narodnomu obrazovaniiu, sostoiavshaias' v 1902 godu v Kurske)*. Chernigov, 1903.

Kir'iakov, V. and Akramovskii, S. *Golos narodnago uchitelia. Otchet o Moskovskom s"ezde predstavitelei uchitel'skikh obshchestv vzaimopomoshchi 28.XII. 1902–6.I.1903 g*. Moscow: O. Somova, 1903.

Kir'iakov, V. V. *Shag za shagom: K istorii ob"edineniia narodnykh uchitelei-iz lichnykh vospominanii i perezhivanii*. Moscow: "Dlia narodnago uchitelia," 1914.

Kolesnichenko, D. A. *Trudoviki v period pervoi rossiiskoi revoliutsii*. Moscow: "Nauka," 1985.

Kratkii obzor deiatel'nosti Obshchestva popecheniia ob uluchshenii byta uchashchikh v nachal'nykh uchilishchakh g. Moskvy za 1895–1901 g.g. Comp. V. F. Borodich. Moscow, 1903.

Kurskoe zemstvo. *Otchet po revizii proizvedennoi v 1904 godu senatorom N. A. Zinov'evym*. 2 vols. St. Petersburg, 1906.

Lapshin, N. P. *Iz istorii russkoi dorevoliutsionnoi inspektsii narodnykh uchilishch (1869–1917 gg.)*. Elabuga, 1963.

Leikina-Svirskaia, V. R. *Intelligentsiia v Rossii vo vtoroi polovine XIX veka*. Moscow: "Mysl'," 1971.

Leikina-Svirskaia, V. R. *Russkaia intelligentsiia v 1900–1917 godakh*. Moscow: "Mysl'," 1981.

Litvinov, V. V. *Voronezhskaia uchitel'skaia seminariia (1875–1910 g.): istoricheskii ocherk*. Voronezh: Voronezhskii gub. statisticheskii komitet, 1911.

Malinovskii, N. A. *Narodnyi uchitel' v revoliutsionnom dvizhenii*. Moscow: "Novaia Moskva," 1926.

Manning, Roberta T. *Crisis of the Old Order in Russia: Gentry and Government*. Princeton: Princeton University Press, 1982.

Maslov, P. P. *Agrarnyi vopros v Rossii*. 2 vols. St. Petersburg: "Obshchestvennaia pol'za," 1905–1908.

Miagkova, K. *O polozhenii narodnykh uchitelei*. Velikii Ustiug: "Severnoe ekho," 1905.

Miliukov, P. N. *Ocherki po istorii russkoi kul'tury*, Vol. II, part 2. Paris: "Sovremennye zapiski," 1931.

Mitskevich, S. I. *Na grani dvukh epokh: ot narodnichestva k marksizmu*. Moscow: Gosudarstvennoe sotsial'no-ekonomicheskoe izd., 1937.

Mitskevich, S. I. *Revoliutsionnaia Moskva, 1888–1905*. Moscow: "Khudozhestvennaia literatura," 1940.

Nachal'noe narodnoe obrazovanie v Tul'skoi gubernii v 1896–1897 uchebnom godu. Tula: izd. Tul'skago gub. zemstva, 1898.

Narodnoe obrazovanie v Rossii (is vol. 10 of *Narodnaia entsiklopediia nauchnykh i prikladnykh znanii)*. Moscow: I. D. Sytin, 1910.

Obozrenie zemskikh uchrezhdenii Tverskoi gubernii: otchet direktora Departamenta Obshchikh Del Ministerstva Vnutrennykh Del Gofmeistera Shtiurmera 1903 g. n. p., n. d.

Obshchestvennoe dvizhenie v Rossii v nachale XX-go veka. Eds. L. Martov, P. Maslov, A. N. Potresov. 4 vols. St. Petersburg: "Obshchestvennaia pol'za," 1909–14.

Obukhov, M. I. *Itogi deiatel'nosti Obshchestva vzaimnago vspomoshchestvovaniia uchiteliam i uchitel'nitsam Nizhegorodskoi gubernii za 10 let sushchestvovaniia ego 1894–1904 g*. Nizhnii-Novgorod, 1905.

Obukhov, M. I. *Na raznye temy. Stat'i po voprosam narodnago obrazovaniia i uchitel'skago byta*. Ufa, 1915.

Obukhov, M. I. *Pervyi Vserossiiskii s"ezd predstavitelei obshchestv vzaimopomoshchi uchashchikh*. Nizhnii-Novgorod, 1903.

Obzor sostoianiia nachal'nago narodnago obrazovaniia v Kurskoi gubernii za 5 let (1895/96–1900/01 uchebn. g.g). Kursk: tip. Kurskago gub. zemstva, 1902.

Ocherk deiatel'nosti obshchestva vzaimnago vspomoshchestovaniia uchashchim i uchivshim v nachal'nykh uchilishchakh Iaroslavskoi gubernii za 10 let sushchestvovaniia (1902–1912 g.g). Iaroslavl: K. F. Nekrasov, 1913.

Odintsev, A., comp. *Uchitel'skii s"ezd*. Moscow, 1904.

Odnodnevnaia perepis' nachal'nykh shkol Rossiiskoi imperii proizvedennaia 18 ianvaria 1911 g. Ed. V. I. Pokrovskii. Vol. 16. Petrograd: izd. MNP, 1916.

Oniani, V. *Bol'shevistskaia partiia i intelligentsiia v pervoi russkoi revoliutsii*. Tiflis: "Sabchota Sakartvelo," 1970.

Ososkov, A. V. *Voprosy istorii nachal'nogo obrazovaniia v Rossii (II pol. XIX- nach. XX vv.)*. 2 vols. Moscow: Moskovskii oblastnoi ped. institut, 1974–75.

Otchet Obshchestva vzaimopomoshchi uchashchim i uchivshim v nachal'nykh uchilishchakh Slavianoserbskago uezda, s 1-go sentiabria 1904 goda po l-e ianvaria 1907 goda (god 5-i i 6-i). Lugansk, 1907.

Otchet obshchestva vzaimopomoshchi uchashchim i uchivshim Samarskoi gubernii za 1905, 1906 i pervuiu polovinu 1907 goda. Samara, 1907.

Otchet po revizii zemskikh uchrezhdenii Moskovskoi gubernii. Ed. N. A. Zinov'ev. 3 vols. St. Petersburg: MVD, 1904.

Otchet po revizii zemskikh uchrezhdenii Viatskoi gubernii. Ed. N. A. Zinov'ev. 2 vols. St. Petersburg: MVD, 1905.

Otchet pravleniia obshchestva vzaimnago vspomoshchestvovaniia uchashchim i uchivshim v nachal'nykh narodnykh shkolakh Chernigovskoi gubernii za 1904, 1905 i 1906 gody. Chernigov, 1907.

Pedagogicheskaia entsiklopediia. Eds. A. G. Kalashnikov, M. S. Epshtein. 3 vols. Moscow: "Rabotnik prosveshcheniia," 1927–30.

Perrie, Maureen. *The Agrarian Policy of the Russian Socialist-Revolutionary Party: From Its Origins through the Revolution of 1905–1907*. New York: Cambridge University Press, 1976.

Petrov, V. V., ed. *Voprosy narodnago obrazovaniia v Moskovskoi gubernii*. 4 vols. Moscow: izd. Moskovskago gub. zemstva, 1897–1901.

Petrunkevich, I. I. *Iz zapisok obshchestvennogo deiatelia*. (is vol. 21 of *Arkhiv russkoi revoliutsii*). Berlin, 1934.

Pirumova, N. M. *Zemskaia intelligentsiia i ee rol' v obshchestvennoi bor'be do nachale XX veka*. Moscow: "Nauka," 1986.

Pirumova, N. M. *Zemskoe liberal'noe dvizhenie: sotsial'nye korni i evoliutsiia do nachala XX veka*. Moscow: "Nauka," 1977.

Polozhenie nachal'nago narodnago obrazovaniia v Novgorodskoi gubernii. 4 vols. Novgorod: izd. Novgorodskago gub. zemstva, 1901–4. Especially vol. 1 *(Polozhenie narodnykh uchitelei)*.

Protokoly III-go delegatskago s"ezda Vserossiiskago soiuza uchitelei i deiatelei po narodnomu obrazovaniiu 7–10 iulia 1906 g. n. p.: izd. VSU, 1906.

Protokoly vtorogo delegatskago s"ezda Vserossiiskago soiuza uchitelei i deiatelei po narodnomu obrazovaniiu, 26–29 dekabria, 1905 goda. St. Petersburg: izd. VSU, 1906.

Rabochee i professional'noe dvizhenie v Nizhegorodskom krae 1869–1917: materialy. Ed. V. T. Illarionov. Nizhnii-Novgorod: izd. Nizhegorodskogo gub. soveta professional'nykh soiuzov, 1923.

Reichman, Henry. *Railwaymen and Revolution: Russia, 1905*. Berkeley: University of California Press, 1987.

Rozhdestvenskii, S. V. *Istoricheskii obzor deiatel'nosti ministerstva narodnago prosveshcheniia, 1802–1902 gg*. St. Petersburg: MNP, 1902.

Rozhkov, N. A. and Sokolov, A. V. *O 1905 gode: vospominaniia*. Moscow: "Moskovskii rabochii," 1925.

Salomatin, P. *Kak zhivet i rabotaet narodnyi uchitel' (lichnye vpechatleniia)*. St. Petersburg: N. N. Mikhailov, 1914.

Samsonov, V. A. *Byt uchashchikh v Novgorodskoi gubernii*. Novgorod: izd. Obshchestva vzaimopomoshchi uchashchikh, 1907.

Sedel'nikova, M. V. *N. V. Chekhov: vidnyi deiatel' narodnogo prosveshcheniia*. Moscow: Gos. uchebno-pedagog. izd-vo Ministerstva prosveshcheniia RSFSR, 1960.

Semenov, S. T. *Dvadtsat' piat' let v derevne*. Petrograd: Kn-vo "Zhizn' i znanie," 1915.

Sergeev, G. I., comp. *Narodnaia shkola v Nizhegorodskom uezde*. Nizhnii-Novgorod: izd. Nizhegorodskago uezdnago zemstva, 1905.

Seropolko, S. O. *Polozhenie uchashchikh v zemskikh shkolakh Tul'skoi gubernii*. Tula: Tul'skoe Obshchestvo vzaimnago, 1904.

Shanin, Teodor. *Russia, 1905–07: Revolution as a Moment of Truth*. New Haven: Yale University Press, 1986.

Shchurov, L. and Glovatskii, L. *Professional'noe dvizhenie prosveshchentsev (istoricheskii ocherk)*. Leningrad: Gub. Otdel soiuza rabotnikov prosveshcheniia, [1927].

Shipov, D. N. *Vospominaniia i dumy o perezhitom*. Moscow: izd-vo M. i S. Sabashnikovykh, 1918.

Sinel, Allen. *The Classroom and the Chancellery: State Educational Reform in Russia under Count Dmitry Tolstoi.* Cambridge, Mass.: Harvard University Press, 1973.

Sistematicheskii svod ukazov Pravitel'stvuiushchago Senata, posledovavshikh po zemskim delam, 1866–1912. Comp. N. I. Kuznetsov. 9 vols. St. Petersburg-Voronezh, 1902–13.

Soveshchanie direktorov narodnykh uchilishch pri upravlenii Moskovskago uchebnago okruga 6–9 maia 1907 g. Moscow, 1907.

Spiridovich, A. I. *Partiia Sotsialistov-Revoliutsionerov i ee predshestvenniki, 1886–1916.* Petrograd, 1916.

Spravochanaia kniga po nizshemu obrazovaniiu. God tretii (svedeniia za 1905 god). Comp. S. I. Antsyferov. part II. St. Petersburg: izd. MNP, 1908.

Spravochnaia kniga po nizshemu obrazovaniiu. God chetvertyi (svedeniia za 1906 god). Comp. S. I.Antsyferov. part II, St. Petersburg: MNP, 1909.

Spravochnaia kniga uchitel'skikh obshchestv vzaimopomoshchi. Moscow: I. D. Sytin, 1905.

Superanskii, M. F. *Byt uchashchikh v nachal'nykh shkolakh Simbirskoi gubernii.* Simbirsk, 1905.

Superanskii, M. F. *Nachal'naia narodnaia shkola v Simbirskoi gubernii: istoriko-statisticheskii ocherk.* Simbirsk, 1906.

Svod vysochaishikh otmetok po vsepoddanneishim otchetam za 1881–1904 general-gubernatorov, gubernatorov, nachal'nikov oblastei i gradonachal'nikov. St. Petersburg, 1893–1907.

Tatarchukov, A. N. *Istoricheskii ocherk professional'nogo dvizheniia v Voronezhskoi gubernii.* Part I. Voronezh: Voronezhskii gub. sovet professional'nykh soiuzov, 1921.

Tekushchaia shkol'naia statistika Kurskago gub. zemstva: god odinnadtsatyi 1906–1907 ucheb. god. Part I. Kursk: tip: Kurskago gub. zemstva, 1908.

Tomashevich, E. *Istoricheskii ocherk deiatel'nosti Tul'skago Obshchestva vzaimopomoshchi uchashchim i uchivshim za istekshee desiatiletie 19 sentiabria 1895–18 sentiabria 1905 gg.* Tula, 1907.

Trudy I-go vserossiiskago s"ezda predstavitelei obshchestv vspomoshchestvovaniia litsam uchitel'skago zvaniia Ed. V. M. Evteev. 2 vols. Moscow: "Beseda," 1907.

Trudy s"ezda upravlenii Moskovskago uchebnago okruga po voprosam narodnago obrazovaniia, 1-11 marta 1901 goda. Eds. A. A. Flerov, A. D. Samarin. 2 vols. Moscow, 1902.

Tulupov, N. V. and Shestakov, P. M. *K voprosu ob ustroistve Vserossiiskago uchitel'skago soiuza.* Moscow: I. D. Sytin, 1905.

Tulupov, N. V. and Shestakov, P. M. *Pervyi vserossiiskii s"ezd predstavitelei obshchestv vspomoshchestvovaniia litsam uchitel'skago zvaniia (Mertialy dlia vyrabotki mer po uluchsheniiu uchitel'skago byta).* Moscow: I. D. Sytin, 1903.

Tulupov, N. V. *Pervyi vserossiiskii s"ezd predstavitelei obshchestv vspomoshchestvovaniia litsam uchitel'skogo zvaniia (Moskva 1902–1903).* Moscow-Leningrad: "Rabotnik prosveshcheniia," 1930.

1905 god v Kurskoi gubernii: sbornik statei. Kursk: "Sovetskaia derevnia," 1925.

1905 god v Samarskom krae: materialy po istorii R. K. P. (b.) i revoliutsionnogo dvizheniia. Ed. N. Speranskii. Samara: izd. Samarskogo Gubkoma R.K.P.(b.), 1925.

Uchitel'stvo Severnogo Kavkaza v 1905 godu. Rostov-na-Donu: izd. Sev. Kav. kraevogo otdela soiuza rabotnikov prosveshcheniia, 1925.

Ushakov, A. V. *Revoliutsionnoe dvizhenie demokraticheskoi intelligentsii v Rossii, 1895–1904.* Moscow: "Mysl'," 1976.

Vakhterova, E. O. *V. P. Vakhterov, ego zhizn' i rabota.* Moscow: Akademiia pedagogicheskikh nauk RSFSR, 1961.

Vasilevich, V. [Kir'iakov, V. V.]. *Moskovskii s"ezd predstavitelei uchitel'skikh obshchestv vzaimopomoshchi 28.XII.1902–6.I.1903 g.* Moscow: I. D. Sytin, 1905.

Veselovskii, B. B. *Istoricheskii ocherk deiatel'nosti zemskikh uchrezhdenii Tverskoi gubernii (1864–1913 gg.).* Tver: izd. Tverskoi gub. zemskoi upravy, 1914.

Veselovskii B. B. *Istoriia zemstva za sorok let.* 4 vols. St. Petersburg: O. N. Popova, 1909–11.

Veselovskii, B. B. *Krest'ianskii vopros i krest'ianskoe dvizhenie v Rossii, 1902–1906 gg.* St. Petersburg: "Zerno," 1907.

Vsepoddanneishii otchet ministra narodnago prosveshcheniia za 1903 god. St. Petersburg: izd. MNP, 1905.

Zapankov, N. A. *Uchitel' narodnoi shkoly.* St. Petersburg, 1906.

Zemskie obshcheobrazovatel'nye kursy dlia uchitelei: sbornik statei. St. Petersburg: izd. Komissii imeni K. D. Ushinskago, 1906.

Zhbankov, D. N. *Kratii obzor deiatel'nosti obshchestv vzaimopomoshchi uchashchim i uchivshim.* Smolensk, 1900.

Zhil'tsov, P. A. and Velichkina, V. M. *Uchitel' sel'skoi shkoly,* Part I *(Uchitel' sel'skoi dorevoliutsionnoi shkoly).* Moscow: Moskovskii oblastnoi ped. institut, 1973.

Zhurnal Obshchego sobraniia 22 aprelia 1905 goda. Ekaterinoslav: izd. Ekaterinoslavskago gub. ob-va vzaimopomoshchi narodnykh uchitelei, 1905.

Zhurnaly uchilishchnoi komissii Saratovskago uezdnago zemstva pri uchastii gg. uchashchikh zemsko-obshchestvennykh uchilishch Saratovskago uezda. Saratov, 1901.

Zhurnaly zasedanii komissii po narodnomu obrazovaniiu pri gubernskoi zemskoi uprave 21 i 22 noiabria 1905 goda. Vladimir-na-Kliazme, 1905.

Zviagintsev, E. A. *Inspektsiia narodnykh uchilishch (Russkoe obshchestvo i uchebnoe vedomstvo v shkol'nom dele).* Moscow: "Zadruga," 1914.

Zviagintsev, E. A. *Polveka zemskoi deiatel'nosti po narodnomu obrazovaniiu.* 2d ed. Moscow: "Zadruga," 1917.

Zviagintsev, E. A., ed. *Voprosy i nuzhdy uchitel'stva: sbornik statei.* 10 vols. Moscow: I. D. Sytin, 1909–11.

Zviagintsev, E. A., Obukhov, A. M., Seropolko, S. O. and Chekhov, N. V., eds. *Narodnoe obrazovanie v zemstvakh: osnovy organizatsii i prakita dela.* Moscow: "Zadruga," 1914.

Zviagintsev, E. A., et al. *Shkola, zemstvo i uchitel': sbornik statei.* Moscow: izd. zhurnala "Narodnyi uchitel'," 1911.

Index